NEW WAR TECHNOLOGIES AND INTERNATIONAL LAW

The desire for humanity and the desire for security have co-existed as long as humans have been alive. As science has become increasingly sophisticated, so have the methods of self-defence by States. Nanotechnology is already changing warfare by increasing capabilities upon which armed forces are heavily reliant: more efficient energy storage, advanced photovoltaics, and improved military protective equipment to name a few of these developments. Some applications of nanomaterials by the military are both powerful and subtle, and have neurological and biological applications: 'devices that can infiltrate electronics and seize control at crucial moments, artificial "disease" agents that can rest harmlessly in victims' bodies until activated by an external signal'. The advance of the use or contemplation of use of these types of nanoscale applications by the military requires urgent analysis in light of existing international law, particularly in light of their potential effects on humans and on the environment.

KOBI LEINS is Visiting Senior Research Fellow at King's College, Department of War Studies, London; Expert for Standards Australia providing technical advice to the International Standards Organisation on AI Standards; Co-founder of IEEE's Responsible Innovation of AI and the Life Sciences; Non-Resident Fellow of the United Nations Institute for Disarmament Research, and Advisory Board Member of the Carnegie Initiative on AI and Equality.

NEW WAR TECHNOLOGIES AND INTERNATIONAL LAW

The Legal Limits to Weaponising Nanomaterials

KOBI LEINS
King's College, London

CAMBRIDGE
UNIVERSITY PRESS

CAMBRIDGE
UNIVERSITY PRESS

Shaftesbury Road, Cambridge CB2 8EA, United Kingdom

One Liberty Plaza, 20th Floor, New York, NY 10006, USA

477 Williamstown Road, Port Melbourne, VIC 3207, Australia

314–321, 3rd Floor, Plot 3, Splendor Forum, Jasola District Centre, New Delhi – 110025, India

103 Penang Road, #05–06/07, Visioncrest Commercial, Singapore 238467

Cambridge University Press is part of Cambridge University Press & Assessment, a department of the University of Cambridge.

We share the University's mission to contribute to society through the pursuit of education, learning and research at the highest international levels of excellence.

www.cambridge.org
Information on this title: www.cambridge.org/9781108799843

DOI: 10.1017/9781108891974

First published 2022
First paperback edition 2026

A catalogue record for this publication is available from the British Library

Library of Congress Cataloging-in-Publication data
Names: Leins, Kobi, 1977– author.
Title: New war technologies and international law : the legal limits to weaponising nanomaterials / Kobi Leins, University of Melbourne.
Description: Cambridge, United Kingdom ; New York, NY : Cambridge University Press, 2022. | Based on author's thesis (doctoral – University of Melbourne Law School, 2019) issued under title: International law applicable to the use of nanomaterials in war. | Includes bibliographical references and index.
Identifiers: LCCN 2021024864 (print) | LCCN 2021024865 (ebook) | ISBN 9781108835244 (hardback) | ISBN 9781108799843 (paperback) | ISBN 9781108891974 (epub)
Subjects: LCSH: Military weapons–Law and legislation. | War (International law) | Nanostructured materials–Law and legislation. | Nanostructured materials–Military applications.
Classification: LCC KZ5624.L45 2022 (print) | LCC KZ5624 (ebook) | DDC 341.6–dc23
LC record available at https://lccn.loc.gov/2021024864
LC ebook record available at https://lccn.loc.gov/2021024865

ISBN 978-1-108-83524-4 Hardback
ISBN 978-1-108-79984-3 Paperback

In loving memory of Sheila Singh.

Sheila Singh's passion for international law, her profound integrity and her heartfelt humour remain an inspiration to me and many others. You are missed.

Dedicated also to Professor Diana Bowman, without whom the will, the way and the wonder would have been lost. Thank you.

CONTENTS

FIGURES

ACKNOWLEDGEMENTS

I am very grateful to my supervisors, Professor Alison Duxbury and Professor Christine Parker, whose patience and encouragement have been endless, whose wisdom has been boundless and without whom I could not have completed this work. You helped me to find my voice.

I wish to express immense gratitude for the Faye Marles Scholarship (2016–2018) and for the James and Valerie McNiff Scholarships (2016 and 2018), both of which enabled this work. I would also like to express gratitude for the Australian Research Council's *Discovery Projects* funding scheme (project number DP130100432), with which this project was affiliated, and funding from the Defence Science Institute, which enabled the first steps of research in this area, as well as providing experts and technical support.

Thank you to Gwen Pascoe, whose life and work remain an inspiration, and to Treasa Dunworth, who recommended that I do a PhD 15 years earlier. If only I had listened. And to Treasa Dunworth, again, who didn't let me quit when the situation would have excused it.

I am also grateful to many colleagues who have become friends and supported me: R. E. Burnett, Maddy Chiam, Damian Clifford, Monique Cormier, Regina Crameri, Maria Elander, Rosemary Grey, Anna Hood, Jonathan Kolieb, Margaret Kosal, Marnie Lloyd, Bob Matthews, Katina Michaels, Emma Nyhan, Rose Parfitt and Laura Petersen, and all those who have supported me in many small and often big ways. Also, a huge thank you to my non-academic friends who have accepted that I have been absent (in more ways than one) for the years that it took to research and write this text and provided me with unwavering support and encouragement: Olivia Craze, Ciar Foster, Rayma Gupta, Jayne Huckerby, Kaz Manning, Jaclynn Markham, Craig Memery, Emma Phillips, Melanie Szydzik, Simon Thomas and Natasha Van Rijn. Thank you to Rhys Ryan and Chantal Morton for your support in helping me to get over the line, and Christina Ward, university librarian extraordinaire.

Thank you to Hilary Charlesworth for being a role model to whose elegance and statesman-like fortitude at all times I can only aspire. Thank you to Margaret Young for the opportunity to teach with, and learn from, you at the University of Melbourne and for your extremely insightful review of this text. Thank you to Megan Richardson for your encouragement and for connecting me with other lawyers with different skill sets also looking at governance of new and emerging technology, and for allowing me to reside in your cubicle all those years. Thank you also to Bruce ('Oz') Oswald for including me in his stable. Thank you also to Professor Stuart Kaye, Associate Professor Cameron Moore and Dr Heather Harrison Dinnis. Most of all, thank you to my loves, my life – Luka, Gustav and Ben.

ABBREVIATIONS

Additional Protocol I	API
Additional Protocol II	APII
Biodiversity Beyond National Jurisdiction	BBNJ
Biological Weapons Convention	BWC
Convention against Torture	CAT
Convention on Certain Conventional Weapons	CCW
Convention on the Elimination of All Forms of Discrimination against Women	CEADW
Committee on Economic, Social and Cultural Rights	CESCR
Convention on the Rights of the Child	CRC
Chemical Weapons Convention	CWC
dense inert metal explosives	DIME
European Convention on Human Rights	ECHR
European Court of Human Rights	ECtHR
Environmental Modification Convention	ENMOD
International Criminal Court	ICC
International Covenant on Civil Political Rights	ICCPR
International Covenant on Economic, Social and Cultural Rights	ICESCR
International Court of Justice	ICJ
International Committee of the Red Cross	ICRC
International Criminal Tribunal for the Former Yugoslavia	ICTY
International Law Commission	ILC
non-governmental organisation	NGO
Organisation for the Prohibition of Chemical Weapons	OPCW
Scientific Advisory Board	SAB
Universal Declaration of Human Rights	UDHR
United Nations	UN

United Nations Compensation Commission	UNCC
United Nations General Assembly	UNGA
United Nations Human Rights Committee	UNHRC
United Nations Security Council	UNSC
United Nations Security Council Resolution	UNSCR
Vienna Convention on the Law of Treaties	VCLT

All errors, inaccuracies and mistakes, however, remain mine alone.

The most commonly asked question is how I came to work at the intersection of the law of war and technology. The answer, like those that many would give for their careers, is a combination of serendipity and passion. I worked on minimising the risks of biological and chemical advances. As research in nanomaterials advanced, I kept reading that there were risks but found no literature identifying where and how nanomaterials could play a part in warfare. This book aims to start a conversation where that gap was.

While writing this book, I became interested in the same questions, but about numerous other technologies. We have now seen protests against algorithms being used to predict students' results. This is not the end of automation, but rather the beginning. The framework used in this book is also applicable to other technologies used in warfare (along with other laws). We do not live in a world without law. We live in a world with multiple, fragmented laws that take time to apply to new advances in technology. Laws are important, but so are cultural practices, standards and other forms of governance that we should not ignore. I hope that this book contributes to helping those trying to understand the international law landscape and new technologies.

1

International Law and the Use of Nanomaterials in War

The desire for humanity and the desire for security have co-existed as long as humans have been alive. Often these desires are in conflict. In 2013, 'Skull 5', a 1.8 million-year-old hominid, was found in Georgia on the Armenian border.[1] Skull 5 'was ill, his jaw was worn away from infections, and he had lost all but one tooth. No longer able to provide for himself, someone must have fed him and kept him safe from harm'.[2] Skull 5's level of nurturing by his clan ensured that he received food and care when he was unable to do so himself – evidence of a sense of humanity 1.8 million years ago.

Skull 5 was found near a stockpile of rounded stones, most probably some of the earliest weapons that were ever used by hominids. This recent discovery illustrates that over 1.8 million years ago, humans also had a deep desire, arguably even a need, to be able to defend themselves. This very tension is at the heart of the international laws of war. States, much like individuals, deeply desire the ability to defend themselves. States also do not wish for war to be without limits, requiring that some humanity, or care for others, be retained even during times of armed conflict. This tension is reflected in many of the treaties and much of the customary international law and legal principles that constitute the laws of war.

As science has become increasingly sophisticated, so too have the methods of self-defence. On the one hand, science initially developed to benefit mankind is often co-opted in war. Many scientific developments undertaken for unrelated purposes have been reappropriated for use in warfare. On the other hand, militaries often engage scientists to

[1] Brian Switek, 'Beautiful Skull Spurs Debate on Human History' (19 October 2013) *National Geographic* <http://news.nationalgeographic.com/news/2013/10/131017-skull-human-origins-dmanisi-georgia-erectus/>.

[2] Ramona Koval, 'On the Whispering of Bones', Speech delivered at Wheeler Centre Gala Night: Stories for the Dead, Melbourne, Australia, 26 February 2017.

advance their own needs.[3] Particularly as science and technology are proving increasingly decisive in fighting wars, there is an unarguable advantage for the side that exploits this scientific knowledge. At the same time, as scientists, academia, industry, governments, lawmakers, lawyers and the armed forces all consider the use of nanomaterials during war, the need to collaborate, clarify parameters of use, prevent dual use and identify the appropriate timing for legal reviews has become urgent.

Nanotechnology is already changing warfare by increasing capabilities on which armed forces are already heavily reliant: more efficient energy storage,[4] advanced photovoltaics[5] and improved military protective equipment,[6] to name a few of the developments that are already under way.[7] Some uses of nanomaterials in war are both powerful and subtle, and have neurological and biological uses: 'devices that can infiltrate electronics and seize control at crucial moments, artificial "disease" agents that can rest harmlessly in victims' bodies until activated by an external signal'.[8] The advance of the use, or contemplation of use, of these types of nanoscale in war requires urgent analysis in light of existing international law, and particularly in light of their potential

[3] Robert Jungk, *Brighter Than A Thousand Suns: A Personal History of the Atomic Scientists* (Houghton Mifflin Harcourt, 1958); Rebecca Slayton, *Arguments that Count* (Massachusetts Institute of Technology, 2013); Sharon Weinberger, *The Imagineers of War: The Untold Story of DARPA, the Pentagon Agency That Changed the World* (Vintage Books, 2017); Neil de Grasse Tyson and Avis Lang, *The Unspoken Alliance between Astrophysics and the Military: Accessory to War* (W W Norton & Company, 2018).

[4] Eun Seon Cho et al, 'Graphene Oxide/Metal Nanocrystal Multilaminates as the Atomic Limit for Safe and Selective Hydrogen Storage' (23 February 2016) *Nature Communications* <www.nature.com/articles/ncomms10804.pdf>.

[5] Photovoltaics refers to the method of converting solar energy into electricity using semiconducting materials, usually solar panels, which convert the sun to useable power. The importance of improved efficiency in this function has direct and widespread use for any means of warfare that requires an energy source.

[6] Much research is being undertaken by militaries to incorporate nano-elements to enhance the function of existing military uses, including gas filters, masks and materials for tanks and protective clothing for soldiers. See Defence Science Institute and Defence Science and Technology Organisation, Symposium, 'Future Technologies for Personal Protection' (7–8 November 2013) <www.defencescienceinstitute.com/2012/09/10/dsi-dsto-symposium-future-technologies-personal-protection/>.

[7] Jun Wang and Peter Dortmans, 'Nanotechnology: Selected Topics and Potential Military Application' (Paper presented at Land Warfare Conference, Melbourne, Australia, 27–30 September 2004) 69–81 <http://dspace.dsto.defence.gov.au/dspace/handle/1947/2559>.

[8] Kelly Hearn, 'Future Soldiers Could Get Enhanced Minds' (19 March 2001) *United Press International* <www.geocities.ws/marksrealm/project457.html>. This article describes the planned use of nanotechnology to create enhanced soldiers. The issue of the 'bio-enhanced' soldier is gaining increased attention but is beyond the scope of my writing.

effects on humans and on the environment. It is not just the laws of war that regulate the use of nanomaterials in armed conflict, as demonstrated in Chapter 5 on international environmental law, as well as in Chapter 6 on international human rights law.

Further, the need to consider the existing legal frameworks governing nanomaterials is urgent, given developments surrounding the interplay and capabilities of multiple technologies, such as the use of new computing algorithms to manipulate artificial intelligence and data. Not since the nuclear bomb has the convergence of technological capabilities posed such profound potential for changing how wars are fought. Since this book was written, the Treaty on the Prohibition of Nuclear Weapons came into force on 22 January 2021.[9]

Although humans have long been dissatisfied with the defence provided by the sticks and stones of our ancestors 1.8 million years ago, the manipulation of matter at the nanoscale opens a whole new world of potential humanitarian uses, along with a swathe of new uses for defence and militaries. As knowledge of human biology and particularly nanomaterials and their role in the function of the human body increases, so too does the desire to use this knowledge to improve lives through medical treatment alongside the desire to gain the upper hand in warfare.

In the last three decades, debates surrounding the use of new and emerging technologies have risen to a crescendo, from suggestions of imminent threats of future unemployment[10] to apocalyptic warnings of killer robots[11] and that robots will replace humans.[12] Since the first use of the word 'robot' in 1920,[13] a cacophony of debate has surrounded the legal frameworks required to respond to the evolution and increased use of interconnected developments in new and emerging technologies such

9 *Treaty on the Prohibition of Nuclear Weapons*, opened for signature 20 September 2017 (came into force 22 January 2021).

10 Shona Ghosh, 'One of Europe's Most Influential Investors Gave a Brutal Example of How AI Could Wipe Out White-Collar Jobs' (13 June 2017) *Business Insider UK* <http://uk.businessinsider.com/fred-destin-artificial-intelligence-will-wipe-out-white-collar-jobs-2017-6?r=US&IR=T>.

11 Campaign to Stop Killer Robots <www.stopkillerrobots.org>.

12 Bill Joy, 'Why the Future Doesn't Need Us' (1 April 2000) *Wired* <www.wired.com/2000/04/joy-2/>. Joy lists robotics, genetics and nanotech as the three game-changing technologies.

13 Karel Čapek, *R.U.R. (Rossum's Universal Robots)* (Claudia Novack trans, Penguin Books, 2004) [trans of: *R.U.R. (Rossumovi Univerzální Roboti* (first published 1920)]. This novel foreshadowed the potential of robots to bring about humanity's gruesome end but was not entirely without hope for humankind.

as automated systems, computer networks and nanotechnology. These discussions have predominantly taken place in the civilian context, and within multiple silos in their respective disciplines.

The broader debates surrounding the use of new and emerging technologies evidence the significance, the complexity and the challenges of governing new and emerging technologies in our lives. While debates regarding the use of automated systems and cyber-attacks in armed conflict have proliferated, consideration of the use of nanomaterials has lagged and consideration of these technologies together requires greater urgency. Much has been written about the regulation of nanotechnology in the civilian sector, and potential risks and challenges in its regulation,[14] but very little has been written about the application of existing legal regimes to the use of nanomaterials in war. By analysing the legal framework applicable to three specific uses of nanomaterials, I address this gap in the literature and illustrate three main points.

First, the analysis that I undertake illustrates that weapons reviews, as provided for in Article 36 of Additional Protocol I (API), are required for all 'means or methods of warfare' containing nanomaterials to ensure compliance with well-established existing treaties and customary international law and legal principles of the laws of war, environmental law

[14] European Commission, *Nanoscience and Nanotechnologies: An Action Plan for Europe 2005–2009* (2005) European Commission Community Research and Development Information Service <https://cordis.europa.eu/pub/nanotechnology/docs/action_plan_brochure.pdf>; Jürgen Altmann, *Military Nanotechnology: Potential Applications and Preventive Arms Control* (Routledge, 2006); Jeffrey Matsuura, *Nanotechnology Regulation and Policy Worldwide* (Artech House, 2006); Graeme Hodge, Diana Bowman and Karinne Ludlow (eds), *New Global Frontiers in Regulation: The Age of Nanotechnology* (Edward Elgar, 2007); Margaret Kosal, *Nanotechnology for Chemical and Biological Defense* (Springer, 2009); Kenneth Abbott, Douglas Sylvester and Garry Marchant, 'Transnational Regulation: Reality or Romanticism?' in Graeme Hodge, Diana Bowman and Andrew Maynard (eds), *International Handbook on Regulating Nanotechnologies* (Edward Elgar, 2010); Eleni Kosta and Diana Bowman, 'Treating or Tracking? Regulatory Challenges of Nano-Enabled ICT Implants' (2011) 33(2) *Law and Policy* 256; National Research Council of the National Academies, *Review of the Federal Strategy for Nanotechnology-Related Environmental, Health, and Safety Research* (National Academies Press, 2009); Diana Bowman and Michael Bennett, 'The Current State of Australia's Evolving Approach to Regulating Nanotechnologies' (2013) 9 *Nanotechnology Law & Business* 330; Graeme Hodge, Andrew Maynard and Diana Bowman, 'Nanotechnology: Rhetoric, Risk and Regulation' (2014) 41(1) *Science and Public Policy* 1; Hitoshi Nasu and Thomas Faunce, 'Nanotechnology and the International Law of Weaponry: Towards International Regulation of Nano-Weapons' (2009) 22 *Journal of Law, Information and Science* 21 <https://law.anu.edu.au/sites/all/files/users/u9705219/nanoweapons_int_law_0.pdf>.

and human rights law. Despite the speed of the scientific development, it is important that the existing laws of war are thoughtfully applied. As already discussed, the tension between the desire for security and humanity is not new; what is new is the speed and scale at which the tools are being developed and interconnected.[15] This speed and scale of development should not be an impediment to thoughtful review and consideration regarding compliance with the law.

Second, the analysis illustrates that it is not only the laws of war that regulate the use of nanomaterials in armed conflict. Legal principles from environmental law, international human rights law and even ancient laws of usufruct may apply to different uses of nanomaterials.

Third, some existing legal frameworks, such as protection of the environment during armed conflict, are not adequate and urgently require strengthening.

Section I will introduce nanomaterials and the impetus for undertaking this project. In Section II, I will provide a summary of the existing literature in the field of regulation of nanomaterials. Section III will introduce the methodological approach used in this book. Section IV will further explain the basis for the Article 36 review that States are required to review new or modified means or methods of warfare prior to use in war as a matter of practice to ensure compliance with the international law applicable in war.[16]

I conclude that there is no need for additional international law specifically regulating nanomaterials as a category, and that such an approach would not be helpful. Unlike the field of computing, where Microsoft has requested a 'Geneva-type Convention' to govern potential misuse or hostile use,[17] I do not recommend a treaty to govern nanomaterials.

[15] Robert Mathews and Timothy McCormack, 'The Relationship between International Humanitarian Law and Arms Control' in Helen Durham and Tim McCormack (eds), *The Changing Face of Conflict and the Efficacy of International Humanitarian Law* (Martinus Nijhoff, 1999) 70. There is 'a gap between the articulation of commitment to the general principles and the effective application of those general principles to specific weapons categories'.

[16] See, e.g., the practice of Sweden and the United States, both of which established formal weapons review mechanisms as early as 1974, three years before the adoption of Additional Protocol I, noted in International Committee of the Red Cross, 'A Guide to the Legal Review of New Weapons, Means and Methods of Warfare: Measures to Implement Article 36 of Additional Protocol I of 1977' (2006) 88(864) *International Review of the Red Cross* 933.

[17] Aarti Shahani, 'Microsoft President Urges Nuclear-Like Limits on Cyberweapons' (16 May 2017) *National Public Radio* <www.npr.org/sections/alltechconsidered/2017/05/16/528555400/microsofts-president-reflects-on-cyberattack-helping-pirates-and-the-nsa>.

Even if a new treaty governing nanomaterials were politically viable, it would not be the most effective approach to govern nanomaterials, given the diverse legal considerations required for the use of nanomaterials in war. For example, nanomaterials used in ballistics require consideration of entirely different legal regimes to nanomaterials used in neuroscience. Regimes refer to broader fields of specialisation (such as trade, human rights, international criminal law and environmental law).[18] Within these different regimes, there may be multiple legal frameworks.

As the technologies develop rapidly and become more complex, the existing legal regimes that govern them require clarification and strengthening to explicitly include relevant new military uses of nanomaterials. As a first point, I make the case that legal reviews must occur in order to comply with existing international treaty and customary law and legal principles. Although I conclude that existing treaty law, such as the Biological Weapons Convention[19] (BWC) and the Chemical Weapons Convention[20] (CWC), applies to nanomaterials, I also recommend that States and governments strengthen the interpretation of the existing prohibitions on chemical and biological weapons. Explicitly including nanomaterials within the mandate of the BWC and CWC under the existing framework of the Review Conferences of the BWC and within the Scientific Advisory Board for the CWC will strengthen already existing prohibitions. States need to be clear that any materials that contravene the BWC or CWC, whether at the regular, micro or nanoscale, remain prohibited, and reiterate that States will be held to account for upholding these treaties.

I Introducing Nanomaterials

'Nano' is a prefix meaning 'a billionth' (a factor of 10^9 of a metre), and it is derived from the Greek νᾶνος, meaning 'dwarf'. By way of illustration, a nano-sized object is to an apple what an apple is to the size of the earth.

18 Stephen Humphreys, 'Structural Ambiguity: Technology Transfer in Three Regimes' in Margaret A Young (ed), *Regime Interaction in International Law: Facing Fragmentation* (Cambridge University Press, 2012) 184.

19 *Convention on the Prohibition of the Development, Production and Stockpiling of Bacteriological (Biological) and Toxin Weapons and on Their Destruction*, opened for signature 10 April 1972, 1015 UNTS 163 (entered into force 26 March 1975) ('*Biological Weapons Convention*').

20 *Convention on the Prohibition of the Development, Production, Stockpiling and Use of Chemical Weapons and on Their Destruction*, opened for signature 3 September 1992, 1974 UNTS 45 (entered into force 29 April 1997) ('*Chemical Weapons Convention*').

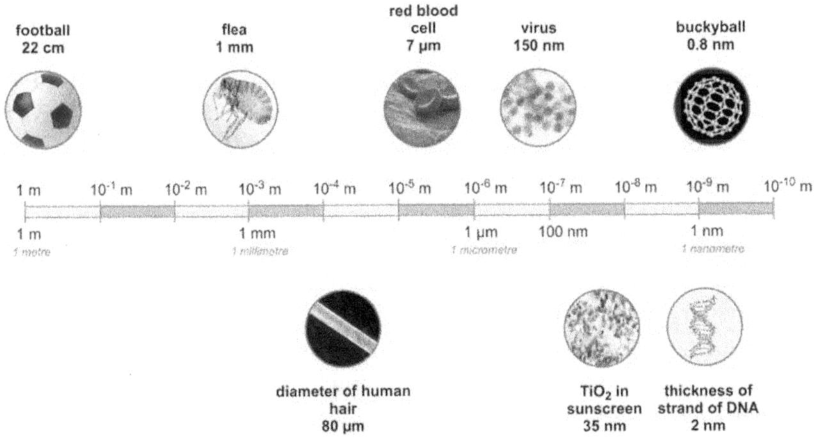

Figure 1.1 Nanoscale map.
Source: University of York Centre for Industry Education Collaboration, 'The Essential Chemical Industry – Online' <www.essentialchemicalindustry.org/images/stories/160_nanotech/03-16-nano_Fig_03.jpg>.

Or to give another example, one nanometre particle could fit approximately 80,000 times across a human hair (see Figure 1.1).[21] In the last two decades, the ability to deliberately create, manipulate or modify existing matter at the nanoscale has resulted in rapid innovation in, and across, many fields. Most of this development is driven by the fact that materials at the nanoscale have different properties when compared to their microscale counterparts, such as increased permeability due to their large surface area to volume ratio, greater strength, higher chemical resistance or heightened conductivity.

Nanoparticles are not new. They have occurred naturally for thousands, perhaps millions, of years in volcanic ash, in sea spray and as mineral deposits, to name just a few examples.[22] These naturally occurring nanoparticles, for the most part, pose few challenges to human health, as human bodies have adapted to deal with these materials over the years.[23] It is not these types of nanomaterial that attracted concern in

[21] Jennifer Kahn, 'Nano's Big Future' (2006) 209(6) *National Geographic* 98.
[22] Vijay Kumar Thakur and Manju Kumari Thakur, *Handbook of Sustainable Polymers: Structure and Chemistry* (Taylor & Francis, 2016) 688.
[23] Christine Buzea, Ivan Pacheco and Kevin Robbie, 'Nanomaterials and Nanoparticles: Sources and Toxicity' (2007) 2(4) *Biointerphases* 17 <https://link.springer.com/content/pdf/10.1116/1.2815690.pdf>.

the early 2000s from consumer groups, non-governmental organisations (NGOs) and academics in relation to potential harm and great uncertainties. Rather, it was the increase in creation and use of purposefully engineered nanoparticles that generated discussion and debate across multiple disciplines and jurisdictions.[24] Commercially, nanoparticles are being used in the manufacture of scratchproof eyeglasses, crack-resistant paints, anti-graffiti coatings for walls, transparent sunscreens, stain-repellent fabrics, self-cleaning windows and ceramic coatings for solar cells, to name a few examples. Promoters of the use of nanomaterials have argued that the technology has the potential to improve the performance of existing products, to offer new capabilities – especially through convergence with other emerging technologies – and to be of fundamental assistance in addressing global problems such as climate change and food security.[25] It is therefore not surprising that a number of national governments have heavily invested in a nanomaterials future, given the seemingly endless number of potential uses (see Figure 1.2).[26]

It is these purposefully engineered particles that will be considered. Most writers use the terms 'nano-enhanced', 'nanomaterials' or 'nanotechnology' to refer to situations where one or more components of matter have been deliberately manipulated to benefit from the special properties of matter exhibited at the nanoscale. The nomenclature 'nano' will refer to human-made materials that have one or more dimensions at this scale.[27] 'Nanotechnology' includes the engineering and fabrication of

[24] See, e.g., P H Hoet, I Brüske-Hohlfeld and O V Salata, 'Nanoparticles–Known and Unknown Health Risks' (2004) 2(1) *Journal of Nanobiotechnology* 12; Andrew D Maynard et al, 'Safe Handling of Nanotechnology' (2006) 444(7117) *Nature* 267; Paul J A Borm et al, 'The Potential Risks of Nnomaterials: A Review Carried Ot for ECETOC' (2006) 3(1) *Particle and Fibre Toxicology* 11; Steffen Foss Hansen et al, 'Late Lessons from Early Warnings for Nanotechnology' (2008) 3(8) *Nature Nanotechnology* 444; John M Balbus et al, 'Meeting Report: Hazard Assessment for Nanoparticles – Report from an Interdisciplinary Workshop' (2007) 115(11) *Environmental Health Perspectives* 1654.

[25] Claudia Som et al, 'The Importance of Life Cycle Concepts for the Development of Safe Nanoproducts' (2010) 269 *Toxicology* 160.

[26] Mihail C Roco, 'International Perspective on Government Nanotechnology Funding in 2005' (2005) 7(6) *Journal of Nanoparticle Research* 707.

[27] There is some controversy surrounding the methodologies of measuring nanometers and, more recently, suggestions that these methodologies may result in vastly different measurements and results: *How to Tell When a Nanoparticle Is Out of Shape* (21 December 2016) National Institute of Standards and Technology <https://m.phys.org/news/2016-12-nanoparticle.html>. Some authors go so far as to specifically request that there be no definition of nanomaterials: see Andrew Maynard, 'Don't Define Nanomaterials' (2011)

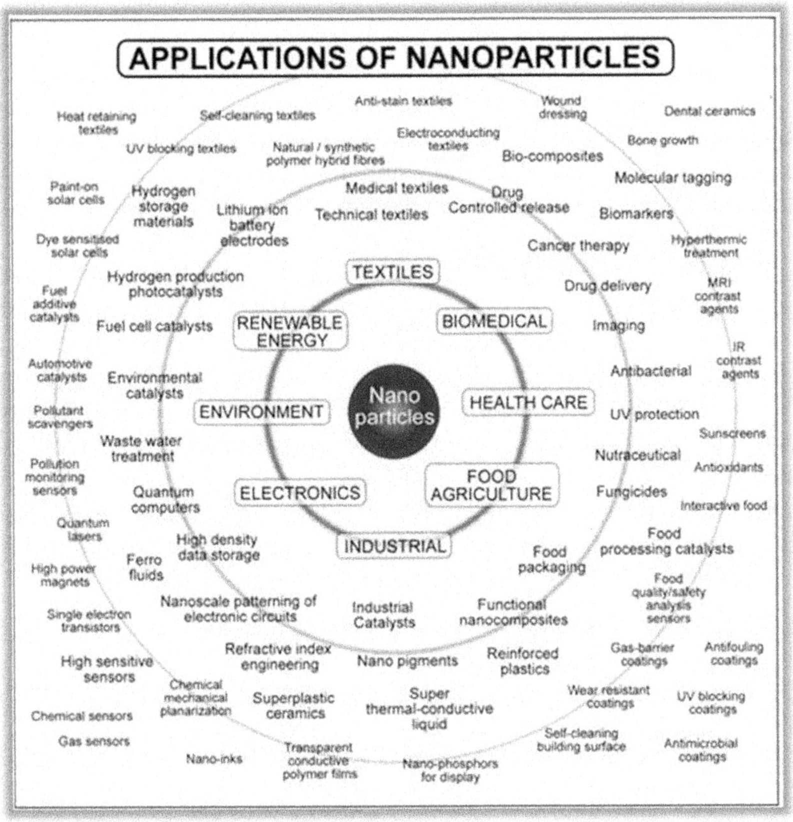

Figure 1.2 Applications of nanoparticles.
Source: Munusamy Thirumavalavan, Kalpana Settu and Jiunn-Fwu Lee, "A Short Review on Applications of Nanomaterials in Biotechnology and Pharmacology" (2016) 2(2) *Current Bionanotechnology* (Discontinued). https://doi.org/10.2174/2213529402666161125143644.

functional systems at the atomic and molecular scales and spans disciplines as diverse as agriculture, biological science, biotechnology, chemistry, defence, energy conversion and storage, engineering, information technology, material sciences, medicine, microelectronics and

475(7354) *Nature* 31. See also Maynard et al., n 24: 'Nanotechnology ... is about controlling matter at near-atomic scales to produce unique or enhanced materials, products and devices'.

pharmaceuticals.[28] In many instances, the uses between these categories overlap as scientists increasingly collaborate and draw from other fields to improve their own technologies.[29]

It has also become clear that some of these engineered nanoparticles or nanotechnologies may be harmful to human health or cause as-yet-unknown side effects.[30] The many unknowns of engineered nanomaterials pose governance challenges in the face of increasing knowledge about how nanomaterials affect the human body.[31]

Military interest in nanomaterials is significant.[32] For some years, there has been extraordinary investment in both military and civilian uses of nanomaterials (see Figure 1.3). The US 2017 federal budget alone provided more than $1.4 billion for the National Nanotechnology Initiative (NNI),[33] a US government research and development initiative involving the nanomaterials-related activities of twenty departments and independent agencies, including academia, government and industry laboratories across the United States. Since its inception in 2001, a cumulative total of nearly $24 billion has been invested in nanomaterials by the US government alone (including the 2017 budget).[34]

[28] Abbott, Sylvester and Marchant, n 14:

> While the term 'nanotechnology' was first coined by Taniguchi in 1974, this simple word does not in itself acknowledge the complexity of ideas, meanings and historical pedigrees embedded in it. It has become a handy shorthand label for a wide range of scientific domains and applications that draw on the diversity of fields that underpin the technology.

[29] Lea Kivivali, *Swinburne Researchers Mimic Butterfly Wing for Compact New Technology* (1 June 2016) Swinburne Institute of Technology <www.swinburne.edu.au/news/latest-news/2016/06/swinburne-researchers-mimic-butterfly-wing-for-compact-new-technology.php>; Elizabeth Pennisi, *Robot Stingray Powered by Light-Activated Muscle Cells* (7 July 2016) Science <www.sciencemag.org/news/2016/07/robotic-stingray-powered-light-activated-muscle-cells>.

[30] Linda Abbott and Andrew Maynard, 'Exposure Assessment Approaches for Engineered Nanomaterials' (2010) 30(11) *Risk Analysis* 1634.

[31] Dexter Johnson, 'Nanoparticles Found in Brains Come from External Sources' (8 September 2016) *IEEE Spectrum* <http://spectrum.ieee.org/nanoclast/semiconductors/materials/nanoparticles-found-in-brains-comes-from-external-sources>.

[32] Defense Advanced Research Projects Agency, 'Atoms to Product: Aiming to Make Nanoscale Benefits Life-Sized' (22 August 2014) *Media Release* <www.darpa.mil/news-events/2014-08/22>.

[33] Subcommittee on Nanoscale Science, Engineering, and Technology, Committee on Technology, and National Science and Technology Council, *NNI Supplement to The President's Budget for Fiscal Year 2017* (31 March 2016) The National Nanotechnology Initiative, Executive Office of the President <www.nano.gov/node/1573>.

[34] Ibid.

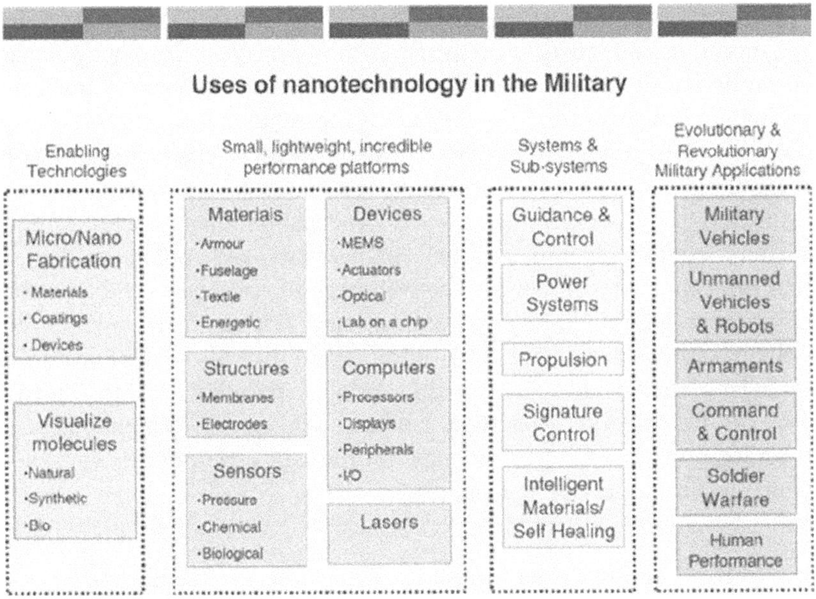

Figure 1.3 Military uses of nanotechnology.
Source: *Nanotechnology Now* <www.nanotech-now.com/images/military_uses.gif>.

Military and civilian research in nanomaterials continues to slowly forge new frontiers with direct implications for new military equipment and associated regulatory mechanisms. Detailed predictions for the possibility of storage, dispersal and transport of chemical and biological agents in the bodies of humans, animals[35] and plants[36] have been provided by scientists in the field looking forward to the future.[37] Nanomaterials, it has been suggested, will enable nanorobots to self-replicate, with no currently developed countermeasures. These nanorobots could, just as one example, be used as 'markers' for individuals to be targeted or, conversely, provide specific protections for particular populations.[38]

[35] Jérôme de Hemptinne, 'Challenges Regarding the Protection of Animals during Warfare' in Anne Peters (ed), *Studies in Global Animal Law* (Springer, 2020) 173.
[36] Ben Richardson, *Time and Environmental Law: Telling Nature's Time* (Cambridge University Press, 2017).
[37] Jürgen Altmann and Mark Gubrud, 'Risks from Military Uses of Nanotechnology – The Need for Technology Assessment and Preventive Control' (Paper presented at Nanotechnology – Revolutionary Opportunities and Societal Implications, 3rd JOINTEC-NSF Workshop on Nanotechnology, Lecce, Italy, 31 January – 2 February 2002) 2–3.
[38] Ibid.

Much of the military research (including research undertaken in collaboration with civilian scientists) does not result in readily available scientific reports or public patents and is therefore difficult to track or evaluate. The Institute for Soldier Nanotechnologies (ISN) is one example of an organisation where 'team members collaborate on basic research to create new materials, devices, process and systems ... to transition promising results toward practical products useful to the soldier'.[39] Although militaries will, of necessity, seek out technologies that meet their needs, they also actively seek to collaborate with civilian researchers to find innovative uses of new science that could be of potential military use. ISN seeks 'promising outcomes of that research in collaboration with our Army and industry partners'.[40] This point is relevant because the separation between science and the military is blurring, posing particular challenges for the legal review of new weapons which will be addressed in Chapter 7.

II The Big Little: Literature Regarding the Regulation of Nanomaterials

Although much has been written about the regulation of nanomaterials over the past decade,[41] very little has been written about the regulation of

[39] *Institute for Soldier Nanotechnologies* <http://isnweb.mit.edu/what-is-isn.html>.

[40] John Joannopoulos and Francis Davis, *Institute for Soldier Nanotechnologies* (18 June 2015) Massachusetts Institute of Technology 1 <http://web.mit.edu/annualreports/pres15/2015.18.06.pdf>:

> This mission includes not only decreasing the weight that soldiers carry but also improving blast and ballistic protection, creating new methods of detecting and detoxifying chemical and biological threats, and providing physiological monitoring and medical treatment. The ultimate goal is to help the Army create integrated systems of nanotechnologies that combine high-tech protection and survivability capabilities with low weight, increased comfort, improved performance, and better compatibility with the end user ... Approximately 30 faculty members from a dozen MIT academic departments, as well as more than 100 graduate students and postdoctoral associates, participate in ISN research. The Institute for Soldier Nanotechnologies website breaks these areas of research into three, namely lightweight, multifunctional nanostructured materials and fibres, soldier medicine, and blast and ballistic threats.

[41] European Commission, *Nanoscience and Nanotechnologies: An Action Plan for Europe 2005–2009* (2005) European Commission Community Research and Development Information Service <https://cordis.europa.eu/pub/nanotechnology/docs/action_plan_brochure.pdf>; Altmann, n 14; Matsuura, n 14; Hodge, Bowman and Ludlow, n 14;

individual weapons systems containing nanomaterials.[42] A small body of literature exists that focuses specifically on the use of nanomaterials by the armed forces. These types of analyses fall loosely into two camps.

The first camp consists of those whose position it is that the existing law has relevance and call for a strengthening of existing international law specifically in relation to nanomaterials.[43] I fall firmly within this camp. The second camp consists of those calling for greater regulation, or new laws, that specifically regulate the use of nanomaterials for military purposes.[44] They argue along the lines that nanomaterials are new, in fact, so new and different that '[t]echnological developments in the methods of conducting war have increased the extent to which the written law is inadequate or absent'.[45] I argue that existing law applies and, in most cases, is adequate but should be carefully considered. This opinion is supported by others considering the legal review of nanomaterials in weapons.[46]

Leading voices in the first camp argue that existing laws should be upheld but strengthened by explicitly including nanomaterials within their mandate.[47] Much of the strengthening of treaties comes from the simple act of clarifying definitions, rather than redrafting the text. The text already provides adequate oversight but requires subsidiary clarification to support an interpretation that includes nanomaterials. Such

Kosal, n 14; Abbott, Sylvester and Marchant, n 14; Kosta and Bowman, n 14; National Research Council of the National Academies, n 14; Bowman and Bennett, n 14; Hodge, Maynard and Bowman, 'Nanotechnology: Rhetoric, Risk and Regulation', n 14.

42 Three such examples are Hitoshi Nasu and Robert McLaughlin (eds), *New Technologies and the Law of Armed Conflict* (Asser Press, 2014); Wang and Dortmans, n 7; William Boothby, *Weapons and the Law of Armed Conflict* (Oxford University Press, 2009) 258–262; Louis A Del Monte, *Nanoweapons: A Growing Threat to Humanity* (University of Nebraska Press, 2017).

43 Altman, n 14; Matsuura, n 14; Kosal, n 14; Abbott, Sylvester and Marchant, n 14; Nasu and Faunce, n 14.

44 Braden R Allenby, 'Are new Technologies Undermining the Laws of War?' (2014) 70(1) *Bulletin of the Atomic Scientists* 21; Robert Pinson, 'Is Nanotechnology Prohibited by the Biological and Chemical Weapons Conventions?' (2004) 22 *Berkeley Journal of International Law* 278; Glenn Reynolds, 'Environmental Regulation of Nanotechnology: Some Preliminary Observations' (2001) 31(6) *Environmental Law Reporter* 10681.

45 Adam Roberts and Richard Guelff (eds), *Documents on the Laws of War* (Oxford University Press, 3rd ed, 2000) 7.

46 Article 36, *Nanoweapons* (November 2017) <www.article36.org/wp-content/uploads/2017/11/Nano-Final-17Nov17.pdf>.

47 Kosal, n 14, Altmann and Gubrud, n 37, 2–3; Altmann, n 14.

clarifications are currently being considered by review bodies under both the BWC and the CWC and will be explored further in Chapter 3.

Some legal writers propose that the BWC, CWC and provisions of the laws of war already govern the military use of nanomaterials.[48] Each of these authors' writings will be discussed in the following chapters. Marcus, also in the first camp, notes that if nanomaterials are 'functionally equivalent' to microscale materials prohibited under the Geneva Protocol,[49] BWC or CWC, then they logically remain prohibited, regardless of their size, and without further clarification.[50] These arguments are supported by scientific evidence: matter at the nanoscale exhibits both biological and chemical properties on the human body, and, as is clarified in Chapter 3, therefore clearly falls within the mandate of these existing treaty regimes.

More broadly, specific uses of nanomaterials in war aside, much has been written about the relationships between nanomaterials and policy and law. A distinction is drawn between 'exploratory research' and that 'aimed at informing decisions'. This distinction is important in that the purpose for which scientific evidence is created is clear. Not creating this distinction may lead to unusual policy and legal positions.[51] This is a concern echoed in a call for nuance in the assessment of whether international law adequately governs emerging technologies in weapons. Often this nuance is lost as technological advancement is made at the cost of adverse effects on humans or the environment that may not be immediately apparent.[52] Judge Weeramantry, regarding the principle of specialty, in the International Court of Justice (ICJ) went so far as to say that international law does not adequately acknowledge that 'complex

[48] William Boothby, 'How Will Weapons Reviews Address the Challenges Posed by New Technologies?' (2013) 52(1) *Military Law and the Law of War Review* 58; Nasu and McLaughlin, n 42, 145; Nasu and Faunce, n 14; *Biological Weapons Convention*; *Chemical Weapons Convention*; Hitoshi Nasu, 'Nanotechnology and Challenges to International Humanitarian Law: A Preliminary Legal Assessment' (2012) 94(886) *International Review of the Red Cross* 653.

[49] *Protocol for the Prohibition of the Use in War of Asphyxiating, Poisonous or Other Gases, and of Bacteriological Methods of Warfare*, opened for signature 17 June 1925, 94 LNTS 65 (entered into force 8 February 1928) ('*Protocol to the BWC*').

[50] David Marcus, 'Famine Crimes in International Law' (2003) 97(2) *American Journal of International Law* 245, 262–264. Marcus proposes that international law should extend to man-made famines as 'famines are often functionally equivalent to genocide': 248.

[51] Andrew Maynard, 'Is Novelty Overrated?' (2014) 9(6) *Nature Nanotechnology* 409.

[52] Laurent Hourcle, 'Environmental Law of War' (2001) 25(1) *Vermont Law Review* 653.

problems have ramifications in many specialized directions'.[53] Judge Weeramantry went on to remark that such instances of 'mutual interdependence' are the result of '[a] world order in which every sovereign state depends on the same global environment'.[54] According to the then President of the Court, Judge Bedjaoui, commenting on the same case, interdependence also has important implications for international law. Judge Bedjaoui also noted that every lawyer is required to interpret language based on reason and a sense of moral judgement, not just on the face of the law.[55] In this sense, every interpretation requires placing the treaty obligations in their historical or social context. This 'moral judgement' requirement also demands the application of international law by analogy to new technologies, including nanomaterials, where they are applicable.

Those in the second camp call for substantially revised or new law. These include commentators variously suggesting that the existing law is not adequate; that the law is outdated; that States need to renegotiate the laws of war; or that States need to create new international laws to respond to rapidly changing technology which poses entirely new legal problems.[56] By calling for substantially new treaties, the direct implication is that the existing law is not sufficient and does not govern nanomaterials. There is ample law governing the use of nanomaterials in war. Calling for more or different law requires mapping the existing international law first and concluding that nanomaterials are not adequately regulated. My analysis concludes that the area which does require more regulation is the protection of the environment in armed conflict more generally and, more specifically, as it pertains to potentially toxic nanomaterials.

My approach falls within the first camp because an analysis of individual technologies with nanomaterials makes it clear that a wide range of international legal treaties, customary law and legal principles apply,

[53] *Legality of the Use by a State of Nuclear Weapons in Armed Conflict* (*Advisory Opinion*) [1996] ICJ Rep 66, 151 (Judge Weeramantry).

[54] Ibid.

[55] Ronald Dworkin, *Law's Empire* (Harvard University Press, 1986) 254–258.

[56] Allenby, n 44; Sean Howard, 'Nanotechnology and Mass Destruction: The Need for an Inner Space Treaty' (2002) 65 *Disarmament Diplomacy*. Howard's vision for a treaty is vast and includes a somewhat unrealistic suggestion for an abolitionist treaty of all uses of nanotechnology, a draft of which is attached as an appendix to his writing. He suggests '[a] rough transposition of the Outer Space Treaty [to seek] peaceful exploitation ... of the nanosphere'; Pinson, n 44; Reynolds, n 44.

either directly or by way of analogy. I conclude that the existing international law is adequate in most instances, except environmental law. I conclude that, in addition to Article 36 Reviews, States need to strengthen existing law by including nanomaterials in official statements and expert advice provided to the treaty advisory bodies. Much like my like-minded colleagues, I call on States and governments to strengthen the existing prohibition on chemical and biological weapons by providing interpretation guidance to include materials at the nanoscale, within the existing framework of the Review Conferences of the BWC and within the Science Advisory Board for the CWC. States need to be clear that any materials that contravene the BWC or CWC, whether at the regular, micro or nanoscale, remain prohibited, and reiterate that States will be held to account for non-compliance with these obligations.

My aim and purpose is to demonstrate that the existing law is far from irrelevant. In some cases, applying international law to new or modified 'means or methods of warfare' involving nanomaterials may require creative interpretation of laws that did not foresee these scientific developments but nonetheless still have application and limit their use. In these cases, minor revisions and strengthening of language are proposed. In the area of international environmental law, new laws are urgently required that take into account the potentially toxic, long-lasting and wide-spread effect of toxic nanomaterials, and other environmental degradation caused by war.

III Methodology

I will examine how existing international law regulates the use of nanomaterials, which is a prerequisite of any new or modified 'means or method of warfare' prior to deployment.[57] The approach taken is that of an Article 36 weapons review for three specific new weapons being reviewed as new or modified, given their inclusion of nanomaterials.[58] It is a logical extrapolation that the inclusion of nanomaterials in new or existing means or methods of warfare should trigger an Article 36 legal review to ensure compliance with existing international treaty law,

[57] *Protocol Additional to the Geneva Conventions of 12 August 1949, and Relating to the Protection of Victims of International Armed Conflicts (Protocol I)*, opened for signature 8 June 1977, 1125 UNTS 3 (entered into force 7 December 1978) art 36 ('*Additional Protocol I*').

[58] Ibid art 36.

customary law and legal principles. The alternative is that States do not undertake reviews of 'means or methods of warfare' containing nanomaterials, and run the risk of non-compliance with their international treaty and customary law obligations. The requirement to review new or modified weapons under Article 36 of API will be discussed in further detail in Section IV of this chapter.

My writing is primarily doctrinal,[59] analysing the existing treaty and customary international law, and case law where relevant. Specific examples of nanomaterials will be used to demonstrate the application of these codified rules and principles, as required by Article 36 of API.[60] Article 38(1) of the Statute of the ICJ[61] has achieved 'an almost canonical status as a codification of the sources of international law'.[62] The binding nature of treaties rests on the *pacta sunt servanda* principle, namely that agreements must be observed in good faith, a principle applicable in many national legal systems. In accordance with the Vienna Convention on the Law of Treaties (VCLT),[63] the approach taken is a textual one.[64] Beyond these sources, the 'judicial decisions and the teachings of the

[59] Terry Hutchinson and Nigel Duncan, 'Defining and Describing What We Do: Doctrinal Legal Research' (2012) 17(1) *Deakin Law Review* 83, 101–104.

[60] *Additional Protocol I* art 36.

[61] *Statute of the International Court of Justice* art 38:

> The Court, whose function is to decide in accordance with international law such disputes as are submitted to it, shall apply: a) international conventions, whether general or particular, establishing rules expressly recognized by the contesting states; b) international custom, as evidence of a general practice accepted as law; c) the general principles of law recognized by civilized nations; d) subject to the provisions of Article 59, judicial decisions and the teachings of the most highly qualified publicists of the various nations, as subsidiary means for the determination of rules of law.

[62] Hilary Charlesworth, 'Law-Making and Sources' in James Crawford and Martii Koskienniemi (eds), *The Cambridge Companion to International Law* (Cambridge University Press, 2012) 188.

[63] *Vienna Convention on the Law of Treaties*, opened for signature 23 May 1969, 1155 UNTS 331 (entered into force 27 January 1980) arts 31, 32 ('*VCLT*'). See also Jean-Marc Sorel, 'Article 31 General Rule of Interpretation' in Olivier Corten and Pierre Klein (eds), *The Vienna Conventions on the Law of Treaties: A Commentary* (Oxford University Press, 2011) 804, 807–808.

[64] *Prosecutor v Delalić (Judgment)* (International Criminal Tribunal for the Former Yugoslavia, Trial Chamber, Case No IT-96-21-T, 16 November 1998) [161]: 'If only one construction is possible, to which the clear, plain or unambiguous word is unequivocally susceptible, the word must be so construed. In cases of ambiguity, however, all legal systems consider methods for determining how to give effect to the legislative intention'.

most highly qualified publicists of the various nations' are also relied on as 'subsidiary means' of interpreting the law where and as required.[65] As such, frequent references are made to the authoritative International Committee of the Red Cross (ICRC) Commentaries to the Geneva Conventions.[66]

It is important to bear in mind that customary international law is a combination of actual State practice and *opinio juris*, or the intention of States to undertake a practice. Both are required to form customary international law.[67] State practice must be 'both extensive and virtually uniform'.[68] The International Law Commission (ILC) has used the language of 'sufficiently widespread and representative, as well as consistent'.[69] In the case of nanomaterials being used during war, there is not enough public information regarding use to indicate any kind of consistent approach or custom in international law based on State practice. As such, considering the legality of the use of nanomaterials during armed conflict requires judicial consideration of customary law and treaty law in other contexts and, from these historical decisions, analogising how courts might make decisions regarding their use, given previous opinions offered in other similar circumstances.

I focus on technology that is advancing rapidly, and which is not developing in isolation but alongside many other technologies simultaneously. Contemporary times are frequently referred to as the beginning of a 'fourth industrial revolution'.[70] For this reason, I not only survey the current state of the law but also suggest how the law should develop (*lege ferenda*) in relation to treaty law. This includes an assessment of commentaries, statements from States and influential NGOs, and academic literature. By way of analysis of the under-examined legal frameworks governing the weaponisation of nanomaterials, I explore the existing constraints that would govern the use of nanomaterials as 'a means or

[65] *Statute of the International Court of Justice* art 38(d).

[66] International Committee of the Red Cross, *The Geneva Conventions of 12 August 1949 – Commentary* (1952–1960) vols I–IV.

[67] See *Military and Paramilitary Activities in and against Nicaragua (Nicaragua v United States) (Merits)* [1986] ICJ Rep 14, 100–101 [190]; *North Sea Continental Shelf (Federal Republic of Germany v Denmark) (Merits)* [1969] ICJ Rep 3.

[68] *North Sea Continental Shelf (Federal Republic of Germany v Denmark) (Merits)* [1969] ICJ Rep 3, 42-43 [73]-[74]. The consistency of State practice may vary and these standards may vary from situation to situation.

[69] See International Law Commission, *Draft Conclusions of Identification of Customary International Law, with Commentaries*, UN GAOR, UN Doc A/73/10 (2018) art 8(1).

[70] Klaus Schwab, *The Fourth Industrial Revolution* (World Economic Forum, 2016).

method of warfare', as well as where the constraints may be lacking. As such, and at times using subsidiary sources such as expert writings, I provide an indicator of what the law should be, as it is reflective of the current state of the law (*lex lata*). The tension between the desire for increasingly sophisticated and powerful weaponry and the desire for an expression or retention of the principle of humanity remains as relevant as it did 1.8 million years ago, regardless of the increasing complexity of the science. Where this line is drawn between principles of humanity and the desire for self-defence is what I will indicate based on an analysis of the existing international legal frameworks, just as an Article 36 legal review would require of a state. By discussing specific examples, this work demonstrates the challenges posed by the use of nanomaterials. Although the considerations in this work are legal, the challenges extend beyond the legal and into challenges for national security, public health, environmental security and sustainability. Consideration of these broader challenges is largely beyond the scope of this book, but remains highly relevant.

IV Legal Requirement to Review Weapons under Article 36 of API to the Geneva Conventions

Article 36 of API requires review of new or modified weapons:

> [i]n the study, development, acquisition or adoption of a new weapon, means or method of warfare, a High Contracting Party is under an obligation to determine whether its employment would, in some or all circumstances, be prohibited by this Protocol or by any other rule of international law applicable to the High Contracting Party.

It follows that it is incumbent on all States to comply with their customary and, in some cases, treaty law obligations.[71] The only way in which States can effectively do this is by undertaking a robust Article 36 legal review of weapons. Before any technology is deployed in armed conflict as a 'means or method of warfare', the legality of its use is required to be determined by legal review. This requirement is customary international

[71] See, e.g., the practice of Sweden and the United States, both of which established formal weapons review mechanisms as early as 1974, three years before the adoption of *Additional Protocol I*, noted in International Committee of the Red Cross, 'A Guide to the Legal Review of New Weapons, Means and Methods of Warfare: Measures to Implement Article 36 of Additional Protocol I of 1977' (2006) 88(864) *International Review of the Red Cross* 933.

law because regardless of whether a Party to API, all States have an obligation to ensure that the weapons they use, and the method of use, comply with international law. It is therefore a truism that the

> [F]aithful and responsible application of its international law obligations would require a State to ensure that the new weapons, means and methods of warfare it develops or acquires will not violate these obligations. Carrying out legal reviews of new weapons is of particular importance today in light of the rapid development of new weapons technologies.[72]

This is despite the fact that it has been suggested that Article 36 is not itself customary international law because of the lack of State practice and *opinio juris*.[73]

Ultimately, it is moot whether weapons reviews are customary international law or not, as ongoing review of weapons is necessary to ensure compliance with obligations under the existing laws of war, particularly as systems and technologies converge and become more complex. Also, of the specially affected States that produce or purchase weapons, many do undertake Article 36 reviews.[74]

In contrast to the use of new or modified weapons, the mere trade or transfer of weapons does not inherently require an Article 36 review, but it may be 'prudent for a State to conduct a review of those weapons which are subject to international scrutiny'.[75]

Subsequent analysis will suggest that any weapon that incorporates nanomaterials should be considered to be 'new' and attract a legal review, given the novel nature of the nanomaterials under consideration, our nascent understanding of these materials, as well as their potential longevity and toxicity to humans. Considerations of environmental

[72] International Committee of the Red Cross, 'A Guide to the Legal Review of New Weapons, Means and Methods of Warfare: Measures to Implement Article 36 of Additional Protocol I of 1977' (2006) 88(864) *International Review of the Red Cross* 933.

[73] Natalia Jevglevskaja, 'Weapons Review Obligation under Customary International Law' (2018) 94 *International Law Studies* 186.

[74] Article 36, *Article 36 Reviews and Addressing Lethal Autonomous Weapons Systems* (April 2016) <www.article36.org/wp-content/uploads/2016/04/LAWS-and-A36.pdf>.

[75] Justin McClelland, 'The Review of Weapons in Accordance with Article 36 of Additional Protocol I' (2003) 85(850) *International Review of the Red Cross* 397, 404. Such an interpretation is consistent with the commentary in Yves Sandoz, Christophe Swinarski and Bruno Zimmermann (eds), *Commentary on the Additional Protocols of 8 June 1977 to the Geneva Conventions of 12 August 1949* (Martinus Nijhoff, 1987), which states 'Without necessarily being "new" in a technical sense . . . arms are new for the State which is intending to acquire them after becoming a Party to the Protocol' at [1472].

impact, which are particularly relevant in the case of nanomaterials and are discussed in further detail in Chapter 5, need to be included.[76] Given the complexity of nanomaterials and their behaviour, the breadth and depth of applicable international law and the speed at which these nanomaterials are being developed, the requirement to undertake a legal review of 'means and methods of warfare' has greater significance and potential legal and practical implications than ever before.

A *Article 36 Weapons Review Considerations*

1 Timing of the Article 36 Review

Not all research or advances in science and technology require review under Article 36 of API. Determining when these advances constitute the 'study' or 'development of a new weapon, means or method of warfare' is the first challenge. The laws of war only apply to a modified or new weapon, means or method of warfare, not advances in science and technology generally. Consequently, when the technologies using nanomaterials are overtly under consideration as a means or method of warfare they would, and should, be subject to the Article 36 review process.[77] Unlike traditional weapons, developing nanomaterial-enhanced means or methods of warfare may be time consuming and expensive. It is in States' interests to establish whether they would be legal prior to outlaying enormous expense on developing a potentially illegal means or method of warfare.

Although not all research and advances have to be reviewed, the question of the timing of the review is becoming more complicated. Despite a long-standing relationship between defence and science, an increasing amount of research in emerging technologies is being funded

[76] Robert Mathews, 'The 1980 Convention on Certain Conventional Weapons: A Useful Framework despite Earlier Disappointments' (Paper presented at the Australian Defence Force Conference on 'Pushing the Envelope: The ADF Contribution to International & Operations Law', University of Melbourne, 20–22 February 2002). With regard to the number of weapons review processes, see Isabel Daoust, Robin Coupland and R Ishoey, 'New Wars, New Weapons? The Obligation of States to Assess the Legality of Means and Methods of Warfare' (2002) 84(846) *International Review of the Red Cross* 354.

[77] For a more detailed discussion of the timing and complexity of Article 36 reviews pertaining to nano-enhanced weapons, means or methods of warfare, see Rain Liivoja, Kobi Leins and Tim McCormack, 'Emerging Technologies of Warfare' in Rain Liivoja and Tim McCormack (eds), *Routledge Handbook of the Law of Armed Conflict* (Routledge, 2016) 603, 620.

by the military. What obligation does the military have to ensure that research undertaken with military funding or military uses in mind complies with Article 36 requirements? Even though the final decision regarding legality of a weapon will rest with the lawyers, it is incumbent on scientific experts to provide accurate information regarding the new technologies to the lawyers. The exact timing required of a review when research is funded or commissioned by a military also remains an open question in the face of rapidly advancing science, and the question of when this research reaches the level of a 'means or methods of warfare' remains yet to be answered.

2 Ability to Independently Provide Review with Narrow Field of Experts

The second point concerns the designated authority responsible for the review. Traditionally, it has been legal advisors within the military wishing to adopt the new means or method of warfare, or military or civilian lawyers, or committees who were tasked with the responsibility for undertaking any weapons review. As the science becomes more sophisticated, unilateral review may not provide the knowledge required to ensure compliance with, for example, environmental legal obligations, given that most of the information regarding toxicity is held within the civilian sector. In the past, reviewers have sought technical advice about the intended use and expected effects of a proposed weapons system. For example, in the case of an old-fashioned kinetic weapon, with a particular kind of ammunition, the questions to be asked would be reasonably straightforward and based on predictable and well-known laws of physics. Now, however, the science is often multidisciplinary, and increasingly complicated, with many more variables and, in the case of nanomaterials, often many unknowns. These unknowns pose challenges to compliance with the existing law. Those setting the requirements for projects need to ensure that their initial specifications are assessed to determine whether they can conduct an Article 36 review. This is important not just to avoid a conflict of interest but also for the ability to provide an objective independent view more generally. At the time when the weapon is being developed or procured, particularly if it involves advanced technologies (in which I would include nanoparticles), this distinction may come too late.[78]

[78] Personal communication with Rob Sparrow, Professor of Philosophy, Monash University, PREMT Conference, Future Wars and Public Conscience, 29–30 May 2017. Sparrow raised this point in the context of a conversation about the requirement for all

In addition to an extensive legal understanding, weapons reviewers are required to have an understanding of the 'engineering design, production and testing (or validation) methods and the ways in which the weapon might be employed on the battlefield'.[79] The legal review of emerging technologies in general, and those involving medical nanomaterials in particular, raises similar issues.[80] Boothby correctly concludes that the inclusion of nanomaterials is 'likely to mean that the weapons reviewer is likely to need more scientific information'.[81]

With the increasing complexity of and rapid advances in technology, evaluations of new weapons systems will require intimate collaboration between the traditional reviewers, lawyers, scientists and engineers. This type of collaboration is not typically how the military has worked and will require changes in focus and culture. In addition, lawyers conducting the legal reviews will need to sufficiently familiarise themselves with the germane science and engineering, not only to analyse compliance with the law but also to be able to ask scientists the right questions to ensure that reviews comply with national legal obligations.[82]

B Rethinking the Article 82 Requirement to Advise Regarding Contextual Use of Nanomaterials in Warfare

Article 82 of API requires not only a one-off review of weapons but also an ongoing availability of legal advisors during conflict to ensure compliance with existing law. Article 82 requires that legal advisers be available at all times to advise military commanders on the laws of war and 'on the appropriate instruction to be given to the armed forces on this subject'.[83]

technology to be reviewed by experts who were 'outside' of those proposing the technology, but who were familiar with it, to avoid conflicts of interest. It was discussed that, with emerging technologies in general, finding experts with this level of objectivity and distance from their colleagues to perform such reviews is becoming increasingly difficult.

79 Alan Backstrom and Ian Henderson, 'New Capabilities in Warfare: An Overview of Contemporary Technological Developments and the Associated Legal and Engineering Issues in Article 36 Weapons Reviews' (2012) 94 *International Review of the Red Cross* 483.

80 Diana Bowman and Jake Gatof, 'Reviewing the Regulatory Barriers for Nanomedicine: Global Questions and Challenges' 2015 10(21) *Nanomedicine* 3275.

81 William Boothby, 'How Will Weapons Reviews Address the Challenges Posed by New Technologies?' (2013) 52(1) *Military Law and the Law of War Review* 58.

82 Lyria Bennett Moses, 'How to Think about Law, Regulation and Technology: Problems with "Technology" as a Regulatory Target' (2013) 5(1) *Law, Innovation and Technology* 1.

83 *Additional Protocol I* art 82.

In conjunction with Article 36 of API, Article 82 provides a framework for ensuring that legal guidance be provided before deployment of any means or method of warfare but also during any deployment, ensuring compliance with the laws of war. Article 82 is a requirement in addition to Article 36, as the context of the use of a weapon may alter the legality of its use.

> A weapon or means of warfare cannot be assessed in isolation from the method of warfare by which it is to be used. It follows that the legality of a weapon does not depend solely on its design or intended purpose, but also on the manner in which it is expected to be used on the battlefield. In addition, a weapon used in one manner may "pass" the [weapon review] "test", but may fail it when used in another manner.[84]

The legal advisor must advise the military commander about the legality of the use of weapons, through the chain of command.[85] Article 82 requires legal advisors of States party to the Protocol 'to advise military commanders at the appropriate level on the application of the Conventions and this Protocol and on the appropriate instruction to be given to the armed forces on this subject'.[86] Beyond the requirement of legal advisors, as the complexity and convergence of technology continues to escalate rapidly, advisors with scientific expertise particular to materials, situations and contexts will also be required to advise the lawyers *in situ*. It is not possible for lawyers to be materials experts, engineers, physicists, biologists and chemists, and yet, without access to these experts, this is in effect what is being asked of those legal teams that provide advice under Article 82. Furthermore, even if lawyers could be one or more of those things, context on the battlefield matters now more than ever, and the interplay between the technologies and the specialists is key. Given the esoteric and highly technical nature of the 'new means and methods of warfare', the requirement additional to Article 36 of ongoing review during use poses very particular challenges in the case of nanomaterials that cannot be seen with the naked eye.

Considering nanomaterials and their impact when that impact is not necessarily immediately apparent or the full risks even known will be a challenge for States. Compliance with Article 82 by providing well-

[84] International Committee of the Red Cross, 'A Guide to the Legal Review of New Weapons', n 72, 938.

[85] Dieter Fleck (ed), *The Handbook of International Humanitarian International Law* (Oxford University Press, 2008) 43.

[86] G I A D Draper, 'Role of Legal Advisers in Armed Forces' (1978) 18(202) *International Review of the Red Cross* 6, 9.

equipped lawyers and independent specialists, on whom the lawyers will have to rely and who understand the potential risks of nanomaterials, will be a necessary but not sufficient condition.

V Outline of Book

For each of the three technologies utilising nanomaterials, I will first consider how the existing international treaty law, customary law and legal principles may have relevance and apply them. In some cases, this will require consideration of some of the history of the formation of the law in order to analogise. I will analyse the adequacy of the existing international legal framework, either applicable directly or by way of analogy.

Chapter 2 will introduce the specific uses of nanomaterials reviewed in this book, namely thermobaric weapons, genetic modification and optogenetics, and explain their particular scientific properties and foreshadow the potentially relevant legal issues to each. I apply international law to three very different examples of 'means or methods of warfare' that include nanomaterials to analyse how the existing legal framework applies and where it may be inadequate. The term 'means and methods' of warfare extends the requirement to review beyond physical weapons. There is a long history to this treaty provision, which is traditionally two-pronged, and attempts to 'control the manner in which weapons are used' as well as to ensure regulation of 'particular types of weapons'.

Chapter 3 will explore international treaty law obligations, including the prohibition of the use of biological or chemical weapons and laser weapons that permanently blind. Chapter 4 will extend the analysis of the international legal framework to consider customary law and legal principles, such as the balancing of military necessity and humanity, the prohibition on unnecessary suffering, the principle of proportionality and the principle of distinction. It will also explain and explore the potential of the Martens Clause to protect from environmental harm and conclude that a lot of heavy lifting is left to the Martens Clause, which, although providing some guidance, requires better regulation. I am not the first to suggest that the Martens Clause be used to protect the environment – the idea was proposed in 2000 as a way to bridge the gap between where the law currently is in protecting the environment during armed conflict and where the law needs to be.[87]

[87] Dinah Shelton and Alexandre Kiss, 'Martens Clause for Environmental Protection' (2000) 30(6) *Environmental Policy and Law* 285.

Given the potential toxicity of particular synthetic nanoparticles, the international environmental law frameworks governing the use of nanomaterials in war will be canvassed in Chapter 5. Chapter 5 differs from the other chapters in that it does not separately examine the three examples of 'means or methods' of warfare. The reason for this is that optogenetics and genetic modification do not provide a threat to the environment, and the potential environmental risks posed by nano-enhanced thermobaric weapons are not clear. What this chapter will discuss is the rise in the use of nanomaterials in 'means or methods' of warfare and how they need to be incorporated in any discussion of risks to the environment.

Chapter 6 will consider applicable governance under the international human rights law framework.

Chapter 7 will provide concluding remarks regarding the regulation of the use of nanomaterials in times of war. I conclude that international law governs nanomaterials, but that the use of nanomaterials requires particular attention by States to ensure compliance with international law.

VI Conclusion

By approaching nanomaterials through the lens of undertaking a weapons review, I aim to achieve two things. First, I have chosen to model an Article 36 review of nanomaterials, which indicates the breadth and richness of law required to be considered for an Article 36 review of any new or emerging technologies. Second, this approach works as a proof of concept to demonstrate that in most instances – environmental law as an exception – existing international law is sufficient to govern military use of nanomaterials. Whether considered customary law or not, the requirement to review new 'means or methods of warfare' is a necessary process for States to ensure compliance with their international treaty, customary law and legal principle obligations.[88] This requirement is imperative in the face of complex and often converging science to ensure compliance with States' international law obligations. In effect, I have chosen to undertake a speculative and extended weapons review, such as a State is required to undertake for new or modified weapons.

[88] *Additional Protocol I* art 36.

2

The Three Technologies Using Nanomaterials

'Nanotechnologies' cannot be legally reviewed as one single category. In this chapter, the three technologies utilising nanomaterials to be discussed in this book will be introduced in some technical detail: thermobaric weapons, optogenetics and genetic modification. Each use of nanomaterials needs to be considered individually to ensure compliance with existing international laws during war. The three uses of nanomaterials considered in this book have been chosen because they raise different existing international law (illustrating the breadth and depth of existing international law) and finally, because they are each at a different stage of development and use.

In the civilian sector, the scientific community has been grappling for some years with the safety of nanomaterials, and its health and environmental implications, as well as the best ways to regulate their development and use in the face of inadequate information regarding long-term risks.[1] Since its inception, the term 'nanotechnologies' has been used to describe a homogenous category. Over time, this terminology has become more nuanced, as it has become understood that the term nanotechnologies is not singular but rather describes a series of platforms on which other technologies are built. Writings and policy documents regarding military uses of nanomaterials have not progressed in the same way or with the same understanding. Conversations about the use of nanoscale science in war lack the nuance of similar conversations in the civilian sphere, and conversations about regulation remain largely at the level of a singular category of 'nanotechnology', rather than analysing individual technologies that use nanoscale science. It is not particularly helpful to speak in generalised terms about the regulation of nanoscale science. Indeed, it is potentially harmful in that risks may be underplayed

[1] Matthew Hull and Diana Bowman, *Nanotechnology Environmental Health and Safety: Risks, Regulation and Management* (Elsevier, 2nd ed, 2014).

or overlooked in the lack of understanding of the specific technology enabled or enhanced by nanoscale science.

Not only is the treatment of technology containing nanomaterials as 'nanotechnologies' problematic but even within an individual scientific discipline, each sub-category of use of nanomaterials may raise different legal issues. Lasers are such an example. Traditional lasers are at the macro scale, while optogenetics functions at the nanoscale. Optogenetics poses completely different challenges to traditional lasers, largely because of the ways in which nanolasers can target human cells with such specificity, including temporarily altering functions of the human brain.

Finally, I have selected these areas for temporal reasons. Each of the three areas selected for analysis in this book, thermobaric weapons, optogenetics and genetic modification, is at a different stage of development or use. Although there are many areas of nascent nanomaterials research that may have a profound impact on the military, I have limited my research to uses of nanomaterials which have been suggested by scientific experts to enable or enhance potential military activity. I have deliberately confined my analysis to areas of research that involve manipulated nanoparticles that are already well advanced, rather than merely in the realm of the hypothetical. Nanoparticles have already been included in thermobaric weapons to increase their intensity and heat. Research in optogenetics is rapid and extremely well-funded in the civilian context. The modification of genes that can be passed to future generations is currently being used, and research on humans has already been documented.[2]

I Thermobaric Weapons

A thermobaric weapon is a 'subcomponent of a larger family of weapons systems commonly known as volumetric weapons, which also include fuel-air explosives',[3] that are frequently 'designed to kill or injure by primary blast effect and incendiary or thermal effects as a secondary source of injury and damage'.[4] Thermobaric weapons have three primary

[2] David Cyranoski, 'CRISPR Gene-editing Tested in a Person for the First Time' (2016) 539 (7630) *Nature* 479.

[3] Anna Wildegger-Gaissmaier, 'Aspects of Thermobaric Weaponry' (2003) 4 *Australian Defence Force Health* 3.

[4] James Bean, 'Enhanced Blast Weapons and Forward Medical Treatment' (April 2004) *US Army Medical Department Journal* 48.

mechanisms for injury. The first injury mechanism of thermobaric weapons is blast and heat. The secondary injury mechanism is flying fragments created by the blast interacting with the surrounding environment (such as bricks, rock walls, or other building materials). The tertiary injury mechanism is suffocation through toxic gases and smoke. The type of injury depends on where the person is in relation to the thermobaric blast.

The capacity of nano-enhanced thermobaric weapons is important for legal analysis because the capacity of these weapons to cause harm is far greater than traditional thermobaric weapons. Thermobaric explosions can cause similar injuries to those created by other regular explosive weapons but have a functional difference.[5] By way of explaining the actual functional difference between traditional kinetic thermobaric weapons and thermobaric weapons with nanomaterials, regular kinetic weapons contain two or more materials (typically a fuel and an oxidizer). Gunpowder, for example, contains approximately 25 per cent fuel and 75 per cent oxidizer. When two substances interact, this causes an explosion. A thermobaric explosion relies on one primary substance igniting on contact with the air. It 'consists of a monopropellant and energetic particles that, upon interaction, ignite and cause a rapid release of energy'.[6] The oxidant is supplied by oxygen in the surrounding air. The almost 100 per cent combustible fuel is most frequently ethylene oxide or propylene oxide. This type of ignition triggers a more intense, higher temperature and farther reaching explosion than that of which conventional kinetic weapons are presently capable.[7] Weapons containing thermobaric explosions create a pressure wave, followed by a vacuum that sucks air and debris into the area of the explosion, effectively sucking the air out of lungs and shredding internal organs of human and/or animal victims alike. Temperatures in the immediate vicinity of a thermobaric blast may be as high as 2,500–3,000 degrees Celsius,[8] increasing the burn threat from flame contact and thermal radiation.[9]

5 Toney Baskin and John Holcomb, 'Bombs, Mines, Blast, Fragmentation and Thermobaric Mechanisms of Injury' in Peter Mahoney et al (eds), *Ballistic Trauma: A Practical Guide* (Springer, 2nd ed, 2005) 45.

6 Thomas Klapötke, *Chemistry of High-Energy Materials* (de Gruyter, 2011) 1972.

7 Baskin and Holcomb, n 5, 45.

8 Lester Grau and Timothy Smith, 'A "Crushing" Victory: Fuel-Air Explosives and Grozny 2000' (2000) 84(8) *Marine Corps Gazette* 30.

9 David Andrew, 'Thermobaric Munitions and Their Medical Effects' (2003) 12(1) *Australian Military Medicine* 9, 9–10.

In terms of their physical effects, each tissue type is compressed, stretched, sheared or disintegrated by overload according to its material properties. Internal organs that contain air (sinuses, ears, lungs and intestines) are particularly vulnerable to blast. The whole body may also be thrown by blast wind, which can result in fractures. Beyond the obvious blast injuries, recent research has shown that there are neurological, biochemical and blood chemistry changes caused by blast effects.[10] These physiological effects are not exclusive to thermobaric weapons, but rather characteristic of any kind of blast weapon.

Thermobaric weapons can be enhanced by using nanomaterials to detonate on contact with air. '[G]reat efforts have been spent on the development of new weapons which are able to generate higher blast, higher impulse and capable of using its energy not to destroy corners or walls only, but to travel around them efficiently and collapse the hardened targets'.[11] Specific research is ongoing in this area to increase the size of the lethal fire ball and the blast radius of the secondary combustion, and to make thermobaric weapons capable of reaching targets outside of caves and bunkers.[12]

As nanoparticles have a greater surface area to mass ratio, the surface area available in nanoparticles is far greater for the same quantity of reactive material than the same material at microscale. The inclusion of nanoparticles increases the intensity, heat and the radius of the blast.[13] Conversely, the quantity of explosive matter required to activate the same

[10] Ibid.

[11] Waldemar Trzciński and Lotfi Maiz, 'Thermobaric and Enhanced Blast Explosives: Properties and Testing Methods' (2015) 40(5) *Propellants, Explosives, Pyrotechnics* 632.

[12] Ahmed Mohamed, Hasem Mostafa and Sherif Elbasuney, 'Nanoscopic Fuel-rich Thermobaric Formulations: Chemical Composition Optimization and Sustained Secondary Combustion Shock Wave Modulation' (2015) 301 *Journal of Hazardous Materials* 491.

[13] Lemi Türker, 'Thermobaric and Enhanced Blast Explosives (TBX and EBX)' (2016) 12 *Defence Technology* 423, 425:

> New reactive metallic materials such as nano-sized aluminum [stat] to increase the reactivity, titanium and boron alloy to improve the thermal output, and magnesium/aluminum alloy to lower the ignition temperature are among the most promising and favorable approaches to increase the overall efficiency of metal combustion ... Furthermore, the research for new formulations and new warhead designs are expected to produce more powerful thermobaric warheads in the future as compared to the already existing weapon systems.

intensity of a blast is smaller, resulting in a smaller weapon with the same explosive capability as an ordinary thermobaric weapon.[14]

Although it is public knowledge that work has been underway by the military to enhance thermobaric weapons using nanoparticles for some time,[15] specific data regarding the details of increased heat production, larger radius or overall enhanced impact of thermobaric weapons with nanomaterials has only latterly become available in scientific journals.[16] The fundamental behaviour of the thermobaric weapon does not change with the inclusion of nanoparticles, and thermobaric weapons with nanomaterials are not necessarily used for a bigger bang. The inclusion of nanomaterials, while increasing the intensity, heat and radius of the blast, can also be used in such a way as to be more contained with a greater intensity.

Thermobaric weapons with nanomaterials will be used as an analytic example in Chapters 3 through 6, testing the application of different areas of international law to the use of nanomaterials in war. Chapters 3 and 4 analyse the existing treaty law, including the prohibition on incendiary weapons under Protocol III to the Convention on Certain Conventional Weapons (CCW),[17] and the prohibition on chemical weapons under the CWC. Thermobaric weapons using nanomaterials demonstrate that the existing treaties have relevance and actually limit the use of nanomaterials if used in this prohibited way. Chapter 4 will explore the customary international law prohibition on causing superfluous injury and unnecessary suffering, which has applicability to thermobaric weapons, as well as the customary international law principles of distinction and proportionality in attack, both of which have relevance for the use of thermobaric weapons with nanomaterials. Chapter 4 concludes that the considerations for thermobaric weapons with nanomaterials do not differ greatly from the considerations for regular-sized thermobaric weapons. International environmental law,

[14] 'The tailored thermobaric charge [using nanoscopic fuel] exhibited an increase in the total impulse by 40–45% compared with reference charge … effective lethal fire-ball duration up to 50ms was achieved': Mohamed, Mostafa and Elbasuney, n 12, 491, 494.

[15] Kim Kibong, 'Thermobarics: Promises, Challenges, and Recommendations' (Paper presented at 7th Joint Bombs/Warheads & Ballistics Symposium, Monterey, USA, 2004).

[16] A van der Heijden et al, 'Modification and Characterization of (Energetic) Nanomaterials' (2010) 71(2) *Journal of Physics and Chemistry of Solids* 59.

[17] *Protocol on Prohibitions or Restrictions on the Use of Incendiary Weapons (Protocol III) to the Convention on Prohibition or Restrictions on the Use of Certain Conventional Weapons Which May Be Deemed to Be Excessively Injurious or to Have Indiscriminate Effects*, opened for signature 10 October 1980, 1342 UNTS 171 (entered into force 2 December 1983) art 2(1) ('*Protocol III to the CCW*').

which is explored in detail in Chapter 5, has particular relevance for thermobaric weapons with nanomaterials and other uses of nanomaterials that may remain long after battles end. Nanomaterials enter water tables and food chains, with an ability to transfer across human membranes, potentially with toxic effects that are only beginning to be understood. Chapter 5 concludes that new law is required to adequately protect the environment during war. Finally, Chapter 6 will analyse the three different technologies through the lens of international human rights law, concluding that the right to life has relevance to thermobaric weapons with nanomaterials even in war.

II Optogenetics

'Laser' is an acronym for 'light amplification by stimulated emission of radiation'. Use of laser technology by the military is ubiquitous.[18] Einstein laid the foundation for the laser when he introduced the concept of stimulated emission in 1917,[19] and, in 1960, Theodore Maiman published a paper demonstrating the first actual laser.[20] Novel nanolasers, however, differ significantly from traditional lasers in three key ways: their size, their novel uses and their ability to be used and developed alongside other emerging technologies to target human bodily functions. This ability to target specific bodily functions, particularly neural networks, would have previously been in the realm of science fiction but is now possible to use as 'means or methods of warfare'.

Optogenetics is the use of light to activate and manipulate or control specific cells, called opsins, in the brain. Optogenetics consists of

> a set of neuromodulation tools that are activated by light ('opto') and are genetically encoded ('genetics'). Like other transgenes, optogenetic tools can be delivered with high spatial precision to specific cell types in the nervous system.[21]

[18] For more history on the development of the laser, see Mario Bertolotti, *The History of the Laser* (Institute of Physics Publishing, 2005) 219.

[19] Alan Chodos (ed), *Einstein Predicts Stimulated Emission* (August 2005) American Physical Society <www.aps.org/publications/apsnews/200508/history.cfm>; Abraham Pais, *Subtle Is the Lord: The Science and the Life of Albert Einstein* (Oxford University Press, 2005) 410–418.

[20] Theodore H Maiman, 'Stimulated Optical Radiation in Ruby' (1960) 187(4736) *Nature* 493.

[21] Matt Carter and Jennifer Shieh, *Guide to Research Techniques in Neuroscience* (Elsevier, 2nd ed, 2015) 193.

New lasers are dramatically smaller than previous generations of laser technology. Lasers built on this scale enable the creation of different wavelengths of light. Indeed, developments in nanolasers are now being driven by the development of optogenetics, as the study of the human brain requires greater specificity of lasers to isolate and target individual opsins and neurons within the brain. Opsins are proteins found within neurons that can be remotely affected by light external to the skull to control neural behaviour.[22] Each different opsin responds to a slightly different range of wavelengths of light. To isolate the behaviour of a target opsin, and to successfully study the individual neuron (i.e. a specific neuron containing the opsin), it needs to be illuminated with only the wavelengths of light to which that specific opsin will respond. Nanolasers satisfy this need by creating very specific wavelengths of light to stimulate individual opsins,[23] and they can be coupled to fibre optics with high efficiency. Nanolasers enable simulation of this natural function within the brain from a source external to the brain more effectively than any other technique currently available,[24] and they continue to advance rapidly in their ability to understand and control the human brain. Recent research indicates the ability to remove or modify memories using this technique.[25]

This relatively new method is enabling profound progress in our understanding of the function of the brain, with potential uses in not only neuroscience and psychology but also for defence,

> Fundamental questions that neuroscientists have previously approached with classical biochemical and electrophysiological techniques can now be addressed using optogenetics. The term optogenetics reflects the key program of this emerging field, namely, combining optical and genetic techniques. With the already impressively successful application of light-driven actuator proteins such as microbial opsins to interact with intact neural circuits, optogenetics rose to a key technology over the past few years.[26]

[22] See generally, Amy Chong et al, 'Non-invasive Optical Inhibition with a Red-Shifted Microbial Rhodopsin' (2014) 17(8) *Nature Neuroscience* 1123.

[23] Marvin Weber, *Handbook of Laser Wavelengths* (CRC Press, 1999).

[24] Kobi Leins, 'Shining a Regulatory Spotlight on New Lasers: Regulation of the Use of Nanolaser Technologies in Armed Conflict' (2016) 56 *Jurimetrics* 261.

[25] Przemysław Zawadzki and Agnieszka K Adamczyk, 'Personality and Authenticity in Light of the Memory-modifying Potential of Optogenetics' (2020) *Nanoethics* <https://doi.org/10.1007/s11569-020-00377-1>.

[26] Guillaume Dugué, Walther Akemann and Thomas Knöpfel, 'A Comprehensive Concept of Optogenetics' in Thomas Knöpfel and Edward Boyden (eds), *Optogenetics: Tools for Controlling and Monitoring Neuronal Activity* (Elsevier, 2012).

Nanolasers are enabling this technology. This ability has potential for the military to manipulate human behaviour and memory, or to induce fear or anger. Recent advances involving lasers are increasingly not applied in a 'traditional' weapons sense, in that their effects are neurological and reversible. There are other non-traditional means and methods of warfare that may also be reversible.[27] This does not mean that international law does not need to be considered in their use.

The international law governing laser weapons will be explored in Chapters 3 through 6. Chapter 3 will explore the relevance of the 1972 BWC, the 1992 CWC and, in limited circumstances, the 1995 Blinding Laser Protocol[28] to the potential use of optogenetics. Chapter 4 will explore the customary international law prohibition on superfluous injury and unnecessary suffering, which has applicability to optogenetics. International environmental law, explored in detail in Chapter 5, has little relevance for optogenetics, and so optogenetics is not specifically considered in Chapter 5. In Chapter 6, the importance of human rights law in governing the use of optogenetics becomes clear. The ability to control human functions, analogised with barbiturates and other forms of reversible control of human behaviour, presents a strong case for human rights law limiting the use of optogenetics, including through the prohibition on torture (which includes reversible effects) and the human right to health.

III Genetic Modification

Genetic modification, which takes place in deoxyribonucleic acid (DNA) at the nanoscale, can now precisely be edited in humans to modify the

[27] For example, electromagnetic radiation is a non-traditional means of warfare already used as a technique in electronic defence and electronic attack. The use of electromagnetic radiation demonstrates the effectiveness of 'nonconventional' methods of warfare, as well as its need to be considered within the frameworks of the laws of war. The potential use of nanolasers requires similar consideration under the laws of war. For more information about electromagnetic radiation, see United States Department of Army, *Field Manual No 3–36 Electronic Warfare* (9 November 2012) 1-1 <https://fas.org/irp/doddir/army/fm3–36.pdf>. Electronic warfare is defined as 'military action involving the use of electromagnetic and directed energy to control the electromagnetic spectrum or to attack the enemy'.

[28] *Protocol on Blinding Laser Weapons (Protocol IV) to the Convention on Prohibition or Restrictions on the Use of Certain Conventional Weapons Which May Be Deemed to Be Excessively Injurious or to Have Indiscriminate Effects*, opened for signature 13 October 1995, 1380 UNTS 370 (entered into force 30 July 1998) art 1 ('*Protocol IV to the CCW*').

very genes that make us who we are and who our offspring become. 'The technology may also be used as a potential "surgical knife" to correct genomic mutations or create new creatures by changing the inherited phenotypes'.[29] It is imaginable that this technology may be used to manipulate or control enemy combatants. Alternatively, genetic modification could protect soldiers from means or methods of warfare that may then kill those without the modification. This technology is included here, as it not only manipulates cells at the nanoscale but provides for permanent changes to germline cells, or the genetic material we pass down to our children. In February 2016, the US Director of National Intelligence added gene editing to the list of threats 'posed by weapons of mass destruction and proliferation',[30] highlighting the perceived potential threat. Although no public literature exists regarding military uses of this type, the technology exists, and the ability for militaries to modify human genes is now real.

In Chapters 3 and 4, I will argue that this particular use of nanomaterials (to modify or alter the human body) during war is clearly prohibited. The use of genetic modification in humans during war is prohibited by both the BWC and the CWC. Further, the genetic modification of non-humans and synthetic biology require States to strengthen existing law by including genetic modification of non-human organisms in official statements and expert advice provided to the treaty advisory bodies. States need to be clear that any genetic modification during war

[29] Li Chun-xiao and Qian Hai-li, 'A Double-Edged Sword: CRISPR-Cas9 Is Emerging as a Revolutionary Technique for Genome Editing' (2015) 2 *Military Medical Research* 25.

[30] James Clapper, *Statement for the Record: Worldwide Threat Assessment of the US Intelligence Community* (9 February 2016) Office of the Director of National Intelligence 9 <www.dni.gov/files/documents/SASC_Unclassified_2016_ATA_SFR_FINAL.pdf>

> Research in genome editing conducted by countries with different regulatory or ethical standards than those of Western countries probably increases the risk of the creation of potentially harmful biological agents or products. Given the broad distribution, low cost, and accelerated pace of development of this dual-use technology, its deliberate of unintentional misuse might lead to far-reaching economic and national security implications. Advances in genome editing in 2015 have compelled groups of high-profile US and European biologists to question unregulated editing of the human germline (cells that are relevant for reproduction), which might create inheritable genetic changes. Nevertheless, researchers will probably continue to encounter challenges to achieve the desired outcome of their genome modifications, in part because of the technical limitations that are inherent in available genome editing systems.

will contravene the BWC or CWC, whether at the regular, micro or nanoscale, and to reiterate that States will be held to account for any breaches of these obligations. Finally, the Martens Clause also prohibits genetic modification, as it prohibits the development of any means or methods of warfare which are against 'dictates of public conscience'.

In Chapter 5, the prohibition on the potential genetic modification of crops used in such a way as to prevent civilians from being able to access food is considered.[31] Human rights law is analysed in Chapter 6 and has particular potential relevance for genetic modification. The right to life could prohibit genetic modification, as could the prohibition on torture and the right to health. The conclusion of this chapter is that to meaningfully undertake an Article 36 review considering the legal obligations of a State during conflict, all international law obligations must be considered. Each different use of nanomaterials will attract different international human rights law, which will therefore require an analysis of different law for each use of nanomaterials.

IV Conclusion

In this chapter, the three technologies utilising nanomaterials were introduced: thermobaric weapons, optogenetics and genetic modification. The reasoning behind the selection of these uses of nanomaterials was explained. Each of the technologies was then explained in some detail, to facilitate a better legal analysis in Chapters 3 to 6 of the book, including a brief summary of the conclusions of each of the chapters and how each of the legal frameworks prohibits or limits each of these three technologies.

Chapter 3 will analyse international treaties that are relevant to regulating these three technologies, namely thermobaric weapons, optogenetics and genetic modification. Each treaty will then be applied individually to the relevant technologies to showcase how international treaty law either prohibits or provides clear limitations for the use of most, if not all, aspects of these three technologies.

[31] *Convention (IV) Respecting the Laws and Customs of War on Land and Its Annex: Regulations Concerning the Laws and Customs of War on Land*, signed 18 October 1907, 205 CTS 277 (entered into force 26 January 1910) art 23(g) ('*Hague Convention (IV)*').

3

International Treaty Law

As discussed in Chapter 1, there has always been tension between the desire to demonstrate humanity and the desire for security, which requires 'continual adaptation following the needs of a changing world'.[1] Attempts to address this tension have resulted in many treaties and agreements. Prior to written agreements, the behaviour of professional soldiers was, to a large extent, regulated by unwritten rules and customs.[2] It has been suggested that 'a large part of the modern law of war has developed simply as a codification and universalization of the customs and conventions of the vocational/professional soldiery'.[3] However, these understandings were not codified, nor did States seek their codification, in an international form until the late nineteenth and early twentieth centuries: the Lieber Code in 1861,[4] *A Memory of Solferino* (a text calling for codification of the principles of the laws of war in 1886),[5] the Brussels Declaration in 1874,[6] the Oxford Manual in

1 Hermann Göring, *Trial of the Major War Criminals before the International Military Tribunal, Nuremberg, 14 November 1945 – 1 October 1946* (1947) vol 1, 221, cited in René van der Wolf and Willem-Jan van der Woolf (eds), *Laws of War and International Law* (Wolf Legal Publishers, 2002) 7.

2 James Turner Johnson, *Just War Tradition and the Restraint of War: A Moral and Historical Inquiry* (Princeton University Press, 1981) 179, 295.

3 Geoffrey Best, *Humanity in Warfare* (Columbia University Press, 1980) 60, cited in Rain Liivoja, 'Chivalry without a Horse: Military Honour and the Modern Law of Armed Conflict' in Rain Liivoja and Andres Saumets (eds), *The Law of Armed Conflict: Historical and Contemporary Perspectives* (Tartu University Press, 2012) 75.

4 'Instructions for the Government of Armies of the United States in the Field (Lieber Code)' (adopted 24 April 1863) International Committee of the Red Cross <https://ihl-databases.icrc.org/ihl/INTRO/110>.

5 François Bugnion, 'From Solferino to the Birth of Contemporary International Humanitarian Law' (22 April 2009) International Committee of the Red Cross <www.icrc.org/eng/resources/documents/article/other/solferino-article-bugnion-240409.htm>.

6 'Project of an International Declaration Concerning the Laws and Customs of War' (adopted 27 August 1874, not in force) International Committee of the Red Cross <https://ihl-databases.icrc.org/ihl/INTRO/135>.

1880,[7] the 1899 Hague Regulations (revised in 1907)[8] and, more recently, the four Geneva Conventions[9] and their three additional Protocols.[10] These principles and rules, now codified, exemplify the behaviour that States expected from each other prior to treaties being negotiated that codified these expectations.

Figure 3.1 illustrates the range of documents in volume and across time that have attempted to regulate the use of specific weapons. It also summarises the conclusion of this thesis as to whether each treaty applies to the three uses of nanomaterials reviewed in this book.

I will argue that, although no treaties have been created regarding nanomaterials specifically, much existing treaty law has relevance and should be applied to weapons utilising nanomaterials. In accordance with Article 38(1)(a) of the Statute of the ICJ, treaties that could be of relevance are the starting point for any analysis of international law during war.[11] In this chapter, I will analyse the application of treaties

[7] 'The Laws of War on Land' (adopted 9 September 1880) International Committee of the Red Cross <https://ihl-databases.icrc.org/ihl/INTRO/140?OpenDocument>.

[8] *Convention (IV) Respecting the Laws and Customs of War on Land and Its Annex: Regulations Concerning the Laws and Customs of War on Land*, opened for signature 18 October 1907, 205 CTS 227 (entered into force 26 January 1910) art 23 ('*Hague Convention (IV)*').

[9] *Geneva Convention (I) for the Amelioration of the Condition of the Wounded and Sick in Armed Forces in the Field*, opened for signature 12 August 1949, 75 UNTS 31 (entered into force 21 October 1950) ('*First Geneva Convention*'); *Geneva Convention (II) for the Amelioration of the Condition of Wounded, Sick and Shipwrecked Members of Armed Forces at Sea*, opened for signature 12 August 1949, 75 UNTS 85 (entered into force 21 October 1950) ('*Second Geneva Convention*'); *Geneva Convention (III) Relative to the Treatment of Prisoners of War (Third Geneva Convention)*, opened for signature 12 August 1949, 75 UNTS 135 (entered into force 21 October 1950) ('*Third Geneva Convention*'); *Geneva Convention (IV) Relative to the Protection of Civilian Persons in Time of War*, opened for signature 12 August 1949, 75 UNTS 287 (entered into force 21 October 1950) ('*Fourth Geneva Convention*').

[10] *Protocol Additional to the Geneva Conventions of 12 August 1949, and Relating to the Protection of Victims of International Armed Conflicts (Protocol I)*, opened for signature 8 June 1977, 1125 UNTS 3 (entered into force on 7 December 1978) ('*Additional Protocol I*'); *Protocol Additional to the Geneva Conventions of 12 August 1949, and Relating to the Protection of Victims of Non-International Armed Conflicts (Protocol II)*, opened for signature 8 June 1977, 1125 UNTS 609 (entered into force on 7 December 1978) ('*Additional Protocol II*'); *Protocol Additional to the Geneva Conventions of 12 August 1949, and Relating to the Adoption of an Additional Distinctive Emblem (Protocol III)*, opened for signature 8 December 2005, 2404 UNTS 261 (entered into force 14 January 2007).

[11] *Statute of the International Court of Justice* art 38(1).

Technology/ Applicable Treaty Law	1925 Geneva Protocol	1972 Biological Weapons Convention	1992 Chemical Weapons convention	1980 Prohibition on Non-Detectable Fragments (Protocol I of the CCW)	1980 Protocol on Prohibitions or Restrictions of Incendiary Weapons (Protocol II of the CCW)	1998 Protocol on Blinding Laser Weapons (Protocol IV of the CCW)
Thermobaric Weapons	No	No	Under specific circumstances	Under specific circumstances	Yes	No
Optogenetics	Yes	Yes	Yes	No	No	Under specific circumstances
Genetic Modification	Yes	Yes	Yes	No	No	No

Figure 3.1 Table of potentially applicable international law instruments to thermobaric weapons, optogenetics and genetic modification (please note that this is not an exhaustive list – it is for illustrative purposes only).

to the technologies in question, namely the 1925 Geneva Protocol,[12] the 1972 BWC,[13] the 1992 CWC[14] and the relevant Additional Protocols of the 1983 Convention on Certain Conventional Weapons,[15] including Protocol I of the CCW prohibiting non-detectable fragments (Protocol I),[16] Protocol III of the CCW prohibiting incendiary weapons

[12] *Protocol for the Prohibition of the Use of Asphyxiating, Poisonous or Other Gases, and of Bacteriological Methods of Warfare*, opened for signature 17 June 1925, 94 LNTS 65 (entered into force 8 February 1928) ('*Protocol to the BWC*').

[13] *Convention on the Prohibition of the Development, Production and Stockpiling of Bacteriological (Biological) and Toxin Weapons and on Their Destruction*, opened for signature 10 April 1972, 1015 UNTS 163 (entered into force 26 March 1975) ('*Biological Weapons Convention*').

[14] *Convention on the Prohibition of the Development, Production, Stockpiling and Use of Chemical Weapons and on Their Destruction*, opened for signature 3 September 1992, 1974 UNTS 45 (entered into force 29 April 1997) ('*Chemical Weapons Convention*').

[15] *Convention on Prohibition or Restrictions on the Use of Certain Conventional Weapons Which May Be Deemed to Be Excessively Injurious or to Have Indiscriminate Effects*, opened for signature 10 October 1980, 1342 UNTS 137 (entered into force 2 December 1983) ('*Convention on Certain Conventional Weapons*').

[16] *Protocol on Non-detectable Fragments (Protocol I) to the Convention on Prohibition or Restrictions on the Use of Certain Conventional Weapons Which May Be Deemed to Be Excessively Injurious or to Have Indiscriminate Effects*, opened for signature 10 October 1980, 1342 UNTS 171 (entered into force 2 December 1983) ('*Protocol I to the CCW*').

(Protocol III)[17] and Protocol IV of the CCW prohibiting blinding laser weapons (Protocol IV).[18] Each of these specific treaties is applicable to one or more of the technologies under consideration. The treaties considered are not an exhaustive source of treaty law pertaining to weapons containing nanomaterials, but they are the treaties that have application to these technologies. There may be other legal frameworks relevant to non-military uses of nanomaterials, or other uses of nanomaterials not considered in this book.

I will analyse secondary literature and other relevant documentation that shows that nanomaterials have been explicitly or implicitly regulated under international law. As we shall see, although not all treaties are applicable to all weapons using nanomaterials, the applicable treaties cover a broad range of uses of nanomaterials in warfare in some depth, which shows the breadth and depth of treaty law to different uses of nanomaterials. The history of the negotiations of the treaties is of particular significance in understanding the intention of the drafters in the absence of specific reference to nanomaterials. For this reason, the history of the negotiation of some of the relevant treaties will be considered.

I do not consider the Arms Trade Treaty,[19] as my focus is on the use of the technologies in question, rather than their trade or transfer. Nor do I consider the Treaty on the Prohibition of Nuclear Weapons.[20] Although nanomaterials may be used to facilitate miniaturised nuclear weapons,[21] miniaturised nuclear weapons are not one of the three uses of nanomaterials that I consider because they were not one of the three uses of nanomaterials selected for review in this book. Finally, the consideration

[17] *Protocol on Prohibitions or Restrictions on the Use of Incendiary Weapons (Protocol III) to the Convention on Prohibition or Restrictions on the Use of Certain Conventional Weapons Which May Be Deemed to Be Excessively Injurious or to Have Indiscriminate Effects*, opened for signature 10 October 1980, 1342 UNTS 171 (entered into force 2 December 1983) ('*Protocol III to the CCW*').

[18] *Protocol on Blinding Laser Weapons (Protocol IV) to the Convention on Prohibitions or Restrictions on the Use of Certain Conventional Weapons Which May Be Deemed to Be Excessively Injurious or to Have Indiscriminate Effects*, opened for signature 13 October 1995, 1380 UNTS 370 (entered into force 30 July 1998) ('*Protocol IV to the CCW*').

[19] *Arms Trade Treaty*, opened for signature on 3 June 2013, UN Doc A/CONF.217/2013/L.3 (27 March 2013) (entered into force 24 December 2014).

[20] *Treaty on the Prohibition of Nuclear Weapons*, opened for signature 7 July 2017 (not yet entered into force).

[21] Jeff Daniels, *Mini-nukes and Mosquito-like Robot Weapons being Primed for Future Warfare* (17 March 2017) CNBC <www.cnbc.com/2017/03/17/mini-nukes-and-inspect-bot-weapons-being-primed-for-future-warfare.html>.

of national domestic legislation implementing international law obligations, as well as legislation governing commercial uses of nanomaterials, although relevant, is also beyond the scope of these chapters that seek to analyse the legality, pursuant to international law, of the use of nanomaterials in armed conflict (*jus in bello*). Private or trade international treaty obligations will also not be considered. Each treaty will be applied individually to the relevant technologies. By considering potentially relevant international law treaties, I will establish that weapons systems using or containing nanomaterials are, to a large extent, governed by existing treaty law. International treaty law provides clear limits for the use of most, if not all, aspects of the three technologies under consideration.

As specified in Article 31(1) of the VCLT, '[a] treaty shall be interpreted ... in the light of its object and purpose'.[22] As the drafters of the treaties under consideration could not have envisaged the capabilities of nanomaterials, my approach is teleological. This means that I interpret the law with the goal or purpose of the law in mind and then apply it to the technologies under consideration. In the absence of judicial decisions regarding military uses of nanomaterials specifically, I apply the law in a way that serves the goal and purpose of the treaty. Where relevant, I also refer to the intention of the drafters. Any treaties need to be viewed through the prism of the principles of military necessity and humanity, which underpin all the laws of war.[23] The approach to treaty interpretation is a two-step process, in which the factors contained in Article 31 are examined first, to determine the ordinary meaning of the law in question. Where there is ambiguity or further clarification is necessary, then Article 32 permits consideration of other factors in addition to those considered under Article 31.[24] In the *Kasikili/Sedudu Islands Case (Botswana/Namibia)*,[25] the ICJ reiterated this approach, noting that Articles 31 and 32 are customary international

[22] *Vienna Convention on the Law of Treaties*, opened for signature 23 May 1969, 1155 UNTS 331 (entered into force 27 January 1980) art 31 (emphasis added) ('*VCLT*').

[23] Nils Melzer, 'Keeping the Balance between Military Necessity and Humanity: A Response to Four Critiques of the ICRC's Interpretative Guidance on the Notion of Direction Participation in Hostilities' (2010) 42 *New York University Journal of International Law and Politics* 831, 907.

[24] John Merrills, 'Two Approaches to Treaty Interpretation' (1969) 4 *Australian International Law* 55.

[25] *Kasikili/Sedudu Island (Botswana v Namibia) (Judgement)* [1999] ICJ Rep 1045, 1059–1060.

law.[26] For this reason, in the absence of specific judicial decisions or State practice regarding nanomaterials, the history of each of the treaties and the context and considerations of the drafters preceding the actual texts are relevant and will be considered where helpful in understanding the intent and purpose of the treaty. In some cases, statements made by delegates attending meetings, or other additional sources of relevant contextual information, will be referenced to provide a greater understanding of the intention of the drafters at the time. The drafting history is relevant, including the *traveaux préparatoires*,[27] and other relevant documentation from treaty negotiations, as are more modern clarifications of understandings by States (such as Review Conference documents).

State practice by way of analogy is required to understand how courts might approach the use and effects of the three technologies under consideration. Given the absence of official State practice relating to weapons using nanomaterials, the practice around the use of biological and chemical weapons is drawn on heavily. Given the absence of case law pertaining specifically to the use of nanomaterials, at times interpretation is made by way of thoughtful analogy to extrapolate the intention of the drafters of the treaty to apply to nanoscale materials.[28]

While I conclude that treaties regulating particular weapons do, to a large extent, cover these three technologies, I also conclude that States need to strengthen existing law by including nanomaterials in official statements and expert advice provided to the treaty advisory bodies. I call on States and governments to strengthen the existing prohibition on chemical and biological weapons to include materials at the nanoscale, within the existing framework of the Review Conferences of the BWC, and within the Science Advisory Board for the CWC. States need to clarify in public statements that any materials that contravene the BWC or CWC, whether at the regular, micro or nanoscale, remain prohibited, and reiterate that States will be held to account.

[26] For a more thorough discussion of what comprises customary international law, see Hilary Charlesworth, 'Customary International Law the Nicaragua Case' (1984) 11 *Australian Yearbook of International Law* 1 and Roozbeh B Baker, 'Customary International Law in the 21st Century: Old Challenges and New Debates' (2010) 21 *European Journal of International Law* 173.

[27] *VCLT* art 32.

[28] See Melzer, n 23, but note Kevin Jon Heller, 'The Use and Abuse of Analogy in IHL' in Jens Ohlin (ed), *Theoretical Boundaries of Armed Conflict and Human Rights* (Cambridge University Press, 2016).

I Continuity of Treaties during War

The International Law Commission (ILC) provides some guidance on how armed conflict affects the continuity of treaties in its Draft Articles on the Effects of Armed Conflicts on Treaties.[29] In this authoritative report, the ILC concluded that the traditional rules of interpretation contained within the VCLT continued to be relevant during armed conflict. The ability of a party to withdraw from, or suspend participation in, a treaty is governed by the VCLT during times of armed conflict. 'Armed conflict' is defined by the ILC as 'a situation in which there is resort to armed force between States or protracted resort to armed force between governmental authorities and organised armed groups'.[30] The definition of 'non-international armed conflict' reflects the definition employed by the International Criminal Tribunal for the Former Yugoslavia (ICTY) in the *Tadič* decision, while an 'international armed conflict' is defined as per Common Article 2 of the 1949 Geneva Conventions.[31] In a time of either non-international or international armed conflict, reference should first be made to the treaty under consideration to ascertain whether the provisions under consideration were intended to have continued effect during armed conflict.[32] In the absence of such a reference, unless there was a specific reason for non-application, it was assumed that the treaty would prevail unless there was a compelling reason for the treaty not to apply.[33]

Clearly, where the purpose of a treaty is to regulate armed conflict, as is the case with the Geneva Conventions or disarmament treaties, there is a presumption that the treaty will continue to apply. Other subject matter, such as human rights, environmental protection and protection of watercourses and aquifers (all of which have been considered in relation to nanomaterials, and which may have relevance during armed conflict), continues to apply.[34] The ILC noted in its report that

[29] See Draft Articles on the Effects of Armed Conflicts on Treaties, with Commentaries in 'Report on the Work of the International Law Commission Sixty-Third Session (26 April–3 June and 4 July–12 August 2011)' [2011] II(2) *Yearbook of the International Law Commission* 108 ('*Draft Articles on the Effects of Armed Conflicts on Treaties*').

[30] Ibid 110, art 2(b).

[31] *First Geneva Convention* art 2; *Second Geneva Convention* art 2; *Third Geneva Convention* art 2; *Fourth Geneva Convention* art 2.

[32] *Draft Articles on the Effects of Armed Conflicts on Treaties*, n 29, 112, art 4, comments (1)–(3).

[33] Ibid 114, art 7.

[34] Ibid 114, art 7; 120–130, annex, comments (1)–(77).

> A State exercising its inherent right of individual or collective self-defense in accordance with the Charter of the United Nations is entitled to suspend in whole or in part the operation of a treaty to which it is a Party insofar as that operation is incompatible with the exercise of that right.[35]

This means that States, where they can justify an entitlement to suspend a treaty, may suspend the treaty in part or in whole. Suspension means that the treaty does not apply for the time during which the justification continues. Once this situation justifying suspension of the treaty ends, the treaty will apply again. States must consider the treaties analysed in this book, and perhaps other treaties for other uses of nanomaterials, and whether this entitlement to suspend 'in whole or part' of an applicable treaty is relevant. This is an additional consideration of the international legal frameworks in relation to nanomaterials, before considering how these legal regimes and treaty obligations may potentially conflict or overlap.

II History of Weapons Treaty Negotiations

A Pre-twentieth Century

The first Hague Peace Conference, hosted in 1899, was initiated by the Czar of Russia, Nicholas II, 'with the object of seeking the most effective means of ensuring to all peoples the benefits of a real and lasting peace, and, above all, of limiting the progressive development of existing armaments'.[36] A more critical view of the Czar's motives reveals that Russia did not have the advanced technology of many of its neighbours and sought to limit the armament race that it clearly could not win.[37] Whatever his motivation, Russia's Czar brought together 26 countries to discuss limiting armaments in the first multilateral meeting of its kind. At the conference, which consisted of a series of 10 meetings from May until July of 1899,[38] three broad matters were considered which resulted in three separate declarations being adopted.[39]

35 Ibid 117, art 14.

36 Russian note of 30 December 1898/11 January 1899.

37 Betsy Baker, 'Hague Peace Conferences (1899 and 1907)' (November 2009) *Max Planck Encyclopedia of Public International Law* [C10].

38 Ministry for Foreign Affairs, *The International Peace Conference, The Hague, May 18–29 July 1899* (Martinus Nijhoff, 1907).

39 The three broad matters were pacific settlement of international disputes, arms limitation and the laws of war.

The second declaration, adopted at the first Hague Peace Conference in 1899, concluded that projectiles containing 'asphyxiating or deleterious gases' should not be used in the battlefield.[40] Interestingly, the Russian delegate who submitted this proposal suggested that all 'asphyxiating or deleterious gases' should be banned but was overruled by his fellow delegates from Siam, Great Britain and France.[41] Count Soltyk, of then Austria-Hungary, objected to the original phraseology as 'all explosives contain gas more or less injurious'.[42] Captain Scheine of Russia, subsequently redefined the prohibition to 'include only those projectiles *whose object* is to diffuse asphyxiating gases, and not to those whose explosion produces incidentally such gases'.[43] Representatives of Russia, Denmark, France, Austria-Hungary, Great Britain and Portugal supported this proposal, with some additional arguments, noting that, 'the task of the conference' was to 'restrict the means of destruction', and therefore it followed that,

> [I]t is logical to prohibit new means, above all when they have such projectiles of a barbarous character and partake of treachery and cruelty similar to the poisoning of drinking water . . . they would destroy more non-combatants than ordinary projectiles; death from asphyxiation is more cruel than death from bullets; means should be sought for putting enemies out of the battle, but not out of this world.[44]

Of the 26 countries present, only the United States and Great Britain voted against the prohibition, and all the other countries voted in favour.[45] Particularly interesting is the broader conversation at the Conference about what was deemed to be abhorrent. In particular, the idea that certain weapons were of a barbarous nature and therefore prohibited was a fairly novel one at the time. This discussion, captured in the preamble to the Hague Declaration, known as the Martens Clause, still resonates today, and will be discussed in more detail in Chapter 4. The idea of poisons or 'barbarous' uses of nanomaterials should be just as

[40] *Hague Declaration (II) on the Use of Projectiles the Object of Which Is the Diffusion of Asphyxiating or Deleterious Gases*, opened for signature 29 July 1899, 187 CTS 453 (entered into force 4 September 1900) ('*Hague Declaration (II)*'). The first declaration was one 'Prohibiting the Discharge of Projectiles and Explosives from Balloons'.

[41] William Hull, *The Two Hague Conferences and Their Contributions to International Law* (Athenaeum Press, 1908) 87.

[42] Ibid.

[43] Ibid (emphasis added).

[44] Ibid.

[45] Ibid 89.

abhorrent as the similar use of regular-sized materials was a hundred years ago.

B Twentieth Century

In 1921, Victor Lefebure, a forward-thinking French chemical liaison officer, spoke to the Grotius Society for a *Problems of Peace and War* seminar series, noting how the concerns about chemical warfare extended to the development of all new weapons, even those not yet created at the time of his talk.[46] He devoted much of his address to explaining that each step of research, development and manufacturing of new chemical weapons all required treaty controls, sentiments that Ludwig Fritz Haber echoed years later. Ludwig Fritz Haber was the son of Fritz Haber, considered by many to be the 'father of chemical warfare', and the man held responsible for Germany's use of chlorine gas in 1915.[47] Lefebure used language that easily applies to the use of nanomaterials today,

> These remarks are not limited to chemical warfare, but the development of all new weapons. Taking a long-distance view, no distinction should be made. If sub-atomic forces can eventually be harnessed for war they must be subjected to the same control and attempts at suppression during their development stages.[48]

Haber Junior also raised the issue of the Hague Conventions, pointing out that any international agreements to abandon poison gas would be meaningless unless there were verification measures and sanctions put in place.[49]

Both the BWC and the CWC extended the 1925 Geneva Protocol prohibition on 'asphyxiating, poisonous or other gases, and *of all analogous* liquids, materials or devices' and 'bacteriological methods of warfare'[50] to a broader prohibition of the development, production, stockpiling and transfer of all such weapons. The adherence to, and

[46] Victor Lefebure, 'Chemical Warfare: The Possibility of Its Control' (1921) 7 *Transactions of the Grotius Society* 153.

[47] Ludwig Fritz Haber, *The Poisonous Cloud: Chemical Warfare in the First World War* (Clarendon Press, 1986) 189, 192.

[48] Victor Lefebure, *The Riddle of the Rhine: Chemical Strategy in Peace and War* (Collins Clear-Type Press, 1921) 12.

[49] Haber, n 47, 189, 192.

[50] United Nations Office for Disarmament Affairs, *Protocol for the Prohibition of the Use in War of Asphyxiating, Poisonous or Other Gases, and of Bacteriological Methods of*

support for, the BWC is not as comprehensive as that of the CWC. Because the CWC has a well-established review body and inspection mechanisms that support compliance of the CWC, and the Geneva Protocol and the BWC do not have such mechanisms, calls for compliance with the Geneva Protocol and the BWC are more frequent. Each of these treaty obligations will now be analysed individually in more detail.

1 The Geneva Protocol: History and Context

Rapid advances in chemistry enabled the manufacture and use of chlorine, phosgene and mustard gas and its deployment in massive quantities on the battlefield in World War I. There were an estimated 1,300,000 casualties from exposure to gas during World War I[51] and at least 300,000 of those were fatalities.[52] The 1899 Hague ban, which was reiterated in the 1907 Hague Convention, did not prevent ongoing attempts to revive the use of chemical weapons.[53] The only applicable treaty was the 1868 Declaration of St Petersburg that specifically prohibited, 'the use of projectiles the object of which is the diffusion of asphyxiating or deleterious gases'.[54] At the time of World War I, views still diverged about the use of chemical warfare.

In 1915, Germany used canisters to release chlorine gas at the Battle of Ypres, relying heavily on winds to disperse their contents. Germany later argued that they did not use projectiles (which was technically true) and did not breach the specific prohibition on projectiles.[55] Later, when Germany did switch to projectiles, they argued that the purpose of the projectiles was to injure personnel with their shrapnel and that the gas contained therein was incidental. Despite Germany's semantic justifications regarding their behaviour, they were held to have been in violation of the prohibition by the Commission on the Responsibility of the Authors of the War and on Enforcement of Penalties, although no individual was ever held responsible.[56] Germany argued that the use of

Warfare: Status of the Treaty <http://disarmament.un.org/treaties/t/1925> (emphasis added).

51 Joseph Kelly, 'Gas Warfare in International Law' (1960) 9 *Military Law Review* 1, 3.

52 'Chemical Weapons' (1986) 11 *United Nations Disarmament Yearbook* 241, 241.

53 *Hague Convention (IV)* art 23.

54 *Hague Declaration (II)*.

55 Howard Levie, 'Humanitarian Restrictions on Chemical and Biological Weapons' (1982) 13 *University of Toledo Law Review* 1192.

56 The Commission on the Responsibility of the Authors of the War and on Enforcement of Penalties nonetheless included the 'use of deleterious and asphyxiating gases' 'as one of

such materials during World War I was justified, with the German commander of the Army Corps at Ypres explicitly expressing the view that, '[w]ar is necessity and knows no exception'.[57] Germany's behaviour clearly violated the requirement to uphold treaties in good faith, now codified in Article 26 of the VCLT.[58] There is a long-standing requirement of good faith in international law, even prior to its codification in the VCLT. Grotius noted that 'good faith should be preserved, not only for other reasons, but also in order that the hope of peace may not be done away with'.[59] Good faith is also included in numerous major international legal instruments, 'some or all of which may collectively be regarded as codifying customary international law'.[60] The ICJ has

the war Crimes committed by Germany during World War I': 'Commission on the Responsibility of the Authors of the War and on Enforcement of Penalties' (1920) 14 (1/2) *American Journal of International Law* 95, 115. Levie (n 55) submits that this may have been incorrect, as the effect of the chlorine gas was totally reliant on 'fickle prevailing winds' and that the cylinders 'had not been made available for this purpose': 1194 n 10. The Commission's recommendations were not carried through at the time, but some suggest that the negotiations around the existence of the Commission laid the preliminary groundwork for the current International Criminal Court: Harry Rhea, 'The Commission on the Responsibility of the Authors of the War and on Enforcement of Penalties and Its Contribution to International Criminal Justice after World War II' (2014) 25(1/2) *Criminal Law Forum* 147.

[57] 'I must confess that the commission for poisoning the enemy, just as one poisons rats, struck me as it must any straightforward soldier; it was repulsive to me. If, however, the poison gas were to result in the fall of Ypres, we would win a victory that might decide the entire campaign. In view of this worthy goal, all personal reservations had to be silent . . . War is necessity and knows no exception': Berthold von Deimling, *Aus der Alten in die Neue Zeit: Lebenserinnerungen von Berthold von Deimling* (Verlag Ullstein, 1930) 201.

[58] *VCLT* art 26.

[59] Hugo Grotius, *De Jure Belli ac Pacis Libri Tres* (1625), quoted in John O'Connor, *Good Faith in International Law* (Dartmouth Publishing, 1991) 56.

[60] Andrew Mitchell, 'Good Faith in WTO Dispute Settlement' (2006) 7(2) *Melbourne Journal of International Law* 339. Major international law instruments that include a good faith requirement include the following: *United Nations Convention on the Law of the Sea*, opened for signature 10 December 1982, 1833 UNTS 3 (entered into force 16 November 1994) arts 105, 157, 300; *Peaceful Settlement of Disputes between States*, GA Res 37/10, UN GAOR, 37th sess, 68th plen mtg, UN Doc A/RES/37/10 (15 November 1982) Annex I(1), II(2) ('*Manila Declaration on Peaceful Disputes*'); *Report of the Secretary-General on the Work of the Organization*, GA Res 37/67, UN GAOR, 37th sess, 91st plen mtg, UN Doc A/RES/37/67 (3 December 1982) [2]; *Charter of Economic Rights and Duties of States*, GA Res 3281 (XXIX), UN GAOR, 29th sess, 2315th plen mtg, UN Doc A/RES/29/3281 (12 December 1974) ch 1(j); *Permanent Sovereignty over Natural Resources*, GA Res 1803 (XVII), UN GAOR, 17th sess, UN Doc A/RES/17/1803 (14 December 1962) [8]; International Institute for the Unification of Private Law, *UNIDROIT Principles of International Commercial Contracts* (UNIDROIT, 2004) art 1.7. See also comments of Lord Phillimore in Permanent Court of International Justice:

stated that the principle of good faith is customary international law.[61] Germany's unsuccessful attempt to obfuscate responsibility for violating the 1868 Declaration of St Petersburg that specifically prohibited 'the use of projectiles the object of which is the diffusion of asphyxiating or deleterious gases'[62] on the basis of semantic arguments is a good example of not acting in good faith.

Where existing treaty language captures nanomaterials, such as in the case of the language in the 1925 Protocol for the Prohibition of the Use in War of Asphyxiating, Poisonous or Other Gases, and of Bacteriological Methods of Warfare (Geneva Protocol) that is reiterated in the preamble of the BWC, any nanomaterial that mimics or has the same effect as a banned chemical or toxin would be prohibited under the existing legal framework. States are required to interpret the existing treaties to include new technologies as a matter of good faith where their properties are captured in existing language. Should States argue that there is some exception to nanomaterials to attempt to avoid the existing ban, then it would be difficult to find that this position was being argued in good faith.

Fritz Haber, Ludwig Fritz Haber's father, the infamous recipient of the Nobel Prize for Chemistry for his discovery of the Haber–Bosch Process, was extremely vocal about his support for the use of gas in warfare, arguing that the more brutal wars were, the shorter and less likely they were to occur in the first place.[63] The sheer scale and horror of the devastation of World War I, however, provided a catalyst for serious reflection and an appetite for significant multilateral negotiation.[64] In 1918, the ICRC launched an appeal condemning the use of chemicals in warfare.

Advisory Committee of Jurists, *Procès-verbaux of the Proceedings of the Committee, June 16th–July 24th, 1920, with Annexes* (The Hague, 1920) 335.

61 *Nuclear Tests (Australia v France) (Merits)* [1974] ICJ Rep 253, 268; *Legal Consequences for States of the Continued Presence of South Africa in Namibia (South West Africa) notwithstanding Security Council Resolution 276 (1970) (Advisory Opinion)* [1971] ICJ Rep 16, 56–57. See also Gillian White, 'The Principle of Good Faith' in Vaughan Lowe and Colin Warbrick (eds), *The United Nations and the Principles of International Law: Essays in Memory of Michael Akehurst* (1994) 230, 241.

62 *Hague Declaration (II)*.

63 Dietrich Stoltzenberg, *Fritz Haber: Chemist, Nobel Laureate, German, Jew* (Chemical Heritage Foundation, 2004).

64 'Gas was looked on as something particularly wicked, something unfair and cowardly, against which a "fair fight" was impossible': William Moore, *Gas Attack!: Chemical Warfare 1915–1918 and Afterwards* (Leo Cooper, 1987) 195.

In 1925, the Geneva Protocol was adopted. It allowed reservations for 'first use' (of asphyxiating, poisonous or other gases or bacteriological methods of warfare) which, somewhat counter-intuitively, allows a State to reserve the right to respond to first use by another State. There are 21 reservations to the 1925 Geneva Protocol retaining a right to respond to first use. Sixteen of those States are now party to the CWC, which prohibits all use and to which no reservations are allowed. As a result, today only five States, namely Angola, Iraq, Israel, Democratic People's Republic of Korea and Libyan Arab Jamahiriya could theoretically, under treaty law obligations, retaliate in kind to the first use of chemical weapons. Of these, Israel, Democratic People's Republic of Korea and Libyan Arab Jamahiriya have stated that they will never use chemical weapons or are strongly committed to their elimination, which leaves only two States that could try to legally justify responding like with like to a 'first use' attack. The 1925 Geneva Protocol is still in force and currently has 140 States Parties.[65]

Given Germany's previous attempts to circumvent the language of the Hague Conventions, States were loath to leave technical loopholes. For this reason, the terminology 'analogous devices', which was first adopted in the Treaty of Versailles and then the Washington Naval Conference in 1922,[66] was also included in the 1925 Geneva Protocol. The 1925 Geneva Protocol prohibits the use of 'asphyxiating, poisonous or other gases, and *of all analogous* liquids, materials or devices' and 'bacteriological methods of warfare', but does not regulate production, storage or transfer.[67] The prohibition on 'analogous devices' would cover any nanomaterials used deliberately for their toxic properties. Any use of nanomaterials which are similar to 'analogous devices' defined in the treaty would sit firmly under the prohibition agreed to by States, embodied in the 1925 Geneva Protocol.

The deliberate inclusion of the language 'analogous devices' is often overlooked by those calling for further regulation. Any nanomaterial used in armed conflict that acts in a way that mimics a poison, or a chemical or biological weapon, would be in contravention of

65 United Nations Office for Disarmament Affairs, *Protocol for the Prohibition of the Use in War of Asphyxiating, Poisonous or Other Gases, and of Bacteriological Methods of Warfare: Status of the Treaty* <http://disarmament.un.org/treaties/t/1925>.

66 *Treaty Relating to the Use of Submarines and Noxious Gases in Warfare*, opened for signature 6 February 1922, 25 LNTS 202 (not yet in force).

67 *Protocol to the BWC* (emphasis added).

international law.[68] The 1925 Geneva Protocol, with deliberately broad language of 'all analogous liquids, materials or devices', as well as the terminology included in the BWC and the CWC, captures a prohibition on nanomaterials in a good faith interpretation of the language of the treaties.[69] Wallach's approach is a similarly pragmatic one, in which he argues that 'functional equivalence' prohibits nanoparticles being used in any way that is not compliant with the existing legal framework. If nanomaterials are 'functionally equivalent' to prohibited microscale materials that are prohibited under the Geneva Protocol, BWC or CWC, they remain prohibited, regardless of their size.[70] This approach relies on the function of matter, rather than focusing on its size. Poisoning, or any hostile use of biological or chemical matter, regardless of size, is clearly prohibited under the existing law. The prohibition on poisoning does not specify the scale of the poison and includes poisonous matter of all sizes, including all matter at the nanoscale.

2 Biological Weapons Convention

While the 1925 Geneva Protocol prohibited use, it did not cover development and stockpiling. As States continued to work on developing these prohibited weapons in the heightened post-WWII Cold War context, the international community came together to agree on a broader and more comprehensive treaty that prohibited not only 'use'. Negotiations resulted in the 1972 BWC, which incorporated the 1925 Geneva Protocol into its preamble, in part, to avoid any potential argument that

[68] Jürgen Altmann and Mark Gubrud, 'Risks from Military Uses of Nanotechnology – The Need for Technology Assessment and Preventive Control' (Paper presented at Nanotechnology – Revolutionary Opportunities and Societal Implications, 3rd JOINTEC-NSF Workshop on Nanotechnology, Lecce, Italy, 31 January – 2 February 2002) 2–3; Jürgen Altmann, *Military Nanotechnology: Potential Applications and Preventive Arms Control* (Routledge, 2006); Hitoshi Nasu and Robert McLaughlin (eds), *New Technologies and the Law of Armed Conflict* (Asser Press, 2014); Robert Pinson, 'Is Nanotechnology Prohibited by the Biological and Chemical Weapons Conventions?' (2004) 22(2) *Berkeley Journal of International Law* 279.

[69] Evan J Wallach, 'A Tiny Problem with Huge Implications – Nanotech Agents as Enablers or Substitutes for Banned Chemical Weapons: Is a New Treaty Needed?' (2010) 33(3) *Fordham International Law Journal* 858, 940. The term Wallach uses is 'jejeune'.

[70] David Marcus, 'Famine Crimes in International Law' (2003) 97(2) *American Journal of International Law* 245, 262–264. Marcus proposes that international law should extend to man-made famines as 'famines are often functionally equivalent to genocide': 248. Famines are mentioned here, given the potential of nanomaterials' toxicity to permeate food chains and water tables, and their potential to have adverse effects on humans' health.

the 1925 Geneva Protocol was superseded by the BWC, as well as to provide explicit support for adherence to the Geneva Protocol.[71] When they became signatories to the BWC, 37 States insisted on a 'first use' reservation (which means that they can respond in the case of first use by another State), of which 21 reservations remain. Of these 21 States with reservations, 18 of these States are party to the BWC, which prohibits any possession of biological weapons, and therefore makes it unlawful to retaliate with them.[72] Therefore the issue of first use seems to be moot in relation to the BWC.[73]

The ICRC notes that State practice indicates that the prohibition on biological weapons is customary international law for both international and non-international conflicts.[74] The BWC currently has 178 States Parties,[75] meaning it is not as widely supported as the CWC[76] but is still thought to represent customary international law in both international and non-international armed conflict by the ICRC.[77] Several General Assembly Resolutions have called for States to comply with the

[71] Note language included in the preamble acknowledging the significance of the 1925 Geneva Protocol

> Recognizing the important significance of the Protocol for the Prohibition of the Use in War of Asphyxiating, Poisonous or Other Gases, and of Bacteriological methods of Warfare, signed at Geneva on June 17, 1925, and conscious also of the contribution which the said Protocol has already made, and continues to make, to mitigating the horrors of war.

[72] *Biological Weapons Convention* art 1.

[73] States were aware that the next generation of chemical weapons were more reliable and no longer relied on favourable climactic conditions. Prior to the negotiation of the CWC, many States had developed protective equipment in anticipation of chemical attack. Thomas Stock, 'Chemical and Biological Weapons: Developments and Proliferation' in Stockholm International Peace Research Institute, *1993 SIPRI Yearbook: World Armaments and Disarmament* (Oxford University Press, 1993) 278, 285–286.

[74] International Committee of the Red Cross, *Customary IHL – Rule 73. Biological Weapons* (2005) <https://ihl-databases.icrc.org/customary-ihl/eng/docs/v1_rul_rule73>. When the Geneva Protocol was signed, 37 States reserved the right to retaliate with biological weapons. Seventeen of these 'no first use' reservations have been withdrawn, meaning that 20 still remain, of which 18 are party to the BWC, and are therefore prohibited from first use. At this stage, only Angola and Israel have retained their first use right of biological weapons.

[75] United Nations Office for Disarmament Affairs, *Convention on the Prohibition of the Development, Production and Stockpiling of Bacteriological (Biological) and Toxin Weapons and on Their Destruction: Status of the Treaty* <http://disarmament.un.org/treaties/t/bwc>.

[76] Ibid.

[77] International Committee of the Red Cross n 74.

1925 Geneva Protocol or the BWC.[78] These General Assembly Resolutions are indicative of the customary international law status of the Protocol and the BWC.

Article 1 of the BWC obliges States to not 'develop, produce, stockpile or otherwise acquire or retain'

1. Microbial or other biological agents, or toxins whatever their origin or method of production, of types and in quantities that have no justification for prophylactic, protective or other peaceful purposes;
2. Weapons, equipment or means of delivery designed to use such agents or toxins for hostile purposes or in armed conflict.

The five-yearly BWC Review Conferences play an important role in ensuring compliance with the BWC as well as clarifying and charting the ongoing role of the BWC. Particularly given the brevity of the BWC, the Review Conferences are an important resource that provides interpretations, instructions, guidelines and recommendations to the States Parties. Resolutions are not legally binding but may be indicative of *opinio juris* in international law.[79] Review Conferences are part of the decision-making processes that make up the wider activities of the regime for the regulation of biological weapons. If one adopts the definition of regimes as 'sets of norms, decision-making procedures and organisations coalescing around functional issue-areas and dominated by particular modes of behaviour, assumptions and biases',[80] it is clear

[78] *Chemical and Bacteriological (Biological) Weapons*, GA Res 3256 (XXIX), UN GAOR, 29th sess, 2309th plen mtg, UN Doc A/RES/3265(XXIX) (9 December 1974); *Chemical and Bacteriological (Biological) Weapons*, GA Res 32/77, UN GAOR, 32nd sess, 100th plen mtg, Agenda Item 39, UN Doc A/RES/32/77 (12 December 1977); *Chemical and Bacteriological (Biological) Weapons*, GA Res 33/59, UN GAOR, 33rd sess, 84th plen mtg, UN Doc A/RES33/59 (14 December 1978). All of these resolutions were adopted without a vote. More recently, the President of the General Assembly, after consultation with Member states, moved that resolutions be adopted without a vote in order to achieve more consistent consensus.

[79] *Legality of the Threat or Use of Nuclear Weapons (Advisory Opinion)* [1996] ICJ Rep 226, 254-5 [70] applied in *Legal Consequences of the Separation of the Chagos Archipelago from Mauritius in 1965 (Advisory Opinion)* (International Court of Justice, General List No 169, 25 February 2019) [151]; Marko Divac Öberg, 'The Legal Effects of Resolutions of the UN Security Council and the General Assembly in the Jurisprudence of the ICJ' (2006) 16(5) *The European Journal of International Law* 879.

[80] Margaret A. Young, 'Introduction: The Productive Friction between Regimes' in Margaret A Young (ed), *Regime Interaction in International Law: Facing Fragmentation* (Cambridge University Press, 2012) 1, 11. This builds on definitions common in international relations scholarship and socio-legal studies. See, e.g., Stephen

that the Review Conferences and their outputs can be as important to evaluate in the biological weapons regime as the BWC itself, especially in setting expectations for States Parties as against other regimes of which they may be members.

The Final Document of the Seventh Review Conference of the BWC in 2011[81] does not mention nanomaterials specifically. However, it does state in Article I, paragraph 3 of its final statement that,

> The Conference reaffirms that the use by the States Parties, in any way and under any circumstances of microbial or other biological agents or toxins that is not consistent with prophylactic, protective or other peaceful purposes, is effectively a violation of Article I.

It is important to note that toxins are included within this definition. Delivery of medicines and collection of toxins within the body would be allowed, as falling under the category of 'prophylactic purposes'. Any use of nanoparticles to deliver poisons or disperse toxins, unless for prophylactic purposes, would be illegal under the BWC. The BWC prohibits toxins, regardless of their properties.[82] It is advisable that subsequent Review Conferences consistently and explicitly include nanomaterials as being within their ambit so that States understand their obligations under the BWC and ensure that nanomaterials are only used for 'prophylactic, protective or other peaceful purposes'.

In 2004, United Nations Security Council Resolution (UNSCR) 1540 provided further restrictions on the use of biological and chemical weapons, including that,

> [A]ll States shall refrain from providing any form of support to non-State actors that attempt to develop, acquire, manufacture, possess, transport, transfer or use nuclear, chemical or biological weapons and their means of delivery.[83]

Krasner, 'Structural Causes and Regime Consequences: Regimes as Intervening Variables' in Stephen Krasner (ed), *International Regimes* (Cornell University Press, 1983) 1; Andreas Fischer-Lescano and Gunther Teubner, 'Regime-Collisions: The Vain Search for Legal Unity in the Fragmentation of Global Law' (2004) 25 *Michigan Journal of International Law* 999.

81 *Final Review Document of the Seventh Review Conference*, Seventh Review Conference of the States Parties to the Convention on the Prohibition of the Development, Production and Stockpiling of Bacteriological (Biological) and Toxin Weapons and on Their Destruction, UN Doc BWC/CONF.VII/COW/CRP.2 (5–22 December 2011) 10.

82 Levie, n 55.

83 SC Res 1540, UN SCOR, 59th sess, 4956th mtg, UN Doc S/RES/1540 (28 April 2004).

Article 25 of the UN Charter[84] specifies that resolutions of the Security Council made under Chapter VII of the UN Charter are binding on all UN members.[85] UNSCR 1540 was made under Chapter VII of the UN Charter, and is therefore legally binding on all States.[86] This prohibition is extended to non-State armed groups and any other non-State participants in any context unless being used for prophylactic, protective or other peaceful purposes, as specified in the text of the Resolution.[87]

In 2015, a meeting was convened to identify and discuss 'Trends in Science and Technology Relevant to the Biological and Toxin Weapons Convention' in preparation for the 8th Review Conference of the 1972 BWC. A summary report noted that '[i]t is now easier to deliver a biological agent given advances in areas such as nanoparticles and sophisticated modelling of dispersal patterns using the techniques of aerobiology'.[88] This report suggests that the risks surrounding the hostile use of nanomaterials are already of concern to scientists advising the BWC. The 2016 Review Conference did not make any major advances, though there were references made to nanomaterials by the United Kingdom,[89] the United States[90] and Cuba (with a code of proposed

[84] 'The Members of the United Nations agree to accept and carry out the decisions of the Security Council in accordance with the present Charter': *Charter of the United Nations* art 25.

[85] Hilary Charlesworth, 'Law-making and Sources' in James Crawford and Martii Koskienniemi (eds), *The Cambridge Companion to International Law* (Cambridge University Press, 2012) 198.

[86] Kelvin Widdows, 'Security Council Resolutions and Non-Members of the United Nations' (1978) 27 *International and Comparative Law Quarterly* 459, 461–462; Phillipe Cahier, 'La Charte des Nations Unies et les Etats tiers' [in French] in Antonio Cassese (ed), *Current Problems of International Law: Essays on UN Law and on the Law of Armed Conflict* (A Giuffrè, 1975) 99–100.

[87] SC Res 1540, UN SCOR, 59th sess, 4956th mtg, UN Doc S/RES/1540 (28 April 2004).

[88] The Global Network of Science Academies, *The Biological and Toxin Weapons Convention: Implications of Advances in Science and Technology* (2015) <https://royalsociety.org/~/media/policy/projects/biological-toxin-weapons-convention/bwc-trends-summary.pdf>.

[89] *Review of Developments in Science and Technology: Key Points from the 2012–2015 Biological and Toxin Weapons Convention Intersessional Programme: Submitted by the United Kingdom, Eighth Review Conference of the States Parties to the Convention on the Prohibition of the Development, Production and Stockpiling of Bacteriological (Biological) and Toxin Weapons and on Their Destruction*, UN Doc BW C/CONF.VIII/WP.17 (1 November 2016).

[90] *Article I: Reinforcing the Core Prohibition of the Biological Weapons Convention: Submitted by the United States of America, Eighth Review Conference of the States Parties to the Convention on the Prohibition of the Development, Production and*

ethical code of conduct for the use of nanomaterials),[91] and in other assorted presentations.[92]

Actors such as the Review Conference members or the Organisation for the Prohibition of Chemical Weapons (OPCW) Scientific Advisory Board (SAB) play a significant role in the role of 'soft law', bringing the makers closer to the subjects of international law.[93] As noted by Charlesworth, 'The binding character of soft law principles may be debated, but they often address issues of almost universal agreement ... and can provide powerful justifications for action' and joint understandings between States.[94]

In the face of rapidly developing technologies, such as nanomaterials, these joint understandings are important for States to clarify with each other what is included within the mandate of the treaty, unanimously based on the opinion of expert scientists. Young and Sullivan have argued that where there has been cooperation in the past between State parties to the relevant treaty, there is a duty of cooperation created for the future.[95] Young and Sullivan have argued that a duty of cooperation arises in international law over time as States cooperate to comply with a

Stockpiling of Bacteriological (Biological) and Toxin Weapons and on Their Destruction, UN Doc BWC/CONF.VIII/WP.14 (25 October 2016) 2.

91 *Code of Professional Ethics for Science Workers in Cuba: Submitted by Cuba* [unofficial English translation], *Eighth Review Conference of the States Parties to the Convention on the Prohibition of the Development, Production and Stockpiling of Bacteriological (Biological) and Toxin Weapons and on Their Destruction*, UN Doc BWC/CONF.VIII/WP.2 (30 September 2016).

92 See, e.g., *Common Understandings Reached by the Meetings of States Parties during the Intersessional Programme Held from 2012 to 2015, Eighth Review Conference of the States Parties to the Convention on the Prohibition of the Development, Production and Stockpiling of Bacteriological (Biological) and Toxin Weapons and on Their Destruction*, UN Doc BWC/CONF.VIII/PC/5 (2 June 2016); Ralf Trapp, 'Advances in the Life Sciences: Between Hype and Caution' (Workshop on the Eighth Review Conference of the Biological Weapons Convention, Geneva, 19 September 2016). <www.unog.ch/80256EDD006B8954/(httpAssets)/2735DBE154902ADBC1258035002C1F09/$file/Trapp+Science+and+technology.pdf>; The Global Network of Science Academies, n 88.

93 S Besson, 'Theorizing the Sources of International Law' in S Besson and J Tasioulas (eds), *The Philosophy of International Law* (Oxford University Press, 2008) 163–164.

94 Charlesworth, n 85, 198.

95 Margaret A. Young and Sebastian Sullivan, 'Evolution through the Duty to Cooperate: Implications of the *Whaling Case* at the International Court of Justice' (2015) 16(2) *Melbourne Journal of International Law* 15, citing Judge ad hoc Charlesworth commenting on the *International Convention for the Regulation of Whaling*, opened for signature 2 December 1946, 161 UNTS 74 (entered into force 10 November 1948) in *Whaling in the Antarctic (Australia v Japan: New Zealand Intervening) (Judgment)* (International Court of Justice, General List No 148, 31 March 2014). See also Alastair Neil Craik, 'The

treaty. Such compliance, Young and Sullivan argue, indicates that States, over time, become obliged to continue to cooperate in a similar manner. Such consensus may relate to a 'duty of cooperation', which may be interpreted as having 'some consequence' for 'States, international organisations and other actors'. I would argue that this duty of cooperation also extends to other treaties, including the BWC, where States have historically cooperated. The BWC clearly prohibits the use of all biological materials that are not for prophylactic, peaceful or protective purposes, which includes biological materials at any scale, including biological matter at the nanoscale. Where States have complied with this prohibition and continued to cooperate to do so, through regular meetings and acquiescence to the advice of scientific experts, States have extended the prohibition to analogous matter at the nanoscale.

3 Chemical Weapons Convention

Iraq's use of chemical weapons against Iranian soldiers throughout the 1980s, and then against their own Kurdish civilians in Halabja in 1988, provided the appetite for negotiation of a multilateral treaty regarding chemical weapons and their use.[96] Between 1986 and 1988, several resolutions made by the Security Council condemned the use of chemical weapons in the Iran–Iraq war, without any differentiation as to whether there was first use or retaliation,[97] indicating that any potential attempt to claim self-defence under 'first use' exceptions would almost certainly be unsuccessful under the current state of the law.

In 1992, the CWC was opened for signature and, in 1997, the CWC entered into force.[98] The CWC extended the prohibition to any chemical used for hostile purposes, beyond the prohibition on the use of

Duty to Cooperate in International Environmental Law: Constraining Discretion through Due Respect' (2020) <https://dx.doi.org/10.2139/ssrn.3596981>.

96 Timothy McCormack, 'International Law and the Use of Chemical Weapons in the Gulf War' (1990–91) 21(1) *California Western International Law Journal* 1, 10–16.

97 SC Res 582, UN SCOR, 41st sess, 2666th mtg, UN Doc S/RES/582 (24 February 1986); SC Res 598, UN SCOR, 42nd sess, 2750th mtg, UN Doc S/RES/598 (20 July 1987); SC Res 612, UN SCOR, 43rd sess, 2812nd meeting, UN Doc S/RES/612 (9 May 1988); SC Res 620, UN SCOR, 43rd sess, 2825th mtg, UN Doc S/RES/620 (26 August 1988).

98 *Convention on the Prohibition of the Development, Production, Stockpiling and Use of Chemical Weapons and on Their Destruction*, opened for signature 3 September 1992, 1974 UNTS 45 (entered into force 29 April 1997); Julian Perry Robinson, 'The Negotiations on the Chemical Weapons Convention: An Historical Overview' in Michael Bothe, Natalino Ronzitti and Allan Rosas (eds), *The New Chemical Weapons Convention: Implementation and Prospects* (Kluwer Law International, 1998) 17–36.

'analogous liquids', and adopted a robust verification mechanism to ensure compliance. Language governing poisons can also be found in the CWC, namely, 'chemical substances, whether gaseous, liquid or solid, which might be employed because of their direct toxic effects on man, animals and plants'.[99] Hays Parks has defined the relevant theme as the effect and the use through chemical properties.

> Chemical warfare is a generic term applied to all efforts and material related to lethal and incapacitating chemical agents and munitions or weapons systems, as well as to the protection and defense of forces against an adversary's employment of such agents or munitions/weapons systems. A chemical agent is a substance which is intended for use in military operations to kill, severely injure or incapacitate combatants through its chemical properties . . .[100]

The prohibition of chemical weapons became widely accepted as customary international law,[101] applicable in both international and non-international armed conflicts,[102] and this prohibition in non-international armed conflicts is contained in several other instruments,[103] as well as military manuals which apply in situations of

99 *Chemical and Bacteriological (Biological) Weapons and the Effects of Their Possible Use: Report of the Secretary-General*, 24th sess, Agenda Item 2, UN Doc A/7575/Rev/1 (1 August 1969) [19].

100 W Hays Parks, 'Classification of Chemical-Biological Warfare' (1981–82) 13 *University of Toledo Law Review* 1165, 1166.

101 See International Committee of the Red Cross, *Customary IHL – Rule 74. Chemical Weapons* (2005) <https://ihl-databases.icrc.org/customary-ihl/eng/docs/v1_rul_rule74>; Lisa Tabassi, 'Impact of the CWC: Progressive Development of Customary International Law and Evolution of the Customary Norm against Chemical Weapons' (2004) 63 *The CBW Conventions Bulletin* 1.

102 At present, only 13 States are party to neither the 1925 Geneva Protocol nor the Chemical Weapons Convention (Bahamas, Chad, Comoros, Democratic Republic of the Congo, Congo, Djibouti, Haiti, Honduras, Marshall Islands, Myanmar, Niue, Somalia and Vanuatu). Of these, the Democratic Republic of the Congo, Haiti and Honduras have all made statements that they consider the use of chemical weapons unlawful in international and non-international armed conflict. International Committee of the Red Cross n 101.

103 See, e.g., *Joint Declaration on the Complete Prohibition of Chemical and Biological Weapons*, Argentina–Brazil–Chile (signed and entered into force 5 September 1991); *Cartagena Declaration on Renunciation of Weapons of Mass Destruction* (signed and entered into force 4 December 1991); *Comprehensive Agreement on Respect for Human Rights and International Humanitarian Law between the Government of the Republic of the Philippines and the National Democratic Front of the Philippines* (signed and entered into force 16 March 1998), pt IV, art 4(4); *Secretary-General's Bulletin – Observance by United Nations Forces of International Humanitarian Law*, UN Doc ST/SGB/1999/13 (6 August 1999) section 6.2.

non-international armed conflict[104] and legislation of many States and judicial opinion.[105] With authority delegated by the CWC, the SAB is an OPCW subsidiary body that enables the Director-General to provide specialised advice in science and technology to the Conference, Executive Council or States Parties to the Convention. The SAB reports to the Director-General, who submits its reports, alongside his own response. Every five years, a large report is prepared by the SAB on developments in science and technology, which is presented to the Review Conferences of the CWC, traditionally without controversy. States accept that the SAB has a strong influence on how States interpret the CWC. This inclusion of nanomaterials as being within the remit of the CWC is included in Review Conference statements and recommendations of Member States through this process. With nearly universal membership, including all five permanent members of the United Nations Security Council (UNSC), it is easy to argue that the CWC with 192 States Parties[106] reflects customary international law.[107] The prohibitions on the use of biological and chemical weapons are both considered to have reached the status of customary international law.[108]

In the 1995 case of *Tadić*, which was decided not long after the CWC was agreed, it was noted by the ICTY that there 'undisputedly emerged a general consensus in the international community on the principle that the use of [chemical] weapons is also prohibited in internal armed

[104] See, e.g., the military manuals of Australia, Belgium, Bosnia and Herzegovina, Cameroon, Canada, Colombia, Ecuador, France, Germany, Israel, Italy, Kenya, Netherlands, New Zealand, Nigeria, Russian Federation, South Africa, Spain, Switzerland, United Kingdom, United States of America and Yugoslavia cited in International Committee of the Red Cross n 101.

[105] See, e.g., the legislation of Armenia, Australia, Belarus, Canada, Croatia, Czech Republic, Ecuador, Estonia, Finland, France, Georgia, Germany, India, Ireland, Italy, Japan, Kazakhstan, Republic of Korea, Luxembourg, Netherlands, New Zealand, Norway, Panama, Peru, Poland, Romania, Russian Federation, Singapore, Slovenia, South Africa, Sweden, Switzerland, Tajikistan, Ukraine, United Kingdom, United States of America, Yugoslavia and Zimbabwe cited in International Committee of the Red Cross n 101.

[106] United Nations Office for Disarmament Affairs, *Convention on the Prohibition of the Development, Production, Stockpiling and Use of Chemical Weapons and on Their Destruction: Status of the Treaty* <http://disarmament.un.org/treaties/t/cwc>.

[107] It is worth noting that the issue of customary international law status of the CWC is not as significant as for the BWC, given that 192 States Parties have ratified, and one party has signed but not ratified (Israel). Only three States have neither signed nor ratified (Egypt, North Korea and South Sudan).

[108] Hans Blix, 'Means and Methods of Combat' in Henry Dunant Institute, *International Dimensions of Humanitarian Law* (Martinus Nijhoff, 1988) 141.

conflicts'.[109] An example of State practice can be found in *Constitutional Case No C-225/95*, which was decided by the Colombian Constitutional Court, where it was explicitly held that customary international law prohibits the use of chemical weapons even in non-international armed conflict.[110] In conclusion, it appears that chemical weapons are universally understood as being prohibited under international law. No State has claimed that chemical weapons may be used in either international or non-international armed conflicts.

The CWC states that each State Party 'undertakes never under any circumstances'

> To develop, produce, otherwise acquire, stockpile or retain chemical weapons, or transfer, directly or indirectly, chemical weapons to anyone.[111]

There is no explicit reference to nanoparticles, nor weapons containing nanomaterials, in the CWC. The reason for this is simple: knowledge about the potential uses of the technology did not exist at the time of the agreement of the treaty, and even if it had, categorically it would not have been helpful to attempt to regulate matter by size.

Like the BWC, the CWC convenes regular Review Conferences as a forum for the assessment and evaluation of the CWC's implementation, and the identification of areas where further explanation or clarification might be required. These types of documents do not change the effect of the treaty but enrich the understanding, as mentioned earlier, and are usually made in consensus. The SAB does not provide binding decisions but rather provides technical guidance on how to interpret the existing treaty. Most recent SAB meetings have considered nanomaterials in each meeting.[112] The most recent SAB meeting on 30 April 2018 explicitly referred to nanomaterials, noting that, 'nanotechnologies used to deliver chemical or biological agents would make nanoparticles a type of delivery

[109] *Prosecutor v Tadić (Decision on the Defence Motion for Interlocutory Appeal on Jurisdiction)* (International Criminal Tribunal for the Former Yugoslavia, Appeals Chamber, Case No IT-94-1-A, 2 October 1995) [124].

[110] Colombia Constitutional Court, *Constitutional Case No C-225/95* (18 May 1995).

[111] *Chemical Weapons Convention.*

[112] It is worth noting that the last three meetings of the SAB have discussed nanomaterials, namely on 25 March 2017, 26 July 2017 and 26 October 2017: Organisation for the Prohibition of Chemical Weapons, *Reports* <www.opcw.org/about-opcw/subsidiary-bodies/scientific-advisory-board/documents/reports/>.

system, which would prohibit them under the Convention and under the Biological Weapons Convention'.[113]

The OPCW plays a key role in ensuring that the CWC is upheld and includes new advances which attract their governance and assurance of compliance. The approach of the OPCW in extending its mandate to encompass new technologies that scientifically fall within its mandate is a practical and logical approach, particularly considering the current political climate and hesitation to negotiate new international legal instruments.

The OPCW is aware that some nanomaterials 'show greater toxicity than micronized material'.[114] Such notes provided by the Director General of the SAB indicate that States who might try to argue that nanomaterials fall outside the scope of the BWC or CWC would have a difficult time doing so, and so strengthen the breadth and depth of application of these existing legal frameworks.

This level of analysis by the OPCW of nanomaterials shows an awareness of, and active engagement with, developments in this field. In contrast to those writers who argue that existing law is insufficient and a whole new treaty is required, the OPCW deliberately views nanomaterials as within its mandate, drawing attention to them and the need to keep providing guidance by means of interpretative material.

The SAB remains an excellent venue for strengthening the CWC by including nanomaterials within its remit. In 2014, the SAB published a report that focuses specifically on the convergence of biology and chemistry.[115] In June 2014, the SAB of the OPCW again made explicit references to advances in 'nanotechnology' and their implications for the CWC, including a recommendation that they should,

[113] Organisation for the Prohibition of Chemical Weapons, *Report of the Scientific Advisory Board on Developments in Science and Technology for the Fourth Special Session of the Conference of the States Parties to Review the Operation of the Chemical Weapons Convention* (30 April 2018) <www.opcw.org/fileadmin/OPCW/CSP/RC-4/en/rc4dg01_e_.pdf>.

[114] Organisation for the Prohibition of Chemical Weapons, *Note by the Director-General: Report of the Scientific Advisory Board on Developments in Science and Technology* (28 February 2008) [2.5]–[2.8]. <www.opcw.org/fileadmin/OPCW/CSP/RC-2/en/RC-2_DG.1-EN.pdf>. Micronised materials refer to those materials at the micro level, which is a magnitude of order bigger than the nanoscale.

[115] Organisation for the Prohibition of Chemical Weapons, *Convergence of Chemistry and Biology: Report of the Scientific Advisory Board's Temporary Working Group* (27 June 2014) <www.opcw.org/fileadmin/OPCW/SAB/en/TWG_Scientific_Advsiory_Group_Final_Report.pdf>.

> [M]onitor advances in nanotechnology prior to the next review conference. Regular engagement with subject matter experts will be required. A broad range of scientific disciplines are converging, including: chemistry: biology; materials science; computer science; engineering; information theory; network theory; mathematics; and quantum mechanics. Scientific practices, across all fields, continue to evolve using multidisciplinary approaches.[116]

Many chemicals of interest at the nanoscale remain firmly under the mandate of the CWC. The report clearly reaffirms this proposition, stating that,

'Nanotechnology has some potential for application to purposes prohibited by the CWC.'[117]

Kosal examines the relationships among technology, strategy and governance; suggests an urgent need to contemplate measures to counter the use of biological and chemical nanomaterials, given the likelihood of their potentially hostile use; and notes the difficulties of regulating, managing, tracking and policing their use. Referring to the CWC, Kosal points out the absence of domestic export control legislation and the lack of updates to the schedules of the CWC since 1997, arguing that further attention should be paid to these existing requirements to avoid misuse of nanomaterials.[118] Kosal also argues that the use of nanomaterials may have profound implications for offensive and defensive strategic considerations, given the nature of nanomaterials and the difficulties confronting tracking and detecting them.[119] Kosal's approach is a practical one, ensuring that the existing multilateral framework is implemented in a timely and effective manner, rather than calling for new laws to address what is already well regulated under existing international treaties.

Altmann's approach regarding modification of the legal framework, like that of Kosal and Wallach, is equally compelling, noting that changing the wording of the CWC will be too arduous and suggesting clarification that,

> [t]oxic substances that are not of biological origin or are not produced by biological systems would not count as toxins, but would fall under the CWC, i.e. be prohibited if directed against humans or animals.[120]

[116] Ibid.

[117] Ibid.

[118] Margaret Kosal, *Nanotechnology for Chemical and Biological Defense* (Springer, 2009).

[119] Ibid.

[120] Altmann, n 68, 171–172.

These clarifications can be made by States under the auspices of the BWC Secretariat or the SAB of the CWC, and even be regular statements clarifying that it is understood that nanomaterials remain under the mandate of the BWC and CWC.

4 Prohibition on Non-detectable Fragments (Protocol I of the CCW)

As already noted, in the laws of war, guidance regarding the regulation of specific types of weapons is sparse. It was not until 1983 that the CCW came into force.[121] The CCW, an umbrella Convention with a number of subsidiary protocols, straddles the somewhat semantic divide between a disarmament treaty and humanitarian law, having captured a number of principles that evolved over time. The CCW prohibits and regulates specific weapons and how they are used. For the purpose of this analysis, the CCW illustrates that different parts of the same treaty may be relevant to different uses of nanomaterials.

In the 1970s, medical personnel treating those from the battlefield witnessed an increasing number of weapons that were deliberately employing glass or other shrapnel that was impossible to detect and complicated to remove. The overwhelming view was that the superfluous suffering was unnecessary and wasted medical resources, and further, that engaging such a mechanism did not serve any military purpose. This view, which prohibited weapons the 'primary effect' of which is to injure by broken glass fragments, was supported by the UK Military Manual, which was drafted before the adoption of Protocol I.[122]

At the time of its adoption, Protocol I to the CCW applied only to international armed conflicts. On ratification, however, France, Israel and the United States stated that they would apply the Protocol to non-international armed conflicts as well,[123] and it is suggested that this prohibition now applies to non-international as well as international armed conflicts.[124]

[121] *Convention on Prohibition or Restrictions on the Use of Certain Conventional Weapons Which May Be Deemed to Be Excessively Injurious or to Have Indiscriminate Effects*, opened for signature 10 October 1980, 1342 UNTS 137 (entered into force 2 December 1983) ('*Convention on Certain Conventional Weapons*').

[122] See International Committee of the Red Cross, *Customary IHL – Rule 79. Weapons Primarily Injuring by Non-detectable Fragments* (2005) <https://ihl-databases.icrc.org/customary-ihl/eng/docs/v1_rul_rule79> n 14.

[123] Ibid n 6.

[124] See International Committee of the Red Cross n 101.

Protocol I to the CCW states that,

> It is prohibited to use any weapon the primary effect of which is to injure by fragments that are not detectable in the human body or x-rays.[125]

It is important to note that the terminology *primary effect* is very specific, and the Protocol does not extend to any weapons the secondary effect of which might be injury by undetectable fragments.

There are three parts to the question of whether nanoparticles could ever fall under this provision, both of which rely on further information about nanoparticles that is not yet publicly available. The first part of the question is whether nanoparticles could be considered 'fragments' and the second is whether they could 'lodge' within the human body. Very recently, it became known that nanoparticles can travel from lungs to the blood, which possibly explains why heart diseases can be caused by nanoparticles.[126] Nanomaterials can also enter the brain through the olfactory system if inhaled. What is not yet understood is the way that engineered nanomaterials interact with the human body, nor whether they can 'lodge' in the body as prohibited by the CCW.[127] More recent research is linking metallic nanoparticles in the body to all kinds of potential long-term risks.[128]

The third part to the question is whether nanoparticles lodged within the body would cause an injury under the language of the Protocol. This area of research is still nascent and the full effects of nanoparticles on the human body are still not entirely understood. With a nascent understanding of movement and toxicity, it is unclear whether the use of nanomaterials would be prohibited under this specific Protocol.

It is most likely that nanoparticles would be prohibited because of their chemical or biological function in the human body under the BWC or CWC, but not as 'undetectable fragments' under this Protocol. If a causal link were to be established between nanoparticles lodged in the body as a source of injury, then it could be argued that if nanoparticles were used in such a way that their *primary effect* were to deliberately lodge within the body and be undetectable, and if they caused injury, they could be prohibited under this Protocol.

[125] *Protocol I to the CCW.*

[126] Mark Miller et al, 'Inhaled Nanoparticles Accumulate at Sites of Vascular Disease' (2017) 11 *ACS Nano* 4542.

[127] Andrew Maynard, 'Old Materials, New Challenges?' (2014) 9(9) *Nature Nanotechnology* 658; Hitoshi Nasu, 'Nanotechnology and Challenges to International Humanitarian Law: A Preliminary Legal Assessment' (2012) 94(886) *International Review of the Red Cross* 653.

[128] Maynard, n 127.

5 Prohibition or Restrictions on the Use of Incendiary Weapons (Protocol III of the CCW)

Another additional Protocol to the CCW prohibits incendiary weapons.[129] This treaty gives effect to the prohibition of unnecessary suffering in relation to certain weapons, in this case particularly by reducing the likelihood of civilian casualties. During discussions in the 1970s, many States proposed a complete ban on incendiary weapons, including against combatants,[130] and some States do prohibit the use of incendiary weapons completely.[131] The use of napalm in Vietnam led the General Assembly to adopt a resolution on general and complete disarmament in which it deplored the use of napalm (and other incendiary weapons) in all armed conflict.[132] Further, several States have made the pertinent point that incendiary weapons should not be permitted even against combatants, as such use would constitute unnecessary suffering.[133]

Most uses of incendiary weapons would be in violation of the laws of war by virtue of the prohibition on superfluous and unnecessary suffering.[134] In 2001, amendments were proposed to extend Protocol III to non-international armed conflicts. The negotiations were not controversial and the Protocol entered into force on 18 May 2004. To date, 29 States have ratified the amended version of the Protocol.[135] The Protocol is very specific about what constitutes an incendiary weapon,

129 *Protocol III to the CCW.*

130 Formal proposals were submitted to the Ad Hoc Committee on Conventional Weapons of the Diplomatic Conference to this effect by Afghanistan, Algeria, Austria, Colombia, Cote d'Ivoire, Egypt, Iran, Kuwait, Lebanon, Lesotho, Mali, Mauritania, Mexico, Norway, Romania, Sudan, Sweden, Switzerland, Tanzania, Tunisia, Venezuela, Yugoslavia and Zaire. See International Committee of the Red Cross, *Customary IHL – Rule 85. The Use of Incendiary Weapons against Combatants* (2005) <https://ihl-databases.icrc.org/customary-ihl/eng/docs/v1_rul_rule85>.

131 See, e.g., Andorra, Colombia, Hungary and Yugoslavia cited in International Committee of the Red Cross n 130.

132 *General and Complete Disarmament*, GA Res 2932 A (XXVII), UN GAOR, 27th sess, 2093rd plen mtg, UN Doc A/RES/2932(XXVII) (29 November 1972) (adopted by 99 votes in favour, none against and 15 abstentions).

133 See, e.g., Belgium, Colombia, Norway, Sweden and the USSR cited in International Committee of the Red Cross n 130.

134 The principle of the prohibition on superfluous injury, which has a long history, will be explored in more detail in Chapter 4. *Additional Protocol I* arts 35(1), 35(2).

135 Argentina, Australia, Austria, Belgium, Bulgaria, Burkina Faso, Canada, China, Croatia, Estonia, Finland, France, Holy See, Hungary, Japan, Latvia, Liechtenstein, Lithuania, Mexico, Netherlands, Norway, Republic of Korea, Romania, Serbia and Montenegro, Slovakia, Spain, Sweden, Switzerland and the United Kingdom. See International Committee of the Red Cross n 130.

> [A] weapon or munition ... primarily designed to set fire to objects or to cause burn injury to persons through the action of flame, heat or a combination thereof.[136]

The key term is *primarily designed.* Excluded from the definition of incendiary weapons in Protocol III are those,

> [M]unitions designed to combine penetration, blast or fragmentation effects with an additional incendiary effect, such as ... explosive bombs and similar combined-effects munitions in which the incendiary effect is not specifically designed to cause burn injury to persons, but to be used against military objectives, such as armored vehicles, aircraft and installations or facilities.[137]

The term 'primarily designed' is an improvement to its predecessor text in the 1899 Hague Declaration, namely 'the sole object of which', as it provides a lower standard by which a weapon may fall foul of Protocol III.[138] Either definition would not provide a high enough standard to hold a State to account if the dispersion of an undetonated thermobaric weapon were to leak and have the same effect as a chemical weapon, as a thermobaric weapon with nanomaterials would not be primarily designed, nor have as its sole object, to behave as a chemical weapon. If it were ever designed in such a way, it would also fly in the face of the 'good faith' obligation discussed earlier in this chapter to comply with a treaty.

6 Prohibition on Blinding Laser Weapons (Protocol IV of the CCW)

This Protocol is the one multilateral treaty specifically focused on a particular category of laser weapons, and the only modern weapon which was prohibited before its actual use on the battlefield.[139] In fact, prior to the adoption of Protocol IV, many States involved in its negotiation called for a broader ban on any weapons that blind, and not just to those

[136] *Protocol III to the CCW* art 1.

[137] Ibid art 1(b)(iii).

[138] Parties were to 'abstain from the use of projectiles the sole object of which is the diffusion of asphyxiating or deleterious gases': *Hague Declaration (II)* (emphasis added).

[139] The Declaration of St Petersburg prohibited anti-personnel projectile missiles before they were used in battle in 1868. See *Declaration Renouncing the Use, in Time of War, of Explosive Projectiles under 400 grammes Weight*, signed 29 November 1868, 138 CTS 297 (entered into force 11 December 1868) ('*Declaration of St Petersburg*').

that are specifically designed to blind, or that blind permanently.[140] The current understanding is that this prohibition applies in both international and non-international armed conflicts.[141]

This Protocol has 107 State Parties. Although it is not yet a party to Protocol IV, the United States has stated that 'the Department [of Defense] has no intent to spend money developing weapons we are prohibited from using'.[142] At the time of adopting the Protocol, China noted that, 'this is the first time in human history that a kind of inhumane weapon is declared illegal and prohibited before it is actually used'.[143] Protocol IV to the CCW bans the use and the transfer of any laser weapon specifically designed to cause permanent human blindness.[144]

The most important aspect of this Protocol for present purposes is the scope of the ban. The Protocol bans the use and the transfer of laser weapons designed to 'cause permanent blindness to unenhanced vision, that is to the naked eye, or to the eye with corrective eyesight devices'.[145] The Protocol does not ban all laser weapons and certainly does not constitute a general ban on either the enhancement or the use of existing laser weapons, or even necessarily the use of lasers in optogenetics, one of the technologies under consideration in this book.

III Regulation of the Uses of Nanomaterials in War

Not all of the treaties discussed in this chapter have relevance for all three of the technologies, namely thermobaric weapons, optogenetics and genetic modification. Each use of nanomaterials will be discussed separately in this section in the context of their applicable treaty regimes.

A Thermobaric Weapons

In this section, I will consider how Protocol III to the CCW, the 1980 Protocol on Non-Detectable Fragments (1980 Protocol), the BWC

140 See, e.g., Australia, Austria, Belgium, Denmark, Ecuador, Finland, France, Germany, Mexico, Netherlands, Norway, Poland, Romania, Russian Federation and Sweden cited in International Committee of the Red Cross, *Customary IHL – Rule 86. Blinding Laser Weapons* (2005) <https://ihl-databases.icrc.org/customary-ihl/eng/docs/v1_rul_rule86> n 20.

141 See International Committee of the Red Cross n 141.

142 Ibid n 9.

143 Ibid n 10.

144 *Protocol IV to the CCW* art 1.

145 Ibid.

and the CWC limit or prohibit the use of thermobaric weapons with nanomaterials. Thermobaric weapons are not illegal *per se* pursuant to Protocol III to the CCW, the BWC, the CWC or the 1980 Protocol, but the existing legal framework does provide limits to their use.

Given that the main function of nanomaterials in thermobaric weapons is to produce heat and vacuum, the use of thermobaric weapons with nanomaterials in war is prohibited or limited by the prohibition on incendiary weapons under Protocol III to the CCW. In some circumstances, the 1980 Protocol can prohibit or limit the use of thermobaric weapons – this would extend to thermobaric weapons with nanomaterials. Nanoparticles 'enhance' the thermobaric weapon by increasing the blast and temperature of the weapon. Regular thermobaric weapons have a core temperature exceeding 3,000 degrees centigrade.[146] On the face of it, the primary injury mechanisms – blast and heat – are at such an intensity that the addition of nanoparticles will make little or no difference to the overall function of the weapon. Nonetheless, the weapon remains regulated by general principles and cannot be used indiscriminately (discussed in more detail in Chapter 4).

> The future of nano-energetics offers immense promise to minimize collateral damage. Nano-energetics relies on nanostructured explosives and fuel additives, as well as catalytics and photovoltaics. The technology provides more effective control of blast, resulting in the direction of energy and impact to a designated target.[147]

The CWC limits the use of thermobaric weapons with nanomaterials where a weapon contains chemicals that do not detonate but subsequently have the same toxic effect as a chemical weapon. It has been suggested that undetonated thermobaric fuels would prove as lethal as most chemical agents to personnel caught within their cloud.[148] One of the more common ingredients in thermobaric weapons is ethylene oxide,

[146] Lester Grau and Timothy Smith, 'A "Crushing" Victory: Fuel-Air Explosives and Grozny 2000' (2000) 84(8) *Marine Corps Gazette* 30.

[147] Ray Nelson, 'Nano-technology and Biotechnology for Future Defense' (2015) 3(22) *Space & Missile Defense Report*, cited in Jefferson Reynolds, 'Collateral Damage on the 21st Century Battlefield: Enemy Exploitation and the Law of Armed Conflict, and the Struggle for a Moral High Ground' (2005) 56 *The Air Force Law Review* 1, 99.

[148] Defence Intelligence Agency, 'Future Threat to the Soldier System, Volume I; Dismounted Soldier–Middle East Threat' (September 1993) 73, cited in *Backgrounder on Russian Fuel Air Explosives ('Vacuum Bombs')* (1 February 2000) Human Rights Watch <www.hrw.org/report/2000/02/01/backgrounder-russian-fuel-air-explosives-vacuum-bombs>.

which is a gas used as a sterilising agent in the health industry. Ethylene oxide is toxic if inhaled. Human Rights Watch has argued that explosives containing ethylene oxide that do not detonate would have similar effects to a chemical weapon.[149] The fact that a thermobaric weapon may contain a substance that may act unintentionally as a toxic chemical if undetonated does not mean that it would automatically be prohibited. The key term is 'deliberate use'. Deliberate use of thermobaric weapons with nanomaterials, or traditional thermobaric weapons, to exploit the properties of the toxic chemicals would be prohibited under the CWC. Non-primary impacts of thermobaric weapons with nanomaterials will be discussed further in Chapter 4 in relation to the SIrUS project.

The 1980 Protocol may restrict the use of thermobaric weapons with nanomaterials under some circumstances. The first question under the 1980 Protocol is whether the 'primary effect' of thermobaric weapons with nanomaterials is to injure by fragments that are 'non-detectable in the human body or x-rays'.[150] The ICRC explanation of the Rule explains that the rationale behind Protocol I was to avoid wounds that had no military utility, were difficult to treat and therefore caused unnecessary suffering.[151] If it could be shown that the primary effect of the thermobaric weapon with nanomaterials was intended to be injury by the dispersion of non-detectable fragments (which is unlikely, given that the primary purpose of thermobaric weapons is almost inevitably their blast and vacuum effect), the second question would be whether nanoparticles constitute fragments for the purposes of this treaty. The first part of the answer to whether nanoparticles constitute fragments derives from their size and function, which I would argue that they may do.

The second question is whether the nanoparticles 'injure' within the meaning of the 1980 Protocol. While nanoparticles can enter the brain through the olfactory system if inhaled, and can move between membranes within the body, we do not yet understand fully the risks

[149] *Backgrounder on Russian Fuel Air Explosives ('Vacuum Bombs')* (1 February 2000) Human Rights Watch <www.hrw.org/report/2000/02/01/backgrounder-russian-fuel-air-explosives-vacuum-bombs>.

[150] *Protocol I to the CCW*.

[151] Reference is made to the UK military manual, which was drafted before the adoption of *Protocol I to the CCW* and included 'projectiles filled with broken glass.' See International Committee of the Red Cross n 122. Weapons that contain plastic as part of their design are not illegal if the plastic is not part of the primary injuring mechanism, according to the United States: International Committee of the Red Cross n 122.

presented by engineered nanomaterials. As already mentioned in Chapter 1, there is very recent research showing that metallic nanoparticles lodged in the brain may lead to a higher risk of certain diseases, such as Alzheimer's.[152] However, even where nanoparticles can be identified, their source is not always clear.[153] Researchers involved in this study concluded that further research is needed in this area. For this reason, it is unlikely that the 1980 Protocol would apply.

By way of analogy, following Wallach's suggestion of 'functional equivalence' that was mentioned earlier in this chapter, another weapon which has been written about extensively regarding its legality under Protocol I is Dense Inert Metal Explosive weaponry (DIME). DIME has been suggested by some authors, including Faunce, to fall within the scope of this Protocol because particles lodge within the body and cause harm.[154] Faunce also suggests that if nanoparticles were included in any weapons system for the primary purpose of causing injury, the 1980 Protocol would

152 German Plascencia-Villa et al, 'High-resolution analytical imaging and electron holography of magnetite particles in amyloid cores of Alzheimer's disease' (2016) 6 *Scientific Reports* <www.nature.com/articles/srep24873>.

153 Barbara Maher et al, 'Magnetite Pollution Nanoparticles in the Human Brain' (2016) 113 (39) *PNAS* 10797

> We identify the abundant presence in the human brain of magnetite nanoparticles that match precisely the high-temperature magnetite nanospheres, formed by combustion and/or friction-derived heating, which are prolific in urban, airborne particulate matter (PM). Because many of the airborne magnetite pollution particles are <200 nm in diameter, they can enter the brain directly through the olfactory nerve and by crossing the damaged olfactory unit. This discovery is important because nanoscale magnetite can respond to external magnetic fields, and is toxic to the brain, being implicated in production of damaging reactive oxygen species (ROS). Because enhanced ROS production is causally linked to neurodegenerative diseases such as Alzheimer's disease, exposure to such airborne PM-derived magnetite nanoparticles might need to be examined as a possible hazard to human health.

154 Thomas Faunce, *Nanotechnology for a Sustainable World* (Edward Elgar, 2012) 149

> Owing to the undetectable nature of tungsten micro-particles in human tissue, the question arises whether a nanotechnology weapon similar to this would fall within the scope of the 1980 Protocol I to the CCW . . . To do so the design intent must meet the threshold for the prohibition, for example, because the primary effect of metal dust sprayed with DIME is to kill, injure or damage by blast without leaving much trace of fragments . . . DIME also could be prohibited owing to the seriousness of injury it causes given the minute size of the fragments that are beyond practical surgical manipulation or removal.

apply. There is compelling evidence that undetectably fine 'energy-charged, heavy metal tungsten alloy (HMTA) powder released by DIMEs is tumour-generating and capable of genotoxic effects'.[155] This analogy may also have relevance for thermobaric weapons with nanomaterials.

Thermobaric weapons are not illegal *per se* pursuant to Protocol III to the CCW, the BWC, the CWC or the 1980 Protocol. Their use, however, has legal constraints. Any inclusion of nanoparticles included primarily to cause long-term human harm would clearly be prohibited, just as DIME, at the microscale, would be prohibited if it were found that this were the function for which it was 'primarily designed'.[156]

Ordinarily, thermobaric weapons are used because of their blast and subsequent vacuum effect, particularly within closed spaces. The idea behind using nanoparticles in thermobaric weapons is not only to extend their reach and increase their temperature but also potentially to create smaller bombs with the same impact as a bigger non-nano version.

Even without nanomaterials,[157] it is difficult to imagine a scenario where it could be argued that thermobaric weapons are 'primarily designed to set fire to objects or to cause burn injury to persons', as required by Protocol III to the CCW.[158] With the increasing prevalence of FAEs (fuel air explosions) and thermobaric weapons that have a larger and longer lasting fire-ball, the incidence of burns may increase. Flash burns, flame burns from secondary fires and inhalation injury from toxic substance may complicate an already severe mechanism of injury.[159]

155 Erik Roedel et al, 'Pulmonary Toxicity after Exposure to Military-Relevant Heavy Metal Tungsten Alloy Particles' (2012) 259(1) *Toxicology and Applied Pharmacology* 74; John Kalinich et al, 'Embedded Weapons-Grade Tungsten Alloy Shrapnel Rapidly Induces Metastatic High-Grade Rhabdomyo-Sarcomas in F344 Rats' (2005) 113(6) *Environmental Health Perspective* 729; Alexandra Miller et al, 'Neoplastic Transformation of Human Osteoblast Cells to the Tumorigenic Phenotype by Heavy Metal Tungsten Alloy Particles: Induction of Genotoxic Effects' (2001) 22(1) *Carcinogenesis* 115.

156 *Protocol III to the CCW* art 1.

157 'The injuries caused by blast are as unpleasant as anything on the battlefield. Most damage is caused when the shockwave passes from tissue to fluid or air, resulting in collapsed lungs and multiple internal haemorrhages. Anyone inside the cloud when it is detonated will probably be killed instantly': David Hambling, 'Deadly blast from the past', *The Guardian* (online), 18 January 2001 <www.theguardian.com/science/2001/jan/18/technology2>.

158 *Protocol III to the CCW* art 1.

159 Toney Baskin and John Holcomb, 'Bombs, Mines, Blast, Fragmentation and Thermobaric Mechanisms of Injury' in Peter Mahoney et al (eds), *Ballistic Trauma: A Practical Guide* (Springer, 2005) 56.

The increase in burns, even if enabled or enhanced by nanomaterials, does not translate to the interpretation that thermobaric weapons are 'primarily designed to set fire to objects'.[160] This is a very high threshold that appears unlikely to be met by thermobaric weapons except in a very small selection of specific uses, given that their primary action is almost inevitably blast and vacuum. Thermobaric weapons are most probably already prohibited because of their cause of superfluous injury and unnecessary suffering (discussed in greater detail in Chapter 4), or the challenges they may pose to the law of distinction; therefore it is unlikely that traditional thermobaric weapons would be prohibited under Protocol III of the CCW, which prohibits incendiary weapons.

B *Optogenetics*

The 1995 Blinding Laser Protocol[161] and the BWC prohibit certain uses and limit other uses of optogenetics. Now is precisely the time to identify relevant legal issues for any potential use of optogenetics during war, as interest by the military in the interface between the human brain and other systems is growing.[162] As we learn more about the mind and how it works, further advances will be made in the ability to control it.

The 1995 Blinding Laser Protocol[163] could have relevance to optogenetics, as it prohibits the use of deliberate permanent blindness as a technique in warfare. In early 2016, trials were undertaken using optogenetics on humans to remediate retinal diseases.[164] There is no question that, in the future, optogenetics could be used to temporarily or permanently damage sight. Thus far, the science appears not to be developed with any intent to cause permanent human blindness or to be irreversible, presuming the reversibility of the current uses. In fact, at present, one of the potential uses of optogenetics, with the help of nanolasers, is

[160] *Protocol III to the CCW* art 1.
[161] *Protocol IV to the CCW* art 1.
[162] Michael Gross, 'The Pentagon's Push to Program Soldiers' Brains' (November 2018) *The Atlantic* <www.theatlantic.com/magazine/archive/2018/11/the-pentagon-wants-to-weaponize-the-brain-what-could-go-wrong/570841/?utm_source=eb>.
[163] *Protocol IV to the CCW* art 1.
[164] Sara Reardon, 'Light Controlled Genes and Neurons Poised for Clinical Trials' (19 May 2016) *Nature* <www.nature.com/news/light-controlled-genes-and-neurons-poised-for-clinical-trials-1.19886>.

specifically to help to restore sight.[165] The Protocol bans the use and the transfer of laser weapons designed to 'cause *permanent* blindness to unenhanced vision, that is to the naked eye, or to the eye with corrective eyesight devices'.[166] If optogenetics were applied for the purposes of blinding irreversibly, such use would unequivocally be banned under Protocol IV. If optogenetics were used to blind temporarily, then it would comply with Protocol IV, although it may be in violation of other international law, which is considered later in this chapter.

Previously, imaging permitted scientists to only observe specific kinds of disparate activity within the brain. Now, functions of the brain are being mapped in the same way that the human genome was being mapped during the 1990s. Optogenetics provides the opportunity to influence the brain, at specific times, to exhibit specific behaviours. Increased understanding of how memory, emotion and cognition work will also almost certainly result in the manipulation of these functions. Coupled with neuro-prostheses, neural probes and intra-neural tissue implants,[167] and other developments in neurological research, the ability to control the brain remotely is becoming increasingly more real. The legal implications of one kind of brain control, optogenetics, will be considered, but the same legal frameworks will be relevant to other developments that could be used to cerebrally manipulate or control human behaviour.

Optogenetics could involve activation by the use of biological matter, namely a virus or genetic modification. The BWC is relevant because the use of biological matter for any hostile purposes is banned. This section puts that aside for a moment to analyse the use of nanolasers as a stand-alone technology. Germany's Military Manual specifically states that the prohibitions described under the BWC 'shall apply both to biotechnological and synthetic procedures serving other but peaceful purposes. They also include genetic engineering procedures and microorganisms altered through genetic engineering'.[168] This specific terminology does not

165 Mohammed Mehdi Doroudchi et al, 'Virally Delivered Channelrhodopsin-2 Safely and Effectively Restores Visual Function in Multiple Mouse Models of Blindness' (2011) 19 (7) *Molecular Therapy* 1220, 1228.

166 *Protocol IV to the CCW* art 1 (emphasis added).

167 Stuart Mason Dambrot, 'Your Brain on Mesh: Injectable Flexible Probe Melds with Neurons, Causes Little or No Chronic Immune Response' (5 July 2017) *Phys Org* <https://phys.org/news/2017-07-brain-mesh-flexible-probe-melds.html>.

168 The Federal Ministry of Defence of the Federal Republic of Germany, *Humanitarian Law in Armed Conflicts: German Manual, VR II 3* (1992) [trans of: *Humanitäres*

appear in other military manuals, which leaves the potential for Defence Forces to be unclear that these uses remain prohibited under the BWC and CWC.

Light-activated genes permit laser light to remotely 'excite' or activate neural functions, or alternatively to inhibit their function.[169] Hall suggests that

> Even more recent genome-editing methods can be used to precisely alter the genetics of living cells in the lab. Along with optogenetics, these tools mean scientists can begin to pinpoint the function of the thousands of different types of nerve cells among the roughly 86 billion in the human brain.[170]

Without the critical step of activation by nanolasers, the genetic modification and the virus remain latent and without effect.[171] Even if a virus were used against the other side in a conflict, and it remained latent and without effect, it would be in contravention of Article 1 of the BWC, which prohibits States Parties from using biological matter that is not permitted by the BWC.[172] The customary international law prohibition of the use of biological weapons binds non-States Parties and States Parties alike. A review of any such use of a virus with enemy combatants would not be approved, as it would clearly contravene the BWC.[173]

Despite being nascent, this research has direct implications for the potential ability to manipulate the human brain and involuntarily change human behaviour. A soldier could hypothetically, via the use of

Völkerrecht in bewaffneten Konflikten (first published 1992)] [438]–[439] <www.humanitaeres-voelkerrecht.de/ManualZDv15.2.pdf>.

169 Lief Fenno, Ofer Yizhar and Karl Deisseroth, 'The Development and Application of Optogenetics' (2011) 34 *Annual Review of Neuroscience* 389, 396.

170 Stephen S Hall, 'Neuroscience's New Toolbox' (17 June 2014) *MIT Technology Review* <www.technologyreview.com/s/528226/neurosciences-new-toolbox/>.

171 Shrivats Mohan Iyer et al, 'Virally Mediated Optogenetic Excitation and Inhibition of Pain in Freely Moving Nontransgenic Mice' (2014) 32(3) *Nature Biotechnology* 274.

172 *Biological Weapons Convention* art 1.

173 Should the military use these techniques with their own armed forces, questions of consent and ethics within the military itself would arise. Beyond these discussions, the technology could potentially be used for 'prophylactic, protective or other peaceful purposes', such as those that would help to manage or inhibit pain, or potentially have uses for PTSD or other trauma. As mentioned earlier, questions of human enhancement and their legality and ethics are beyond the scope of this book. Adam Henschke, '"Supersoldiers": Ethical Concerns in Human Enhancement Technologies' in International Committee of the Red Cross, *Humanitarian Law & Policy* (3 July 2017) <http://blogs.icrc.org/law-and-policy/2017/07/03/supersoldiers-ethical-concerns-human-enhancement-technologies-2/>.

nanolasers, have reactions or emotions that are virtually 'remote controlled'. As more information is being acquired about the brain, attempts to control it, via optogenetics or other means, are likely to proliferate. The consideration of this particular modification of function is relevant for optogenetics, but also for future potential technologies that may effectively hijack the brain using other techniques enabled by the combination of neuroscience and advances in the use of nanomaterials. Although many other methods of human control already exist, it is the immediate reversibility of this technology that makes it unique, and unlike other weapons contemplated by treaty law.

Traditional nanolasers do not require novel application of the law.[174] Similar general legal principles as those that govern kinetic weapons apply, in addition to specific treaty law governing lasers. However, the use of nanolasers in a non-traditional way, namely to manipulate brain cells, attracts other legal regimes that are not traditionally associated with lasers. Even within the category of nanolasers, the type of use of nanomaterials needs to be differentiated and analysed individually for legal implications.

In conclusion, the impact of nanolaser-enabled technology has the potential to be magnified by other emerging technologies. Innovative uses of science may be game-changers for the military, particularly in conjunction with other emerging technologies, including motes, which are already in use.[175] Any review of weapons would need to consider not only the law applicable to optogenetics, as this section has done, but also the amplified effects if coupled with other new and emerging technologies. In the meantime, any use of optogenetics 'specifically designed, as their sole combat function or as one of their combat functions, to cause

[174] Information about a High Energy Liquid Laser Area Defense System (HELLADS) suggests that further research on a liquid-state laser for aircraft is already well under way. As David Shaver states, 'The goal of the HELLADS program is to develop a 150 kilowatt (kW) laser weapon system that is ten times smaller and lighter than current lasers of similar power, enabling integration onto tactical aircraft to defend against and defeat ground threats.' David Shaver, *High Energy Liquid Laser Area Defense System (HELLADS)*, Defense Advanced Research Projects Agency <www.darpa.mil/news-events/2015-05-21-2>. See also Richard Whittle, 'Silent, Invisible, Deadly: The Weapon that Could Change Warfare', *New York Post* (online), 27 December 2015 <http://nypost.com/2015/12/27/air-force-will-test-first-aircraft-mounted-laser-weapon-in-january>.

[175] Smart dust, also known as microelectrical mechanisms (MEMS), comprises components that are micrometres in size and often contain sensors. Anil Ananthaswamy, 'The March of the Motes' (2003) 179(2409) *New Scientist* 26.

permanent blindness' would be prohibited, and under Article 2 of the 1995 Blinding Laser Protocol, States would need to use 'all feasible precautions' in the use of laser systems to avoid incidents of permanent blindness.

C *Genetic Modification*

Genetic modification includes the modification of genes both of the individual and of the germline, affecting future offspring. Genetic modification using a new technique called CRISPR-Cas9 was listed as the breakthrough of the year for 2015. CRISPR-Cas9 uses bacteria to modify genes. CRISPR-Cas9 is not the first tool developed to edit DNA; in fact, it is one of many techniques that have been used. It is, however, by far the most reliable, cost-effective and accessible of the techniques developed. Unlike previous tools, it uses the same techniques as naturally occurring bacteria and single-celled micro-organisms, and, unlike some previous techniques, is not man-made. CRISPR is an acronym for 'clustered regularly interspaced short palindromic repeats'. The Cas9 component of the name refers to an enzyme associated with the immune system of bacteria. CRISPR's hallmark is the naturally occurring bacterial defence system that forms the basis for CRISPR-Cas9 genome editing technology.[176] It is a technology that enabled the deliberate editing of DNA in embryos for the first time, and the modification of human genomes that will pass on to subsequent generations, affecting what is known as the germline. It has been noted that there is a 'potential use of genetic markers to target an ethnic group or even a specific individual'.[177] Switzerland explicitly mentioned CRISPR as one of the technologies about which it was concerned at the 2019 Meeting of the States Parties to the Convention on the Prohibition of the Development, Production, and Stockpiling of Bacteriological (Biological) and Toxin Weapons and on their Destruction.[178] In 2006, Doswald-Beck, an international lawyer, noted the possibility of genetic modification being used as a method of

[176] John Travis, 'And Science's 2015 Breakthrough of the Year is . . .' (17 December 2015) *Science* <www.sciencemag.org/news/2015/12/and-science-s-breakthrough-year>.

[177] Altmann and Gubrud, n 68, 2–3.

[178] *Scientific and Technological Developments of Relevance to the Convention and the Assessment of Benefits and Risks: Submitted by Switzerland*, Meeting of the States Parties to the Convention on the Prohibition of the Development, Production and Stockpiling of Bacteriological (Biological) and Toxin Weapons and on Their Destruction, UN Doc BWC/MSP/2019/MX.2/WP.2 (10 July 2019).

warfare, and the attention that it had garnered from States. She noted that it was prohibited in law and that States had already been motivated in 2007 to take steps to prevent its use in armed conflict,

> Mention must be made of a potential new method of warfare that is already prohibited in law but that could have horrific effects if developed, namely, genetic weapons. The spectre of this as well as of new and obviously preliminary developments in bio-technology has already motivated States to begin negotiations for the development of verification methods for the Biological Weapons Convention.[179]

Both the BWC and the CWC prohibit genetic modification of humans in war. States need to be clear in official statements and expert advice that any genetic modification during war will contravene the BWC or CWC, whether at the regular, micro or nanoscale, and therefore remains prohibited, and reiterate that States will be held to account for any breaches of these obligations. In this section, these laws will be applied to genetic modification and their adequacy analysed.

States will have varying degrees of willingness to facilitate regulation on potential weaponisation for a number of reasons, the most prominent of which is the likelihood of other States possessing similar weapons, or whether they might be susceptible to attack by them. 'The prospect of States agreeing to accept limits on their weaponry depends on variables ranging from whether they possess or are likely to be attacked with them, to the degree of international and domestic concern about their impact on the civilian population'.[180] This argument is, of course, applicable to all technologies, not just those involving nanoparticles. Currently, the technological capability to modify human genomes is held by a handful of States. That said, the newest technique of CRISPR-Cas9 is much simpler than previous techniques, making it accessible to more State and non-State actors. This accessibility of the technology, and the ease with which it may be transferred, increases the urgency for regulation which differs from that governing the use of more traditional weapons and can be created and transferred more easily.

[179] Since 2006, some States, including the United States and the United Kingdom, have permitted modifications of germlines under some circumstances. Louise Doswald-Beck, 'Humanitarian Law in Future Wars' in Michael Schmitt and Leslie Green (eds), *The Law of Armed Conflict: Into the Next Millennium* (US Naval War College, 1998) 39.

[180] Michael Schmitt, 'War, Technology, and the Law of Armed Conflict' in Anthony Helm (ed), *The Law of War in the 21st Century: Weaponry and the Use of Force* (Naval War College, 2006) 137.

International law provides limits to the use of germline modification, applicable to embryos, sperm or eggs, to alter the genes in all the resultant person's cells, including their eggs and their subsequent offspring. Scientists describe a situation where '[t]he technology may also be used as a potential "surgical knife" to correct genomic mutations or create new creatures by changing the inherited phenotypes'.[181] I will review both potential uses of genetic modification: the genetic modification of humans and the genetic modification (and synthetic creation) of non-human organisms, including those that are synthetically created.

1 Genetic Modification in Humans

In the civilian sector, some prominent scientists called for a moratorium on permanent modification of genetics for germlines (those that will be passed on to future generations).[182] These calls were for moratoriums for the civilian population only during times of peace (I assume that the use in armed conflict was not even contemplated in this context), and made four key recommendations: a hold on clinical uses; the creation of expert forums; suggestions for more transparent research; and a globally representative group to recommend policy approaches. Given how complicated the ethics and social ramifications of this kind of modification are in the civilian sector and how divided the scientific community is without even having considered potential uses for the military, it would seem that at least the same level of consideration should be given to any potential military uses of genetic modification of germlines.

(a) The BWC The use of a part of a bacterium for hostile purposes, i.e. not for 'prophylactic, protective or other peaceful purposes',[183] would be prohibited under the BWC. CRISPR-Cas9 uses bacteria to modify genes. If a part of a bacteria were to be used for hostile purposes, unless for 'prophylactic, protective or other peaceful purposes',[184] it would clearly be prohibited under the BWC.

In February 2017, the National Academy of Science and the National Academy of Medicine published a report on Human Genome Editing,

[181] Li Chun-Xiao and Qian Hai-li, 'A Double-Edged Sword: CRISPR-Cas9 Is Emerging as a Revolutionary Technique for Genome Editing' (2015) 2 *Military Medical Research* 25.
[182] David Baltimore et al, 'A Prudent Path Forward for Genomic Engineering and Germline Gene Modification' (2015) 348(6230) *Science* 36.
[183] *Biological Weapons Convention* art 1.
[184] Ibid.

Science, Ethics and Governance,[185] largely due to concerns about the explosion in CRISPR-Cas9 system genome editing. In this report, a committee defined a set of criteria under which heritable germline editing could be permitted when US restrictions were permitted, or if countries without legal prohibitions were to proceed with this line of research. Both the United States and the United Kingdom now permit genome editing under some circumstances.[186] This original position of the scientists is relevant, as it indicates States' reluctance to permit germ editing, even where consent is provided in times of peace. Given the serious concerns expressed regarding the use of this technology during peacetime, and the constraints required, it is unlikely that the use of genetic modification in war would be tolerated under any circumstances.

(b) The CWC The CWC requires that each State Party:

> [U]undertakes never under any circumstances:

(a) To use chemical weapons;
(b) To engage in any military preparations to use chemical weapons.[187]

Both of these terms have traditionally applied to widespread use of chemicals during war. Given the specificity of the use of enzymes to modify genetic codes permanently, this provision needs to be interpreted to include modification of the human genome.

The Cas9 refers to an enzyme produced by the bacteria. Enzymes are not alive but are complex proteins made up of chemicals produced by bacteria. Although it may be argued that proteins are not chemicals, this distinction would seem artificial and arbitrary. If Cas9 were to be weaponised, then it would be prohibited under the CWC, as it is a type of chemical. The weaponisation of any chemical is clearly prohibited under the CWC, and the technique of CRISPR-Cas9 would be captured under this prohibition by the nature of using a chemical action to bring about its effect.

[185] National Academy of Sciences and National Academy of Medicine, *Human Genome Editing: Science, Ethics and Governance* (2017) <http://nationalacademies.org/cs/groups/genesite/documents/webpage/gene_177260.pdf>.

[186] Haroon Siddique, 'British Researchers Get Green Light to Genetically Modify Human Embryos', *The Guardian* (online), 2 February 2016 <www.theguardian.com/science/2016/feb/01/human-embryo-genetic-modify-regulator-green-light-research>.

[187] *Chemical Weapons Convention* arts 1(b), 1(c).

There may be situations in the future where both the BWC and the CWC apply. In November 2017, new research indicated that genetic modification could be undertaken without using any bacteria, but rather simply by using roaming nanoparticles.[188] Such use would be prohibited by the BWC and the CWC, as the tools used would be able to be categorised as either chemical and/or biological matter, even at the nanoscale. States need to be clear that any use of genetic modification in war is prohibited, as this would ensure that a common understanding exists and would assist with compliance.[189] States should clarify this prohibition under both the BWC and the CWC. States need to strengthen existing law by including nanomaterials in official statements and expert advice provided to the treaty advisory bodies, ensuring that genetic modification of humans is included, including within the existing framework of the Review Conferences of the BWC and within the SAB for the CWC. States need to be clear that any materials that contravene the BWC or CWC, whether at the regular, micro or nanoscale, remain prohibited, and reiterate that States will be held to account if techniques involving genetic modification are used during war.

2 Genetic Modification in Non-humans

As research in nanomaterials advances, ongoing scientific developments create '[a] continuous biochemical threat spectrum, with the CWC and BWC overlapping in their coverage of mid-spectrum agents such as toxins and bioregulators'.[190] A specific example of such a threat is the creation of synthetic DNA within which nanorobots can reside.[191] This modification of DNA can occur within plants and animals, not just within humans, with potentially serious detrimental effects to the ecosystem, reproductive capabilities or nutritional values of animals or plants to humans. Although I am not aware of any such modification in the course of hostilities, it is imaginable that such genetic modification of plants could potentially be weaponised in the future.

[188] Hao Yin et al, 'Structure-guided Chemical Modification of Guide RNA Enables Potent Non-viral in vivo Genome Editing' (2017) 35 *Nature Biotechnology* 1179.

[189] *Chemical Weapons Convention* arts 1(b), 1(c).

[190] Mark Wheelis and Malcolm Dando, 'Neurobiology: A Case Study for the Imminent Militarization of Biology' (2005) 87(859) *International Review of the Red Cross* 560.

[191] Dan Ferber, *Cloaked DNA Nanodevices Survive Pilot Mission* (22 April 2014) Harvard Medical School <http://hms.harvard.edu/news/cloaked-dna-nanodevices-survive-pilot-mission-4-22-14>.

The weaponisation of any genetic modification, whether human or non-human, would be prohibited under the BWC and the CWC if used for hostile purposes. Clarifying this prohibition would ensure that this common understanding is reflected and assist with compliance.[192] States need to strengthen existing law by including nanomaterials in official statements and expert advice provided to the treaty advisory bodies, ensuring that genetic modification of non-humans is included, including within the existing framework of the Review Conferences of the BWC and within the SAB for the CWC. In addition, calls have been made for strengthening of the monitoring body of the BWC.[193] States need to be clear that any materials that contravene the BWC or CWC, whether at the regular, micro or nanoscale, remain prohibited, and reiterate that States will be held to account if techniques involving non-human genetic modification are used during war.

3 Digital Genomes

In 2002, the danger of creation of synthetic genetic sequences was evidenced by the creation of an artificial polio virus from scratch using tailor-made DNA sequences that were subsequently brought to life to become a living parthenogenetic virus.[194] In principle,

> [T]his method could be used to synthesize other viruses with similarly short DNA sequences. This includes at least five viruses that are considered to be potential bio warfare agents, among them Ebola virus, Marburg virus and Venezuelan equine encephalitis virus.[195]

The US military has repeatedly discussed possible uses of biotechnology for warfare scenarios, including the development of material-degrading microorganisms to destroy fuel, construct materials or create stealth paints.[196]

192 *Chemical Weapons Convention* arts 1(b), 1(c).

193 Katherine Nixdorff et al, 'Dual-Use Nano-neurotechnology: An Assessment of the Implications of Trends in Science and Technology' (2018) 37(2) *Politics and the Life Sciences* 180.

194 Jeronimo Cello, Aniko V Paul and Eckard Wimmer, 'Chemical Synthesis of Poliovirus cDNA: Generation of Infectious Virus in the Absence of Natural Template' (2002) 297 (5583) *Science* 1016.

195 Jan Van Aken and Edward Hammond, 'Genetic Engineering and Biological Weapons' (2003) 4 *EMBO Reports* S57.

196 US Army War College, Summary Report on Biotechnology Workshop 2020 (29 and 30 May 1996, document number 96-6963) cited in Jan Van Aken and Edward Hammond, 'Genetic Engineering and Biological Weapons' (2003) 4 *EMBO Reports* S57.

Fabrication and assembly using non-biological and biological substrates opens up endless possibilities in the physical and biological realms. The ability to program biological functions is known as 'digital biology', 'digital programming' or 'digital coding'. All of these, in effect, mean a similar thing – the ability to reprogram existing biological signalling pathways and networks. Digital biology refers to the code itself, and synthetic biology refers to the synthetic construction of that biological code. The ability to construct biological functions also allows the programming and assembling of new organisms based on the knowledge of existing rules underlying biological systems. A good example of this can be found in a recent publication in *Science* which evidences the ability to completely artificially construct synthetic biological matter,

> Recoding – the repurposing of genetic codons – is a powerful strategy for enhancing genomes with functions not commonly found in nature. Here, we report computational design, synthesis, and progress toward assembly of a 3.97-megabase, 57-codon *Escherichia coli* genome in which all 62,214 instances of seven codons were replaced with synonymous alternatives across all protein-coding genes. . . . This work underscores the feasibility of rewriting genomes and establishes a framework for large-scale design, assembly, troubleshooting, and phenotypic analysis of synthetic organisms.[197]

This work is ground-breaking because it means not only being able to tamper with existing organisms' biological code but also points to the ability to synthetically create entirely new organisms. Beyond the existing ability to program and assemble new functions, this knowledge expands research into the ability to design and construct new organisms with no known biological counterparts. Digital genomes enable scientists to create life through synthetic biology, which occurs at the nanoscale. The weaponisation of digital genomes would be prohibited under the BWC and the CWC, as hostile use of biological or chemical matter is prohibited under these Conventions. Clarifying this position would ensure that this common understanding is reflected and would help secure compliance.

Strategic investment is being made on a national scale in enabling technologies, resulting in acceleration of the technology and rapid diffusion of the knowledge enabling synthetic biology. These technologies have major implications for regenerative medicine and for military uses. There are major strategic national investments in enabling technologies,

[197] Nili Ostrov et al, 'Design, Synthesis and Testing toward a 57-codon Genome' (2016) 353 (6301) *Science* 819.

and particularly in synthetic biology, as well as rapid acceleration and diffusion of the technology. This wave of research has clear national security and military implications, including a dramatic expansion in the range of dual-use capabilities, which will be discussed in more detail in Chapter 7. There are also eugenic implications, as not only can genomes be edited but also synthetically created. Altmann notes that, '[a]t some point in nanotechnology development, the difference between living and artificial will probably blur, e.g. when bio molecular computers are connected to neurons, new traits are programmed genetically, or synthetic organisms are created'.[198] It seems that that time is becoming ever closer, as the ability to synthetically create organisms is already possible.

Genome sequencing is terminology that includes the reading of code, synthesis (creating new code by writing) and targeted modification (editing); assembly, delivery and integration of novel genes (targeting); and designed regulation and control of complex genetic networks (system states). It is relevant to understand genome sequencing, as each of these steps is required to undertake what is simply referred to as synthetic biology. This technology has many potential uses across industrial sectors as diverse as healthcare, textile, novel materials, sensor networks and industrial enzymes, to name just a few.

Genome sequencing may also be used as a form of therapy to modify human genomes. These therapies might be comparable to military enhancements (and may, in fact be used to similar effect, such as the ability to stay awake, memory retention or increased focus). This possibility of human enhancement has been touched on by Coleman, who suggested that '[m]embers of the military might be required to have microchips or other devices implanted into them in order to enable them to achieve a better interface with military equipment, or in order to improve their performance in other ways, such as by improving one or more of their senses'.[199] As synthetic biology, implants and modified humans become a reality, the legality of the use of these technologies in the battlefield needs to be considered urgently.

The weaponisation of synthetic biology would be prohibited under the BWC and the CWC, but clarifying that this prohibition would apply to

198 Altmann, n 68, 96.

199 Stephen Coleman, 'Ethical Challenges of New Military Technologies' in Hitoshi Nasu and Robert McLaughlin (eds), *New Technologies and the Law of Armed Conflict* (Asser Press, 2014) 29, 40 citing Keith Bauer, 'Wired Patients: Implantable Microchips and Biosensors in Patient Care' (2007) 16(3) *Cambridge Quarterly of Healthcare Ethics* 281, 283.

nanomaterials would ensure that this common understanding is reflected and secure compliance.[200] States need to strengthen existing law by including nanomaterials in official statements and expert advice provided to the treaty advisory bodies, ensuring that genome sequencing is included, including within the existing framework of the Review Conferences of the BWC and within the SAB for the CWC. States need to be clear that any materials that contravene the BWC or CWC, whether at the regular, micro or nanoscale, remain prohibited, and reiterate that States will be held to account if techniques involving genome sequencing are used during war.

IV Conclusion

Analysing international treaty law reveals that each of the different technologies using nanomaterials is governed by different treaties (see Figure 3.1). In the case of nanolasers (optogenetics and laser weapons), different treaties may restrict or prevent their use. Some of the treaties are clearly directly applicable. Some require reliance on external sources to assist in interpretation to include new and emerging technologies under the VCLT, or consideration of 'functional equivalence'. All could benefit from explicit language in statements by their supporting bodies to ensure that it is clear that their use by States in war is prohibited under the specific relevant treaties.

Prohibitions and principles still require distillation into specific rules to ensure that they are respected during conflict. Esteemed disarmament specialist Goldblat noted that the rules of conduct 'may not resist the pressure of military expedience' and that, for this reason, there is an 'intrinsic link' between the regulation of weaponry and the development of what is traditionally referred to as humanitarian law.[201] In other words, whether speaking of weapons or the use of weapons in armed conflict, it is exactly in high pressure military contexts that the laws and

[200] *Chemical Weapons Convention* arts 1(b), 1(c).

[201] Jozef Goldblat, *Agreements for Arms Control: A Critical Survey* (Taylor & Francis, 1982) 89

> All laws of war suffer from one common weakness: the rules of conduct established for belligerents in time of peace may not resist the pressure of military expedience generated in the course of hostilities, and the attempts to "humanise" war may sometimes prove futile. The danger that the weapons prohibited may, under certain circumstances, be resorted to – as has occurred on several occasions – will not disappear if these weapons remain in the arsenals of States. Hence the intrinsic link between the development of the humanitarian laws of war and progress in the field of disarmament.

specific rules regarding specific weapons must be taken into account to ensure compliance with international law. These specific rules must embody and reflect the much older custom, treaty obligations, and customary international law, which will be discussed in more detail in Chapter 4.

Having considered the major arms control and disarmament treaties that are of potential relevance to the regulation of weapons with nanomaterials, the next chapter will consider general laws of war principles that potentially prohibit or regulate the use of the technologies under consideration in this book. I will also consider judicial decisions in order to understand how courts approach comparable technologies, and the likely application of existing legal frameworks to the existing technologies under consideration.

4

International Customary Law and Principles

As noted in Chapter 1, customary international law is a combination of State practice and *opinio juris*, or the intention of States to undertake a practice. Both are required to form customary international law.[1] State practice must be 'both extensive and virtually uniform'.[2] Official State documents may evidence *opinio juris*.[3] The distinction between treaty law and custom and principles is, in part, an artificial one. Custom is, over time, often embodied in treaty language.[4] Treaty ratification can also contribute to State practice for the purposes of customary international law.[5] Nevertheless, customary law can be established as an individual source of law.[6] This chapter will provide an analysis of the general customary law and principles applicable to the laws of war, and then apply them to the three technologies, namely thermobaric weapons with nanomaterials, optogenetics and genetic modification.

First, this chapter will set out the relevant legal principles. Second, this chapter will consider the applicability of these principles to the weapons

[1] See *Military and Paramilitary Activities in and against Nicaragua (Nicaragua v United States) (Merits)* [1986] ICJ Rep 14, 100–101 [190]; *North Sea Continental Shelf (Federal Republic of Germany v Denmark) (Merits)* [1969] ICJ Rep 3, 43 [74].

[2] *North Sea Continental Shelf (Federal Republic of Germany v Denmark) (Merits)* [1969] ICJ Rep 3, 43 [74]. 'Extensive' refers to the States contributing to the practice, so that 'specially affected' States practice will carry more weight: 42–43 [73]–[74].

[3] See *Military and Paramilitary Activities against Nicaragua (Nicaragua v United States)* [1986] ICJ Rep 14, 100–101 [190].

[4] Monica Hakimi, 'Custom's Method and Process: Lessons from Humanitarian Law' in Curtis A Bradley (ed), *Custom's Future: International Law in a Changing World* (Cambridge University Press, 2016) 153.

[5] *North Sea Continental Shelf (Federal Republic of Germany v Denmark) (Merits)* [1969] ICJ Rep 3.

[6] Maurice Mendelson, 'The Formation of Customary International Law' (1998) 272 *Receuil des Cours* (1998) 155, 250, 289.

under consideration. Not all of these principles are relevant to the three technologies under consideration. This chapter will consider the balancing principles of military necessity and humanity, which underly all customary international humanitarian law. It will also consider the following specific requirements of the laws of war under customary international law; (I) the prohibition on superfluous injury and unnecessary suffering (which includes an academic project to attempt to define the term more precisely) and the Martens Clause, which, being against 'the dictates of public conscience' would also prohibit superfluous injury and unnecessary suffering; (II) the principle of proportionality; and (III) the principles of distinction and precaution. This body of customary international law also applies to the use and modifications of weapons including nanomaterials.

In the case of nanomaterials being used during war, there is not enough public information regarding use to indicate any kind of consistent approach or custom in international law based on State practice. As such, considering the legality of the use of nanomaterials during armed conflict requires consideration of State practice with regard to other technologies, and then applying this practice to nanomaterials. Where this State practice is discussed in the context of the consideration of other technologies, given that no such commentary exists on nanomaterials yet, I analogise by considering how the rationale used in existing international law judgments might be applied to the three uses of nanomaterials under consideration.

Underpinning all laws of war is the requirement that a balance be struck between what is necessary from a military point of view (military necessity) and what is desirable from a humanitarian point of view (avoiding unnecessary suffering) when setting targets.[7] These are not clear lines drawn in the sand, and it is not only the weapon *per se* that may be regulated but also its context and specific use. Military necessity permits measures which are necessary to accomplish a legitimate military purpose and are not otherwise prohibited by international humanitarian law. In the case of an armed conflict the only legitimate military purpose is to weaken the military capacity of the other parties to the conflict.

[7] Michael Schmitt, 'Military Necessity and Humanity in International Humanitarian Law: Preserving the Delicate Balance' in Michael Schmitt, *Essays on War and Law at the Faultlines* (Springer, 2012) 89.

This requirement underpins all other laws of war. An example of this principle would be that using weapons that cause extreme suffering (such as that caused by nuclear weapons) would be difficult to justify as militarily necessary under any circumstances.

In this chapter, the ICJ's position will be set out that States 'do not have unlimited freedom in the choice of means in the weapons they use'.[8] States are also not permitted to use 'weapons that are incapable of distinguishing between civilian and military targets'.[9] States are also prohibited from using weapons that cause superfluous injury to combatants or involve 'uselessly aggravating their suffering'.[10] I apply each of these international customary laws and principles to the three technologies including nanomaterials, as a weapons review would require, and provide examples where possible, by way of analogy.

I Prohibition on Causing Superfluous Injury and Unnecessary Suffering

Closely linked to the requirement to weigh up military necessity with humanity, and reinforcing it, is the prohibition on causing superfluous injury and unnecessary suffering.[11] The principle behind the prohibition is to protect the combatant from injury or suffering greater than is necessary to put him or her out of action. Examples of weapons that have been cited in practice as causing unnecessary suffering are weapons such as lances or spears with a barbed head, explosive bullets, poisons and poisoned weapons, including projectiles smeared with substances that inflame wounds, certain booby-traps and nuclear weapons, just to give a few examples.[12]

[8] *Legality of the Threat or Use of Nuclear Weapons (Advisory Opinion)* [1996] ICJ Rep 226, 257 [78].

[9] Ibid. See also Judge Higgins' Dissenting Opinion at 588–589, [24] (Judge Higgins).

[10] Ibid 257 [78].

[11] International Committee of the Red Cross, *Customary IHL – Rule 70. Weapons of a Nature to Cause Superfluous Injury or Unnecessary Suffering* (2005) <https://ihl-databases.icrc.org/customary-ihl/eng/docs/v1_rul_rule70>.

[12] See, e.g., the military manuals of Ecuador, Germany, Netherlands, New Zealand, Russian Federation, South Africa, United Kingdom and United States of America cited in International Committee of the Red Cross, *Customary IHL – Rule 70. Weapons of a Nature to Cause Superfluous Injury or Unnecessary Suffering* (2005) <https://ihl-databases.icrc.org/customary-ihl/eng/docs/v1_rul_rule70> n 43, 46, 47, 50.

Attempts to define the contents of this principle were made in the late 1990s, with specific attempts to quantify effects of certain weapons and the injuries that they cause,[13] noting that, prior to these attempts through the project on 'superfluous injury or unnecessary suffering', or SIrUS, the definition of 'superfluous injury or unnecessary suffering' remained 'within the realm of emotional reaction or philosophical argument'.[14] Project SIrUS will be discussed in greater detail in Part A of this section.

In Part B of this section, I will also consider the Martens Clause, which is a principle that has particular relevance to certain militarisation of nanomaterials because it is a catch-all legal requirement that requires compliance with 'the dictates of public conscience', which is another source of law prohibiting 'superfluous injury and unnecessary suffering'.

The prohibition of 'superfluous injury or unnecessary suffering' is specifically about the effects of the weapon on combatants, and the limits on those effects. This rule is applicable in both international and non-international armed conflicts.[15] Numerous military manuals apply the rule,[16] and it has also been applied in national

[13] Robin Coupland (ed), *The SIrUS Project: Towards a Determination of Which Weapons Cause "Superfluous Injury or Unnecessary Suffering"* (1997) International Committee of the Red Cross <www.loc.gov/rr/frd/Military_Law/pdf/SIrUS-project.pdf>.

[14] Ibid 12.

[15] International Committee of the Red Cross, *Customary IHL – Rule 70. Weapons of a Nature to Cause Superfluous Injury or Unnecessary Suffering* (2005) <https://ihl-databases.icrc.org/customary-ihl/eng/docs/v1_rul_rule70>.

[16] See, e.g., the military manuals of Argentina, Australia, Belgium, Benin, Bosnia and Herzegovina, Burkina Faso, Cameroon, Canada, Colombia, Congo, Croatia, Dominican Republic, Ecuador, France, Germany, Hungary, Indonesia, Israel, Italy, Kenya, Republic of Korea, Madagascar, Mali, Morocco, Netherlands, New Zealand, Nigeria, Romania, Russian Federation, Senegal, South Africa, Spain, Sweden, Switzerland, Togo, United Kingdom, United States of America and Yugoslavia cited in International Committee of the Red Cross, *Customary IHL – Rule 70. Weapons of a Nature to Cause Superfluous Injury or Unnecessary Suffering* (2005) <https://ihl-databases.icrc.org/customary-ihl/eng/docs/v1_rul_rule70> n 5. See also the oral and written statements of Ecuador, Egypt, India, Iran, Japan, Lesotho, Marshall Islands, Sweden and Zimbabwe in *Legality of the Threat or Use of Nuclear Weapons (Advisory Opinion)* [1996] ICJ Rep 226 and the written statements of Samoa and Solomon Islands in *Legality of the Use by a State of Nuclear Weapons in Armed Conflict (Advisory Opinion)* [1996] ICJ Rep 66.

law.[17] Multiple UN General Assembly resolutions have also recalled support for this rule over many decades.[18] This principle is also codified in Article 35 of API to the Geneva Conventions, which states,

[17] See, e.g., *Ryuichi Shimoda et al v The State* (1966) 32 ILR 626 (District Court of Tokyo, Judgment date 7 December 1963) ('*Shimoda Case*').

[18] See, e.g., *Napalm and Other Incendiary Weapons and all Aspects of Their Possible Use*, GA Res 3076 (XXVIII), UN GAOR, 28th sess, 2192nd plen mtg, Agenda Item 34, Supp No 30, UN Doc A/RES/3076(XXVIII) (6 December 1973); *Respect for Human Rights in Armed Conflicts*, GA Res 3102 (XXVIII), UN GAOR, 28th sess, 2197th plen mtg, Agenda Item 96, Supp No 30, UN Doc A/Res/3102(XXVIII) (12 December 1973); *Napalm and Other Incendiary Weapons and all Aspects of Their Possible Use*, GA Res 3255 (XXIX), 29th sess, 2309th plen mtg, Agenda Item 27, Supp No 31, UN Doc A/RES/3255(XXIX)A-B (9 December 1974); *United Nations Conference on Prohibitions or Restrictions of Use of Certain Conventional Weapons Which May Be Deemed to Be Excessively Injurious or to Have Indiscriminate Effects*, GA Res 33/70, UN GAOR, 33rd sess, 84th plen mtg, Agenda Item 49, Supp No 45, UN Doc A/RES/33/70 (14 December 1978); *United Nations Conference on Prohibitions or Restrictions of Use of Certain Conventional Weapons Which May Be Deemed to Be Excessively Injurious or to Have Indiscriminate Effects*, GA Res 34/82, UN GAOR, 34th sess, 97th plen mtg, Agenda Item 41, Supp No 46, UN Doc A/RES/34/82 (11 December 1979); *United Nations Conference on Prohibitions or Restrictions of Use of Certain Conventional Weapons Which May Be Deemed to Be Excessively Injurious or to Have Indiscriminate Effects*; GA Res 37/79, UN GAOR, 37th sess, 98th plen mtg, Agenda Item 51, Supp No 51, UN Doc A/Res/37/79 (9 December 1982); *Convention on the Prohibitions or Restrictions on the Use of Certain Conventional Weapons Which May Be Deemed to Be Excessively Injurious or to Have Indiscriminate Effects*, GA Res 38/66, UN GAOR, 38th sess, 97th plen mtg, Agenda Item 51, Supp No 47, UN Doc A/RES/38/66 (15 December 1983); *Convention on Prohibitions or Restrictions on the Use of Certain Conventional Weapons Which May Be Deemed to Be Excessively Injurious or to Have Indiscriminate Effect*, GA Res 39/56, UN GAOR, 39th sess, 97th plen mtg, Agenda Item 50, Supp No 51, UN Doc, A/RES/39/56 (12 December 1984); *Convention on Prohibitions or Restrictions on the Use of Certain Conventional Weapons Which May Be Deemed to Be Excessively Injurious or to Have Indiscriminate Effects*, GA Res 45/64, UN GAOR, 45th sess, 54th plen mtg, Agenda Item 64, Supp No 49, UN Doc A/RES/45/64 (4 December 1990); *Convention on Prohibitions or Restrictions on the Use of Certain Conventional Weapons Which May Be Deemed to Be Excessively Injurious or to Have Indiscriminate Effects*, GA Res 46/40, UN GAOR, 46th sess, 65th plen mtg, Agenda Item 64, Supp No 49, UN Doc A/RES/46/40 (6 December 1991); *Convention on Prohibitions or Restrictions on the Use of Certain Conventional Weapons Which May Be Deemed to Be Excessively Injurious or to Have Indiscriminate Effects*, GA Res 47/56, UN GAOR, 47th sess, 81st plen mtg, Agenda Item 65, Supp No 49, UN Doc A/RES/47/56 (9 December 1992); *Convention on Prohibitions or Restrictions on the Use of Certain Conventional Weapons Which May Be Deemed to Be Excessively Injurious or to Have Indiscriminate Effects*, GA Res 48/79, UN GAOR, 48th sess, 81st plen mtg, Agenda Item 75, Supp No 49, UN Doc A/RES/48/79 (7 January 1994); *Convention on Prohibitions or Restrictions on the Use of Certain Conventional Weapons Which May Be Deemed to Be Excessively Injurious or to Have Indiscriminate Effects*, GA Res 49/79, UN GAOR, 49th sess, 90th plen mtg, Agenda Item 66, Supp No 49, UN Doc A/RES/49/79 (11 January 1995); *Convention on Prohibitions or Restrictions on the Use of Certain Conventional*

1. In any armed conflict, the right of the Parties to the conflict to choose methods or means of warfare is not unlimited.
2. It is prohibited to employ weapons, projectiles and material and methods of warfare of a nature to cause superfluous injury or unnecessary suffering.[19]

The *Legality of the Threat or Use of Nuclear Weapons (Advisory Opinion)* provides guidance about the importance of considering superfluous injury in the use of any means or methods of warfare.[20] This discussion occurred in the context of the potential use of nuclear weapons, where it was determined that, in the absence of a specific treaty prohibiting nuclear weapons, it was necessary for the Court to examine various treaties that might be relevant to the regulation of nuclear weapons as well as the general principles of the laws of war.[21] For the first time in its then fifty-year history, every member of the ICJ delivered an individual and different opinion in the *Nuclear Weapons Advisory Opinion*.[22]

Weapons Which May Be Deemed to Be Excessively Injurious or to Have Indiscriminate Effects, GA Res 50/74, UN GAOR, 50th sess, 90th plen mtg, Agenda Item 74, Supp No 49, UN Doc A/RES/50/74 (10 January 1996); *Convention on Prohibitions or Restrictions on the Use of Certain Conventional Weapons Which May be Deemed to be Excessively Injurious or to Have Indiscriminate Effects*, GA Res 51/49, UN GAOR, 51st sess, 79th plen mtg, Agenda Item 75, Supp No 49, UN Doc A/RES/51/49 (8 January 1997); *Conventional weapons convention*, GA Res 52/42, UN GAOR, 52nd sess, 67th plen mtg, Agenda Item 75, Supp No 49, UN Doc A/RES/52/42 (31 December 1997); *Conventional Weapons Convention*, GA Res 53/81, UN GAOR, 53rd sess, 79th plen mtg, Agenda Item 75, Supp No 49, UN Doc A/RES/53/81 (8 January 1999); *Convention on Prohibitions or Restrictions on the Use of Certain Conventional Weapons Which May Be Deemed to Be Excessively Injurious or to Have Indiscriminate Effects*, GA Res 54/58, UN GAOR, 54th sess, 69th plen mtg, Agenda Item 80, Supp No 49, UN Doc A/RES/54/58 (31 December 1999).

19 *Protocol Additional to the Geneva Conventions of 12 August 1949, and relating to the Protection of Victims of International Armed Conflicts (Protocol I)*, opened for signature 8 June 1977, 1125 UNTS 3 (entered into force 7 December 1979) arts 35(1), 35(2) ('*Additional Protocol I*').

20 *Legality of the Threat or Use of Nuclear Weapons (Advisory Opinion)* [1996] ICJ Rep 226, Summary of the Advisory Opinion, paragraph D.

21 The specific language is that the use of nuclear weapons must 'be compatible with the requirement of the international law applicable in armed conflict particularly those of the principles and rules of international humanitarian law, as well as with specific obligations under treaties and other undertakings which expressly deal with nuclear weapons': *Legality of the Threat or Use of Nuclear Weapons (Advisory Opinion)* [1996] ICJ Rep 226, 266.

22 Dapo Akande, 'Nuclear Weapons, Unclear Law? Deciphering the *Nuclear Weapons* Advisory Opinion of the International Court' (1998) 68(1) *British Yearbook of International Law* 165, 168.

In their Advisory Opinion, the ICJ discussed the limitations provided by the principle of prohibition of superfluous injury and unnecessary suffering. While this conclusion was concerned with nuclear weapons, the considerations may be extrapolated to apply to the weaponisation of other technological advances, including nanomaterials.

The *Nuclear Weapons Advisory Opinion* noted unanimously that any weapons causing combatants unnecessary harm or uselessly aggravating their suffering are prohibited, and that States do not have unlimited freedom of choice of means in the weapons they use.[23] The lesson is that, either in the presence or absence of specific treaties governing their use, all weapons, including those utilising nanomaterials, are required to comply with the general principles and rules of the laws of war. More specifically, the ICJ provided specific guidance regarding this principle, noting that unnecessary suffering was 'a harm greater than that unavoidable to achieve legitimate military objectives'.[24] In other words, the general principles and rules of the laws of war always apply, regardless of the new or emerging technology, and, more specifically, to any 'means or methods' of warfare that incorporate nanomaterials. The Opinion ultimately ruling that nuclear weapons could, under a very narrow range of circumstances, be permitted does not change the arguments made in this chapter. The strong support for the *Treaty on the Prohibition of Nuclear Weapons*, having come into effect on 22 January 2021, may indicate that State attitudes, and potentially *opinion juris*, have changed somewhat since 1996. Hopefully, the tolerance for weapons using nanomaterials will be tested in a legal context before they are tested in the battlefield.

A The SIrUS Project

The best-known attempt to provide a more concrete definition of superfluous injury and unnecessary suffering was the SIrUS project (SIrUS stands for 'superfluous injury or unnecessary suffering'). SIrUS was an academically sound attempt to quantify the long-used but ill-defined terminology using data.[25] Coupland, a former war surgeon who

[23] *Legality of the Threat or Use of Nuclear Weapons (Advisory Opinion)* [1996] ICJ Rep 226, 256–257 [77]–[78], 262–263 [95].

[24] Ibid 238.

[25] Robin M Coupland, 'The Effect of Weapons: Defining Superfluous Injury and Unnecessary Suffering' (1996) 3 *Medicine and Global Survival* <www.ippnw.org/pdf/mgs/3-coupland.pdf>.

conceived this approach, explained that it was a 'first attempt to apply the epidemiology of the effects of weapons to international law'.[26] As Coupland clarified, '[a]s weapons systems that have differing effects on the human body are being developed for potential military use, creating some yardstick of suffering to which the effects of weapons are applied becomes essential'.[27] In order to enable this, Coupland composed a matrix of data, quantifying certain injuries and types of suffering.

The attempt to use data to create a specific standard to uphold this principle, rather than a vague principle, was met with strong resistance. Some States were displeased with an attempt to define and quantify what unnecessary suffering would mean in practice. For example, Russia and France, in their submissions to the ICJ in the *Nuclear Weapons Advisory Opinion*, noted that their position was that a weapon can only be prohibited by this rule if a State agreed to prohibit a weapon by treaty.[28] As noted previously, the ICJ did not hold this view, but rather held that the prohibition on superfluous injury and unnecessary suffering was one of the cardinal principles of the laws of war, and, as such, governs all States without going so far as defining what exactly constituted superfluous injury and unnecessary suffering in the *Nuclear Weapons Advisory Opinion*. Although this submission was not in relation to the SIrUS project specifically, the Judges took the position that, in the absence of a treaty prohibition, there is a fundamental rule to avoid superfluous injury or unnecessary suffering. This is a rule which every State has an obligation to uphold. Any use of nanomaterials that results in superfluous and unnecessary suffering would be prohibited.

B The Martens Clause

Any analysis of the legality of means or methods of warfare containing nanoscale components must comply with existing legal principles in how they are used. Another such principle which would inevitably prohibit 'superfluous injury and unnecessary suffering' would be the Martens Clause. The Martens Clause is a principle that has particular relevance to certain militarisation of nanomaterials because it is a catch-all legal requirement that requires compliance with 'the dictates of public conscience'.

[26] Ibid.
[27] Ibid.
[28] *Legality of the Threat or Use of Nuclear Weapons (Advisory Opinion)* [1996] ICJ Rep 226.

In 1899, a Russian delegate named Friedrich Martens presented a Declaration to the Hague Peace Conference. After the delegates failed to agree on a negotiated preamble, they adopted the language from this Declaration, which has been translated into the English version as,

> Populations and belligerents remain under the protection and the rule of the principles of nations, as they result from usages established among civilised peoples, from the laws of humanity and the dictates of the public conscience.[29]

What is known as the Martens Clause was subsequently adopted as the preamble to the 1899 Hague Convention.[30] Similar language to the Martens Clause is repeated in the General Provisions of API[31] and the preamble of Protocol II.[32] Further, the ICJ has observed the Martens Clause to be 'an effective means of addressing rapid evolution of military technology'.[33] As succinctly stated by Meron, '[w]here there already is some legal basis for adopting a more humanitarian position, the Martens Clause enables decision makers to take the extra step forward'.[34] Although some consider the Martens Clause to be the ultimate legal contingency plan,[35] the Martens Clause underpins the existing legal framework, and supports existing law, in addition to providing legal

[29] *Convention (IV) Respecting the Laws and Customs of War on Land and Its Annex: Regulations Concerning the Laws and Customs of War on Land*, signed 18 October 1907, 205 CTS 277 (entered into force 26 January 1910) Preamble ('*Hague Convention (IV)*').

[30] *Convention (II) Respecting the Laws and Customs of War on Land and Its Annex: Regulations Concerning the Laws and Customs of War on Land*, signed 29 July 1899, 187 CTS 429 (entered into force 4 September 1900) ('*Hague Convention (II)*').

[31] *Additional Protocol I.*

[32] *Protocol Additional to the Geneva Conventions of 12 August 1949, and Relating to the Protection of Victims of Non-International Armed Conflicts (Protocol II)*, opened for signature 8 June 1977, 1125 UNTS 609 (entered into force 7 December 1978) ('*Additional Protocol II*').

[33] *Legality of the Threat or Use of Nuclear Weapons (Advisory Opinion)* [1996] ICJ Rep 226, 259 [84]. In a slightly different context, Schmitt argues that the Martens Clause only applies in the absence of treaty law: Michael Schmitt and Jeffrey Thurnher, '"Out of the Loop": Autonomous Weapon Systems and the Law of Armed Conflict' (2013) 4 *Harvard National Security Journal* 231, 275.

[34] Theodor Meron, 'The Martens Clause, Principles of Humanity and Dictates of Public Conscience' (2000) 94(1) *The American Journal of International Law* 78.

[35] Rob Sparrow, 'Ethics as a Source of Law: The Martens Clause and Autonomous Weapons' on International Committee of the Red Cross, *Humanitarian Law & Policy* (14 November 2017) <http://blogs.icrc.org/law-and-policy/2017/11/14/ethics-source-law-martens-clause-autonomous-weapons/>.

guidance where there is an absence.[36] This position was reiterated by the ILC, which noted that '[the Martens Clause] … provides that even in cases not covered by specific international agreements, civilians and combatants remain under the protection and authority of the principles of international law derived from established custom, from the principles of humanity and from the dictates of public conscience'.[37] Both the Geneva Conventions of 1949 and its two additional Protocols restate the Martens Clause.[38]

The SIrUS project also referred to the fact that the Martens Clause was determined to be customary international law by the ICJ's *Nuclear Weapons Advisory Opinion*,[39] and the ICJ noted that this principle 'has proved to be an effective means of addressing the rapid evolution of military technology'.[40] An alternative view is that States view the Martens Clause as merely normative and not enforceable on its own merits. However, in the ICJ decision, the Court determined that the Martens Clause was a customary rule of normative status, meaning that the Clause is a norm that regulates State conduct, thereby elevating it to the status of being a binding legal principle. Justice Shahabuddeen went further to note a General Assembly resolution that condemned nuclear war as

[36] Antonio Cassese, 'The Martens Clause: Half a Loaf or Simply Pie in the Sky?' (2000) 11(1) *European Journal of International Law* 187.

[37] 'Report of the Commission to the General Assembly on the Work of Its Forty-Sixth Session' [1994] II(2) *Yearbook of the International Law Commission* 317.

[38] *Hague Convention (IV)* Preamble; *Geneva Convention (I) for the Amelioration of the Condition of the Wounded and Sick in Armed Forces in the Field*, opened for signature 12 August 1949, 75 UNTS 31 (entered into force 21 October 1950) art 63 ('*First Geneva Convention*'); *Geneva Convention (II) for the Amelioration of the Condition of Wounded, Sick and Shipwrecked Members of Armed Forces at Sea*, opened for signature 12 August 1949, 75 UNTS 85 (entered into force 21 October 1950) art 62 ('*Second Geneva Convention*'); *Geneva Convention (III) relative to the Treatment of Prisoners of War (Third Geneva Convention)*, opened for signature 12 August 1949, 75 UNTS 135 (entered into force 21 October 1950) art 142 ('*Third Geneva Convention*'); *Geneva Convention (IV) relative to the Protection of Civilian Persons in Time of War*, opened for signature 12 August 1949, 75 UNTS 287 (entered into force 21 October 1950) art 158 ('*Fourth Geneva Convention*'); *Additional Protocol II*; *Convention on Prohibition or Restrictions on the Use of Certain Conventional Weapons Which May Be Deemed to Be Excessively Injurious or to Have Indiscriminate Effects*, opened for signature 10 October 1980, 1342 UNTS 137 (entered into force 2 December 1983) Preamble ('*Convention on Certain Conventional Weapons*').

[39] *Legality of the Threat or Use of Nuclear Weapons (Advisory Opinion)* [1996] ICJ Rep 226, 256 [78], 259 [84] referred to in Coupland, n 13, 13.

[40] See Rupert Ticehurst, 'The Advisory Opinion of the International Court of Justice on the Legality of the Threat or Use of Nuclear Weapons' (1996) 2(1) *War Studies Journal* 107.

being 'contrary to human conscience and reason', using language similar to that of the Martens Clause, evidencing the significance of the terminology 'public conscience' in international law.[41] This discussion is relevant because it supports the Martens Clause being a source of international law that may provide governance or protection where other law is silent, and, for this reason, it has particular relevance for the regulation of nanomaterials in armed conflict.

II Principle of Distinction

The principle of distinction and the rule of precaution, although separate principles, are closely related. The rule of precaution will be discussed separately in the next section. Another cardinal rule under the laws of war is that one must distinguish between civilians and combatants; never target civilians who are not participating in hostilities; and only direct attacks against military targets. This rule is fundamental to the protection of civilians on the battlefield. Given State practice, this is a rule that applies as a norm of customary international law in both international and non-international armed conflict.[42]

Under the principle of distinction, there must be a distinction drawn between civilians and combatants in armed conflict at all times. Attacks are never to be directed intentionally at civilians. The civilian population

[41] *Legality of the Threat or Use of Nuclear Weapons (Advisory Opinion)* [1996] ICJ Rep 226, 256 [78], 259 [84]. See also Sean McBride, 'The Legality of Weapons of Social Destruction' in C Swinarski (ed), *Studies and Essays on International Humanitarian Law and Red Cross Principles in Honour of Jean Pictet* (Martinus Nijhoff, 1984) 406,

> Many resolutions adopted by the General Assembly of the United Nations have, either directly or by inference, condemned completely the use, stockpiling, deployment, proliferation and manufacture of nuclear weapons. While such resolutions may have no formal binding effect in themselves, they certainly do represent 'the dictates of public conscience' in the 20th century, and come within the ambit of the 'Martens Clause' prohibition.

For a more detailed discussion of the Nuclear Advisory Opinion and the Martens Clause, see Rupert Ticehurst, 'The Martens Clause and the Laws of Armed Conflict' (1997) 37(317) *International Review of the Red Cross* 125.

[42] International Committee of the Red Cross, *Customary IHL – Rule 1. The Principle of Distinction between Civilians and Combatants* (2005) <https://ihl-databases.icrc.org/customary-ihl/eng/docs/v1_cha_chapter1_rule1>. See also Jean-Marie Henckaerts and Louise Doswald-Beck, *Customary International Humanitarian Law* (Cambridge University Press, 2005) 3–8.

is protected by the law and is to retain immunity from attack. Once a civilian takes part in hostilities, while they are in combat, they lose their civilian protection for the time that they are involved in hostilities.[43] The principle of distinction between civilians and combatants has been codified in Article 48 of API.[44] Combatants must distinguish themselves from the civilian population, and civilians who participate in hostilities lose this immunity under the laws of war.[45] In relation to non-international armed conflict, a similar protection is implicit in the prohibition on attacking the civilian population or individual civilians.[46] Optogenetics and genetic modification are inherently specific and prohibited outright against civilians for the purposes of armed conflict.

Much has been written about those who directly participate in hostilities and where this threshold lies.[47] Also, 'members of the armed forces who have laid down their arms and those placed *hors de combat* by sickness, wounds, detention or any other cause' are protected by Common Article 3 of the 1949 Geneva Conventions[48] and also the Geneva Conventions more generally. This is potentially relevant should weapons containing nanomaterials be used to manipulate or temporarily disable combatants.

The rule of distinction requires that,

> [t]he Parties to the conflict shall at all times distinguish between the civilian population and combatants and between civilian objectives and

43 *Additional Protocol I* art 51(3): 'Civilians shall enjoy the protection afforded by this section, unless and for such time as they take a direct part in hostilities'.

44 *Additional Protocol I* arts 48, 50(1)–(3).

45 Ibid.

46 *Additional Protocol II* art 13(2). For a more detailed discussion of the principle of distinction, see Emanuela-Chiara Gillard, 'Protection of Civilians in the Conduct of Hostilities' in Rain Liivoja and Tim McCormack (eds), *Routledge Handbook of the Law of Armed Conflict* (Routledge, 2016) 159–161.

47 Ian Henderson, *The Contemporary Law of Targeting: Military Objectives, Proportionality and Precautions in Attack under Additional Protocol I* (Martinus Nijhoff, 2009) 213.

48 *Protocol Additional to the Geneva Conventions of 12 August 1949, and Relating to the Adoption of an Additional Distinctive Emblem (Protocol III)*, opened for signature 8 December 2005, 2404 UNTS 261 (entered into force 14 January 2007) arts 3(1) ('*Additional Protocol III*'): 'Persons taking no active part in the hostilities, including members of armed forces who have laid down their arms and those placed "hors de combat" by sickness, wounds, detention, or any other cause, shall in all circumstances be treated humanely, without any adverse distinction founded on race, colour, religion or faith, sex, birth or wealth, or any other similar criteria'. See also Nils Melzer, *Interpretative Guidance on the Notion of Direct Participation in Hostilities under International Humanitarian Law* (2009) International Committee of the Red Cross <www.icrc.org/eng/assets/files/other/icrc-002-0990.pdf>.

> military objectives and accordingly shall direct their operations only against military objectives.[49]

API requires that,

> In the conduct of military operations, constant care shall be taken to spare the civilian population, civilians and civilian objects.[50]

Article 8(2)(b)(ii) of the 1998 Rome Statute, also prohibits,

> Intentionally directing attacks against civilian objects, that is, objects which are not military objectives.[51]

Where the use of a weapon renders it incapable of distinguishing between civilians and combatants it is illegal *per se.* A weapon that can distinguish between combatants and civilians must be used in a way that upholds the principle of distinction. No weapon can be used indiscriminately. Methods of warfare incapable of being directed at specific military objectives – that cannot distinguish between civilian and military objectives – are prohibited.[52]

The ICJ in the *Nuclear Weapons Advisory Opinion* explained that States must 'never make civilians the object of attack and must consequently never use weapons that are incapable of distinguishing between civilian and military targets'.[53] In a later case, *Armed Activities on the Territories of the Congo*, the ICJ also explicitly noted that indiscriminate weapons are prohibited alongside indiscriminate methods of warfare.[54] Methods of warfare are not unlimited and any weapon that is incapable of being directed at specific military objectives – that cannot distinguish between civilian and military objectives – is prohibited.[55]

There is an understanding that decisions must be made on information reasonably available at the time,[56] although there are divergent views whether there is an obligation to use a particular technology or

49 *Additional Protocol I* art 48.
50 Ibid art 57(1).
51 *Rome Statute of the International Criminal Court*, opened for signature 17 July 1998, 2187 UNTS 90 (entered into force 1 July 2002) art 8(2)(b)(ii) ('*Rome Statute*').
52 *Additional Protocol I* arts 54(4), 54(5).
53 *Legality of the Threat or Use of Nuclear Weapons (Advisory Opinion)* [1996] ICJ Rep 226, 257 [78].
54 *Armed Activities on the Territory of the Congo (Democratic Republic of the Congo v Uganda) (Judgment)* [2005] ICJ Rep 168, 240 [208].
55 *Additional Protocol I* arts 54(4), 54(5).
56 William Boothby, *The Law of Targeting* (Oxford University Press, 2012) 152.

type of weapon (for example one that may be more targeted, but extremely expensive).[57] This principle is relevant for the use of nanoparticles, as they are unable to distinguish between civilians and combatants, and may inadvertently cause immediate harm or long-term health issues for civilians in non-medical uses such as optogenetics and genetic modification. The long-term effects of metallic nanoparticles, if released into the environment, will affect all those who live in the area, potentially for a long time. It is therefore important that this principle be respected in the consideration of any new or modified means or method of warfare containing nanoparticles.

Any weapons or components of weapons using nanoparticles would potentially give rise to consideration of this legal principle. The principle of distinction poses a challenge in weapons systems that may include nanoparticles that may have long-term health effects if released into the environment. The environmental impact of residual nanoparticles will be considered in further detail in Chapter 5 on environmental law, with the conclusion that where new knowledge regarding deleterious effects of nanoparticles comes to light, weapons reviews will need to be reconsidered in light of new information.

The terrain where weapons are to be used must be a consideration in weapons review to ensure that the principle of distinction is respected, and to ensure compliance with other international humanitarian law.[58] It is not only the weapon itself that needs to be reviewed but also the way in which it is used, which should include the environment. The US Joint Urban Operations Manual states that '[a]n analysis of the threat is essential as is the intelligence and information on the physical terrain and infrastructure characteristics of the urban environment'.[59] This is demonstrated by the varying types of environment in which thermobaric weapons with nanomaterials may be used, as will be discussed in the latter half of this chapter applying the law to the technologies in question.

[57] See generally Michael Schmitt, 'War, Technology, and the Law of Armed Conflict' in Anthony Helm (ed), *The Law of War in the 21st Century: Weaponry and the Use of Force* (Naval War College, 2006) 131.

[58] James Fry, 'Contextualized Legal Reviews for the Methods and Means of Warfare: Cave Combat and International Humanitarian Law' (2006) 44 *Columbia Journal of Transnational Law* 453, 480.

[59] US Joint Chiefs of Staff, *Joint Urban Operations JP 3-06* (20 November 2013) I-8, cited in Isabel Robinson and Ellen Nohle, 'Proportionality and Precautions in Attack: The Reverberating Effects of Using Explosive Weapons in Populated Areas' (2016) 98(901) *International Review of the Red Cross* 107.

The law is unequivocal that the use of civilians as shields for military targets is prohibited. API, in support of this principle, specifically states,

> The presence or movements of the civilian population or individual civilians shall not be used to render certain points or areas immune from military operations, in particular in attempts to shield military objectives from attacks or to shield, favour or impede military operations. The Parties to the conflict shall not direct the movement of the civilian population or individual civilians in order to attempt to shield military objectives from attacks or to shield military operations.[60]

Where the civilian population voluntarily moves into caves where military facilities are housed, for protection or for other reasons, international humanitarian law provides that the attacker must provide the usual precautions in attack provided for under international humanitarian law.[61] Part of precautions in attacks, flowing from the principle of proportionality, is the requirement to use the type of weapon with the least deleterious implications for the civilians and civilian objects where a choice is available between different weapons with comparable effect. In agreement with Henderson, an Australian military lawyer, the presence of civilians near military targets, whether deliberate or not, must be considered under the laws of war and does not reduce their value as humans in calculating proportionality.[62]

As Henderson succinctly states, '[e]ach civilian is "worth" the same as every other civilian, and where they are counted as collateral damage voluntary human shields are given the normal weighting of any other civilian in the proportionality equation'.[63] A counter-argument to Henderson is that voluntary human shields may be argued to be taking a direct part in hostilities, in which case they become targetable. The difficulty with this position, however, is establishing the intent of civilians under hostile conditions. Henderson concludes that there is no in-between category of civilian and combatant for the purposes of civilians who are located near a military installation, and he notes that it is better to assume civilian status in case of any doubt. Henderson's position would appear to be the most consistent with correct application of the

60 *Additional Protocol I* art 51(7).

61 *Additional Protocol I* art 57(1); *Legal Issues Arising from the War in Afghanistan and Related Anti-Terrorism Efforts* (October 2001) Human Rights Watch <www.hrw.org/campaigns/september11/ihlqna.htm>.

62 Henderson also supports this view in Henderson, n 47, 213.

63 Ibid 218.

principle of distinction, and the only one that could ensure the consistent protection of civilians.

It is not clear whether the civilians in caves and bunkers of many of the current conflicts (Afghanistan, Syria, to name two) are deliberate shields or not but, coming to the same conclusion as Henderson, this is not material in the question of calculating proportionality, and is often impossible to ascertain under the circumstances surrounding conflict. I concur with Henderson's suggestion that a distinction be made between human shields who physically block a route of attack (who are then actively participating in hostilities) and those who are merely providing a 'moral pause' to an attacker. In bunkers and caves, civilians would seldom be blocking a route of attack, and therefore an attack would need to calculate their deaths as collateral damage. In bunkers, where civilians and military personnel are often found intermingled, the principle of precaution for civilians would need to be upheld. Fry clarifies that 'each [use] is *prima facie* unlawful in such settings [bunkers and caves], except in very limited circumstances, because of the difficulty in distinguishing between civilians and combatants within such environments'.[64] The ability to comply with this requirement will differ depending on the use of nanomaterials in question, and will be considered in more detail in the context of the three technologies under consideration.

III Principle of Proportionality

The principle of proportionality states that the launching of an attack that may be expected to cause incidental loss of civilian life, injury to civilians, damage to civilian objects or a combination thereof, which would be excessive in relation to the concrete and direct military advantage anticipated, is prohibited.[65] For a target to be legitimate, the calculation must be taken according to the 'circumstances ruling at the time'.[66] Despite the long history of international humanitarian law treaties, 1977 API was the first time that the rule on proportionality was codified in a multilateral treaty. State practice establishes this as a principle of

[64] Fry, n 58, 490.

[65] *Additional Protocol I* arts 51(5)(b), 52(2), 57.

[66] For a more detailed discussion of the time sensitivity of the assessment criteria, see David Turns, 'Military Objectives' in Rain Liivoja and Tim McCormack (eds), *Routledge Handbook of the Law of Armed Conflict* (Routledge, 2016) 139, 149.

customary international law applicable in both international and non-international armed conflicts.[67]

The term 'proportionality' is not explicitly used in API, and various reasons have been posited as to why.[68] It is clear that the principle of proportionality is being described, nonetheless, in Article 51(5)(b) of API, which describes the indiscriminate attacks that are prohibited, including,

> [A]n attack which may be expected to cause incidental loss of civilian life, injury to civilians, damage to civilian objects or a combination thereof, which would be excessive in relation to the concrete and direct military advantage anticipated.[69]

The concept of proportionality is embodied in rules that prohibit commanders from directing attacks against military objectives,

> which may be expected to cause incidental loss of civilian life, injury to civilians, damage to civilian objects, or a combination thereof, which would be excessive in relation to the concrete and direct military advantage anticipated.[70]

And

> [An] attack shall be cancelled or suspended if it becomes apparent that the objective is not a military one or is subject to special protection or that the attack may be expected to cause incidental loss of civilian life, injury to civilians, damage to civilian objects, or a combination thereof, which would be excessive in relation to the concrete and direct military advantage anticipated.[71]

67 *Prosecutor v Martić (Decision)* (International Criminal Tribunal for the Former Yugoslavia, Trial Chamber, Case No IT-95-11-R61, 8 March 1996); *Prosecutor v Kupreškić (Judgement)* (International Criminal Tribunal for the Former Yugoslavia, Trial Chamber, Case No IT-95-16-T, 14 January 2000); Inter-American Commission on Human Rights, *Third Report on Human Rights in Colombia*, Organization of American States, Doc No OEA/Ser.L/V/II.102 Doc 9 Rev 1 (26 February 1999).

68 For a detailed account as to why the reference to proportionality was avoided, see William J Fenrick, 'The Rule of Proportionality and Protocol I in Conventional Warfare' (1982) 98 *Military Law Review* 91, 102 and Frits Kalshoven, 'Reaffirmation and Development of International Humanitarian Law Applicable in Armed Conflicts: The Diplomatic Conference, Geneva, 1974–1977, Part II' (1978) 9 *Netherlands Yearbook of International Law* 107.

69 *Additional Protocol I* art 51(5)(b).

70 Ibid art 57(2)(a)(iii).

71 Ibid art 57(2)(a)(ii).

An attacker must

> [T]ake all feasible precautions in the choice of means and methods of attack with a view to avoiding, and in any event to minimizing, [collateral damage].[72]

The principle of proportionality requires that in calculating whether an attack is proportional, all civilians present within the same complex or space, indirectly targeted, would need to be taken into account as collateral damage. If civilians are directly targeted then this is a breach of the principle of distinction. A simpler way of conceptualising proportionality has been suggested as asking whether an attack would be considered proportional if it had 'tak[en] place over a part of the country's own territory under enemy occupation, in which case the civilian casualties would be compatriots'.[73] In some cases, this may mean a commander taking on a greater risk to his own forces to reduce the amount of collateral damage to the enemy's civilian population.[74] The principle of proportionality is also codified in Protocol II and amended in Protocol II to the CCW.[75]

In addition to all of these sources, the Statute of the International Criminal Court (ICC) states that, 'intentionally launching an attack in the knowledge that such attack will cause incidental loss of life or injury to civilians or damage to civilian objects . . . which would be clearly excessive in relation to the concrete and direct overall military advance anticipated' constitutes a war crime in international armed conflicts.[76] Numerous States, including States at the time not party to API, invoked the principle of proportionality in their assessments of the legality of the use of nuclear weapons and whether their use would violate the laws of war.[77]

72 Ibid art 57(2)(a)(iii).

73 Javier Gómez, 'The Law of Air Warfare' (1998) 38(323) *International Review of the Red Cross* 347.

74 British Defence Doctrine (JWP-0-01), cited in Anthony Rogers, 'Zero-casualty warfare' (2000) 82(837) *International Review of the Red Cross* 165 n 41.

75 *Amended Protocol II to the CCW* art 3(3); *Protocol II to the CCW* art 3(8).

76 *Rome Statute* art 8(2)(b)(iv). See also *Regulation No 2000/15 On the Establishment of Panels with Exclusive Jurisdiction over Serious Criminal Offences*, UNTAET, UN Doc UNTAET/REG/2000/15 (6 June 2000) section 6(1)(b)(iv).

77 See the statements of Egypt, India, Iran, Malaysia, Netherlands, New Zealand, Solomon Islands, Sweden, United Kingdom, United States of America and Zimbabwe cited in International Committee of the Red Cross, *Customary IHL – Rule 14. Proportionality in Attack* (2005) <https://ihl-databases.icrc.org/customary-ihl/eng/docs/v1_cha_chapter4_rule14> n 14.

In a different context, in this case that of aerial bombing, in *Prosecutor v Stanislav Galić* before the ICTY, the matter of proportionality was discussed. The Tribunal found that,

> certain apparently disproportionate attacks may give rise to the inference that civilians were actually the object of attack. In determining whether an attack was proportionate it is necessary to examine whether a reasonably well-informed person in the circumstances of the actual perpetrator, making reasonable use of the information available to him or her, could have expected excessive civilian casualties to result from the attack.
>
> The rule of proportionality does not refer to the actual damage caused or to the military advantage achieved by an attack, but instead uses the words "expected" and "anticipated".[78]

According to this decision, the onus to prove that an attack is proportional is on the military decision maker, and is prospective, rather than retrospective. That said, the 'reasonably well-informed person' appears to be relevant. The fact that the attacker is ignorant of the presence of civilians in the vicinity of the attack is not sufficient if the attacker has not informed themselves of the possibility of the presence of civilians. Ignorance is not adequate to deny responsibility. The reasonable commander needs to make enquiries on the basis of information that is reasonably available at the time. This is a very important point to note, given the complexity of new technologies. What is 'reasonable' in light of the complexity of new technologies? What is 'reasonably available'? States' interpretation of this remains publicly untested, although many States have taken positions regarding their interpretation of the provision.[79]

[78] *Trial Chambers: The Prosecutor v Stanislav Galič – Case No. IT-98-29-T – "Judgement and Opinion"* (5 December 2003) International Criminal Tribunal for the Former Yugoslavia <www.icty.org/x/file/Legal%20Library/jud_supplement/supp46-e/galic.htm>.

[79] See *Ratification (with Declarations and Reservations) to Protocol Additional to the Geneva Conventions of 12 August 1949, and Relating to the Protection of Victims of International Armed Conflicts (Protocol I): Algeria*, registered 16 August 1989, 1552 UNTS 381 (entered into force 16 February 1990); *Ratification (with Declarations and Reservations) to Protocol Additional to the Geneva Conventions of 12 August 1949, and Relating to the Protection of Victims of International Armed Conflicts (Protocol I): Austria*, registered 13 August 1982, 1289 UNTS 302 (entered into force 13 February 1983); *Ratification (with Declarations and Reservations) to Protocol Additional to the Geneva Conventions of 12 August 1949, and Relating to the Protection of Victims of International Armed Conflicts (Protocol I): Australia*, registered 21 June 1991, 1642 UNTS 473 (entered into force 21 December 1991); *Ratification (with Declarations and Reservations) to Protocol Additional to the Geneva Conventions of 12 August 1949, and Relating to the Protection of Victims of International Armed Conflicts (Protocol I): Belgium*, registered 20 May 1986,

In the ICTY judgment of *Prosecutor v Ljube Boškoski & Johan Tarčulovski*, the concept of proportionality was also discussed, noting that,

> proportionality in this context means the ratio between the military advantage gained and the casualty to the civilian population which is different from the notion of proportionality applicable in *jus ad bellum* in relation to the right to self-defence.[80]

There is some controversy around the elasticity of this test. What is a reasonable person? Is it a reasonable commander in command of his or her troops? Or a reasonable lay-person? What enquiries must be made?

1435 UNTS 367 (entered into force 20 November 1986); *Ratification (with Declarations and Reservations) to Protocol Additional to the Geneva Conventions of 12 August 1949, and Relating to the Protection of Victims of International Armed Conflicts (Protocol I): Canada*, registered 20 November 1990, 1591 UNTS 462 (entered into force 20 May 1991); *Ratification (with Declarations and Reservations) to Protocol Additional to the Geneva Conventions of 12 August 1949, and Relating to the Protection of Victims of International Armed Conflicts (Protocol I): France* in *Official Records of the Diplomatic Conference on the Reaffirmation and Development of International Humanitarian Law Applicable in Armed Conflicts, Geneva (1974–1977), Volume VII* (Federal Political Department, Bern, 1978) 192–194; *Ratification (with Declarations and Reservations) to Protocol Additional to the Geneva Conventions of 12 August 1949, and Relating to the Protection of Victims of International Armed Conflicts (Protocol I): Germany*, registered 14 February 1991, 1607 UNTS 526 (entered into force 14 August 1991); *Ratification (with Declarations and Reservations) to Protocol Additional to the Geneva Conventions of 12 August 1949, and Relating to the Protection of Victims of International Armed Conflicts (Protocol I): Ireland*, registered 12 July 1999, 2073 UNTS 28 (entered into force 19 November 1999); *Ratification (with Declarations and Reservations) to Protocol Additional to the Geneva Conventions of 12 August 1949, and Relating to the Protection of Victims of International Armed Conflicts (Protocol I): Italy*, registered 27 February 1986, 1425 UNTS 438 (entered into force 17 August 1986); *Ratification (with Declarations and Reservations) to Protocol Additional to the Geneva Conventions of 12 August 1949, and Relating to the Protection of Victims of International Armed Conflicts (Protocol I): Netherlands*, registered 26 June 1987, 1477 UNTS 299 (entered into force 26 December 1987); *Ratification (with Declarations and Reservations) to Protocol Additional to the Geneva Conventions of 12 August 1949, and Relating to the Protection of Victims of International Armed Conflicts (Protocol I): New Zealand*, registered 8 February 1988, 1499 UNTS 358 (entered into force 8 August 1988); *Ratification (with Declarations and Reservations) to Protocol Additional to the Geneva Conventions of 12 August 1949, and Relating to the Protection of Victims of International Armed Conflicts (Protocol I): Spain*, registered 21 April 1989, 1537 UNTS 389 (entered into force 21 October 1989); *Ratification (with Declarations and Reservations) to Protocol Additional to the Geneva Conventions of 12 August 1949, and Relating to the Protection of Victims of International Armed Conflicts (Protocol I): United Kingdom*, registered 28 January 1998, 2020 UNTS 73 (entered into force 28 July 1998).

80 *Prosecutor v Boškoski & Tarčulovski (Judgement)* (International Criminal Tribunal for the Former Yugoslavia, Appeals Chamber, Case No IT-04-82-A, 19 May 2010) 15.

The ICJ has defined and upheld responsibility under the principle of proportionality as a customary international law principle in the *Nuclear Weapons Advisory Opinion*.[81] The reason that proportionality is relevant in the use of nanomaterials is that, before their use, whether their use is proportional must always be considered, particularly in light of potential unknown long-term environmental and human health effects, which will be discussed in more detail in Chapters 5 and 6.

IV The Rule of Precaution

The rule of precaution supports the principle of distinction in requiring that, when planning attacks on military objectives in proximity to civilians, precautions must be taken to avoid civilian casualties. Given State practice, this is also a rule that applies as a norm of customary international law in both international and non-international armed conflict.[82] There is a further restriction that attacks must be cancelled if it becomes apparent that an attack is of the type that would be prohibited.[83] If possible, advance warnings must be given for attacks that may affect the civilian population.[84] In choosing an attack, the one that causes the least danger to the civilian population must be taken, when a choice is possible.[85] When the loss of civilian life or destruction of civilian objects outweighs the military advantages of the attack, then that attack should be cancelled.[86]

The Kupreškić Decision in the ICTY discussed the customary nature of the requirement to take precautions prior to any attacks in both international and non-international armed conflicts, and considered this rule customary because it articulated pre-existing norms.[87] The Tribunal also noted that this rule had not been contested by any State, nor was there any counter-indicative practice.[88] In short, before any attack,

[81] Deborah Russo, *The Use of Proportionality in the Recent Case-Law of the ICJ* (4 June 2015) SSRN <https://ssrn.com/abstract=2614316>.

[82] International Committee of the Red Cross, *Customary IHL – Rule 22. Principle of Precautions against the Effects of Attacks* (2017) <https://ihl-databases.icrc.org/customary-ihl/eng/docs/v1_rul_rule22>.

[83] *Additional Protocol I* art 57(2)(b).

[84] Ibid art 57(2)(c).

[85] Ibid art 57(3).

[86] Ibid art 57(2)(a)(iii).

[87] *Prosecutor v Kupreškić (Judgement)* (International Criminal Tribunal for the Former Yugoslavia, Trial Chamber, Case No IT-95-16-T, 14 January 2000).

[88] Ibid.

thoughtful consideration must be given to the balance between military necessary and humanity. The question of how military necessity and humanity should be weighed has been the focus of many tomes, which will not be canvassed here.[89]

The rule of precaution was first codified in Article 2(3) of the 1907 Hague Convention, which stated that the commander of the navy,

> [S]hall take all due measures in order that the town may suffer as little harm as possible.[90]

In support of the principle of distinction, API requires State parties to take feasible precautions to,

> Protect civilians and civilian objects against the dangers resulting from military operations.[91]

While Article 48 sets out the principle of distinction, it does not define what 'military objects' are. This is found in Article 52(2), which states that,

> In so far as objects are concerned, military objectives are limited to those objects which by their nature, location, purpose or use make an effective contribution to military action and whose total or partial destruction, capture or neutralization, in the circumstances ruling at the time, offers a definite military advantage.[92]

Courts have relied on or referred to this rule to varying degrees, even if not explicitly, in their decisions. In the *Nicaragua Case*, concerning the use of force by the United States against Nicaragua, the ICJ noted in relation to mines laid off the coast that 'every possible precaution must be taken for the security of peaceful shipping' and that belligerents are bound,

> to notify the danger zones as soon as military exigencies permit, by a notice addressed to ship owners, which must also be communicated to the Governments through the diplomatic channel (Art. 3).[93]

[89] Henderson, n 47; Michael N Schmitt, 'Military Necessity and Humanity in International Humanitarian Law: Preserving the Delicate Balance' (2010) 50(4) *Virginia Journal of International Law* 795 and Yoram Dinstein, 'The Principle of Proportionality' in Kjetil Mujezinović Larsen, Camilla Guldahl Cooper and Gro Nystuen (eds), *Searching for a 'Principle of Humanity' in International Humanitarian Law* (Cambridge University Press, 2012) 72, just to give a limited sample.

[90] *Hague Convention (IV)* art 2(3).

[91] *Additional Protocol I* art 58.

[92] Ibid art 52(2).

[93] *Military and Paramilitary Activities in and against Nicaragua (Nicaragua v United States of America) (Judgment)* [1986] ICJ Rep 14, 102.

In other words, it is incumbent on those making attacks to take 'every possible precaution', although exactly what this would mean is unclear. The ICJ has noted the application of 'certain general and well recognized principles, namely: elementary considerations of humanity, even more exacting in peace than in war'.[94]

In the 2003 *Galić* case, a prosecution for serious violations of international humanitarian law, the ICTY stated, *inter alia*, that,

> The presence of individual combatants within the population does not change its civilian character. In order to promote the protection of civilians, combatants are under the obligation to distinguish themselves at all times from the civilian population; the generally accepted practice is that they do so by wearing uniforms, or at least a distinctive sign, and by carrying their weapons openly. In certain situations, it may be difficult to ascertain the status of a particular person in the population. The clothing, activity, age, or sex of a person are among the factors which may be considered in deciding whether he or she is a civilian. A person shall be considered to be a civilian as long as there is a doubt as to his or her real status.[95]

The Commentary to API notes that civilian status is assumed for 'persons who have not committed hostile acts, but whose status seems doubtful because of the circumstances. They should be considered as civilians until further information is available, and therefore should not be attacked'. The Trial Chamber in the *Galić* case appears to apply the standard of 'reasonable to believe', that is, if it is not reasonable to believe that someone is a combatant in the circumstances of the case, then the person shall be considered a civilian and not made the object of attack.[96] The onus is on the person making the decision to justify that their presumption that a person was a combatant was reasonable.

The principle of precaution is relevant when combat takes place in densely populated areas, or in areas where military and civilian targets may be intermingled. This principle may have relevance to nanomaterials if they were weaponised in a way that made it impossible to issue precautions.

[94] *Corfu Channel (United Kingdom v Albania) (Merits)* [1949] ICJ Rep 4, 22 cited in *Military and Paramilitary Activities in and against Nicaragua (Nicaragua v United States of America) (Judgment)* [1986] ICJ Rep 14, 102.

[95] *Prosecutor v Galič (Judgement)* (International Criminal Tribunal for the Former Yugoslavia, Trial Chamber I, Case No IT-98-29-T, 5 December 2003) [50].

[96] Ibid.

V Application of the Principles to Specific Uses of Nanomaterials during War

Not all of the customary international law and principles discussed in this chapter have relevance for all three of the technologies, namely thermobaric weapons, optogenetics and genetic modification. Each use of nanomaterials will be discussed separately next, and relevant customary international law or principles will be applied. The customary international law prohibition on causing superfluous injury and unnecessary suffering as well as the customary international law principles of distinction and proportionality in attack apply to thermobaric weapons, given their intensity and indiscriminate nature. Optogenetics and genetic modification, on the other hand, raise completely different legal issues to thermobaric weapons. Optogenetics provides a level of specificity of targeting (i.e. individual cells) that currently seems like science fiction. As has already been discussed in Chapter 3, the use of optogenetics specifically would be prohibited under the BWC and the CWC. Beyond these treaty prohibitions, the customary international law prohibition on causing superfluous injury and unnecessary suffering would apply, but for entirely different reasons than the use of thermobaric weapons with nanomaterials. As this kind of specificity, and potentially, reversibility, has not been previously possible, analogies with other new and emerging technologies must be made, as well as considerations of regulation of the same technologies in the civilian sector.

A Thermobaric Weapons

This section explores the applicability of the customary international law prohibition on causing superfluous injury and unnecessary suffering, as well as the customary international law principles of distinction and proportionality in attack, in the context of the use of thermobaric weapons with nanomaterials.

One of the common uses of thermobaric weapons historically has been in underground or bunker warfare. In the 1980s, Afghan caves were used by the Mujahidin for protection from Soviet attacks, and to stage attacks on the Soviets. International coalition forces in Afghanistan and Iraq have seen an increasing number of combatants holed up in deep caves and bunkers. However, caves have long been used for non-military purposes, such as hospitals, schools and places of worship.[97] More

[97] PBS, 'Cave War', *News Hour with Jim Lehrer*, 10 December 2001; Naomi Wax, 'Ideas & Trends: Notes from Underground', *New York Times* (New York), 25 November 2001

recently, civilians have been seeking shelter in caves in Syria, following over 200,000 deaths and more than 11 million people being displaced.[98] Cave warfare has been described by one author as 'humanity's long dark climb out of the caves . . . now being reversed'.[99] The use of thermobaric weapons in enclosed spaces would require careful consideration of the laws of war, regardless of whether nanomaterials were used in the weapons or not. Targeting civilians in such cases would be prohibited in accordance with the principle of distinction.

Where there are both civilian and military installations within caves or bunkers, there are challenges for fulfilling the principles of distinction and precaution, as well as the principle of proportionality. The number of civilian deaths needs to be considered to ensure that it is not excessive in relation to the military advantage expected. Targeting combatants and military objectives would require a proportionality analysis, and a methods and means analysis, as discussed previously in this chapter. Subject to an analysis determining that civilian casualties would not be 'excessive in relation to the concrete and direct military advantage anticipated', and the use of a thermobaric weapon would not cause superfluous injury or unnecessary suffering, then it could, in very specific circumstances, be lawful to use such weapons in caves or bunkers.

Great care must be taken in the use of thermobaric weapons, and particularly thermobaric weapons using nanomaterials, which are by their very nature more powerful than their traditional counterparts, to ensure the principle of distinction is upheld.

Thermobaric weapons, whether traditional or using nanomaterials, should not be used in heavily populated areas where military and civilians intermingle. Nor should they be used in bunkers where civilians reside or hide, as civilians would inevitably be killed by their blast.

If thermobaric weapons using nanomaterials leave nanomaterial residues that may affect the population (research on the toxicity of nanomaterials is still nascent), then their use may violate this rule in that civilians might be inevitably affected by remaining nanoparticles in the environment. The environmental impact of residual nanoparticles, and

<www.nytimes.com/2001/11/25/weekinreview/ideas-trends-notes-from-underground.html>, cited in Fry, n 58, 496.

98 Christian Storm, 'Inside the Secret Cave Hideouts Used by Syrian Rebels and Families' (11 March 2015) *Business Insider Australia* <www.businessinsider.com.au/syrian-secret-cave-hideouts-2015-3>.

99 Kenneth Rose, *One Nation Underground: The Fallout Shelter in American Culture* (New York University Press, 2001) 89.

potential for injury, will be considered in further detail in Chapter 5 on environmental law, including a brief discussion of whether the use of toxic nanomaterials would be prohibited under the Martens Clause, which is explained in some detail earlier in this chapter.[100]

Thermobaric weapons illustrate the increased power which nanomaterials may add to traditional weapons. States have already fielded these weapons, meaning that arguments must have been made in internal policy documents that these weapons are not inherently indiscriminate, or which may have stated restrictions on their use. Such statements do not appear to be publicly available. Traditional thermobaric weapons are powerful. Thermobaric weapons using nanomaterials are even more powerful. Smaller weapons using nanomaterials may have an intensity of blast comparable to a much larger weapon, due to the larger surface area of the materials at the nanoscale. The principle of distinction between combatants and non-combatants is relevant. As thermobaric weapons are extremely powerful, like all other weapons systems, care needs to be taken that they are not used in areas with civilians or where civilians may be harmed. On the one hand, one of the potential advantages of using thermobaric weapons with nanomaterials over traditional thermobaric weapons is that although they may have a more intense blast, it occurs within a more concise radius by using a smaller weapons system, making thermobaric weapons with nanomaterials more likely to avoid civilian casualties and therefore able to uphold the principle of distinction.

B Optogenetics

Chapter 2 established that the use of optogenetics (or any other similar use of nanomaterials) that affect biology but have no justification for 'prophylactic, protective or other peaceful purposes' would be prohibited under the BWC.[101] Beyond this treaty-based prohibition are also the limits established by general principles of law. Any permanent modification of the human brain, I would argue, would be prohibited by the principle prohibiting superfluous injury and unnecessary suffering, by

[100] *Hague Convention (IV)* Preamble.

[101] *Convention on the Prohibition of the Development, Production and Stockpiling of Bacteriological (Biological) and Toxin Weapons and on Their Destruction*, opened for signature 10 April 1972, 1015 UNTS 163 (entered into force 26 March 1975) art 1 ('*Biological Weapons Convention*').

way of analogy to the prohibition on deliberate and irreversible blindness. The use of optogenetics in war, or any other reversible but temporary modification of the brain, tests the existing legal frameworks. As this kind of issue has not arisen before, analogies with other new and emerging technologies must be made, as well as considerations of governance of the same technologies in the civilian sector.

Military uses of optogenetics may be considered so abhorrent as to be banned under the Martens Clause, which is discussed earlier in this chapter. Given the aversion in the international community to permanent blindness, it would be arguable by analogy that temporary changes to cells through laser light, or permanent changes through genetic modification, would be prohibited under the Martens Clause, because it violates the basic 'laws of humanity and the dictates of public conscience'. As the future inevitably holds further advances in research and ability to manipulate neural networks, the questions of what society will tolerate and what they will not become more pertinent, particularly in relation to 'non-lethal' weapons. Much literature has been written about the misnomer of non-lethals (also called less-than lethals) and concerns about their use on the battlefield.[102] This is particularly relevant for optogenetics, where behaviour of an enemy combatant could be temporarily modified, thereby putting them at greater risk of other conventional weapons.

1 The Use of Nanomaterials as 'Non-lethal' Weapons

I have already discussed in some detail how the effects of optogenetics and genetic modification using nanomaterials can be reversible, and not inevitably lead to death. Weapons that do not inevitably result in death are often referred to as 'non-lethal'. 'Non-lethal' became terminology commonly used in the 1990s, when the idea of weapons that 'did not kill' or were 'reversible' became popular. In the mid-1990s, the Institute for Foreign Policy Analysis in the United States wrote a comprehensive paper outlining numerous potential 'non-lethal' weapons. At that time, 'non-lethals' under consideration included what were then referred to as 'biotechnicals', including hemorrhagic conjunctivitis, chronic diarrhea, yellow fever and Crimean Congo, and hemorrhagic fever.[103] Genetic

[102] Coupland, n 13.

[103] Robert Bunker (ed), 'Nonlethal Weapons: Emerging Requirements for Security Strategy' (INSS Occasional Paper 15, Institute for Foreign Policy Analysis, 1996) 11 <www.hsdl.org/?view&did=1145>.

modification, temporary neural modification and non-fatal diseases were also proposed. Although this discourse dates back to the mid-1990s, and some of the technologies discussed are now outdated, this conversation still has relevance for the consideration of the potentially reversible uses of nanomaterials today, and so will be briefly discussed to frame some of the concerns with reversible uses of nanomaterials.

The naming of this proposed new generation of weapons as 'non-lethals' elicited fierce opposition.[104] One of the major concerns expressed by those writing about the topic was the fundamental issue that the term 'non-lethal' was a misnomer and an attempt to romanticise alternative methods of causing harm to humans. Although the proposed techniques may not have always been fatal in and of themselves (which was also argued is not even the case), the reality is that any attempt to use 'non-lethal' means to 'disengage' soldiers leaves them vulnerable to other lethal weapons and means of attack,

> 'Non-lethal' weapons will always be backed up or used in conjunction with conventional weapons. This may mean that the lethality of conventional weapons is potentiated and that doctors may have to treat people suffering from the effects of both conventional and new weapons . . . The medical profession must guard against use of its knowledge for the purposes of weapon development.[105]

Over twenty years after the initial hype around non-lethals, genetic modification and optogenetics are no longer science fiction. As the ability to modify and control humans remotely becomes more practicable, urgent discussions are needed about the legality of these techniques if applied on the battlefield, or even before being used as a means of crowd control. Warnings more than 20 years ago to not be 'seduced' by the term 'non-lethal' remain prescient.

With the case of the two technologies with potential relevance for use as 'non-lethals', namely optogenetics and genetic modification, limitations may be argued to be moot. As with 'non-lethals', specific temporary disabling weapons may contravene the principle on superfluous injury (discussed in detail earlier in this chapter) and even international human rights law (discussed in Chapter 6). The ability to alter or influence human physiology can be as specific as targeting individuals with a

[104] Robin Coupland, '"Non-lethal" Weapons: Precipitating a New Arms Race' (1997) 315 (7100) *British Medical Journal* 72; Malcolm Dando, *A New Form of Warfare: The Rise of Non-lethal Weapons* (Brasseys, 1996).

[105] Coupland, n 104.

specific marker or genetic make-up, making them able to satisfy the principle of distinction. Targeting individuals specifically, rather than using less discriminating traditional weapons, may be argued to be more humane where the effect is non-permanent and reversible. Those who argue in support of the use of 'non-lethal' weapons argue that 'non-lethal' weapons are preferable to traditional weapons. This argument is flawed for the following reasons.

First, on a practical level, very few States will have these technologies, thus increasing the likelihood of asymmetric warfare. As a small number of States have increasingly advanced knowledge, other States will respond with the techniques available to them – techniques such as cyber-attacks, terrorism and other unilateral responses.

Second, even where weapons may be 'non-lethal', as was the case with blinding laser weapons, as discussed in Chapter 3, they may be so abhorrent as to otherwise be banned. In the case of permanently blinding laser weapons, it was found that the idea of permanently blinding soldiers was so abhorrent as to be prohibited outright, despite this method of warfare being 'non-lethal', as discussed in Chapter 3.

Third, the terminology used in the 1925 Geneva Protocol, the BWC and the CWC makes no specific reference to permanence, so whether a physical effect is reversible or not is irrelevant under the existing legal framework. Whether temporary or permanent, any incapacitation by any means involving chemical or biological matter (and nanomaterials within the body often demonstrate both properties) remains prohibited under the existing legal framework.

Fourth, it is time to consider the Martens Clause. As science rapidly evolves our ability to modify and control humans remotely, discourse around not only the legality but also the ethics of such means or methods of warfare must advance to consider the 'dictates of public conscience'.[106] As uses of nanomaterials advance, as Coupland noted, it is incumbent on those working with these materials, and I would argue also States, to 'guard against the use of its knowledge for the purposes of weapon development'.[107] The Martens Clause also prohibits the use of

[106] Robert Sparrow, 'Ethics as a Source of Law: The Martens Clause and Autonomous Weapons' on International Committee of the Red Cross, *Humanitarian Law & Policy* (14 November 2017) <http://blogs.icrc.org/law-and-policy/2017/11/14/ethics-source-law-martens-clause-autonomous-weapons/>. See also Antonio Cassese, 'The Martens Clause: Half a Loaf or Simply Pie in the Sky?' (2000) 11(1) *European Journal of International Law* 187.

[107] Coupland, n 104.

nanomaterials in any way that would be against the 'dictates of public conscience'.

Historically, the laws of war have tried to minimise human suffering caused by traditional methods on the battlefield. Technologies that can be more targeted and specific in their effect, such as optogenetics or genetic modification, raise interesting questions for the laws of war. Much like thermobaric weapons with nanomaterials, the use of optogenetics is so specific and precise that the principle of distinction does not apply because nanomaterials will operate with such specificity that it falls within permitted uses.

Other areas of science involving nanolasers that require further consideration are photonics,[108] potentially highly toxic quantum dots, and metamaterials.[109] Considering the regulation of optogenetics in armed conflict is a microcosm of the broader challenge of talking about regulating nanomaterials as a singular category. Even within optogenetics, the potential uses of nanolasers are diverse and vast, and each use has different implications and may attract different legal regimes, depending on the category of science within which it falls (i.e. if the materials are used as poisons within the human body,[110] if biological materials are used[111] or if chemicals are used).[112] Clearly, there is no specific prohibition on thermobaric weapons or optogenetics.

[108] Photonics refers to the science used to modulate, emit, generate, process, switch, amplify, sense and detect light. Photonics, manipulating the interactions of light and matter at a very small scale, has many applications for tracking, enabling and controlling the human body that may prove very interesting for use in armed conflict.

[109] Metamaterials are materials created at the nanoscale that are artificially created to have properties that differ from those at their regular scale. For example, a cloak consisting of brick-like blocks of gold nanoantennas that redirect light has been successfully created to scatter light to make microscopic objects invisible. This has not yet been scaled up to work for larger objects. See Richard W Ziolkowski, 'Metamaterials: The Early Years in the USA' (2014) 1 *EPJ Applied Metamaterials* 1.

[110] The 1925 Geneva Protocol prohibits the use of 'asphyxiating, poisonous or other gases, and of all analogous liquids, materials or devices' and 'bacteriological methods of warfare': *Protocol for the Prohibition of the Use in War of Asphyxiating, Poisonous or Other Gases, and of Bacteriological Methods of Warfare*, opened for signature 17 June 1925, 94 LNTS 65 (entered into force 8 February 1928) ('*Protocol to the BWC*').

[111] See generally *Biological Weapons Convention*.

[112] See generally *Convention on the Prohibition of the Development, Production, Stockpiling and Use of Chemical Weapons and on Their Destruction*, opened for signature 13 January 1993, 1974 UNTS 45 (entered into force 29 April 1997) ('*Chemical Weapons Convention*').

The principle of precaution may still be relevant,

> The intrinsically humanitarian character of the legal principles in question ... permeates the entire law of armed conflict and applies to all forms of warfare and to all kinds of weapons, those of the past, those of the present and those of the future.[113]

Consideration needs to be made as to how nanomaterials will distinguish between civilians and combatants, and what rules will apply if those effects are reversible. Biomedical intervention may have different effects on different people, and the effects of interference on any biological function are difficult to predict. It is important that consideration is given to the relevant legal frameworks in applying all new and emerging technology, particularly those incorporating nanomaterials, for the purposes of consideration in this book.

C Genetic Modification

The BWC and the CWC prohibit the use of genetic modification, as discussed in Chapter 3. As noted in *Military and Paramilitary Activities in and against Nicaragua (Nicaragua v United States of America) (Judgment)*, the Court explicitly stated that 'both on the level of treaty law and that of customary international law, these norms retain a separate existence'.[114] To be clear, the ICJ in the *Nicaragua (Merits)* decision was not specifically discussing the co-existence of customary and treaty obligations in relation to the BWC and the CWC, but nevertheless, this decision can be extended to analyse other treaty law and customary international law, such as those that exist in relation to the BWC and the CWC. Even if the BWC and the CWC clearly prohibit the use of genetic modification in war, a separate and further prohibition exists under customary international law. Customary international law principles also prohibit genetic modification, as already discussed in Chapter 2. Given the inevitability of superfluous injury and unnecessary suffering both to those directly affected and to their future offspring, as modifying genetic code is permanent and life-changing in ways we do

[113] *Legality of the Threat or Use of Nuclear Weapons (Advisory Opinion)* [1996] ICJ Rep 226, 86. Although this statement was made by Higgins J in dissent, it is nonetheless relevant.

[114] In *Military and Paramilitary Activities in and against Nicaragua (Nicaragua v United States of America) (Judgment)* [1986] ICJ Rep 14, 95–96 [178], the Court explicitly stated that 'both on the level of treaty law and that of customary international law, these norms retain a separate existence'.

not yet entirely understand, and given the requirement of proportionality under international law, the use of genetic modification as a means or method of warfare would be prohibited under all circumstances.

VI Conclusion

By carefully applying customary international law to three specific uses of nanomaterials at differing stages of use or development, it becomes clear that there is ample room for interpretation of the existing customary international law to comprehend and include new technologies that harness the properties of nanomaterials. This chapter demonstrates that existing customary international law and principles provide limitations, and even prohibitions, to the three uses of nanomaterials in war.

In this chapter, I have defined and analysed four customary international laws or principles and then analysed their application in judicial review, extrapolating this analysis, where relevant, to the three uses of nanomaterials in the last part of this chapter. By looking at decisions of international courts, I analogised how courts may apply customary law to the use of nanomaterials in the future.[115]

Targeting specific cells may violate the prohibition on superfluous injury and unnecessary suffering (particularly if the intervention is reversible), while not violating the principle of distinction or the rule of precaution. The inclusion of nanomaterials in some 'means or methods' of warfare may in fact make the methods of warfare more targeted and discriminate, and therefore better able to comply with the principles of the laws of war. However, being compliant with international custom or principles does not necessarily mean that the use is permissible *per se*, as seen in the discussions of whether these same uses comply with environmental law. This will be discussed in greater detail in Chapter 5, and human rights law in greater detail in Chapter 6.

Finally, this chapter evidences that each type of use of nanomaterials attracts different legal frameworks: optogenetics and genetic modification raise completely different legal issues to thermobaric weapons. Optogenetics provides a level of specificity of targeting (i.e. individual cells) that may seem to some like science fiction. The consideration of

[115] James Crawford interprets this as meaning that judicial opinions are 'evidence of the law . . . Their value, however, stops short of precedent as it is understood in the common law tradition': James Crawford, *Brownlie's Principles of Public International Law* (Oxford University Press, 2012) 37.

these applicable legal principles and custom demonstrates that the use of nanomaterials in war never occurs in a legal vacuum. Even where the use of a weapon with nanomaterials is not necessarily prohibited or limited by treaty or even customary international law, the Martens Clause may have relevance and prohibit certain uses of nanomaterials, such as in the case of genetic modification. In cases of reversible changes to the human body during war, even where potentially not prohibited by treaty or customary international law principles, there remains a prohibition of the use of nanomaterials in such a way as being against the 'dictates of public conscience'.

The next chapter will look at how international environmental law and principles govern the use of nanomaterials during war, and where there are gaps that require further international law to provide adequate protection.

5

International Environmental Law and Principles

International environmental law is important to consider during war, as the environment may be seriously harmed during armed conflict, with long-term impact on the environment and human health long after battles pass. In the case of nanomaterials, this harm may even be intergenerational. Nanomaterials enter water tables and food chains; are able to move across human membranes; and may reside in the human body indefinitely. Scientists are only just beginning to understand the potentially toxic effects of nanomaterials on the environment and the human body in the short and long term. Protection of the environment during armed conflict requires not only high-level international legal agreements but also practical rules and granular guidance in military manuals and instructions that can be correctly applied in any battlefield. For this reason, the perspective of this chapter broadens beyond traditional international laws of war to examine how international environmental law should be used to review and address the effects of nanomaterials from 'means or methods of warfare' to the environment. The risks of potential long-term harm of environmental damage during war are increasingly being discussed in international fora.[1]

Maynard et al. argue that two of the 'five grand challenges' for those using nanomaterials are: (1) to 'learn how harmful nano-materials are', and (2) to 'evaluate the impact of engineered nanomaterials from cradle to grave'.[2] Nanomaterials pose unknown toxicity risks, are difficult to detect, cause intergenerational health issues and are challenging to remove once they have leached into water tables and ecosystems.[3] These properties pose specific challenges to the existing protections

[1] Britta Sjöstedt and Anne Dienelt, 'Enhancing the Protection of the Environment in Relation to Armed Conflicts: Draft Principles of the International Law Commission and beyond' (2020) 10(1) *Goettingen Journal of International Law* 13.

[2] Andrew Maynard et al, 'Safe Handling of Nanotechnology' (2006) 444(7117) *Nature* 267.

[3] Satinder Kaur Brar et al, 'Engineered Nanoparticles in Wastewater and Wastewater sludge – Evidence and Impacts' (2009) 30(3) *Waste Management* 504.

currently provided by international environmental law in peacetime but also during war. The manipulation and use of nanomaterials has been identified as contributing to the breach of one of the nine 'planetary boundaries' that scientists have identified as the limits of Earth systems tolerance to human-induced change to ecological systems at the planetary level.[4] It is well known that anthropogenic rises in greenhouse gas emissions are causing climate change, and thus breaching the planetary boundary of climatic conditions in which 'safe and just' human civilisations can flourish.[5] Another way in which planetary boundaries are potentially at risk is through the introduction of novel entities into the environment, including chemicals and new types of engineered materials and organisms such as plastic polymers in the ocean and nanomaterials.[6] Earth system scientists argue that novel entities, including nanomaterials, are of global environmental concern where they are persistent; mobile across scales with widespread distribution; and potentially impact on vital earth systems processes or subsystems. The problem is that these impacts may not be discovered until they are a problem at the global scale and have become irreversible.[7] Thus, the challenge is to develop the knowledge base to screen new materials (including nanomaterials) before they are released into the environment.[8]

One prominent international jurist observes that '[w]e are only now becoming aware of the tremendous capacity for new technologies to produce harmful effects over extended geographic distances'.[9] Experts have specifically called for consideration of nanomaterial toxicity and its potential environmental consequences in times of peace.[10] In addition,

[4] Will Steffen et al, 'Planetary Boundaries: Guiding Human Development on a Changing Planet' (2015) 347(6223) *Science* 736, 1259855-1. The nine boundaries so far identified are climate change, biodiversity, land-system change, freshwater use, biochemical flows (phosphorous and nitrogen), ocean acidification, atmospheric aerosol loading, stratospheric ozone deletion and novel entities (including nanomaterials) pervading the environment.

[5] Will Steffen and Mark Stafford Smith, 'Planetary Boundaries, Equity and Global Sustainability: Why Wealthy Countries Could Benefit from More Equity' (2013) 5 *Current Opinion in Environmental Sustainability* 403, 404.

[6] Steffen et al, n 4, 1259855-7-8.

[7] Ibid.

[8] Ibid 1259855-8.

[9] Phillippe Sands, *Lawless World: America and the Making and Breaking of Global Rules* (Penguin, 2005) 16.

[10] The Royal Society, *Nanoscience and Nanotechnologies: Opportunities and Uncertainties* (July 2004) 5 <https://royalsociety.org/~/media/Royal_Society_Content/policy/publications/2004/9693.pdf>; Organisation for Economic Co-operation and Development, *Report of the OECD Workshop on the Safety of Manufactured Nanomaterials: Building*

there has been some agitation for a Geneva Convention with the specific purpose of protecting the environment from harm, including the kind of potential long-term harm caused by residual nanomaterials. This would include considering the risks of using nanomaterials in military systems more broadly, and for the purposes of this book, the risks in 'means and methods' of warfare more specifically.[11] Other authors writing about the regulation of nanomaterials in relation to its effect on the environment consider that '[m]ilitary nanotechnology is likely to be less destructive than self-replicating "gray goo", but harmful enough in its own way'.[12]

The nanomaterials that may be significant for the purposes of this book are any 'means or methods' of warfare that will leave residual nanomaterials in quantities that may cause harm. These include, but are not limited to, the use of nanomaterials in membranes and materials; detection and diagnostics of chemical and biological agents; decontamination; and medical countermeasures.[13] Geoengineering, which is the intentional large-scale manipulation of the environment, is also being explored using nanoscale science.[14] The use of such techniques in warfare would have potentially devastating and irreversible long-term effects on environments and their populations.

Optogenetics and human genetic modification do not provide a threat to the environment, and the potential environmental risks posed by nano-enhanced thermobaric weapons are not entirely clear, nor do they

Co-operation, Co-ordination and Communication (2005) <www.oecd.org/officialdocuments/publicdisplaydocumentpdf/?cote=ENV/JM/MONO(2006)19&docLanguage=bi>; Jane Macoubrie, *Informed Public Perceptions of Nanotechnology and Trust in Government* (2005) Woodrow Wilson International Centre for Scholars <www.pewtrusts.org/~/media/legacy/uploadedfiles/wwwpewtrustsorg/news/press_releases/nanotechnologies/nanotech0905pdf.pdf>; Douglas Mulhall, *Our Molecular Future: How Nanotechnology, Robotics, Genetic and Artificial Intelligence Will Transform Our World* (Prometheus Books, 2002) 63–72; Günter Oberdörster, Eva Oberdörster and Jan Oberdörster, 'Nanotoxicology: An Emerging Discipline Evolving from Studies of Ultrafine Particles' (2005) 113(7) *Environmental Health Perspectives* 823.

11 Ensign Florencio J Yuzon, 'Deliberate Environmental Modification through the Use of Chemical and Biological Weapons: "Greening" the International Laws of Armed Conflict to Establish an Environmentally Protective Regime' (1996) 11(5) *American University International Law Review* 793.

12 'Gray goo' is the self-replicating matter that some scientists suggest may continue proliferating indefinitely. Shiv Kant Prasad, *Advanced Nanotechnology* (Discovery Publishing House, 2008) 108.

13 Margaret Kosal, *Nanotechnology for Chemical and Biological Defense* (Springer, 2009).

14 Andrew Maynard and Jack Stilgoe (eds), *The Ethics of Nanotechnology, Geoengineering and Clean Energy* (Routledge, 2017).

exist on a scale that would necessarily cause harm. The technologies that may be significant for the purposes of this book are: batteries, weapons systems containing nanomaterials, nanomaterials used in tracking devices or any other system that may leach into water tables or food chains, fire retardants (already found to pose long-term health risks) or any other 'means or method' of warfare that releases and leaves nanomaterials in the soil, water or air proving to be harmful to humans in the long-term. Genetic modification more broadly, however, may have profound impacts for the environment, as discussed by a recent WTO panel.[15] In this case, the WTO isolated a tiny set of 'applicable law' (which did not cover the precautionary principle) and the WTO panel constrained its use of the 'relevant rules of international law' under VCLT treaty interpretation rules (Article 31(3)(c)), a position that Young argues, and with which I concur, is highly problematic.[16] Who gets to decide what law is applicable in cases involving nanomaterials? In the *Biotech* case, the WTO panel got to decide about the use of the precautionary principle in a case involving a trade moratorium on genetically modified food imports because of the WTO's compulsory dispute settlement body.

It is for this reason that this chapter will review and analyse existing international environmental law relevant to the increasing use of nanomaterials on the battlefield, as well as providing recommendations as to how the law needs to be strengthened to avoid future environmental catastrophes.

This chapter follows the development of international environmental law chronologically, mapping the shifting understanding and evaluation of the environment over time. The use of herbicides in Vietnam was a turning point in the history of international environmental law. Both the Convention on the Prohibition of Military or any Other Hostile Use of Environmental Modification Techniques (ENMOD)[17] and API,[18] the

[15] For the original case and analysis see: Gregory Conko and Henry I Miller, 'WTO and Biotech Food: Who Really Won?' (26 February 2006) *Competitive Enterprise Institute* <https://cei.org/opeds_articles/wto-and-biotech-food-who-really-won/>.

[16] Margaret A Young, 'The WTO's Use of Relevant Rules of International Law: An Analysis of the *Biotech* Case' (2007) *The International and Comparative Law Quarterly* 56(4) 907.

[17] *Convention on the Prohibition of Military or Any Other Hostile Use of Environmental Modification Techniques*, opened for signature 10 December 1976, 1108 UNTS 151 (entered into force 5 October 1978) ('*Environmental Modification Convention*'). The last time States attended a review conference for ENMOD was 1992.

[18] *Protocol Additional to the Geneva Conventions of 12 August 1949, and Relating to the Protection of Victims of International Armed Conflicts (Protocol I)*, opened for signature

first international agreements providing some protection for the environment during armed conflict, arose from the serious harm caused to the environment during the Vietnam War. Both of these international agreements will be analysed in detail in relation to the use of nanomaterials in warfare. This chapter will analyse the Precautionary Principle, as well as looking at how the balance between the Principle of Military Necessity and Humanity may provide protection of the environment during war. The Principle of Distinction and its potential to protect the environment during war will also be considered, as well as the Hague Conventions and the ancient Principle of Usufruct. Some more recent international environmental laws specifically intended to protect the environment during armed conflict will also be examined. Given our changing values and nascent understanding of the risks of the use of nanomaterials, coupled with our appreciation of our reliance on the environment, some older laws require new interpretations.

After the initial legal response to the Vietnam War through ENMOD and API, other international agreements providing various levels of protection followed. The World Charter for Nature[19] was agreed and, much later, the United Nations Compensation Commission (UNCC) specifically considered environmental damage caused by Iraq's invasion of Kuwait in 1991, using innovative methods for assessing the value of environmental damage. Both of these agreements will be considered later in this chapter, linking them back to the potential harm caused by nanomaterials in warfare. Finally, the use of depleted uranium in munitions, already discussed at great length in existing literature, will be considered to see what lessons can be learned for nanomaterials used in 'means or methods of war'. In conclusion, recommendations will be made for implementation and enforcement of international environmental law, as well as recommendations for new international law that provides adequate protection, given the current knowledge of our interdependence with the environment.

I Relevance of International Environmental Law to War

Because of the way environmental law has developed, I analyse applicable international environmental law along its natural timeline,

8 June 1977, 1125 UNTS 3 (entered into force 7 December 1978) arts 35(1), 35(2) ('*Additional Protocol I*').

19 *World Charter for Nature*, GA Resolution 37/7, UN GAOR, 37th sess, 48th plen mtg, UN Doc A/RES/37/7 (28 October 1982).

chronologically from the older laws and principles to trace the development and trajectory of environmental law and principles during war as a body of law. Some of the older laws and principles, which were established prior to the Vietnam War, may be interpreted now to include some of the post–Vietnam War values. For this reason, interpretations of these older laws may be overlaid with more modern approaches to evaluating the environment and, at times, reference interpretative tools that post-date the laws and principles in question. This approach is deliberately taken to show the flexibility and relevance of older laws and principles that, in the face of changing values and standards, can be used as a tool to reflect current understandings. International law is never static, and arguments that no law applies to nanomaterials, or that there is no applicable law to any new or emerging technology for that matter, do not take into account the considerable existing international law.

When use of weapons results in the release of nanomaterials into the environment, causing harm to either the environment per se or to people, then it might be argued that the Martens Clause, with its reference to the 'dictates of public conscience', should protect from this kind of harm. This would reflect our current understanding and appreciation of the environment, as expressed in other international environmental agreements and negotiations such as the Stockholm Declaration,[20] the 1992 Rio Declaration, the Rio 20+ World Summit[21] as well as the Sustainable Development Goals,[22] the 2017 Draft Global Pact for the Environment[23] and the official Working Group for the Global Pact for the Environment as recommended by the General Assembly in May 2018.[24]

[20] *Report of the United Nations Conference on the Human Environment: Stockholm, 5–16 June 1972*, UN Doc A/CONF.48/14/Rev.1 (1972) 3–5 ('*Declaration of the United Nations Conference on the Human Environment*').

[21] *The Future We Want*, GA Res 66/288, UN GAOR, 66th sess, 123rd plen mtg, Agenda Item 19, UN Doc A/RES/66/288 (11 September 2012).

[22] See *Transforming Our World: The 2030 Agenda for Sustainable Development*, GA Res 70/1, UN GAOR, 70th sess, 4th plen mtg, Agenda Items 15 and 116, UN Doc A/RES/70/1 (21 October 2015) 14.

[23] Le Club des Juristes, *Draft Project Global Pact for the Environment* (24 June 2017) International Union for Conservation of Nature <www.iucn.org/sites/dev/files/content/documents/draft-project-of-the-global-pact-for-the-environment.pdf>. Article 19, under the heading 'Armed Conflict', notes that 'States shall take pursuant to their obligations under international law all feasible measures to protect the environment in relation to armed conflicts'.

[24] *Towards a Global Pact for the Environment*, GA Res 72/277, UN GAOR, 72nd sess, Agenda Item 14, UN Doc A/RES/72/277 (14 May 2018).

This seems to be a natural extension of the understanding of the Martens Clause, given the increasing awareness of the precarity of our environment and our shifting understanding of the value of the environment, particularly in the face of a mass extinction[25] in what is now being referred to as the Anthropocene period.[26] Protection of the environment should be included as part of the 'dictates of public conscience' to reflect current knowledge of our dependence on a sustainable environment. The Vietnam War was a turning point for awareness of the impact of war on both the short-term devastation and long-term harm to the environment. This chapter is therefore divided between pre- and post–Vietnam War, given the enormous shift in attitudes to protection of the environment during war, and the rapid development of international environmental law after 1975.[27] After the Vietnam War, new international legal instruments were agreed on to protect the environment, as outlined previously. Looking forward, depleted uranium munitions, about which much has been written, offer an analogy for the challenges of nanomaterials and thus insight into the considerations required for an international environmental legal framework.

The first challenge regarding the protection of the environment under the laws of war is the applicability of the law. While the laws of war were initially conceived in a time of international armed conflicts (IAC), the overwhelming number of conflicts today are non-international armed conflicts (NIAC).[28] Many of the current conflicts causing the most damage to the environment are between armed groups within a single State, either regular armed forces fighting non-governmental armed groups or non-governmental armed groups fighting each other. Such situations would be captured by Common Article 3 of the Geneva Conventions relating to non-international armed conflict.

As almost every armed conflict causes some environmental damage, there is a threshold question as to how much damage is prohibited.

[25] E S Brondizio et al (eds), 'Global Assessment Report on Biodiversity and Ecosystem Services of the Intergovernmental *Science*-Policy Platform on Biodiversity and Ecosystem Services' (2019) *IPBES* <https://ipbes.net/global-assessment>.

[26] J R McNeill, 'Global Environmental History: The First 150,000 Years' in J R McNeill and E S Mauldin (eds), *A Companion to Global Environmental History* (Wiley-Blackwell, 2012) 3.

[27] Eliana Cusato, 'From Ecocide to Voluntary Remediation Projects: Legal Responses to Environmental Warfare in Vietnam and the Spectre of Colonialism' (2018) *Melbourne Journal of International Law* 19(2) 494.

[28] *Uppsala Conflict Data Program Database*, Uppsala University <http://ucdp.uu.se/>.

Articles 35 and 55 of API prohibit damage during armed conflict that is 'widespread, long-term *and* severe'.[29] All three conditions must be proven for a violation to occur. This triple standard is nearly impossible to satisfy and provides a prohibitively high bar for any meaningful protection of the environment. Further, the drafters' failure to define these terms means that the threshold is imprecise and uncertain.[30] Little evidence can be found in the negotiating history of what the delegates intended by the phrase. Other than a statement mentioning battlefield damage in France during World War I, which clarifies that this would not satisfy the articles' requirement,[31] very little is explained about the terminology or intent of the drafters. Even if conflicts occur between States, it is unclear whether Articles 35(3) and 55 apply to those States not party to API, of which there are 18.[32] The United States did not ratify API, largely because of its opposition to the environmental provisions.[33] The United States has rejected these provisions as 'overly broad and ambiguous' and 'not a part of customary law'.[34]

The situation is even more complicated when environmental damage is caused by nanomaterials during war. Around the same time as the Vietnam War, the first commercial explorations of nanomaterials began. Nevertheless, none of the drafters of existing international environmental law instruments contemplated nanomaterials, which necessitates interpretation by reference to analogous cases. Therefore, parallels will be drawn between the discussions of the legality of the use of DIMEs[35] and nanomaterials, which raises similar issues of invisible, widespread,

[29] *Additional Protocol I* arts 35, 55 (emphasis added).

[30] Liesbeth Lijnzaad and Gerard Tanja, 'Protection of the Environment in Times of Armed Conflict: The Iraq-Kuwait War' (1993) 40(2) *Netherlands International Law Review* 169, 180; W Verwey, 'Observation on the Legal Protection of the Environment in Times of International Armed Conflict' in A-C Kiss and Johan Lammers (eds), *Hague Yearbook of International Law Vol 7* (Brill, 1994) 36.

[31] Michael Schmitt, 'Green War: An Assessment of the Environmental Law of International Armed Conflict' (1997) 22(1) *Yale Journal of International Law* 1, 71.

[32] International Committee of the Red Cross, *Protocol Additional to the Geneva Conventions of 12 August 1949, and Relating to the Protection of Victims of International Armed Conflicts (Protocol I), 8 June 1977* <https://ihl-databases.icrc.or5g/applic/ihl/ihl.nsf/INTRO/470?OpenDocument>.

[33] Guy Roberts, 'The New Rules for Waging War: The Case against Ratification of Additional Protocol I' (1985) 26 *Virginia Journal of International Law* 109.

[34] Office of General Counsel, *Department of Defense Law of War Manual* (May 2016) United States Department of Defense 353 <www.defense.gov/Portals/1/Documents/DoD_Law_of_War_Manual-June_2015_Updated_May_2016.pdf>.

[35] *Yugoslavia v United States* (1999) 38(4) ILM 1188.

potentially long-term environmental harm. Finally, the UNCC's precedential model of evaluating the environment beyond its role as an economic asset will be analysed. I will conclude that, despite some post–Vietnam War agreements that attempt to curb environmental damage during armed conflict, the existing environmental law and principles are inadequate in the face of the particular properties of nanomaterials and their potentially long-lasting and deleterious effects.

II Pre–Vietnam War Environmental Protection in War

A The Martens Clause

The relevance of the Martens Clause to environmental use may not have necessarily been foreseen when it was drafted. The language of the Martens Clause is as follows,

> Populations and belligerents remain under the protection and the rule of the principles of nations, as they result from usages established among civilised peoples, from the laws of humanity and *the dictates of the public conscience.*[36]

The legal requirement for consideration of the 'dictates of public conscience' is found in the preamble to the Hague Conventions (otherwise known as the Martens Clause), in the preamble to many of the Geneva Conventions, as well as the preamble of the CCW.[37] The Martens

[36] *Convention (IV) Respecting the Laws and Customs of War on Land and Its Annex: Regulations Concerning the Laws and Customs of War on Land*, signed 18 October 1907, 205 CTS 277 (entered into force 26 January 1910) Preamble (emphasis added) ('*Hague Convention (IV)*').

[37] *Hague Convention (IV)* Preamble; *Geneva Convention (I) for the Amelioration of the Condition of the Wounded and Sick in Armed Forces in the Field*, opened for signature 12 August 1949, 75 UNTS 31 (entered into force 21 October 1950) art 63 ('*First Geneva Convention*'); *Geneva Convention (II) for the Amelioration of the Condition of Wounded, Sick and Shipwrecked Members of Armed Forces at Sea*, opened for signature 12 August 1949, 75 UNTS 85 (entered into force 21 October 1950) art 62 ('*Second Geneva Convention*'); *Geneva Convention (III) Relative to the Treatment of Prisoners of War*, opened for signature 12 August 1949, 75 UNTS 135 (entered into force 21 October 1950) art 142 ('*Third Geneva Convention*'); *Geneva Convention (IV) Relative to the Protection of Civilian Persons in Time of War*, opened for signature 12 August 1949, 75 UNTS 287 (entered into force 21 October 1950) art 158 ('*Fourth Geneva Convention*'); *Protocol Additional to the Geneva Conventions of 12 August 1949, and Relating to the Protection of Victims of Non-International Armed Conflicts (Protocol II)*, opened for signature 8 June 1977, 1125 UNTS 609 (entered into force on 7 December 1978) ('*Additional Protocol II*'); *Convention on Prohibition or Restrictions on the Use of Certain Conventional Weapons*

Clause was already discussed in Chapter 4 but has particular relevance in the context of environmental protection because the terminology, 'dictates of public conscience', entails the notion that the law must reflect values of the time. One of these changes in the values of our time is a change in how the environment is valued. An increasingly ubiquitous use of nanomaterials in war, and the harm they may cause to the environment, makes examination of the use of nanomaterials in war all the more urgent.

The Martens Clause is relevant because the way that humans value the environment has changed dramatically over the past three decades. Previously, the dominant Western approach to the environment was that it was only considered valuable for the ways that it could sustain humans: providing food, clothing and shelter. Even the usefulness of endangered species of plants or animals related to humans' appreciation of the aesthetics of the plants or animals.[38] Our appreciation of the environment has evolved to one of an 'intrinsic worth approach',[39] understanding that the environment has inherent value, even to the extent that some countries are granting environmental features legal personality under the law.[40] Some writers are calling for laws that govern what they refer to as 'ecocide' in an attempt to provide a more holistic approach to protecting the environment, given how interconnected we are with it, or to provide

Which May Be Deemed to Be Excessively Injurious or to Have Indiscriminate Effects, opened for signature 10 October 1980, 1342 UNTS 137 (entered into force 2 December 1983) Preamble ('*Convention on Certain Conventional Weapons*'). The 1980 Convention on Prohibitions or Restrictions on the Use of certain Weapons which may be deemed to be Excessively Injurious or to have Indiscriminate Effects repeats the language from the Martens Clause in its preamble

> Confirming their determination that in cases not covered by this Convention and its annexed Protocols, or by other international agreements, the civilian population and the combatants shall at all times remain under the protection and authority of the principles of international law derived from established custom, from the principles of humanity and from the dictates of public conscience.

38 Andrew Solow and Stephen Polasky, 'The Endangered Species Act as a Tool to Conserve Biological Diversity' (1999) 14 *Choices* 17.

39 For more information about the intrinsic value approach, see Mirka Laurila Pant et al, 'How to Value Biodiversity in Environmental Management?' (2015) 55 *Ecological Indicators* 1.

40 Erin O'Donnell, *Legal Rights for Rivers: Competition, Collaboration and Water Governance* (Routledge, 2019).

legal identity for environmental features or resources.[41] This shift in the dominant conceptions of the environment was triggered by authors such as Rachel Carson,[42] and has been indirectly reflected in international law through a proliferation of international agreements. It has also been explicitly expressed through UNCC decisions in the early 2000s relating to environmental damage sustained during Iraq's invasion of Kuwait.[43] These decisions included an evaluation of the intrinsic value of the environment and not just a narrow economic evaluation.[44] Even when the environment is contemplated, all too often the environment is lost in fora that prioritise other rights, such as human rights or trade agreements.[45]

[41] Erin O'Donnell, Michelle Maloney and Christine Parker, *New Developments in the Legal Status of Rivers* (11 August 2017) <http://law.unimelb.edu.au/__data/assets/pdf_file/0007/2516479/Legal-rights-for-rivers-Workshop-Report.pdf>. For further information regarding suggestions of criminalising ecocide, see Polly Higgins, *Eradicating Ecocide* (Shepheard-Walwyn, 2015).

[42] Rachel Carson, *Silent Spring* (Houghton Mifflin, first published 1962, 2002 ed). Jacqueline Peel has written extensively on the topic of international law and the environment: see Jacqueline Peel, 'Science and Risk Assessment in International Law: Learning from the WTO SPS Experience' (2004) 98 *Proceedings of the Annual Meeting (American Society of International Law)* 283; Jacqueline Peel, *Science and Risk Regulation in International Law* (Cambridge University Press, 2010).

[43] Cymie Payne, 'Developments in the Law of Environmental Reparations: A Case Study of the UN Compensation Commission' in Carsten Stahn, Jens Iverson and Jennifer Easterday (eds), *Environmental Protection and Transitions from Conflict to Peace: Clarifying Norms, Principles and Practices* (Oxford University Press, 2017); Cymie Payne, 'Legal Liability for Environmental Damage: The United Nations Compensation Commission and the 1990–1991 Gulf War' in Carl Bruch, Carroll Muffett and Sandra Nichols (eds), *Governance, Natural Resources and Post-Conflict Peacebuilding* (Routledge, 2016).

[44] Cymie Payne and Peter Sand (eds), *Gulf War Reparations and the UN Compensation Commission: Environmental Liability* (Oxford University Press, 2011) 84: 'At the UNCC, a number of claims successfully demonstrated physical or biological impairment of environmental resources – for example, various terrestrial, groundwater, and marine claims of Kuwait, some terrestrial and marine claims of Saudi Arabia, and certain claims of Iran and Jordan. The F4 Panel recommended compensation for these claims'. This may also have been partially because of the definitions provided in the Governing Council Resolutions that referred to 'depletion of or damage to natural resources' as per Governing Council Decision 7: United Nations Compensation Commission, *Governing Council Decision 7: Criteria for Additional Categories of Claims*, UN SCOR, 3rd sess, 18th mtg, UN Doc S/AC.25/1991/7/Rev.1 (17 March 1992).

[45] Margaret A. Young, *Fragmentation and International Law* in Lavanya Rajamani and Jacqueline Peel (eds), *Oxford Handbook of International Environmental Law* (Oxford University Press, 2nd ed, forthcoming).

Evaluations of environmental damage need to include compensation for intrinsic damage in light of contemporary values attributed to the environment, much in the same way that the World Trade Organization has a mechanism for disputes. All too often, '"the environment" is . . . left behind when the interests of states are shaped by, and pursued through, other regimes, whose functional orientation does not prioritize ecological concerns. Those other regimes have institutional strength and compulsory dispute settlement, while environmental principles are often scattered amongst custom and non-binding instruments'.[46]

As a preamble to the Hague Convention, the Martens Clause is relevant for context in terms of treaty interpretation as per Article 31 of the VCLT.[47] Little has been written on the status of preambles, such as the Martens Clause, in international law, even though they are often negotiated with great care. The topic of preambles is not explicitly singled out for mention in the recent *Oxford Guide to Treaties*, but is mentioned in Hollis[48] and Gardiner[49] as part of the 'context'.

Klabbers states,

> The preamble therewith becomes an extension of the *negotiandum*, and while it may be the case, as Koskenniemi suggests, that the preamble contains the things that were left out of the treaty itself, nonetheless its relevance is keenly felt by the parties: it functions as the garbage can of disagreement, or the dumpster of discord.[50]

There seems to be general agreement that the text of the preamble may be used to help understand the treaty itself as an 'element of context as defined in the Vienna rules'.[51] Even if they are a 'dumpster of discord', as

[46] Ibid.

[47] *Vienna Convention on the Law of Treaties*, opened for signature 23 May 1969, 1155 UNTS 331 (entered into force 27 January 1980) ('*VCLT*') art 31(2).

[48] See D B Hollis (ed), *The Oxford Guide to Treaties* (Oxford University Press, 2012).

[49] Richard Gardiner, *Treaty Interpretation* (Oxford University Press, 2015) 206.

[50] Jan Klabbers, 'Treaties and their Preambles' in Michael J Bowman and Dino Kritsiotis (eds), *Conceptual and Contextual Perspectives on the Modern Law of Treaties* (Cambridge University Press, 2018) 12.

[51] Richard Gardiner, *Treaty Interpretation* (Oxford University Press, 2008) 186–187: 'By stating the aims and objectives of a treaty, as preambles often do in general terms, preambles can help in identifying the object and purpose of the treaty'. Gardiner also notes that, 'if the terms of a substantive provision offered a choice of meanings, those which ran counter to rights and obligations under other instruments would be exclusions. Put more generally, the substantive provisions will usually have greater clarity and precision than the preamble; but where there is doubt over the meaning of a substantive provision, the preamble may justify a wider interpretation, or at least rejection of a

Klabbers refer to preambles, they still comprise the context of the negotiation. Preambles are often contained in the official records of the negotiations.[52] There is some disagreement as to whether preambles may create specific legal obligations.[53] Kritsiotis has referred to the preamble as the 'mood music' of the treaty and, as such, it is unable to be ignored, as it creates the context for the substantive text,[54] a position with which I strongly concur.

The idea that the 'dictates of public conscience' in the Martens Clause may change over time (and therefore, by implication, be potentially consistent with an intrinsic value approach to the environment) was discussed in detail in Judge Shahabuddeen's dissenting judgment in the *Nuclear Weapons Advisory Opinion*. Shahabuddeen noted that, while the principles of the Martens Clause, namely humanity and the dictates of public conscience, were legal principles, 'the precise content of the standard implied by these principles of international law are to be ascertained in the light of changing conditions, inclusive of changes in

restrictive one', paraphrasing Eric Suy, 'Le Préambule' in Emile Yakpo and Tahar Boumedra (eds), *Liber Amicorum Judge Mohammed Bedjaoui* (Kluwer, 1999) 253–269. See also Oliver Dörr and Kirsten Schmalenbach (eds), *Vienna Convention on the Law of Treaties: A Commentary* (Springer, 2012) 544: 'The preamble to a treaty, usually consisting of a set of recitals, may assist in determining the object and purpose of a treaty'.

52

> Recourse to *travaux préparatoires* as a subsidiary means of interpreting the text, as already indicated, is frequent both in State practice and in cases before international tribunals. Today, it is generally recognized that some caution is needed in the use of *travaux préparatoires* as a means of interpretation. They are not, except in the case mentioned . . . an authentic means of interpretation. They are simply evidence to be weighed up against other relevant evidence of the intention of the parties, and the cogency depends on the extent to which they furnish proof of the common understanding of the parties as to the meaning attached to the terms of the treaty. Statements of individual parties during the negotiations are therefore of small value in the absence of evidence that they were assented to by the other parties.

Sir Humphrey Waldock, 'Third Report on the Law of Treaties' [1964] II *Yearbook of the International Law Commission* 58, [20], cited in Richard Gardiner, *Treaty Interpretation* (Oxford University Press, 2008) 307. See also Jan Klabbers, 'International Legal Histories: The Declining Importance of *Travaux Préparatoires* in Treaty Interpretation' (2003) 50(3) *Netherlands International Law Review* 267.

53 Max Hulme, 'Preambles in Treaty Interpretation' (2016) 164(5) *University of Pennsylvania Law Review* 1281, 1284–1285.

54 Dino Kritsiotis, 'An Uncensored History of International Law' (Lecture delivered at Master of Laws program, The University of Melbourne, 2 June 2018). See also Klabbers 'Treaties and their Preambles', n 50.

the means and methods of warfare and the outlook and tolerance levels of the international community'.[55] Judge Weeramantry made similar points in his dissenting opinion, noting that, 'beyond the domain of express prohibitions, there lies the domain of the general principles of humanitarian law ... The general principle is ... applied to the specific situation and out of that particular application a rule of greater specificity emerges'.[56] Definitions of the principles may shift over time.

Although no case involving nanomaterials has yet been heard by an international judicial tribunal, it is still possible to extrapolate that the deliberate misuse or even the use of man-made nanoparticles without regard to their long-term risk during armed conflict may be prohibited under current understandings of the value of the environment and how the law should protect it. Concerns about the use of nanomaterials, potentially causing long-term and invisible harm, should be considered as part of the dictates of public conscience. Assessment of the long-term environmental harm of the use of nanomaterials in weapons should be considered as part of any Article 36 weapons review because it would be required by the Martens Clause. Contemplation of environmental harm as being within the ambit of the Martens Clause may result in limitations on the use of nanomaterials in war in certain circumstances, particularly if the Precautionary Principle (as discussed next) is applied.

B The Precautionary Principle in Environmental Law

The Precautionary Principle is fundamental to international environmental law, and specific reference to it by the judiciary dates back to early twentieth-century Roman law. The concept is generally considered to have first appeared in the English language from a translation of the German term *Vorsorgeprinzip* in the 1980s.[57] The Precautionary Principle is noted in the United Nations Convention on the Law of the Sea,[58] the Stockholm Declaration[59] and the 1992 Rio

[55] *Legality of the Threat or Use of Nuclear Weapons (Advisory Opinion)* [1996] ICJ Rep 226, 406 (Judge Shahabuddeen).

[56] Ibid 493 (Judge Weeramantry).

[57] Sonja Boehmer Christiansen, 'The Precautionary Principle in Germany: Enabling Government' in Tim O'Riordan and James Cameron (eds), *Interpreting the Precautionary Principle* (Earthscan, 1994).

[58] *United Nations Convention on the Law of the Sea*, opened for signature 10 December 1982, 1833 UNTS 397 (entered into force 16 November 1994).

[59] *Declaration of the United Nations Conference on the Human Environment*, n 20, 3–5.

Declaration,[60] and it has been suggested that the principle indicates a rapid widespread emergence of a State's right to environmental protection without exception.[61]

More recent language defining the Precautionary Principles is as follows,

> Where there are threats of serious or irreversible damage, lack of full scientific certainty shall not be used as a reason for postponing cost-effective measures to prevent environmental degradation.[62]

The use of nanomaterials in 'means and methods of warfare' is likely to leave nanomaterials in the environment, the full long-term impacts of which we are not yet aware. This is a classic Precautionary Principle scenario, in which there is reason to believe that there may be potential harm, but there is a lack of scientific certainty about the specific nanomaterials that may be harmful and how they will cause harm. The Precautionary Principle requires 'cost-effective measures to prevent environmental degradation', even where there is a lack of full scientific certainty.

The Precautionary Principle places the responsibility on those developing a technology or technique to consciously and effectively weigh up risk,[63] and it requires regulators to proactively provide protection from future risks, even when the future risks are not entirely scientifically clear.[64] The Precautionary Principle adds another layer of protection to those who may potentially be adversely affected by an action or decision.[65] Ignorance is no protection from responsibility under

[60] Report of the United Nations Conference on Environment and Development: Rio de Janeiro, 3–14 June 1992, UN Doc A/CONF.151/26 (Vol. I) (12 August 1992) annex ('*Rio Declaration on Environment and Development*').

[61] Margaret Okorodudu-Fubara, 'Oil in the Persian Gulf War: Legal Appraisal of an Environmental Warfare' (1992) 23 *St Mary's Law Journal* 123.

[62] *Rio Declaration on Environment and Development*', n 60, Principle 15.

[63] Lesley Wexler, 'Limiting the Precautionary Principle: Weapons Regulation in the Face of Scientific Uncertainty' (2006) 39(2) *University of California Davis Law Review* 459. The leading approach, a military precautionary principle, is often both indeterminate and insensitive to the harms raised by alternative weapons. Rather than fall prey to heuristics and biases, both the military and environmental advocates should be more attentive to the full range of environmental, health, military and financial costs presented by weapon use.

[64] Ronnie Harding, 'Toxics, Industry and Precaution: What Role for Science' in Ronnie Harding and Elizabeth Fisher (eds), *Perspectives on the Precautionary Principle* (Federation Press, 1999) 209–215.

[65] David Adelman, 'Scientific Activism and Restraint: The Interplay of Statistics, Judgment, and Procedure in Environmental Law' (2004) 79(2) *Notre Dame Law Review* 497, 543.

the Precautionary Principle. Supporters of the Precautionary Principle link it to producing information that further protects the environment and, at the very least, requires formal contemplation of risk.[66]

The Precautionary Principle has been criticised for several reasons. First, the Precautionary Principle is not universally accepted, which means that not all States will acknowledge it as a principle, or use it as a tool. Some countries, most notably the United States, reject the Precautionary Principle entirely, or note that it is unenforceable.

Second, opponents of the Precautionary Principle criticise it for having little or no effect. The Precautionary Principle requires a weighing of risk that is not specified but does not require a particular action, such as creating an Environmental Impact Statement or anything similar. The Precautionary Principle is not a catch-all solution, nor does it prevent harm to the environment occurring. It is not the equivalent of a 'do no harm' principle.[67] Harm may still occur, even though the risks have been weighed. The outcome of the Precautionary Principle can therefore vary vastly depending on what methodology is used to assess risk. Certain methodologies may unintentionally create greater risks. Some have argued that the Precautionary Principle, if applied during war, may at best fail to prioritise those actions that best promote public health and the environment,[68] and at worst, fail to protect against the most serious health and environmental hazards.[69]

Although these criticisms are based on valid concerns that must be addressed, the Precautionary Principle remains the best reminder to assess and safeguard against risks that are not yet fully known – precisely the case with human-manipulated nanoparticles still under development and being researched.

In case law, the *Trail Smelter Arbitration* confirmed that no State has the right to allow activities within its boundaries that cause serious environmental harm within another State's borders due to air pollution (the 'transboundary harm' principle).[70]

66 Wendy Wagner, 'Commons Ignorance: The Failure of Environmental Law to Produce Needed Information on Health and the Environment' (2004) 53(6) *Duke Law Journal* 1619.

67 I am indebted to one of my examiners for drawing my attention to this issue.

68 Simon Grant and John Quiggin, 'Bounded Awareness, Heuristics and the Precautionary Principle' (2013) 93 *Journal of Economic Behavior & Organization* 17.

69 Wexler, n 63.

70 *Trail Smelter Case (United States v Canada)* (1938/1941) 3 RIAA 1905.

> The award ... and its finding on the state of international law on air pollution in the 1930s has come to represent a crystallising movement for international environmental law.[71]

As Bratspies argues, the *Trail Smelter* decisional process also demonstrated an inchoate version of the Precautionary Principle.[72] As there was no settled scientific evidence at that time as to what impact pollution from the smelter in Canada had across the border on farmers in the United States, the Tribunal required 'using preliminary measures to prevent harm while information sufficient to create a permanent regime fair to all parties [was] developed'.[73] This was a pragmatic decision the Tribunal made about how to manage a dispute in the interim. Given the high stakes involved in environmental harm, the 'transboundary harm' principle ought to apply in war.

Although the *Trail Smelter Arbitration* did not specifically contemplate nanomaterials, the principles enunciated, including the "(semi) precautionary principle" (as Bratspies calls it)[74] that was applied in the decision process, still have relevance. The *Trail Smelter Case* crystalises various principles that remain important for international environmental law. These principles should be developed and applied to the use of nanomaterials in war. States should contemplate potential future environmental harm caused by the use of nanomaterials, the risks of which are not yet entirely known. As a result, weapons reviews of 'means or methods of war' should contemplate potential harm caused to the environment as a matter of course. States should contemplate potential future environmental harm caused by the use of nanomaterials, the risks of which are not yet entirely known. As a result, weapons reviews of 'means or methods of war' should contemplate potential harm caused to the environment as a matter of course.

Nanomaterials seep into water tables and traverse national boundaries, potentially transferring irreversible and virtually undetectable potential toxicity. Nanomaterials require special consideration prior to their use, and impartial toxicology specialists to review their potential deleterious

[71] Phillippe Sands and Jacqueline Peel, *Principles of International Environmental Law* (Cambridge, 2012) 26.

[72] Rebecca Bratspies, 'Trail Smelter's (Semi) Precautionary Legacy' in Rebecca Bratspies and Russell Miller (eds), *Transboundary Harm in International Law* (Cambridge University Press, 2006) 153, contemplating the implications of the *Trail Smelter Case (United States v Canada)* (1938/1941) 3 RIAA 1905.

[73] Ibid.

[74] Ibid.

effects. States are liable for causing transboundary environmental harm, and this should include where nanomaterials seep into water tables and contaminate air and food.

The Precautionary Principle has been applied in more recent UNCC decisions (discussed in detail later in the chapter)[75] and is included in the principles of the Rio Declaration.[76] These sources are valuable for different reasons. The Rio Declaration, although not having the status of an internationally negotiated treaty, is an indication of *opinio juris* of the principle that the environment requires legal protection. The UNCC's decisions are indicative of the *opinio juris* of States regarding the status and value of the environment.

Despite being fundamental to the protection of environmental law, there is some disagreement around whether the Precautionary Principle should apply during armed conflict, or even at all.[77] Opponents of the Precautionary Principle note its heuristic bias, meaning that it potentially focuses on alleviating one aspect of a complex problem while ignoring or deprioritising other complex issues. By being overly cautious in the employment of new weapons, the full effects of which are not yet known, some authors go so far as to argue that applying the Precautionary Principle to the use of weapons may keep greener weapons off the battlefield because it may cause States to be too risk averse and therefore reluctant to use new and emerging technologies that may actually be better for the environment.[78]

Some States have argued for the applicability of the Precautionary Principle during war. For example, in its request to re-examine the *Nuclear Tests Case*, New Zealand explicitly proposed that the Precautionary Principle apply during armed conflict in its written statement submitted to the ICJ. New Zealand argued that, under customary international law, the Precautionary Principle applies to armed conflict because States are under an obligation to carry out an environmental

[75] Cymie Payne, 'Legal Liability for Environmental Damage: The United Nations Compensation Commission and the 1990–1991 Gulf War' in Carl Bruch, Carroll Muffet and Sandra Nichols (eds), *Governance, Natural Resources and Post-Conflict Peacebuilding* (Routledge, 2016).

[76] *Rio Declaration on Environment and Development*, n 60.

[77] Paul Szasz, 'The Existing Legal Framework, Protecting the Environment during International Armed Conflict' in Richard Grunawalt, John King and Ronald McClain (eds), *Protection of the Environment during Armed Conflict* (Naval War College, 1996) 278–282. The United States dismisses the precautionary principle entirely.

[78] Wexler, n 63, 462.

impact assessment 'in relation to any activity which is likely to cause significant damage to the environment, particularly where such effects are likely to be transboundary in nature'.[79] New Zealand went on to explain the Precautionary Principle as, in the absence of certainty, 'having regard to scientific and technical knowledge at the time … [and] not hold[ing] up the adoption of effective and proportionate measures with *a view to avoiding a risk of serious and irreversible damage to the environment at an economically acceptable cost*'.[80] However, France, in its submissions, questioned whether the Precautionary Principle had become a binding rule of international law, and denied that the principle could have the effect of shifting the burden of proof as New Zealand had asserted.[81] There is no legal conclusion regarding these submissions. This level of legal ambiguity is inadequate for providing protection to the environment.

The Precautionary Principle has particular relevance for nanomaterials, where toxicity and long-term effects on human health are still coming to light. Conflict ravages communities and devastates human made and natural environments. Long-term toxicity resulting in harm to human health needs to be avoided. In the case of nanomaterials, where their impacts are not yet entirely known, and are difficult to detect and remove from food chains and water tables, the Precautionary Principle should apply to any use of nanomaterials in war. Such precaution would also comply with other requirements of the laws of war regarding the long-term effects of war on populations, including the principle of humanity, as discussed next. In conclusion, the Precautionary Principle needs to be explicitly included in judgments and interpretations of treaties as a standard of law during war to ameliorate potential

[79] 'Request for an Examination of the Situation', *Request for an Examination of the Situation in Accordance with Paragraph 63 of the Court's 1974 Judgment in the Case Concerning Nuclear Tests (New Zealand v France)* (International Court of Justice, General List No 97, 21 August 1995) 44 [89] <www.icj-cij.org/files/case-related/97/7187.pdf>.

[80] 'Request for an Examination of the Situation', *Request for an Examination of the Situation in Accordance with Paragraph 63 of the Court's 1974 Judgment in the Case Concerning Nuclear Tests (New Zealand v France)* (International Court of Justice, General List No 97, 21 August 1995) 55 [107] <www.icj-cij.org/files/case-related/97/7187.pdf> (emphasis added).

[81] 'Verbatim Record', *Request for an Examination of the Situation in accordance with Paragraph 63 of the Court's 1974 Judgment in the Case Concerning Nuclear Tests (New Zealand v France)* (International Court of Justice, General List No 97 France, 12 September 1995) 56–62 <www.icj-cij.org/files/case-related/97/097-19950912-ORA-01-00-BI.pdf>.

long-term environmental damage. In order to ensure compliance with this argument, any review of a 'means or method' of warfare should contemplate environmental implications.

C *Custom and Principles of the Laws of War Relevant to Protection of the Environment*

1 The Balance between the Principles of Military Necessity and Humanity and Protection of the Environment

If we agree that the environment has intrinsic value, the principle of humanity, discussed in the introduction to this book, needs to reflect this shift. Environmental protection is important for the principle of humanity because humans cannot survive without a safe and sustainable environment in which to live. The suggestion that military operations should take into account environmental impact is not a new one, but it raises very specific challenges, each of which must be individually considered. The choice of methodology will affect the outcomes of these legal requirements for review of nanomaterials during war. What is measured will be valued. If the impact to the environment is not measured, it will not be valued. If the impact to the environment is included in the definition of humanity in the laws of war, which it has traditionally not been, it will be valued.

There are three specific challenges to the process of weighing military necessity against humanity where the latter includes damage to the environment. Although much has been written about weighing military necessity against humanity, it is not a clear-cut mathematical equation.[82] The first question is whether the environment should be considered as a component of the concept of 'humanity'. Given humans' dependence on a sustainable environment for survival, I argue that this must be the case. The inclusion of the environment as a component of the balance, then, requires a choice about the way the environment is evaluated vis-à-vis humanity.

Different conclusions will be reached depending on the method of evaluation of potential damage to the environment. A utilitarian approach will naturally establish less value for the environment when balancing it against military necessity, whereas an intrinsic valuation of

[82] Ian Henderson, *The Contemporary Law of Targeting: Military Objectives, Proportionality and Precautions in Attack under Additional Protocol I* (Martinus Nijhoff, 2009).

the environment may provide a different outcome. The difficulty in assessing whether an act is militarily necessary is that it must be judged on a case-by-case basis. The lighting of the oil fires during the war in Iraq, for example, would be impossible to legally justify under any interpretation of military necessity. However, many military campaigns causing environmental damage may be later justified with arguments of military necessity, such as bombing a military target located near an area of environmental significance. The lack of clarity around the methodology that should be used in evaluating damage to the environment as a component of considerations of 'humanity' means that the environment is seldom even considered, let alone protected from long-term environmental damage in the battlefield context.

Second, the Rome Statute of the ICC codifies the weighing up of military necessity and humanity in Article 8(2)(iv), which includes under war crimes '[e]xtensive destruction and appropriation of property, not justified by military necessity and carried out unlawfully *and* wantonly'.[83] One question could be whether the environment might be considered property and, as such, offered the protection that other property is given during war. Including the environment as an object of property would mean that only objects with proprietary rights, and not those with broader benefit to the community, would potentially be protected.

Third, the legal standards of both 'unlawfully' and 'wantonly', as outlined in the Rome Statute, are particularly difficult to ascertain when it comes to contemplating harm to the environment. When does the action required by military necessity traverse into the realm of 'wantonly'? And if the requirement of the standard of prevention of environmental harm is 'unlawful', does that 'unlawful' need to reflect the standards of ENMOD and API, which were developed after the Vietnam War? The current thresholds for proving breach of environmental law during war are ill-defined, even for traditional environmental harm. Intent to cause harm is virtually impossible to prove in the context of conflict, a requirement under ENMOD.[84] The use of nanomaterials raises additional challenges for current legal thresholds. The release of toxic nanomaterials into water sources would not need to be widespread

[83] *Rome Statute of the International Criminal Court*, opened for signature 17 July 1998, 2187 UNTS 91 (entered into force 1 July 2002) ('*Rome Statute*') (emphasis added).

[84] Michael Schmitt and Leslie Green (eds), *The Law of Armed Conflict: Into the Next Millennium* (US Naval War College, 1998).

to wreak havoc that caused long-term damage to the environment and human health.

Finally, protection of the environment during armed conflict, given updated understandings of our reliance on the environment, needs to be prioritised. In the past, in the use of traditional weapons, military necessity has been held to almost always supersede the importance of protecting the environment. This approach is outdated but embedded in military manuals and the way that militaries operate. 'The dictates of military necessity, as assessed by opposed leaderships, have taken consistent precedence over the laws of war in almost every critical aspect of belligerent policy'.[85] In other words, those leading wars tend to err on the side of military necessity. Any protection of the environment will almost always be superseded by military necessity unless these protections are made explicit in specific rules of combat and military manuals.

To adequately protect the environment, greater consideration must be given to the inherent complexity and embedded values in the task of weighing military necessity and factoring in environmental considerations.[86] The requirement of commanders to balance the immediacy of decision-making on the battlefield in the face of so many unknowns regarding long-term effects of nanoparticles may be beyond most individuals making these types of decisions. This means that the long-term environmental risks of nanomaterials will most likely not be considered in the moment on the battlefield, even with an effective Article 36 review considering these issues prior to deployment.

2 The Principle of Distinction and Environmental Protection

As was discussed in Chapter 4, the principle of distinction prohibits or limits the use of thermobaric weapons with or without nanomaterials. It is difficult to imagine a situation where their use would comply with this principle. The question arising in this chapter is a slightly different one, namely whether the impact of nanomaterials on the environment requires special consideration under this principle. The principle of distinction, as previously discussed in Chapter 4, is a cornerstone of the laws of war and requires the distinction between military and civilian

85 Richard Falk, *Revitalizing International Law* (Iowa State University Press, 1989) 168.

86 William Arkin, Damian Durrant and Marianne Cherni, *On Impact: Modern Warfare and the Environment: A Case Study of the Gulf War* (1991) Greenpeace <www.greenpeace.org/international/Global/international/planet-2/report/1991/6/on-impact-modern-warfare-and.pdf>.

persons and objects and prohibits attacks that are indiscriminate and direct attacks against civilians and civilian objects.

The Precautionary Principle is one approach to managing scientific risk, and, I propose, the most prudent. But broader questions about the relationship between international law and science remain. The Principle of Distinction could be interpreted or expanded to include the environment, similarly to civilian objects, and therefore make consideration of the environmental impact of the use of nanomaterials in weapons a required part of a weapons review. Assuming this approach, international environmental law principles, such as the Precautionary Principle, would then be relevant to questions of how to assess the risk to the environment. In short, the Principle of Distinction is one way of ensuring that international environmental law is upheld when contemplating the laws of war for an Article 36 weapons review.

Where the science is not yet clear, are there other resources that should be consulted? Fundamentally, how should international law respond to risk?[87] These questions remain but, in the face of the increased use of nanomaterials, the need to find their answers has become more urgent and requires greater analysis and clarity. Even if the legal principles were clearer, the relationship between science and international law would still require clarification.

3 The Hague Conventions, the Ancient Principle of Usufruct and Environmental Protection

The Hague Conventions codify an older principle of usufruct, which is a principle that relates to situations of military occupation. Usufruct is a principle from ancient Roman times and states that the fruits of the land may be used where replaceable, but wholesale exploitation and abuse of the environment is prohibited,[88] which would include leaving potentially toxic nanomaterials in the environment. This principle therefore has relevance for the way in which the environment is left after armed conflict involving occupation of any kind, including the impact that remaining nanomaterials may have on the environment. This principle limits the occupying powers (or those conducting warfare) in their seizure and use of property, and is codified in Article 23(g) of the 1899 and 1907 Hague Regulations regarding the Destruction of Enemy

[87] Peel, *Science and Risk Regulation in International Law*, n 42.

[88] More generally, see Yoram Dinstein, *The International Law of Belligerent Occupation* (Cambridge University Press, 2009).

Property, and also under customary international law.[89] Dating back to ancient Roman law, usufruct requires that entitlements are limited to the 'rights of use' and 'consumption of fruits'.[90] In the words of the 2004 UK Manual of the Law of Armed Conflict, the United Kingdom's interpretation of this principle is that the Occupying Power may not only sell crops but also 'cut and sell timber and work the mines'.[91] Even in the case of mining, where the materials are not renewable, extraction is permitted. The rationale for this is that non-maintenance is liable to lead to long-term decline of the facility.[92] In summary, the concept is that the land may be used where the resources are replaceable, or existing infrastructure would be maintained by doing so. Usufruct could prohibit leaving deposits of potentially toxic nanomaterials during times of military occupation. Usufruct can be seen as a partial recognition of the importance of a safe and healthy environment for the sake of the people of the occupied territory, who need to be able to eat the food. There should be recognition of a considerable extension of this idea to ensure a safe and healthy environment in a range of ways, including that the environment is not contaminated by nanomaterials.

Returning briefly to the outdated idea of the environment only as property, the 1899 and 1907 Hague Conventions provide specific constraints, under which it is prohibited to,

> [D]estroy or seize the enemy's property, unless such destruction or seizure be imperatively demanded by the necessities of war.[93]

The decisions of the UNCC, established under the mandate of UNSCR 687,[94] provide a powerful and extremely useful insight into the

[89] Ibid 210, 214.

[90] International Committee of the Red Cross, *Customary IHL – Rule 50: Practice* (2017) <https://ihl-databases.icrc.org/customary-ihl/eng/docs/v2_rul_rule50>.

[91] United Kingdom Ministry of Defence, *The Manual of the Law of Armed Conflict* (Oxford University Press, 2004) [11.85]–[11.87].

[92] Iain Scobbie, 'Natural Resources and Belligerent Occupation: Mutation through Permanent Sovereignty' in Stephen Bowen (ed), *Human Rights, Self-Determination and Political Change in the Occupied Palestinian Territories* (Martinus Nijhoff, 1997) 238.

[93] *Convention (II) with Respect to the Laws and Customs of War on Land and Its Annex: Regulations Concerning the Laws and Customs of War on Land*, signed 29 July 1899, 187 CTS 429 (entered into force 4 September 1900); *Convention (IV) with Respect to the Laws and Customs of War on Land and Its Annex: Regulations Concerning the Laws and Customs of War on Land*, signed 18 October 1907, 205 CTS 277 (entered into force 26 January 1910) art 23(g).

[94] UNSC Resolution 687 was authorised under Chapter VII of the UN Charter: SC Res 687, UN SCOR, 2981st mtg, UN Doc S/RES/687 (8 April 1991).

application of Article 23(g) of the Hague Conventions during armed conflict. The extensive damage caused to the environment by Iraq was found to have violated Article 23(g) of the Hague Regulations regarding the destruction of enemy property, most famously remembered as the fiery lit oil wells left to burn in Kuwait in 1990. Paragraph 16 of UNSCR 687 stated that 'Iraq … is liable under international law for any … damage, including environmental damage and the depletion of natural resources … as a result of Iraq's unlawful invasion and occupation of Kuwait'.[95] The scale of the damage and the long-term and irreversible nature of the destruction resulted in a specific requirement to compensate for environmental damage.

Toxication of water, soil or crops caused by nanomaterials may reach the standard of 'destruction to enemy property'. The widespread use of nanomaterials in weapons systems that could potentially contaminate water tables, food and air would fall within the same category as the environmental damage deliberately wreaked on Kuwait. With the precedent provided by the UNCC decisions, States can and should be held accountable for environmental damage caused by the use of any nanomaterials during armed conflict that could be considered 'destruction to enemy property'. This could occur in instances where environmental damage in occupied territories affects anything deemed to be 'enemy property', including crops, water tables and similar environmental features. As noted in Chapter 2, the effect of nanomaterials is virtually invisible, widespread and may potentially cause long-term harm. This harm may result from nanomaterials entering water tables and food chains and transferring across human membranes, with potentially toxic effects that are only beginning to be understood.

Another issue is whether new resources may be sought out by those occupying a territory. Some commentators propound that the Occupying Power is forbidden to deplete oil reserves, which must remain unexploited.[96] While the question of whether sovereignty of natural resources is vested in governments or in peoples is interesting,[97] it is not likely that

[95] SC Res 687, UN SCOR, 2981st mtg, UN Doc S/RES/687 (8 April 1991) [16].

[96] Brice Claggett and O Thomas Johnson Jr, 'May Israel as a Belligerent Occupant Lawfully Exploit Previously Unexploited Oil Resources of the Gulf of Suez?' (1978) 72(3) *American Journal of International Law* 558, 575–576.

[97] Emeka Duruigbo, 'Permanent Sovereignty and Peoples' Ownership of Natural Resources in International Law' (2006) 38(1) *George Washington International Law Review* 33, 43–50.

it will be the relevant question for the purpose of considering the use of nanomaterials in war.

For the purposes of the use of nanomaterials during armed conflict or occupation, not harming the environment, or leaving it in a state worse than it was found, may have relevance for nanoparticles' impact on the environment – one of the key principles of usufruct. This would apply to residual nanomaterials left by thermobaric weapons, or any other use of weapons that leaves residual nanomaterials.

III Post–Vietnam War Environmental Protection in Armed Conflict

Agent Orange was used by the United States in the Vietnam War to remove foliage from the trees, to destroy enemy cover, mobility and, in some cases, deliberately contaminate sources of food. Between 1963 and 1972, the United States Air Force also seeded clouds in operations designed to lengthen the rainy season to make life for combatants on the ground unpleasant and unpaved roads impossible to traverse.[98] At the time of these attacks, in 1973, Brownlie concluded that, '[t]hough the position may soon change, general international law (or customary law) contains no rules or standards related to the protection of the environment as such'.[99] He did note that *lex lata* had 'major relevance' for the potential realisation of environmental protection, namely through the rules relating to State responsibility; the territorial sovereignty of States; and, finally, the concept of the freedom of the seas.[100]

It was against this historical backdrop that ENMOD was negotiated in 1976. Negotiators of ENMOD suggested use of the term 'stability of the ecosystems', but this was discarded and replaced by the expression 'widespread, long-term or severe damage'.[101] The following year, in

[98] Arthur Westing, *Ecological Consequences of the Second Indochina War* (Almqvist & Wiksell International, 1976) 27. Three types of herbicides were used: Agents Orange and White interfered with plant metabolism, while Agent Blue dehydrated plants. These herbicides were distributed by aircraft, helicopters and even truck- and boat-mounted sprayers.

[99] Ian Brownlie, 'A Survey of International Customary Rules of Environmental Protection' (1973) 13 *Natural Resources Journal* 179, 179 <http://digitalrepository.unm.edu/cgi/viewcontent.cgi?article=3333&context=nrj>.

[100] Ibid.

[101] Hans Blix, 'Means and Methods of Combat' in Henry Dunant Institute, *International Dimensions of Humanitarian Law* (Martinus Nijhoff, 1988) 150.

1977, API to the Geneva Conventions included two articles prohibiting warfare that may cause 'widespread, long-term and severe damage to the natural environment'.[102] The progression during this period was one of moving from a 'utilitarian' approach towards the value of the environment, and a shift to a more 'intrinsic value' approach. These international treaties remain the most relevant to the protection of the environment during armed conflict. Nonetheless, the required standards are still too high for proving a breach, and are highly problematic in light of the way that nanomaterials may cause harm that is virtually impossible to map or identify.

In 1996, the relevance of international environmental law in armed conflict was recognised by the ICJ in the *Nuclear Weapons Advisory Opinion*, where it was held that environmental protection may be a relevant factor in determining whether the use of a weapon is illegal under circumstances where life is not sustainable,[103] and that, 'the general obligation of States to ensure that activities within their jurisdiction or control respect the environment of other States or of areas beyond national control is now part of the corpus of international law relating to the environment'.[104] As the means and methods of war involve increasingly sophisticated technology, the potential scope and variety of the kinds of irreversible damage that may be caused to future generations require more careful scientific analysis and greater consideration of the risks to the environment than ever before.

Introducing specific standards that protect the environment during armed conflict has been met with some concern by both the ICRC and by some States, although for very different reasons. The ICRC has expressed concerns that applying the intrinsic approach of environmental protection could detract from and ultimately decrease human protection, as humans would not be the primary focus of protection during armed conflict and could therefore be compromised.[105] I do not believe that this is a position that should be seriously countenanced, given the potential risks to humans if the environment is not protected during armed conflict. Both humans *and* the environment need to be protected during armed conflict. Concerns regarding elevating the protection of the

102 *Additional Protocol I* arts 35(3), 55.

103 *Legality of the Threat or Use of Nuclear Weapons (Advisory Opinion)* [1996] ICJ Rep 226, 243 [33].

104 Ibid 241–242 [29].

105 Schmitt, 'Green War', n 31, 7.

environment during armed conflict were shared by some States, but for a very different reason, namely that the added requirement of consideration of the environment may limit the ability to target otherwise legitimate military targets. It was noted that consideration of protection of the environment may 'distort proportionality calculations and thereby immunize valid military objectives'.[106] Whether for the reasons expressed by the ICRC or due to the concerns raised by States, there was an overall acknowledgement of the desirability of providing greater protection of the environment simultaneously coupled with a general reluctance to raise legal standards for protection of the environment for fear that it would unsettle a delicate balance inherent in the laws of war. Ideally, new treaty law providing adequate environmental protection should be negotiated.

A Prohibition of Military or Hostile Use of Environmental Modification Techniques

In 1976, ENMOD was drafted. The ICRC documents and the negotiating history provide no further insights into what the drafters intended beyond the definitions provided by the Committee on Disarmament as an appendix to ENMOD when they presented the draft text to the General Assembly in 1976.[107]

Article 1 requires,

> Each State Party to this Convention undertakes not to engage in military or any other hostile use of environmental modification techniques having widespread, long-lasting *or* severe effects as the means of destruction, damage or injury to any other State Party.[108]

This Convention is only very rarely applicable to the point of irrelevance because the definition of damage to the environment is narrow, and the standard for breach is high: the damage required must be 'widespread, long-lasting or severe', and with the intention of being an 'environmental modification technique'. The definition of 'long-lasting' is held to be 'a period of months, or approximately a season'; widespread 'encompassing

[106] Ibid.

[107] Michael Schmitt, 'War and the Environment: Fault Lines in the Prescriptive Landscape' in Jay Austin and Carl Bruch (eds), *The Environmental Consequences of War: Legal, Economic and Scientific* (Cambridge University Press, 2000) 105–107.

[108] *Environmental Modification Convention* art 1 (emphasis added).

an area on the scale of several hundred square kilometres', and 'severe' involving 'serious or significant disruption or harm to human life, natural and economic resources or other assets'.[109]

In the case of nanomaterials, the area that is affected may be hard to define, and the definition of long-lasting may require decades to show damage, rather than a season. In some instances, the harm may have already occurred but not be evident for some time. These are high thresholds of damage to prove and assess and are different thresholds to those of API (discussed later in the chapter). The temporal threshold for ENMOD is, however, more protective of the environment than that of API. Under ENMOD, the term 'long-lasting' is reasonably defined as a period of months or approximately a season, unlike API, under which 'long-term' is defined as 'a matter of decades', a threshold for which it is virtually impossible to demonstrate a breach.[110] These differences are significant for nanomaterials, such as those used in thermobaric weapons, or in membranes, batteries or any other nanomaterial waste, where longevity of the impact is not yet known. Limiting the period to a 'matter of decades' may be too long, and too late by the time the toxicology profile of nanoparticles is fully known.

The issue of the protection of the environment during armed conflict was raised in the public consciousness again in 1990 during the Gulf War, where deliberate destruction of the environment through the lighting of over 600 oil fires and the destruction of crops drew attention to the significance of the long-term impact of environmental damage.[111] Damage from the oil fires' smoke, also at the nanoscale, was held to attract compensation for damages at the time by the UNCC.

[109] The Understandings were not incorporated into the Convention but were included in the report transmitted by the Conference: *Report of the Conference of the Committee on Disarmament: Volume I*, UN GAOR, 31st sess, Supp No 27, UN Doc A/31/27 (1976) 91–92.

[110] Karen Hulme, *War Torn Environment: Interpreting the Legal Threshold* (Brill Academic Publishers, 2004) 5.

[111] Payne and Sand, n 44. The United Nations Security Council established the ad hoc United Nations Compensation Commission (UNCC) to address reparations as a component of the ceasefire following Iraq's 1990–1991 invasion and occupation of Kuwait. The UNCC addressed important questions of state responsibility, environmental liability, mass claims processing, international law and dispute settlement institutions in the post-armed conflict context.

In 1992, a call was made for a fifth Geneva Convention regarding the environment,[112] and in the same year, the United Nations General Assembly (UNGA) called for a debate specifically on the protection of the environment during armed conflict. This resulted in UNGA Resolution 47/37,[113] which reiterated the existing legal frameworks (1907 Hague Convention, API, ENMOD and the Rio Declaration) and urged 'States to take all measures to ensure compliance with the existing international law applicable to the protection of the environment in times of armed conflict'.[114] This UNGA Resolution also called for the ICRC to report on the protection of the environment in times of armed conflict, 'and to submit to the General Assembly . . . a report on activities reported by the Committee'.[115] Further, the same Resolution stated in its Preamble that 'destruction of the environment, not justified by military necessity and carried out wantonly, is contrary to existing international law'. The UNGA Resolution fell short of identifying specific gaps in the existing international legal framework and did not suggest any amendments or modifications to the existing law. It did not identify nanomaterials as posing one of these risks.

In 1994, the ICRC submitted a proposal, as requested by UNGA Resolution 47/37, in Guidelines for Military Manuals and Instructions on the Protection of the Environment in Times of Armed Conflict.[116] Without formally approving the document, the UNGA invited all States to disseminate the guidelines and to 'give due consideration to the possibility of incorporating them' into their national manuals.[117] This is significant because protection of the environment during armed conflict requires not only high-level international legal agreements but also practical rules in military manuals and instructions to be correctly applied on any battlefield. In the case of the use of nanomaterials, granular instructions about the risks and potential governance structures

[112] Glen Plant (ed), *Environmental Protection and the Law of War: Elements of a 'Fifth Geneva' Convention on the Protection of the Environment in Times of Armed Conflict* (Bellhaven, 1992) 43.

[113] *Protection of the Environment in Times of Armed Conflict*, GA Res 47/37, UN GAOR, 47th sess, 73rd plen mtg, Agenda Item 136, UN Doc A/RES/47/37 (9 February 1993).

[114] Ibid art 1.

[115] Ibid art 4.

[116] 'Guidelines for Military Manuals and Instructions on the Environment in Times of Armed Conflict' (1996) 36(311) *International Review of the Red Cross* 231.

[117] *Protection of the Environment in Times of Armed Conflict*, GA Res 47/37, UN GAOR, 47th sess, 73rd plen mtg, Agenda Item 136, UN Doc A/RES/47/37 (9 February 1993).

required to protect civilian populations and their environment from potential harm are urgently required.

Most recently, in 2018, in a case before the ICJ, Costa Rica claimed compensation for environmental damage caused by the creation of three canals, or canõ, within its territory. It was noted that Nicaragua had removed over 300 trees and cleared 6.19 hectares of vegetation. This case was the first time the Court took a position on the evaluation of environmental damage, noting that it was,

> appropriate to approach the valuation of environmental damage from the perspective of the ecosystem as a whole, by adopting an overall assessment of the impairment or loss of the environmental goods and services prior to recovery, rather than attributing values to specific categories of environmental goods and services and estimating recovery periods for each of them.[118]

The Court went on to note that 'the absence of certainty' as to the extent of the damage did not preclude the Court from awarding damages,[119] both for monitoring and assessment of the damage and for remediation of the damage, noting that the UNCC had set the same precedent. This case demonstrates that the ICJ has internalised the intrinsic value of the environment that must be taken into account in assessing any sustained damage, which will hopefully also be reflected in future judgments, and in particular, any environmental damage sustained as a result of nanomaterials and their release into the environment during armed conflict.

B Additional Protocol I to the Geneva Conventions

The Diplomatic Conference on the Reaffirmation and Development of International Humanitarian Law Applicable in Armed Conflicts, convened by the ICRC, was attended by representatives of over 100 nations and 50 NGO or intergovernmental organisations in four sessions over four years. API borrowed language from both the Hague Conventions and from the Geneva Conventions. Most of the provisions in the laws of war that provide protection to the environment are indirect. This Protocol provided direct protection of the environment for the first time.

118 *Certain Activities Carried Out by Nicaragua in the Border Area (Costa Rica v Nicaragua) (Judgment)* (International Court of Justice, General List No 150, 2 February 2018) [78].
119 Ibid [86].

APII does not address environmental damage, and so is not discussed further here.

The focus of Article 35(3) of API is on the effect on the environment, in comparison with ENMOD where the provisions refer more specifically to the technique used, a response at the time to the use of Agent Orange in Vietnam. The provisions in API provide a wider catch-all protection for the environment than ENMOD, insofar as these provisions cover not only intentional damage but also unintentional and incidental damage. Article 35(3) was included to appease those who believed that the environment had intrinsic value, by pointing to a standard of damage to the environment, rather than assessing the effect on the environment in human terms.[120] In a sense, Article 35(3) extends the traditional protection proffered to humans to protect them in armed conflict to protect the environment in armed conflict as well.

Note the language of Article 35(3) of API, which prohibits,

> methods or means of warfare which are intended, or may be expected, to cause widespread, long-term *and* severe damage to the natural environment.[121]

Article 48 states that,

> In order to ensure respect for and protection of the civilian population and civilian objects, the Parties to the conflict shall at all times distinguish between the civilian population and combatants and between civilian objects and military objectives and accordingly shall direct their operations only against military objectives.

Article 52(2) of API defines military objectives as,

> those that by nature, location, purpose or use make an effective contribution to military action and whose total or partial destruction, capture or neutralization, in the circumstances ruling at the time, offers a definite military advantage.[122]

This language leaves unclear whether environmental targets, such as chemical plants, or natural resources potentially under dispute, could

[120] George Aldrich, 'Progressive Development of the Laws of War: A Reply to Criticisms of the 1977 Geneva Protocol I' (1986) 26 *Virginia Journal of International Law* 693; Schmitt, 'Green War', n 31, 14.

[121] *Additional Protocol I* art 35(3) (emphasis added). It is worth noting that the United States has not ratified Additional Protocol I and does not accept the articles as constituting customary law.

[122] *Additional Protocol I* art 52(2).

be characterised as a 'legitimate military target', even if their attack could have a profoundly detrimental environmental impact. If environmental protection were considered part of the 'humanitarian' equation in balancing against military necessity, it would be difficult to justify attacking targets that would have profound long-term effects on the civilian population. Further, nanomaterials are increasingly being used in military contexts which are not necessarily weapons, but the long-lasting environmental impact of which remains unknown, making their use subject to ENMOD or API.[123]

Article 54(2) of API states,

> It is prohibited to attack, destroy, remove or render useless objects indispensable to the survival of the civilian population, such as foodstuffs, agricultural areas for production of foodstuffs, crops, livestock, drinking water installations and supplies and irrigation works, for the specific purpose of denying them for their sustenance value to the civilian population or to the adverse Party, whatever the motive, whether in order to starve out civilians, to cause them to move away, or for any other motive.

Article 54(2) is somewhat eroded by Article 54(5), which states that military necessity as a principle has priority,

> derogation from the prohibitions contained in paragraph 2 may be made by a party to the conflict within such territory under its own control where required by imperative military necessity.

Article 55(1) of API provides a cumulatively high bar for protection, in that,

1. Care shall be taken in warfare to protect the natural environment against widespread, long-term *and* severe damage. This protection includes a prohibition of the use of methods or means of warfare which are intended or may be expected to cause such damage to the natural environment and thereby to prejudice the health or survival of the population.
2. Attacks against the natural environment by way of reprisals are prohibited.[124]

[123] Homeland Defense and Security Information Analysis Centre, *State of the Art Report: Uses of Nanotechnology on Surfaces for Military Applications* (17 October 2016) <www.hdiac.org/system/files/20161017_HDIAC_SOAR_Nanotech_FINAL_reduced%20size.pdf>.

[124] *Additional Protocol I* art 55(1) (emphasis added).

The definition of severe is unclear, particularly over a long period. It is uncertain whether the use of nanomaterials in 'means or methods' of warfare would reach this standard. In fact, one commentary on Article 35 (3) has suggested that it would,

> not impose any significant limitation on combatants waging conventional warfare. It seems primarily directed instead to high-level decision-makers and would affect such unconventional means of warfare as the massive use of herbicides and chemical agents which could produce widespread, long-term and severe damage to the natural environment.[125]

Further, each of these individual conditions has been interpreted in such a way that they would be difficult to fulfil, even individually. The definition of long-term seems to be a measurement of decades and not years or months – an extremely high standard with enormous long-term repercussions,[126] which may not cover nanoparticles left by thermobaric weapons, using nanomaterials which may be toxic but disperse quickly, and not be able to be proven to cause damage for years in one location. The use of nanomaterials in such a way that harm could be 'reasonably expected' needs to be avoided.

In fact, the very nature of nanoparticles means that they will travel through water tables and enter food chains without being easily detectable. The definition of widespread and severe has been defined as 'damage as would be likely to prejudice over a long term the continued survival of the civilian population or would risk causing it major health problems'.[127] Research to date has indicated that the toxicity of nanomaterials is long-term. Nanomaterials may cause health risks that are not immediately apparent but may result in long-term toxicity and health implications if consumed in food or water. The thresholds provided for in API would almost inevitably be too high to protect against long-term toxicity of nanomaterials, which, even if able to be established, would be too late. It is unlikely that this threshold would provide adequate protection from the potential harm caused by residual nanoparticles.

[125] Michael Bothe et al, *New Rules for Victims of Armed Conflict: Commentary on the Two 1977 Protocols Additional to the Geneva Conventions of 1949* (Martinus Nijhoff, 1982) 348.

[126] Ibid.

[127] Yves Sandoz, Christophe Swinarski and Bruno Zimmermann (eds), *Commentary on the Additional Protocols of 8 June 1977 to the Geneva Conventions of 12 August 1949* (Martinus Nijhoff, 1987) 1454–1455.

When Article 35(3) of API was drafted, the Precautionary Principle, which was discussed earlier in the chapter, was not prominent in discussions, and Article 35(3) remains silent about situations where the risks are unclear. The duty of care requirement of Article 55(1) of API requires the taking of reasonable steps to prevent damage to the environment.[128] I suggest that a reasonable interpretation of this provision should include the Precautionary Principle, and therefore an environmental impact assessment should be required as part of an Article 36 weapons review in every circumstance where a new nanomaterial is included in a weapons system.[129] In order to comply with international environmental legal standards under the Precautionary Principle, the onus is on those using nanomaterials in war to identify and be responsible for the short- and long-term harm they may cause. More recently, negotiations at the UN on the Biodiversity Beyond National Jurisdiction (BBNJ) are moving in the direction of entrenching the precautionary principle in this instrument.[130]

C *World Charter for Nature*

Adopted by a resolution of the UNGA in 1982, the World Charter for Nature[131] was developed by the International Union for the Conservation of Nature (IUCN), formerly known as the World Conservation Union. This resolution tackles head on the need to prevent environmental damage during armed conflict. Principle 5 requires that '[n]ature shall be secured against degradation caused by warfare or other hostile activities'.[132] Principle 11 notes that '[a]ctivities which might have an impact on nature shall be controlled, and the best available technologies that minimise significant risks to nature or other adverse effects shall be used', then continues to categorise specific types of harm and the need to rehabilitate those areas affected.[133] Although useful in its content,

[128] Hulme, n 110, 81.

[129] Ibid 85–86.

[130] United Nations General Assembly, 'Speakers Consider Criteria for Area-Based Management Tools, as Negotiations on Draft Treaty to Protect Marine Biodiversity Enter Third Day' (Media Release, 21 August 2019) <www.un.org/press/en/2019/sea2111.doc.htm>.

[131] *World Charter for Nature*, GA Resolution 37/7, UN GAOR, 37th sess, 48th plen mtg, UN Doc A/RES/37/7 (28 October 1982).

[132] Ibid principle 5.

[133] Ibid principle 11.

given its explicit reference to the impact on the environment, a UNGA resolution does not necessarily have much of an impact on how wars are fought, and is not a strong enough legal source to regulate environmental damage during armed conflict.

There may be other international environmental legal agreements that also apply during armed conflict, even if they do not expressly state this intention. Without specific language that excludes their use during armed conflict, protection would continue to be provided by the Convention for the Protection of the World Cultural and Natural Heritage;[134] the Convention on Wetlands of International Importance especially as Waterfowl Habitat;[135] and the Convention on Biological Diversity.[136] These protections may be significant where the protected areas are targeted during armed conflict, and they may provide another layer of legal protection.

IV Nanomaterials and Parallels with Depleted Uranium Munitions

The legality of the use of nanomaterials has some parallels with long-standing discussions of the legality of the use of DIME.[137] DIME deliberately uses an explosive spray of superheated radioactive micro-shrapnel made from milled and powdered heavy metal tungsten alloy (HMTA), which is highly lethal within a relatively small area over a long period of

[134] *Convention Concerning the Protection of the World Cultural and Natural Heritage*, opened for signature 16 November 1972, 1037 UNTS 151 (entered into force 17 December 1975). The Convention specifically states that 'the outbreak of the threat of an armed conflict' is sufficient to place a property on the World Heritage in Danger list. The inclusion of a provision that applies only during armed conflict indicates that the drafters intend for the Convention to continue to apply during armed conflict.

[135] *Convention on Wetlands of International Importance Especially as Waterfowl Habitat*, opened for signature 2 February 1971, 996 UNTS 245 (entered into force 21 December 1975). It has been suggested that this Convention continues to apply during times of armed conflict, albeit in a slightly modified manner, given the mention of the terminology 'situations of urgent national interest'.

[136] *Convention on Biological Diversity*, opened for signature 5 June 1992, 1760 UNTS 79 (entered into force 29 December 1993). There is no indication as to whether this treaty is considered to continue to apply during armed conflict, although some have argued that it is analogous to a human rights treaty and should continue to apply. See Silja Vöneky, 'A New Shield for the Environment: Peacetime Treaties as Legal Restraints of Wartime Damage' (2003) *Review of European, Comparative and International Environmental* Law <https://doi.org/10.1111/1467-9388.00229>.

[137] *Yugoslavia v United States* (1999) 38(4) ILM 1188.

time.[138] One author notes that, 'the use of weapons containing depleted uranium is having far-reaching consequences for human life' and almost certainly for the environment.[139] The same can be argued of certain man-made metallic nanoparticles.

Although at the microscale rather than the nanoscale, DIME has properties that might be similar to toxic nanoparticles in that they are difficult to detect, cause inter-generational health issues, and are difficult to remove once they have leached into water tables and ecosystems.[140] Like DIME, potential exposure to nanomaterials by military personnel, civilians, post-conflict peacekeepers, relief workers and livestock may have intergenerational effects through inhalation, ingestion or other exposure through the skin. The longer the conflict, the greater the risk of exposure for each of these groups. Unsurprisingly, women and children are most likely to suffer from exposure from DIME,[141] given their interaction with the soil and water through women's frequent exposure to gardening and children to play.[142] Nanomaterials share potential toxicity for human genes with DIME, about which little is yet known.[143] Given these uncertainties, it is hard to imagine a circumstance where DIME, or nanoparticles behaving similarly to DIME, could be legally used in munitions or any other uses on the battlefield, particularly as their risks become 'reasonably foreseeable' as scientific research becomes clearer on their potential long-term harm.

In 1999, the Federal Republic of Yugoslavia (FRY) filed complaints against the then ten countries[144] forming the North Atlantic Treaty Organization (NATO) that bombed FRY. Part of their claim related to the bombing of oil refineries and chemical plants that they argued was in

[138] See David Hambling, 'Cancer Worries for New U.S. Bombs, DefenseTech' (22 May 2006) *Military.com* <www.military.com/defensetech/2006/05/22/cancer-worries-for-new-u-s-bombs>; *Dense Inert Metal Explosive (DIME)* (2017) Global Security <www.globalsecurity.org/military/systems/munitions/dime.htm>.

[139] *Yugoslavia v United States* (1999) 38(4) ILM 1188, 1189.

[140] Brar et al, n 3.

[141] Cristina Giannardi and Daniele Dominici, 'Military Use of Depleted Uranium: Assessment of Prolonged Population Exposure' (2003) 64(2/3) *Journal of Environmental Radioactivity* 227.

[142] Rosalie Bertell, *Depleted Uranium as a Weapon of War* (August 1999) <www.begegnungszentrum.at/texte/bertell/bertell2-du.htm>.

[143] Laila Benameur, Liu Wei and Alain Botta, 'Genotoxicity of Nanoparticles' in Bharat Bhushan (ed), *Encyclopedia of Nanotechnology* (Springer, 2012) 952–962.

[144] The case could not be filed directly against NATO, as the ICJ only has jurisdiction over States. The ten States involved were Belgium, Canada, France, Germany, Italy, Netherlands, Portugal, Spain, the United Kingdom and the United States.

breach of an obligation not to cause environmental damage. The use of DIME was also argued to be in breach of the prohibition not to cause far-reaching health and environmental damage.[145] The ICJ found that the Court lacked jurisdiction *prima facie* for this particular case, but emphasised that its findings 'in no way prejudge(d) the question of the jurisdiction of the Court to deal with the merits' and left 'unaffected the rights of the Government of Yugoslavia (and of the Respondent States) to submit arguments regarding those questions'.[146] The ICJ is a legitimate forum for resolving such disputes between States, and a forum for advisory opinions, such as whether the environment requires protection when using certain means or methods of warfare including nanomaterials. The ICJ has dealt with many cases that have involved decisions regarding the environment since its consideration of the *Nuclear Weapons Advisory Opinion*.[147] Some feel that 'established and commonly referred to environmental principles' are not referred to enough by the ICJ.[148] This may be an indication of the challenge of applying environmental principles, as they stand, to individual disputes. The overall contribution of the ICJ to international environmental law remains modest, despite affirming the obligation of States to protect the environment; to prevent transboundary harm to other areas beyond national jurisdiction; and to carry out environmental impact assessments before potentially harmful activities are authorised.[149] The environmental jurisprudence of the ICJ appears to still be overly cautious compared to the more committed attitude

[145] *Yearbook of the International Court of Justice 1999–2000* (United Nations, 2000) 182.

[146] International Court of Justice, 'Legality of Use of Force: The Court extends by one year the time-limits for the filing by Yugoslavia of written statements on the preliminary objections made by the Respondent States' (Press Release, 23 February 2001) 2 <www.icj-cij.org/files/case-related/107/107-20010223-PRE-01-00-EN.pdf>.

[147] These include: *Gabcikovo-Nagymaros Project (Hungary v Slovakia)* [1997] ICJ Rep 7; *Fisheries Jurisdiction Case (Spain v Canada)* [1998] ICJ Rep 432; *Pulp Mills in the River Uruguay (Argentina v Uruguay) (Request for the Indication of Provisional Measures)* (2006) 45 ILM 1025; and more recently, Ecuador instituted proceedings against Colombia for the aerial spraying of toxic herbicides that is allegedly causing damage to people, animals, crops and the natural environment across its border: see *Aerial Herbicide Spraying (Ecuador v Colombia)* [2013] ICJ Rep 278.

[148] Afshin Akhtarkhavari, 'Environmental Principles and the International Court of Justice' (2009) 28 *Australian Year Book of International Law* 101. In *Certain Activities Carried Out by Nicaragua in the Border Area (Costa Rica v Nicaragua) (Judgment)* (International Court of Justice, General List No 150, 2 February 2018), the focus was on the procedural requirement to undertake environmental impact assessments.

[149] *Certain Activities Carried Out by Nicaragua in the Border Area (Costa Rica v Nicaragua) (Judgment)* (International Court of Justice, General List No 150, 2 February 2018).

adopted by other competing jurisdictions. The ICJ has a role to play in establishing accountability for environmental degradation caused by materials, such as nanomaterials, during war, the full risks of which are not yet known.

V Implementation, Enforcement and Recommendations for Environmental Law

In addition to the decisions made by the ICJ and other courts, frameworks and guidelines that balance scientific research with environmental protection are needed. Careful consideration must be given to the benchmarks for effective assessment of the toxicity of new nanomaterials, particularly given the difficulty of assessing their long-term toxicity. As the ability to use and integrate nanomaterials into military systems increases, the urgency to monitor the effect of nanoparticles on the environment will increase. Publications such as the Organisation for Economic Co-operation and Development's Series on the Safety of Manufactured Nanomaterials[150] provide up to date information about the toxicity of certain nanoparticles and should be coordinated to share information with bodies such as the SAB of the CWC and the Expert Panels for the BWC.[151] It is important that this information is shared with the international legal community to ensure regulatory bodies keep apace of the technologies and include definitions that ensure toxic nanomaterials are not used in the battlefield, either deliberately or inadvertently. The intersection of the laws of war and international environmental law is not well-equipped to deal with the pervasive spread of nanomaterials that may have serious but medium-term effects, and also indirect and unknown effects. States need to address these risks but also gather further information to understand the risks, so that they may be better regulated and the environment better protected.

Ideally, the environment would remain protected at all times during war. In cases where it is not, it is important that those who disregard the environment and cause it harm be held accountable. There has already

[150] OECD, *Publications in the Series on the Safety of Manufactured Nanomaterials* (2018) <www.oecd.org/env/ehs/nanosafety/publications-series-safety-manufactured-nanomaterials.htm>.

[151] Kobi Leins and Diana M Bowman, 'Nanomaterials: A Tale of Two Applications' in William Boothby (ed), *New Technologies: The Law in War and Peace* (Cambridge University Press, 2019) 285–314.

been one United Nations subsidiary body, the UNCC, set up under international law that has comprehensively considered compensation for environmental damage sustained during armed conflict. The decisions of the UNCC, as discussed previously, are a useful resource when considering the application of the laws of war to nanomaterials. The UNCC is often overlooked but is highly relevant because of its rich source of precedents for evaluating environmental damage, perhaps due to the highly politicised nature of the Security Council resolution that established it.[152] The framework and the decisions adopted by the Governing Council of the UNCC provide an extremely useful tool to understand the application of environmental law in armed conflict. One team of international lawyers was assigned claims of an environmental nature, totalling $85 billion, although of those 109 claims, the amount finally awarded in compensation totalled $5.3 billion. Decisions made by the UNCC not only set a precedent in terms of their ability to establish environmental damage but also their progressive methodology in quantifying environmental damage, such as in the case of establishing harm caused by inhaling smoke from the Gulf fires. The methodology of the UNCC has not been widely used, although Payne and Sand argue that it could usefully be applied in other cases where environmental harm is caused by conflict.[153]

The reports of the Governing Council of the UNCC (set up to quantify the damage caused by Iraq's invasion of Kuwait in 1991) are a useful resource in analysing, valuing and deciding how to award financial compensation for environmental harm during armed conflict, and provide an excellent model for future forums or courts tasked with similar mandates. The underlying principle applied was that 'the general rule is to restore what has been damaged to integrity or, if this is not possible, to provide an equivalent for it'.[154] Part of that responsibility was held to

[152] Ruth Wedgwood, 'The Enforcement of Security Council Resolution 687: The Threat of Force Against Iraq's Weapons of Mass Destruction' (1998) 92(4) *American Journal of International Law* 724.

[153] Payne and Sand, n 44.

[154] United Nations Compensation Commission Governing Council, *Report and Recommendations Made by the Panel of Commissioners Concerning the Fifth Instalment of 'F4' Claims*, UN Doc S/AC.26/2005/10 (30 June 2005) 24 [80]; Cymie Payne, 'UN Commission Awards Compensation for Environmental and Public Health Damage from 1990–91 Gulf War' (2005) 9(25) *American Society for International Law* <www.asil.org/insights/volume/9/issue/25/un-commission-awards-compensation-environmental-and-public-health-damage>.

include the provision of money for environmental monitoring and assessment of over $243 million. This approach may have been the first time that actual data was used to review claims, and the Precautionary Principle was applied to identify potential risks, including those linked to human health. Given that the ability to collect and assess data now far surpasses the capabilities available at the time of the UNCC's decision-making, this methodology could now be even more useful.

One forum for prosecuting breaches of international environmental law during armed conflict is the ICC, which was established by the Rome Statute in the summer of 1998. The provisions of the Rome Statute provide an eco-centric shift in the protection of the environment,[155] which may prove useful in regulating nanomaterials in conflict, should harmful inter-generational effects of nanoparticles be established.[156] This Statute provides, among other things, a framework for addressing international environmental law violations and contains provisions that both explicitly and by inference provide for jurisdiction over environmental damage caused during armed conflict. The Statute not only contains a provision that protects the environment but also makes it a criminal offence to cause environmental damage.

Article 8 of the Rome Statute states that the ICC has jurisdiction over war crimes, including grave breaches of the Geneva Conventions. Article 8(2)(a)(iv) of the Rome Statute criminalises 'extensive destruction and appropriation of property, not justified by military necessity and carried out unlawfully and wantonly'.[157] Article 8(2)(b)(ii) of the Rome Statute prohibits,

> Other serious violations of the laws and customs applicable in international armed conflict, within the established framework of international law, namely, any of the following acts ...

155 Jessica Lawrence and Kevin Heller, 'The First Ecocentral Environmental War Crime: The Limits of Article 8(2)(b)(iv) of the Rome Statute' (2007) 20 *Georgetown International Environmental Law Review* 61.

156 Ryan Gilman, 'Expanding Environmental Justice after War: The Need for Universal Jurisdiction over Environmental War Crimes' (2011) 22(3) *Colorado Journal of International Environmental Law and Policy* 447, 448: 'Universal jurisdiction developed because states realized, as they developed rules and customs in international law, that certain criminal offenses are objectionable to such a degree that prosecutions should not be thwarted based on jurisdictional loopholes'. Despite this lack of jurisdiction, some States have chosen to prosecute these crimes on the basis of universal jurisdiction.

157 *Rome Statute* art 8(2)(a)(iv).

> (ii) Intentionally directing attacks against civilian objects, that is, objects which are not military objectives[.][158]

Whether Articles 8(2)(a)(iv) or 8(2)(b)(ii) of the Rome Statute would include the environment under 'property' or 'civilian objects' remains untested. It may be difficult to fit pervasive environmental damage into these terms, particularly if Courts take an intrinsic worth approach to the environment. On the other hand, this provision may provide limited application to the environment where it falls within the category of being a civilian object. The environment needs to be front of mind in the application of the principle of proportionality, and ways to include protection of the environment require clarification and strengthening. This is one example of where the language of international criminal law, international environmental law and international humanitarian law have different meanings and remain ambiguous.

Although not yet invoked, the Prosecutor retains the right to initiate trial proceedings for environmental damage under this clause. This potential protection is an important step in the direction of codifying the protection of the environment during conflict. Article 8(2)(b)(iv) of the Rome Statute, as one of the definitions of war crimes, prohibits,

> Intentionally launching an attack in the knowledge that such attack will cause incidental loss of life or injury to civilians or damage to civilian objects or widespread, long-term and severe damage to the natural environment which would be clearly excessive in relation to the concrete and direct overall military advantage anticipated.

This clause adds the tests of military necessity and proportionality to the cumulative standard of 'widespread, long-term and severe'. It also adds the term 'overall' to qualify the term military advantage. This language incorporates the standard of requiring both the proof of the actual damage and the intention and knowledge that the attack would result in the damage caused. Finally, the inclusion of this terminology under section (b) instead of section (a), which contains grave breaches of the Geneva Conventions, means that States are not obliged to prosecute these crimes. Further, Article 22(2) of the Statute requires that any ambiguity as to definitions be construed in favour of the charged person.[159] Without modification to the Rome Statute, it is likely that interpretations used in ENMOD and API would be used to assist interpretation,

[158] Ibid art 8(2)(b)(ii).
[159] Ibid art 22(2).

providing prohibitively high standards for finding a violation, and inadequate protection from potentially toxic nanomaterials.

In 2016, the Prosecutor of the ICC issued a report on the policy for its case selection, noting that '[t]he Office will also seek to cooperate and provide assistance to States, upon request, with respect to conduct which constitutes a serious crime under national law, such as the illegal exploitation of natural resources ... or the destruction of the environment'.[160] In the same document, it was also noted that '[t]he manner of commission of the crimes may be assessed in light of ... crimes committed by means of, or resulting in, the destruction of the environment or of protected objects'.[161] Finally, the note mentioned the environment a third time, noting that,

> [t]he impact of the crimes may be assessed in light of ... environmental damage inflicted on the affected communities. In this context, the Office will give particular consideration to prosecuting the Rome Statute crimes that are committed by means of, or that result in, *inter alia*, the destruction of the environment, the illegal exploitation of natural resources or the illegal dispossession of land.

This policy does not alter the scope of the Rome Statute, but it does indicate a clear intention of the Office of the Prosecutor to prioritise cases that have caused damage to the environment. The practical impact of this theoretical prioritisation remains to be seen but is likely to be helpful for addressing the risks of using nanomaterials.

The recent 2017 Global Pact for the Environment is an initiative to conclude a legally binding international instrument to protect the environment (including a clause on armed conflict) under the auspices of the United Nations, which synthesises the principles outlined in the Stockholm Declaration, the World Charter for Nature, the Rio Declaration and other instruments, to solidify the environmental rule of law around the world and achieve the 2030 Agenda for Sustainable Development,

> Article 19: Armed conflicts
>
> States shall take pursuant to their obligations under international law all feasible measures to protect the environment in relation to armed conflicts.

160 Office of the Prosecutor, *Policy Paper on Case Selection and Prioritisation* (15 September 2016) International Criminal Court 5 <www.icc-cpi.int/itemsDocuments/20160915_OTP-Policy_Case-Selection_Eng.pdf>.

161 Ibid 13.

In 2018, the UNGA adopted a resolution in relation to the 2017 Global Pact, setting in motion a process to discuss and potentially reach agreement on an international instrument. The Global Pact includes in its text the language that 'States shall take pursuant to their obligations under international law all feasible measures to protect the environment in relation to armed conflicts'.[162] Requirements of intention, severity or long-term damage do not need to be proven: all the Global Pact requires is that States protect the environment as best they can during armed conflict, and that this be done pursuant to their obligations under international law. It remains to be clarified what 'feasible measures' means where the environmental risks may not be immediately apparent, as is the case with nanomaterials.

VI Conclusion

The ILC has concluded that the environmental impact of armed conflict may pose 'a serious threat to the livelihoods and even existence of individual human beings and communities'.[163] The international legal community is appraised of the risks of environmental damage during armed conflicts, and these have been outlined in detail in numerous documents, along with statements outlining a greater need for legal protection, prepared by the Special Rapporteur appointed by the ILC.[164] For this reason, the ILC has considered in much detail the adequacy of the existing legal framework, not just of the laws of war, but of treaty law in general, which it has held continues to apply during armed conflict. The ILC concludes that the protection provided by the laws of war is inadequate.

[162] Le Club des Juristes, *Draft Project Global Pact for the Environment* (24 June 2017) International Union for Conservation of Nature <www.iucn.org/sites/dev/files/content/documents/draft-project-of-the-global-pact-for-the-environment.pdf>.

[163] Marie Jacobsson, *Report of the International Law Commission, Sixty-third Session*, UN GAOR, 66th sess, Supp No 10, UN Doc A/66/10 (2011) Annex E ('*Protection of the Environment in Relation to Armed Conflicts*') 351.

[164] Marie Jacobsson, *Preliminary Report on the Protection of the Environment in Relation to Armed Conflicts*, UN GAOR, 66th sess, UN Docs A/CN.4/674 (30 May 2014) and A/CN.4/674/Corr.1 (11 August 2014); Marie Jacobsson, *Second Report on the Protection of the Environment in Relation to Armed Conflicts*, UN GAOR, 67th sess, UN Doc A/CN.4/685 (28 May 2015); Marie Jacobsson, *Third Report on the Protection of the Environment in Relation to Armed Conflicts*, UN GAOR, 68th sess, UN Doc A/CN.4/700 (3 June 2016).

Increasingly, policymakers are turning their attention to the need to protect 'ecosystem services' or the natural environment on which humans depend for existence. Indeed, concepts such as 'ecosystem services' and 'natural capital' have been developed to signal the need for law and policy to economically value environmental loss – which has intrinsic value, not just for humans – and thus create a greater commitment to preventing destruction in the first place. As sea levels rise and inhabitable land areas diminish, increased conflict, particularly over natural resources, will be inevitable. Population density on decreased land masses will increase pressure on existing natural resources, which are already seriously stretched in some places, to the point of being unsustainable. As discussed earlier in this chapter, the Martens Clause has particular potential to provide protection in response to changing values of the environment.

As noted in Young's upcoming publication,

> 'the environment' is often left behind when the interests of states are shaped by, and pursued through, other regimes, whose functional orientation does not prioritize ecological concerns. Those other regimes have institutional strength and compulsory dispute settlement, while environmental principles are often scattered amongst custom and non-binding instruments.[165]

None of the international environmental law analysed in this chapter adequately protects the environment from toxic nanoparticles with direct, and indirect, and medium- to long-term implications for human health and the environment, and institutions and compulsory dispute settlement mechanisms, as highlighted by Young, are sorely lacking. As this chapter shows, the existing international law and principles attempt to protect against acute short-term direct environmental damage with an impact on humans, and long-term, pervasive direct impacts. The existing law does not protect from the unknown risks of nanomaterials, or the long-term invisible risks to the environment and human health

The extremely high thresholds of geographical reach and lengthy timeframes required by ENMOD and API are entirely inadequate to deal with the risks posed by the as-yet-not-entirely-known toxicity of nanomaterials, as well as the challenges in detecting or removing them from

[165] Margaret A Young, 'Fragmentation and International Environmental Law' in Lavanya Rajamani and Jacqueline Peel (eds), *Oxford Handbook of International Environmental Law* (Oxford University Press, 2nd ed, forthcoming) <https://papers.ssrn.com/sol3/papers.cfm?abstract_id=3441535>.

the environment once released. The existing legal standards, discussed in detail in this chapter, are outdated and not at all suited to the nature of new technologies and materials. New regulatory frameworks contemplating the nature of unseen nanomaterials in the environment and their potential deleterious effects on long-term health that may take years to eventuate need to be contemplated and negotiated now. Protection of the environment from nanomaterials in war is urgently required. As noted by the ILC and in the Global Pact, new standards that reflect new technologies need to be agreed by States to provide adequate and urgent protection that reflects our current scientific knowledge. As previously discussed, nanomaterials may enter water tables and food chains and transfer across human membranes, with potentially toxic effects that are only beginning to be understood.

6

International Human Rights Law

This chapter shows that international human rights law has direct applicability to the three technologies under consideration during war. In arriving at this conclusion, this chapter analyses the decisions of international courts and judicial bodies, which provide a 'subsidiary means for the determination of the rules of law'.[1] Given that Article 36 weapon reviews require consideration of all international law obligations, and given that international human rights law applicable to the uses of nanomaterials is under consideration, it follows that Article 36 reviews require application and careful consideration of international human rights law.

In this chapter, I consider the application of four specific international human rights: the right to life; the prohibition on torture or cruel, inhuman or degrading treatment or punishment; the right to health, including mental health; and the right to food and water.[2] Each of these rights has been held to apply during war, as will be discussed in the second part of this chapter. Other international human rights law might have particular relevance to other uses of nanomaterials in war.

In this chapter, each international human right will be defined, its codification noted and its consideration in judicial decisions analysed. As the use of nanomaterials is relatively nascent, no judicial commentary regarding nanomaterials specifically yet exists, so judicial opinions that are relevant to the principle under consideration will be extrapolated or analogised to indicate how human rights principles would govern the use of thermobaric weapons, optogenetics or genetic modification. By

[1] *Statute of the International Court of Justice* art 38(1)(b) and (d).

[2] Stuart Casey-Maslen, Neil Corney and Abi Dymond-Bass, 'The Review of Weapons under International Humanitarian Law and Human Rights Law' in Stuart Casey-Maslen (ed), *Weapons under International Human Rights Law* (Cambridge University Press, 2014). As is noted in Daragh Murray et al (eds), *Practitioners' Guide to Human Rights Law in Armed Conflict* (Oxford University Press, 2016) 165: 'The rights to health, food and water are primarily brought into play on the basis of a weapon's longer-term effects, for instance, through incubation of disease in the body, or as a result of environmental contamination'.

looking at decisions of international courts, we can understand how courts may apply customary law to the use of nanomaterials in the future.[3] This chapter will also analyse secondary literature to further understand how the use of nanomaterials in armed conflict should be limited by these rights.

Human rights law is of particular significance to the regulation of the use of nanomaterials in war. Historically, the laws of *jus ad bellum* and *jus in bello* were separate and distinct: in times of peace, human rights were understood to apply, and in situations of armed conflict, the laws of war were understood to apply. The two legal regimes were considered mutually exclusive. This separation in the evolution of laws creates its own issues, 'A feature of modern multilateral treaty-making is the tendency for treaty-makers in particular areas to develop specialised concepts and techniques'.[4] This specialised approach to international law is problematic because individual treaties and other legal obligations create inconsistencies and potential conflicts for States, of which specialists may be unaware.

It is generally agreed that both human rights law and the laws of war 'have a shared basis in the fundamental principle of humanity'[5] and that they are complementary. Exactly how they relate requires further examination in practice, as this chapter will evidence.[6] In the last decade, it has been suggested that there has been a 'humanisation' of international humanitarian law, and a 'humanitarianisation' of international human rights law.[7] Multiple decisions of the ICJ have considered and applied international human rights during armed conflict.[8]

[3] James Crawford interprets this as meaning that judicial opinions are 'evidence of the law . . . Their value, however, stops short of precedent as it is understood in the common law tradition': James Crawford, *Brownlie's Principles of Public International Law* (Oxford University Press, 2012) 37.

[4] Hilary Charlesworth, 'Law-making and Sources' in James Crawford and Martii Koskienniemi (eds), *The Cambridge Companion to International Law* (Cambridge University Press, 2012) 192.

[5] Theodor Meron, 'Human Rights in Time of Peace and in Time of Armed Strife: Selected Problems' in Thomas Burgenthal (ed), *Contemporary Issues in International Law: Essays in Honor of Louis B Sohn* (NP Engel, 1984).

[6] Regarding complementarity of international institutions see John Tobin, 'Seeking Clarity in Relation to the Principle of Complementarity: Reflections on the recent Contributions of Some International Bodies' (2007) 8(2) *Melbourne Journal of International Law* 356.

[7] Vera Gowlland-Debbas, 'The Right to Life and the Relationship between Human Rights and Humanitarian Law' in Christian Tomuschat, Evelyne Lagrange and Stefan Oeter (eds), *The Right to Life* (Martinus Nijhoff, 2010) 126.

[8] *Legality of the Threat or Use of Nuclear Weapons (Advisory Opinion)* [1996] ICJ Rep 226, 240; *Legal Consequences of the Construction of a Wall in the Occupied Palestinian Territory*

The first part of this chapter will consider the significance of international human rights law for the use of nanomaterials in general. The second part of this chapter will demonstrate how human rights apply during armed conflict, and how they can apply to nanomaterials by way of analogy. As well as applying human rights to the use of nanomaterials, where relevant, similar protections provided by the laws of war will be analysed and thresholds compared. By undertaking this analysis, the complexity of the relationship between human rights law and the laws of war becomes clear. Most importantly, the need for a human rights analysis, given the impact on and future potential to manipulate human biology that nanomaterials present, becomes evident.

In the third part of this chapter, I apply the international human rights law to thermobaric weapons, optogenetics and genetic modification. I do this by applying the analysis of relevant human rights law by prominent jurists held to be applicable during armed conflict, and analogising their application based on the knowledge that we have about the three specific nanomaterials in question.[9] I will explore this complex area of interaction between human rights law and the laws of war during conflict by practically applying human rights law to the three uses of nanomaterials under question.

As was demonstrated in Chapters 3, 4 and 5, different uses of nanomaterials attract different legal frameworks even within a particular body of international law. On the other hand, international human rights law does not apply across the board to all technologies containing nanomaterials: the right to life has relevance for the use of thermobaric weapons with nanomaterials and genetic modification, but less so for optogenetics. The prohibition on torture and the right to health are relevant to optogenetics and genetic modification, and any other manipulation of human biology on the nanoscale, but not to thermobaric weapons using nanomaterials. The human right to food and water is relevant to the potential danger posed by dispersion of nanomaterials in food chains and water cycles in war. The conclusion of this chapter is that, to meaningfully undertake an Article 36 review considering the legal obligations of a state during conflict, human rights obligations in relation to 'means and methods of warfare' containing nanomaterials must be considered. Each

(Advisory Opinion) [2004] ICJ Rep 136; *Armed Activities on the Territory of the Congo (Democratic Republic of the Congo v Uganda) (Judgment)* [2005] ICJ Rep 168.

[9] Philip Alston and Ryan Goodman, *International Human Rights: Text and Materials* (Oxford University Press, 2013).

different use of nanomaterials will attract different international human rights law, which therefore requires thorough analysis before any nanomaterials are used in war.

I Application of International Human Rights Law to the Use of Nanomaterials in War

Article 36 weapons review requires legal review of the use of a weapon, which includes international human rights law. The conceptual beginnings of human rights and humanitarian law have been described as 'disjointed'.[10] The first interaction or overlap between human rights law and the laws of war was academic, when human rights obligations were considered to apply by certain authors, albeit in a limited fashion, even in war.[11]

None of the original human rights instruments make mention of weapons, or even wars. The only mention of war in either the 1948 Universal Declaration of Human Rights (UDHR) or the International Covenant on Civil and Political Rights (ICCPR) is in Article 20 of the latter, which noted that, '[a]ny propaganda for war shall be prohibited by law'.[12] Nevertheless, human rights law has gained traction in its application in armed conflict over the past twenty years, as it has become apparent that in some cases, human rights law offers broader protection for civilians during armed conflict than the laws of war,

> The manner in which both international human rights and humanitarian law correspond to each other in these areas is, of course, not without friction, but for the most part their rapprochements seem to be driven by a sense of coherence and cross-fertilization.[13]

[10] Francisco Martin et al (eds), *International Human Rights and Humanitarian Law: Treaties, Cases, & Analysis* (Cambridge University Press, 2006) 2.

[11] Monica Hakimi, 'Custom's Method and Process: Lessons from Humanitarian Law' in Curtis A Bradley (ed), *Custom's Future: International Law in a Changing World* (Cambridge University Press, 2016) 155.

[12] *International Covenant on Civil and Political Rights*, opened for signature 19 December 1966, 999 UNTS 171 (entered into force 23 March 1976) art 20 ('*ICCPR*'). For a further discussion of the relationship between disarmament and human rights, see Treasa Dunworth, *Humanitarian Disarmament: An Historical Enquiry* (Cambridge University Press, 2021).

[13] Michael Schoiswohl, 'Human Rights and Disarmament – A Blind Date or Shotgun Marriage?' (2013) 15(1) *Austrian Review of International and European Law* 109, 116.

States need to consider potentially applicable human rights law to ensure compliance with their legal obligations. Regarding jurisdiction, the principle of universal application of the ICCPR has been explicitly held to apply 'for violations of rights under the Covenant which its agents commit upon the territory of another State, whether with the acquiescence of the Government to that State or in opposition to it'.[14]

The ICJ has long affirmed the relevance of international human rights law in armed conflict, but the practical application of human rights law poses many challenges.[15] In the *Nuclear Weapons Advisory Opinion*, the ICJ found that international human rights law continues to apply during armed conflict. The Court confirmed that, 'the protection of the International Covenant on Civil and Political Rights does not cease in times of war'.[16] In the *Advisory Opinion on the Legal Consequences of the Construction of a Wall in the Occupied Palestinian Territory*,[17] the ICJ noted that certain human rights instruments, such as the ICCPR, the International Covenant on Economic, Social and Cultural Rights (ICESCR) and the United Nations Convention on the Rights of the Child (CRC), were all applicable to the Occupied Palestinian Territory.[18] The ICJ considered both the laws of war and human rights law to assess the legality of the construction of the wall.[19] In this Advisory Opinion, it was also found that,

> [a]s regards the relationship between international humanitarian law and human rights law, there are three possible situations: some rights may be exclusively matters of international humanitarian law; others may be exclusively matters of human rights law; yet others may be matters of both these branches of international law.[20]

[14] Human Rights Committee, *Decision: Communication No 52/1979*, 13th sess, UN Doc CCPR/C/OP/1 (19 July 1981) 88 ('*de Lopez v Uruguay*').

[15] Murray et al, n 2, v.

[16] *Legality of the Threat or Use of Nuclear Weapons (Advisory Opinion)* [1996] ICJ Rep 226, 240 [25].

[17] *Legal Consequences of the Construction of a Wall in the Occupied Palestinian Territory (Advisory Opinion)* [2004] ICJ Rep 136.

[18] Ibid.

[19] Eibe Riedel, Gilles Giacca and Christophe Golay (eds), *Economic, Social, and Cultural Rights in International Law: Contemporary Issues and Challenges* (Oxford University Press, 2014) 321.

[20] *Legal Consequences of the Construction of a Wall in the Occupied Palestinian Territory (Advisory Opinion)* [2004] ICJ Rep 136, 178 [106].

Unfortunately, the Advisory Opinion did not go one step further to clarify exactly when each of those situations would arise. Nevertheless, the Opinion found that international human rights law continued to operate during armed conflict.[21] Human rights law has been held to apply in armed conflict in other judicial decisions, such as the European Court of Human Rights (ECtHR) applying the European Convention on Human Rights (ECHR) in *Louizidou v Turkey*[22] and *Cyprus v Turkey.*[23]

Further, the United Nations Human Rights Committee (UNHRC) noted in its General Comment 29 on States of Emergency that both the ICCPR and the laws of war apply unless there is a 'public emergency which threatens the life of a nation',[24] in which case some provisions can be derogated from, while others remain non-derogable at all times. The *Nuclear Weapons Advisory Opinion* also noted that, under Article 4 of the ICCPR, human rights law may be derogated from in the very specific circumstances which 'threaten the life of the nation'.[25] General Comment 29 concluded that the right to life is non-derogable under any circumstances. Other international human rights law, such as the UDHR, also continues to apply, a position supported by prominent legal jurists.[26]

[21] Sir Arthur Watts, 'Israeli Wall Advisory Opinion (Legal Consequences of the Construction of a Wall in the Occupied Palestinian Territory)' (February 2007) *Max Planck Encyclopedia of Public International Law* <http://opil.ouplaw.com/view/10.1093/law:epil/9780199231690/law-9780199231690-e150>.

[22] *Loizidou v Turkey* (1995) 310 Eur Court HR (ser A).

[23] *Cyprus v Turkey* [2001] IV Eur Court HR 1.

[24] Human Rights Committee, *General Comment No 29: States of Emergency (Article 4)*, 1950th mtg, UN Doc CCPR/C/21/Rev.1/Add.11 (31 August 2001) [3]

> Not every disturbance or catastrophe qualifies as a public emergency which threatens the life of the nation, as required by article 4, paragraph 1. During armed conflict, whether international or non-international, rules of international humanitarian law become applicable and help, in addition to the provisions in article 4 and article 5, paragraph 1, of the Covenant, to prevent the abuse of a State's emergency powers. The Covenant requires that even during an armed conflict measures derogating from the Covenant are allowed only if and to the extent that the situation constitutes a threat to the life of the nation. If States parties consider invoking article 4 in other situations than an armed conflict, they should carefully consider the justification and why such a measure is necessary and legitimate in the circumstances.

[25] *ICCPR* art 4.

[26] William Schabas, 'The Right to Life' in Andrew Clapham and Paola Gaeta (eds), *The Oxford Handbook of International Law in Armed Conflict* (Oxford University Press, 2014) 369.

International human rights law therefore continues to apply during armed conflict, including the four human rights discussed later in the chapter. How those relationships continue between human rights and the laws of war is more complicated,[27] and will be discussed in detail later.

The rights that are non-derogable at any time include the right to life (Article 6); freedom from torture, cruel, inhuman, degrading treatment or punishment and freedom from medical or scientific experimentation without consent (Article 7); freedom from slavery (Article 8(1)) or servitude (Article 8(2)); the right not to be imprisoned for contractual debt (Article 11); freedom from retroactive criminal punishment (Article 15); right to recognition as a person before the law (Article 16); and freedom of thought, conscience and religion (Article 18). Article 6 of the Second Optional Protocol to the ICCPR prescribes that the prohibition on capital punishment is non-derogable for parties to that Protocol.[28] In General Comment No 5, the UNHRC explains that 'measures taken under article 4 are of an exceptional and temporary nature and may only last as long as the life of the nation concerned is threatened'.[29] Article 4 (1) also requires that no measure that derogates may be inconsistent with other obligations under international law, such as the laws of war.

II Significance of International Human Rights Law for the Use of Nanomaterials in War

International human rights law is particularly relevant for uses of nanomaterials on the human body that may be non-permanent or actively reversible. The laws of war were drafted to prohibit or limit harm during armed conflict at a time when none of these technologies and capabilities had been imagined. Traditionally, weapons had effects that were permanent, such as disability or death. As established in Chapter 3, in most cases the use of nanomaterials in the human body

[27] O Hathaway et al, 'Which Law Governs during Armed Conflict? The Relationship between International Humanitarian Law and Human Rights Law in Armed Conflicts' (2012) 96(6) *Minnesota Law Review* 1883.

[28] Human Rights Committee, *General Comment No 24: Issues Relating to Reservations Made upon Ratification or Accession to the Covenant or the Optional Protocols thereto, or in Relation to Declarations under Article 41 of the Covenant*, 52nd sess, UN Doc CCPR/C/21/Rev.1/Add.6 (4 November 1994).

[29] Sarah Joseph and Melissa Castan, *The International Covenant on Civil and Political Rights: Cases, Materials, and Commentary* (Oxford University Press, 3rd ed, 2013) [26.59].

for a hostile purpose would be prohibited by the BWC and CWC. In addition to these prohibitions under the BWC and the CWC, international human rights law provides further limitations on their use. Some States may argue, much like the arguments posed in the 'non-lethal' weapon debate, that the reversibility of some uses of nanomaterials makes them exempt from obligations under arms control treaties. International human rights law steps in when these arguments are not legally supported and provides legal limits as to how these technologies may be employed in warfare.

International human rights law has particular relevance in cases where human behaviour may be modified or deliberately altered in war without permanent disability, injury or death. The ability to manipulate human biology in a reversible way is a decidedly new development in science (analogous to the use of barbiturates, discussed in more detail later), and the rate and the specificity with which it can be achieved is moving ahead in leaps and bounds. Whether temporary, permanent, targeted or general, human rights law provides limitations additional to the BWC and CWC for hostile uses that alter human biology.

Finally, international law requires re-evaluation of any weapon if an initial review does not provide adequate information, or if new information comes to light, in order to ensure legal compliance. In the case of nanomaterials, research regarding toxicity to humans and the environment is still ongoing. As long-term health effects come to light regarding the use of nanomaterials, any weapons incorporating nanomaterials would require a new weapons review to reflect compliance with the international human rights law framework, taking into account the current knowledge regarding toxicity of nanomaterials.[30] A failure to do so may result in States being held responsible as they 'knew or ought to have known' of the long-term risks of the weapon in question.[31] Given that these human rights have been held to continue to apply during armed conflict in numerous legal decisions, these rights would, at a minimum, require consideration for any Article 36 review involving nanomaterials.[32]

30 Murray et al, n 2, 173.

31 *Brincat and Others v Malta* (European Court of Human Rights, Chamber, Application Nos 60908/11, 62110/11, 62129/11, 62312/11, 62338/11, 24 July 2014) [105]; *O'Keeffe v Ireland* [2014] I Eur Court HR 155, [152].

32 Stuart Casey-Maslen, *Weapons under International Human Rights Law* (Cambridge University Press, 2014) xviii.

III International Human Rights Law and Thermobaric Weapons, Optogenetics and Genetic Modification

Applying international human rights law to thermobaric weapons, optogenetics and genetic modification requires consideration of different international human rights for each technology. Thermobaric weapons with nanomaterials, with their broad impact and far-reaching explosions, require consideration of the right to life. The prohibition on torture and the right to life have applicability to optogenetics and genetic modification. The right to health has relevance for optogenetics and genetic modification. The right to food and water needs to be considered wherever potentially toxic metallic nanomaterials are dispersed into water sources and food chains.

On the basis of existing jurisprudence considering the application of these rights during conflict, I will analogise how these decisions would be relevant for the use of nanomaterials in the cases under review. Each of the potentially relevant international human rights will be discussed in more detail later in the chapter, including briefly discussing their relationship to the laws of war, which was discussed in detail in Chapters 3 and 4.

A Right to Life

The right to life is explicitly mentioned in Article 6 of the ICCPR,[33] Article 3 of the UDHR[34] and Draft General Comment No 36 of the Human Rights Committee.[35] The 'right to life' has been described as the 'supreme right',[36] and yet it is difficult to precisely define. More recently, the right to life has been noted to have a close relationship with the prohibition on 'torture' and 'ill-treatment', whereby 'torture and ill-treatment, which may seriously affect the physical and mental health of

33 *ICCPR* arts 20, 6.

34 *Universal Declaration of Human Rights*, GA Res 217A (III), UN GAOR, 3rd sess, 183rd plen mtg, UN Doc A/810 (10 December 1948) art 3.

35 Human Rights Committee, *General Comment No 36 on Article 6 of the International Covenant on Civil and Political Rights, on the Right to Life (Advanced Unedited Version)* <www.ohchr.org/Documents/HRBodies/CCPR/GCArticle6/GCArticle6_EN.pdf>.

36 Human Rights Committee, *General Comment No 14: Article 6 (Right to Life)*, 16th sess, UN Doc HRI/GEN/1/Rev.7 (12 May 2004) 128. See also Human Rights Committee, *Decision: Communication No 45/1979*, 15th sess, UN Doc C/CCPR/OP/1 (31 March 1982) 117 ('*de Guerrero v Colombia*').

the mistreated individual ... could also generate the risk of deprivation of life'.[37]

Although it is difficult to define, there are some clear parameters, including both negative limits and positive obligations, under international human rights law. Paragraph 6 of General Comment No 36 notes that,

> Deprivation of life involves an international ... or otherwise foreseeable and preventable life-terminating harm or injury, caused by an act or omission. It goes beyond injury to bodily or mental integrity or threat thereto ... States parties must respect the right to life and have the duty to refrain from engaging in conduct resulting in arbitrary deprivation of life. States parties must also ensure the right to and exercise due diligence to protect the lives of individuals against deprivations caused by persons or entities, whose conduct is not attributable to the State ... The obligation of States parties to respect and ensure the right to life extends to reasonably foreseeable threats and life-threatening situations that can result in loss of life. *States parties may be in violation of article 6 even if such threats and situations do not result in loss of life.*[38]

The right to life standard under human rights law is higher than the rule that prohibits indiscriminate attacks under the laws of war.[39] A State may be held responsible for a violation of the right to life, even if the death is not deliberate.[40]

The 1949 Geneva Conventions set out norms regarding respect for life, particularly in situations of armed conflict. Article 12 common to the first two Geneva Conventions refers to persons who are '*hors de combat*' and states that,

> Any attempts upon their lives, or violence to their persons, shall be strictly prohibited; in particular they shall not be murdered or exterminated, subjected to torture or to biological experiments; they shall not wilfully

[37] Human Rights Committee, *General Comment No 36 (2018) on Article 6 of the International Covenant on Civil and Political Rights, on the Right to Life*, 124th sess, UN Doc CCPR/C/GC/36 (30 October 2018) [54].

[38] Ibid [6] (emphasis added).

[39] Human Rights Committee, *General Comment No 36 (2018) on Article 6 of the International Covenant on Civil and Political Rights, on the Right to Life*, 124th sess, UN Doc CCPR/C/GC/36 (30 October 2018).

[40] Human Rights Committee, Views: *Communication No 1275/2004*, 94th sess, UN Doc CCPR/C/94/D/1275/2004 (30 October 2008) ('*Umetaliev and Tashtanbekova v Kyrgyzstan*').

> be left without medical assistance and care, nor shall conditions exposing them to contagion or infection be created.[41]

A recent publication on the right to life focuses more than half of its text on the right to life in situations of armed conflict, addressing issues such as the status of prisoners, collateral damage and targeted killings.[42]

In the case of *Isayeva et al v Russia*,[43] the protection of the right to life during war was considered to have the potential to be violated because of inadequate consideration of the use of a weapon prior to use (including consideration of non–nano-enhanced thermobaric weapons), although in this particular case the right to life was not violated. The ECtHR considered a case where Chechnyan civilians were hit by bombs from Russian military planes. The Court considered the right to life and found that the operation, or the use of the bombs, 'was planned and executed with requisite care for the lives of the civilian population'.[44]

In another case considering human rights during armed conflict, the ECtHR found that 'the indiscriminate bombing of a village inhabited by civilians – women and children being among their number [was] manifestly disproportionate'. Reference was made to the 1950 European Convention on the Protection of Human Rights and Fundamental Freedoms, and the ECtHR concluded that Russia had 'failed in its obligation to protect the right to life'.[45] This example evidenced a shift in thinking by finding that States can be held responsible for disregarding the right to life during conflict. These precedents mean that any use of nanomaterials that could impinge on the right to life needs to be considered prior to their use. *How* nanomaterials are used in war, not just *when*, also requires careful consideration. If thermobaric weapons with nanomaterials were to be used without adequate precaution or regard for

[41] *Geneva Convention (I) for the Amelioration of the Condition of the Wounded and Sick in Armed Forces in the Field*, opened for signature 12 August 1949, 75 UNTS 31 (entered into force 21 October 1950) art 12 ('*First Geneva Convention*'); *Geneva Convention (II) for the Amelioration of the Condition of Wounded, Sick and Shipwrecked Members of Armed Forces at Sea*, opened for signature 12 August 1949, 75 UNTS 85 (entered into force 21 October 1950) art 12 ('*Second Geneva Convention*').

[42] Tomuschat, Lagrange and Oeter (eds), n 7.

[43] *Isayeva v Russia* (European Court of Human Rights, Chamber, Application Nos 57947/00, 57948/00 and 57949/00, 24 February 2005) [179]-[189], [195].

[44] Ibid [199].

[45] *Esmukhambetov et al v Russia* (European Court of Human Rights, Chamber, Application No 23445/03, 29 March 2011) [150].

civilians, they may not only violate the principles of the laws of war, discussed in Chapter 4, but potentially also violate the right to life.

The standard required of authorities to protect the right to life was considered in more detail by the ECtHR in *Osman v UK*.[46] This case considered a situation where the State was accused of not having done enough to protect the deceased from his murderer. The Court stated,

> For the Court, and having regard to the nature of the right protected by article 2, a right fundamental in the scheme of the Convention, it is sufficient for an applicant to show that the authorities *did not do all that could be reasonably expected of them to avoid a real and immediate risk to life* of which they have or ought to have knowledge. This is a question which can only be answered in the light of all the circumstances of any particular case.[47]

In this case before the ECtHR, the onus is placed on the authorities to do all that could 'reasonably be expected to avoid a real and immediate risk to life'. Although this case is substantially different on the facts, and no nanomaterials are at play, as more becomes known about the toxicity of nanoparticles, this obligation to avoid real risk will become even more relevant. The question of how immediate the risk needs to be remains open.

Even though a weapon may not be prohibited, the way that a weapon is used may breach the right to life. In the case of *Santa Domingo Massacre v Colombia* heard by the Inter-American Court of Human Rights, cluster munitions were dropped by the military on guerrilla fighters.[48] The Court found that the human right to life had been breached, not because the weapons had been used *per se*, but because adequate precautions had not been taken.[49] This interpretation of the human right to life has parallels to its laws of war counterparts, which have been similarly interpreted to require that precautions be taken to protect the right to life.[50]

46 [1998] VII Eur Court HR 3124.

47 *Osman v United Kingdom* [1998] VII Eur Court HR 3124, [116] (emphasis added).

48 *Santa Domingo Massacre v Colombia* (Inter-American Court of Human Rights, Series C No 259, 30 November 2012).

49 Louise Doswald-Beck, 'Human Rights Law and Nuclear Weapons' in Gro Nystuen, Stuart Casey-Maslen and Annie Golden Bersagel (eds), *Nuclear Weapons under International Law* (Cambridge University Press, 2014) 435, 449.

50 International Committee of the Red Cross, *Customary IHL – Rule 22. Principle of Precautions against the Effects of Attacks* (2017) <https://ihl-databases.icrc.org/customary-ihl/eng/docs/v1_rul_rule22>.

There are no specific cases about nanomaterials in this area of law, but other cases, such as those considering toxicity of nuclear waste, may provide an insight into the view of the courts. In *EHP v Canada*,[51] a plaintiff brought a case on behalf of present and future generations, for a town (unironically) called Port Hope, where approximately 200,000 tons of radioactive waste were stored. In its admissibility decision, the UNHRC 'observe[d] that the present communication raise[d] serious issues, with regard to the obligation of States parties to protect human life', and found that the claimant and other residents could legitimately claim a potential breach under Article 6.[52] However, this right did not extend to future generations.[53] Joseph notes that this position would suggest that it is hard to imagine 'many instances where breaches of the "rights" of future generations would be foreseeable enough to establish admissibility'.[54]

In *Concluding Observations on Israel*, by the UNHRC, it was found that a lack of potable water could pose a threat to life.[55] Further, in *Concluding Observations on Kosovo*, it was noted that holding internally displaced persons in camps with lead contamination created a responsibility to relocate them and 'that the victims of lead contamination are provided with adequate medical treatment and access to effective remedies to seek and obtain compensation for any damage caused to their health'.[56] Although no breaches have yet been found, the consideration by the UNHRC of a socio-economic and environmental element into Article 6 so as to require States to attempt to ensure that people within the jurisdiction have access to basic subsistence needs indicates that in future, perhaps where nanomaterials toxify basic subsistence needs, the decision by the HRC might change.

As the ability to modify and manipulate human biology advances, the question of what would violate the right to life becomes more urgent.

[51] Human Rights Committee, Decision: Communication No 67/1980, 17th sess, UN Doc CCPR/C/17/D/67/1980 (27 October 1982) ('EHP v Canada').

[52] Ibid.

[53] Ibid [8(a)].

[54] Sarah Joseph, Jenny Schultz and Melissa Castan, *The International Covenant on Civil and Political Rights: Cases, Materials and Commentary* (Oxford University Press, 2012) 85.

[55] Human Rights Committee, *Consideration of Reports Submitted by States Parties under Article 40 of the Covenant: Concluding Observations of the Human Rights Committee – Israel*, 99th sess, UN Doc CCPR/C/ISR/CO/3 (3 September 2010).

[56] Human Rights Committee, *Consideration of Reports Submitted by States Parties under Article 40 of the Covenant: Concluding Observations of the Human Rights Committee – Kosovo (Serbia)*, 87th sess, UN Doc CCPR/C/UNK/CO/1 (14 August 2006).

The question of where the boundary lies between the desire for humanity and the desire to use advances in nanomaterials for security remains largely unanswered within the human rights law framework. This section of the chapter will address these questions, based on precedents considering non-derogable human rights in the context of conflict. Thermobaric weapons and genetic modification would both be limited in their use by the right to life. As nanomaterials are developed that may undermine or threaten the right to life, international human rights law and case law should limit their use. I will consider each of the uses of nanomaterials in turn, and how the right to life might affect the legality of their use in conflict.

1 Thermobaric Weapons

The right to life is the human right of most relevance to the use of thermobaric weapons with nanomaterials, given thermobaric weapons' potential to indiscriminately kill. As discussed in Chapter 4, precautions prior to use of thermobaric weapons with nanomaterials would need to be undertaken under the laws of war. The laws of war require limitations to the use of thermobaric weapons, with or without nanomaterials. Under international human rights law, the standards to protect life are much higher, including both acts and omissions. Deprivation of life, as per General Comment No 36 of the ICCPR, involves a deliberate or otherwise foreseeable and preventable life-terminating harm or injury. This is a very broad net. Any act, or omission to act, in the use of nanomaterials during armed conflict could result in a violation of the right to life, even if no loss of life occurs, as per paragraph 26 of General Comment No 36, discussed previously. General Comment No 36 of the ICCPR also discusses the role of the right to life in war, noting that the rights are 'complementary, not mutually exclusive'.[57]

Although thermobaric weapons with nanomaterials have been compared to nuclear weapons, and described as 'among the greatest threats to the right to life which confront humankind today',[58] they are not weapons of mass destruction. The Human Rights Committee concluded that 'the procedure laid down in the Optional Protocol was not designed for conducting public debate over matters of public policy, [such as support for

[57] Human Rights Committee, *General Comment No 36 (2018) on Article 6 of the International Covenant on Civil and Political Rights, on the Right to Life*, 124th sess, UN Doc CCPR/C/GC/36 (30 October 2018) [64], [67].

[58] Human Rights Committee, *General Comment No 14: Article 6*, 23rd sess, UN Doc HRI/GEN/1/Rev.1 (2 November 1984) [4].

disarmament and issues concerning nuclear and other weapons of mass destruction]'.[59] A similar conclusion may be drawn about the use of nanomaterials, that is, the Optional Protocol was not designed for conducting public debates about nanomaterials. At the same time, the use of nanomaterials in thermobaric weapons in enclosed spaces where there are humans, for example, would constitute not only a violation of the laws of war but also a violation of the right to life as their use would almost certainly constitute '[d]eprivation of life [involving] an intentional or otherwise foreseeable and preventable life-terminating harm or injury', a violation under Article 6 of the ICCPR[60] and Article 3 of the UDHR.[61]

2 Genetic Modification

The right to life also has implications for genetic modification affecting future generations. There are two types of DNA susceptible to alteration. One is general DNA, and the other is called germline DNA, and is the core DNA humans replicate to pass on to their offspring. Altering germline DNA directly alters the DNA of future generations.

The issue of genetic modification in plants was considered in the HRC decision in *Brun v France*, where a complaint involved a French decision to allow open-field testing of genetically modified organisms. The UNHRC found the claim to be inadmissible on the basis that there was inadequate evidence that the genetically modified fields were a personal risk to life.[62] Genetic modification of an individual, rather than a field of crops, or the use of optogenetics on an individual, would be likely to result in a different conclusion. Permanently modifying future humans must be prohibited by the international human right to life, as it not only affects those whose genes are altered but also their offspring. General Comment No 36 includes in the right to life the right to life with dignity.[63] Modifying the human genetic makeup of an individual or their offspring would violate this right to life with dignity. A right to life with

[59] Human Rights Committee, *Decision: Communication No 429/1990*, 47th sess, UN Doc CCPR/C/47/D/429/1990 (29 April 1993) [6.2] ('*EW v Netherlands*').

[60] *ICCPR* arts 20, 6.

[61] *Universal Declaration of Human Rights*, GA Res 217A (III), UN GAOR, 3rd sess, 183rd plen mtg, UN Doc A/810 (10 December 1948) art 3.

[62] Human Rights Committee, *Decision: Communication No 1453/2006*, 88th sess, UN Doc CCPR/C/88/D/1453/2006 (18 October 2006) ('*Brun v France*').

[63] Human Rights Committee, *General Comment No 36 (2018) on Article 6 of the International Covenant on Civil and Political Rights, on the Right to Life*, 124th sess, UN Doc CCPR/C/GC/36 (30 October 2018) [3].

dignity would include self-determination and one's own genetic material – modification of genetic makeup would violate this right. In addition to any modification being prohibited under the BWC and the CWC (as discussed in Chapter 3), the international human right to life would clearly prohibit genetic modification of the individual's genetic makeup, or to the germline that is passed down to future generations, during times of war or times of peace.

The right to life requires consideration where contamination by nanoparticles may have potentially fatal consequences. The right to life is not limited to immediate killing, and contains a positive obligation to protect life, as discussed earlier in this chapter.[64] Genetic modification of a population, just to give one example, might make a population more susceptible to disease. Where evidence becomes available of toxicity of nanomaterials, there is a positive obligation not to use such materials in war. The ongoing use of nanomaterials, the cumulative effect of which would be to harm the local population immediately, or even well into the future, would be in violation of these obligations. This aspect of the right to life may take on greater importance as the currently unknown toxicity profiles of many human-made nanomaterials come to light, and the impact of nanomaterials affects human lives in future.

B Prohibition on Torture and Other Forms of Cruel, Inhuman or Degrading Treatment

The prohibition on torture is found in the Convention against Torture and Other Cruel, Inhuman or Degrading Treatment or Punishment (CAT),[65] Article 3 of the ECHR,[66] and Article 7 of the ICCPR.[67] The prohibition is a fundamental, non-derogable human right. Torture is prohibited during times of war and times of peace. General Comment

64 *Esmukhambetov et al v Russia* (European Court of Human Rights, Chamber, Application No 23445/03, 29 March 2011) [150].

65 *Convention against Torture and Other Cruel, Inhuman or Degrading Treatment or Punishment*, opened for signature 10 December 1984, 1465 UNTS 85 (entered into force 26 June 1987) art 3 ('*Convention against Torture*').

66 *Convention for the Protection of Human Rights and Fundamental Freedoms*, opened for signature 4 November 1950, 213 UNTS 221 (entered into force 3 September 1953) art 3.

67 *ICCPR* arts 7, 4(2). See also Human Rights Committee, *General Comment No 29: States of Emergency (Article 4)*, 1950th mtg, UN Doc CCPR/C/21/Rev1/Add.11 (31 August 2001) [7].

20 of the UNHRC does not distinguish between the different levels of treatment, and notes that,

> The Covenant does not contain any definition of the concepts covered by article 7, nor does the Committee consider it necessary to draw up a list of prohibited acts or to establish sharp distinctions between the different kinds of punishment or treatment; the distinctions depend on the nature, purpose and severity of the treatment applied.[68]

Torture is also prohibited by Article 3 common to the four Geneva Conventions,[69] Article 12 of the First and Second Conventions,[70] Articles 17 and 87 of the Third Convention,[71] Article 32 of the Fourth Convention,[72] Article 75 (2(a) and (e)) of API and Article 4 (2(a) and (h)) of Additional Protocol II (APII).[73] Under Article 85 of API, these breaches constitute war crimes.[74] In non-international armed conflict, they are considered serious violations. The Rome Statute of the ICC defines torture and cruel, inhuman or degrading treatment as war crimes under Article 8 (2)(a)(ii), (iii) and (xxi), and (2)(c)(i) and (ii)).[75]

[68] Human Rights Committee, *General Comment No 20: Article 7 (Prohibition of Torture, or Other Cruel, Inhuman or Degrading Treatment or Punishment)*, 44th sess, UN Doc A/47/40 (10 March 1992).

[69] *Geneva Convention (I) for the Amelioration of the Condition of the Wounded and Sick in Armed Forces in the Field*, opened for signature 12 August 1949, 75 UNTS 31 (entered into force 21 October 1950) art 3 ('*First Geneva Convention*'); *Geneva Convention (II) for the Amelioration of the Condition of Wounded, Sick and Shipwrecked Members of Armed Forces at Sea*, opened for signature 12 August 1949, 75 UNTS 85 (entered into force 21 October 1950) art 3 ('*Second Geneva Convention*'); *Geneva Convention (III) relative to the Treatment of Prisoners of War*, opened for signature 12 August 1949, 75 UNTS 135 (entered into force 21 October 1950) art 3 ('*Third Geneva Convention*'); *Geneva Convention (IV) Relative to the Protection of Civilian Persons in Time of War*, opened for signature 12 August 1949, 75 UNTS 287 (entered into force 21 October 1950) art 3 ('*Fourth Geneva Convention*').

[70] *First Geneva Convention* art 12; *Second Geneva Convention* art 12.

[71] *Third Geneva Convention* arts 17, 87.

[72] *Fourth Geneva Convention* art 32.

[73] *Protocol Additional to the Geneva Conventions of 12 August 1949, and Relating to the Protection of Victims of International Armed Conflicts (Protocol I)*, opened for signature 8 June 1977, 1125 UNTS 3 (entered into force on 7 December 1978) arts 75(2)(a), 75(2)(e) ('*Additional Protocol I*'); *Protocol Additional to the Geneva Conventions of 12 August 1949, and Relating to the Protection of Victims of Non-International Armed Conflicts (Protocol II)*, opened for signature 8 June 1977, 1125 UNTS 609 (entered into force on 7 December 1978) arts 4(2)(a), 4(2)(h) ('*Additional Protocol II*').

[74] *Additional Protocol I* art 85.

[75] *Rome Statute of the International Criminal Court*, opened for signature 17 July 1998, 2187 UNTS 91 (entered into force 1 July 2002) arts 8 2(a)(ii), 8 2(a)(iii), 8 2(a)(xxi), 8 2(c)(i), 8 2(c)(ii) ('*Rome Statute*').

In the case of *Čelebići*, the customary nature of the prohibition on torture was examined in some detail,[76] particularly in relation to the definition contained in international conventions and human rights instruments. It was upheld that the criminality of torture under customary as well as conventional law was not in question, given that the prohibition was contained in Common Article 3 of the Geneva Conventions as well as the grave breaches provisions.[77] This decision affirmed that the prohibition was reiterated in all of the human rights instruments, including the UDHR, the ICCPR and the ECHR.[78]

Although all three degrees of treatment are prohibited, torture is the most 'reprehensible' of the three forms of treatment.[79] Certain consequences may flow from a finding of torture which do not flow from a finding of a lesser standard of treatment. The definition of torture is largely accepted to be the definition found in Article 1 of CAT, which defines torture as,

> [A]ny act by which severe pain or suffering, whether physical or mental, is intentionally inflicted on a person for such purposes as obtaining from him or a third person information or a confession, punishing him for an act he or a third person has committed or is suspected of having committed, or intimidating or coercing him or a third person, or for any reason based on discrimination of any kind, when such pain or suffering is inflicted by or at the instigation of or with the consent or acquiescence of a public official or other person acting in an official capacity. It does not include pain or suffering arising only from, inherent in or incidental to lawful sanctions.[80]

The ECHR Article 3 states that, 'noone shall be subjected to torture or inhuman or degrading treatment or punishment'.[81] The ICCPR, Article 7 explains the prohibition on torture thus, '[n]o one shall be subjected to torture or to cruel, inhuman or degrading treatment or punishment.

[76] *Prosecutor v Delalić (Judgment)* (International Criminal Tribunal for the Former Yugoslavia, Trial Chamber, Case No IT-96-21-T, 16 November 1998) [452] ('*Čelebići Case*').

[77] Ibid [452].

[78] Ibid [452], [453].

[79] Manfred Nowak, *UN Covenant on Civil and Political Rights: CCPR Commentary* (NP Engel, 2nd ed., 2005) 160.

[80] *Convention against Torture and Other Cruel, Inhuman or Degrading Treatment or Punishment*, opened for signature 10 December 1984, 1465 UNTS 85 (entered into force 26 June 1987) art 3 ('*Convention against Torture*').

[81] *Convention for the Protection of Human Rights and Fundamental Freedoms*, opened for signature 4 November 1950, 213 UNTS 221 (entered into force 3 September 1953) art 3.

In particular, no one shall be subjected without his free consent to medical or scientific experimentation,' but does not in fact define torture.[82] The prohibition on 'medical or scientific experimentation' would have direct relevance for the use of optogenetics or genetic modification in war. The use of optogenetics to alter human behaviour, for example, or the modification of the human genome for medical or scientific experimentation would be prohibited if undertaken without consent in any context, including war.

The ECtHR has noted in articulating the ambit of torture that commonly held views have changed over time. A case involving life imprisonment without the option of parole was found to violate Article 3 of the ECHR,[83] as was juvenile imprisonment.[84] In this case, the ECtHR took the opportunity to note that judicial corporal punishment of juvenile offenders, which was acceptable in 1956, was no longer acceptable by Convention standards in 1978. The Court noted that 'the development of commonly accepted standards' needed to be considered.[85] It is worth noting that the Court's reflection of the changing times and values may potentially reflect attitudes towards the use of nanomaterials in the future. What is tolerated by way of use of nanomaterials today may change in the future.

In 2003, the UN Special Rapporteur on Torture produced a report pursuant to Resolution 2002/38 of the UN Commission on Human Rights, calling for,

> [A]ll Governments to take effective legislative, administrative, judicial or other measures to prevent and prohibit the production, trade, export and use of equipment which is specifically designed to inflict torture or other cruel, inhuman or degrading treatment.[86]

The report does not specify whether these methods are prohibited during armed conflict, or in riot control, but urgently requires States to stop producing or using anything that constitutes torture. Torture was found

[82] Joseph and Castan (2013) [9.19].

[83] *Vinter v United Kingdom* [2016] III Eur Court HR 317.

[84] *Tyrer v United Kingdom* (1978) 26 Eur Court HR (ser A).

[85] Ibid [31].

[86] Commission on Human Rights, *Study on the Situation of Trade in and Production of Equipment Which Is Specifically Designed to Inflict Torture or Other Cruel, Inhuman or Degrading Treatment, Its Origin, Destination and Forms, Submitted by Theo van Boven, Special Rapporteur on Torture, Pursuant to Resolution 2002/38 of the Commission on Human Rights*, 59th sess, Agenda Item 11(a), UN Doc E/CN.4/2003/69 (13 January 2003) [12].

to include any use of materials 'whose medical effects are not fully known or whose use in practice has revealed a substantial risk of abuse or unwarranted injury' and would be prohibited.[87] Any nanomaterial that would be developed and used as a form of torture would be prohibited under international law, supported by national law preventing its use. For example, the use of optogenetics to blind or incite rage, removing even temporarily human bodily functions, could be interpreted to constitute torture, as there would be a substantial risk of abuse or unwarranted injury.

The right has some overlap with the prohibition on superfluous injury or unnecessary suffering, and reflects the purpose of the laws of war to reduce human suffering during armed conflict.[88] One specialist in the laws of war referred to the obligation to provide humane treatment to protected persons under the Geneva Conventions as the '*leitmotif* of the four Geneva Conventions'.[89] Although not the same as an explicit prohibition on torture, the standard of requiring humane treatment would prohibit torture under any understanding of the terminology.

1 Optogenetics and Genetic Modification

Damage to health does not need to be permanent to violate the prohibition on torture or cruel, inhuman or degrading punishment. In the case of *Antipenkov v Russia*, the use of rubber truncheons, despite not causing long-term damage to health, was found to have caused mental and physical suffering. It sufficed that the detainee had been subject to inhuman and degrading treatment by Russian officials.[90] This decision highlights that the reversibility of damage does not mitigate the prohibition on torture. If nanomaterials with reversible effect were to be used without the consent of individuals during peacetime, this would also violate the prohibition on

[87] Commission on Human Rights, *Torture and Other Cruel, Inhuman and Degrading Treatment: Report of the Special Rapporteur on Torture, Theo Van Boven*, 61st sess, Agenda Item 11(a), UN Doc E/CN.4/2005/62 (15 December 2004).

[88] Manfred Nowak, 'Torture and Other Cruel, Inhuman or Degrading Treatment or Punishment' in Andrew Clapham and Paola Gaeta (eds), *The Oxford Handbook of International Law in Armed Conflict* (Oxford University Press, 2014) 387.

[89] International Committee of the Red Cross, *The Geneva Conventions of 12 August 1949 – Commentary: IV Geneva Convention Relative to the Protection of Civilian Persons in Times of War* (1958) 204 ('*GC IV Commentary*'). See also Cordula Droege, '"In Truth the *Leitmotiv*" – The Prohibition of Torture and Other Forms of Ill-Treatment in International Humanitarian Law' (2007) 89(867) *International Review of the Red Cross* 515.

[90] *Antipenkov v Russia* (European Court of Human Rights, Chamber, Application No 33470/03, 15 October 2009) [54], [60], [61].

torture.[91] An example would be where nanomaterials were used to alter human behaviour, which may still constitute torture.

As discussed in Chapter 2, optogenetics has the ability to alter human emotions by activating specific neurons to enhance or reduce fear, aggression or pain. This use of optogenetics is prohibited without the consent of the individual under all circumstances. If optogenetics were used, despite not causing permanent or even long-term damage to health, their use during conflict in any way that could cause mental or physical suffering would be prohibited under international human rights law. Arguably, any loss of cognitive or emotional control would potentially cause mental or physical suffering, and so the use of optogenetics would inevitably violate the prohibition on torture.

Although there are no specific cases referring to the prohibition on torture and nanomaterials, the effect of barbiturates is analogous to the effects of optogenetics. Barbiturates or other chemical substances to lower a subject's inhibitions are already in use by Indian police forces, for example.[92] In May 2010, the Supreme Court of India found that compulsory use of such techniques constituted 'cruel, inhuman or degrading treatment', noting specifically that invading people's mental processes was unacceptable and could constitute either torture or 'cruel, inhuman or degrading treatment',

> [t]he popular perceptions of terms such as 'torture' or cruel, inhuman or degrading treatment' are associated with gory images of blood-letting and broken bones. However, we must recognise that a forcible intrusion into a person's mental processes is also an affront to human dignity and liberty, often with grave and long-lasting consequences.[93]

As neuroscience advances, the science will inevitably enable weaponisation. It is important that we develop and implement rules and practices

[91] This standard is upheld under the *Convention against Torture*. For further discussion of relevant literature and jurisprudence, see Manfred Nowak and Elizabeth McArthur, *The United Nations Convention against Torture: A Commentary* (Oxford University Press, 2008). Under the *Optional Protocol to the Convention against Torture and Other Cruel, Inhuman or Degrading Treatment or Punishment*, opened for signature 4 February 2003, 2375 UNTS 237 (entered into force 22 June 2006), States are also required to establish 'national preventative mechanisms' against torture.

[92] Subhojyoti Acharya, *Is Narco Analysis a Reliable Science? – Present Legal Scenario India* (19 February 2008) Legal Service India <www.legalserviceindia.com/article/l176-Narco-Analysis.html>.

[93] *Selvi v State of Karnataka* (Supreme Court of India, Criminal Appellate Jurisdiction, 5 May 2010) [205].

that prevent neuroscientific advances from being used in hostile ways. In detention, prohibitions on coercion of detainees would also prevent their use. As discussed in Chapter 2, optogenetics already provides the possibility to pinpoint specific neural functions, both emotional and biological, including the ability to see. The use of optogenetics to control, enhance or reduce emotional responses involuntarily would be in contravention of international human rights law under the prohibition on torture, as well as the human right to physical and mental health. The prohibition on torture appears to provide more protection than the prohibition on 'superfluous injury and unnecessary suffering' discussed in Chapter 4. For this reason, international human rights law may be the most relevant legal instrument that considers the legality of manipulation of human behaviour during war.

The use of optogenetics to cause fear or pain would also be prohibited under the prohibition on torture. Whether through optogenetics, or any other advanced medical use of nanomaterials, such use in a way that could 'inflict torture or other cruel, inhuman or degrading treatment' would clearly be forbidden, even where there is no long-term damage to health. By this definition, all manipulation of human physical function, including optogenetics or genetic modification, should be illegal based on the prohibition on torture. Given the reversibility of the technologies, and the way in which they modify the body internally, violations of certain thresholds would be extremely difficult to establish or prove. Using the precedent on barbiturates, which similarly incapacitate, it should be analogised from existing jurisprudence that all instances of controlling the mind would therefore be prohibited.

In the next section, I will consider the limitations provided for the use of nanomaterials by the human right to health, including mental health.

C *Right to Health, Including Mental Health*

The human right to health was first outlined in the Constitution of the World Health Organisation (WHO), the preamble of which defines health as a 'state of complete physical, mental and social well-being and not merely the absence of disease or infirmity'.[94] In 1966, the ICESCR provided a more detailed definition of the human right to health in Article 12,

[94] Office of the United Nations High Commissioner for Human Rights and World Health Organization, *The Right to Health: Fact Sheet No 31* <www.ohchr.org/Documents/Publications/Factsheet31.pdf>.

> The States Parties to the present Covenant recognize the right of everyone to the enjoyment of the highest attainable standard of physical and mental health.

In the ICESCR General Comment, it was noted that the right to health includes the right to medical care. The right to health also requires States to promote conditions in which people can lead a healthy life, and 'extends to the underlying determinants of health, such as food and nutrition, housing, access to safe and potable water and adequate sanitation, safe and healthy working conditions, and a healthy environment'.[95]

Beyond the positive obligations, the obligation to respect the right to health extends to States actively refraining from any act that negatively impacts, directly or indirectly, on this right.[96] States may violate their responsibility to uphold the right to health by permitting either permanent or temporary effects caused by the use of nanomaterials in the environment that directly and intentionally negatively affect human biology, such as using a virus to potentially alter the function of the brain, such as optogenetics. The use of optogenetics might alter behaviour, or genetic modification might alter the body's genetic makeup. Either way, the potential impact on human health should be considered as part of weapons reviews, by studying the long-term effects on the human body and the environment. International law has already recognised that health is a human right affected by conflict. Judicial decisions have already dealt with the right to health, such as the UNCC awarding compensation for harm to health caused by the effects of ingestion of smoke and other health implications from the Gulf fires, discussed in Chapter 5.

1 Optogenetics

Nanomaterials are most likely to undermine the international human right to physical and mental health in situations where the brain is manipulated using optogenetics. The use of torture, or enhancing or decreasing fear, pleasure, anger or pain without consent using optogenetics would all violate the right to health in an armed conflict. Causing temporary blindness would breach the right to human health. The right

[95] Committee on Economic, Social and Cultural Rights, *General Comment No 14: The Right to the Highest Attainable Standard of Health*, 22nd sess, Agenda Item 3, UN Doc E/C.12/2000/4 (11 August 2000).

[96] Manisuli Ssenyonjo, *Economic, Social and Cultural Rights in International Law* (Hart Publishing, 2009) 336.

to health is further defined by the Office of the High Commissioner for Human Rights and the World Health Organisation, noting that 'the obligation to respect requires States to refrain from interfering directly or indirectly with the right to health' and to 'prevent third parties from interfering with the right to health'.[97] Any tampering with human physiology without consent, whether temporary or permanent, is a violation of the right to health and is not permitted, whether during armed conflict or during times of peace. Although there is no case law on this specific point, it is difficult to imagine how intentionally altering someone's physical or mental health to their detriment would not be in violation of this right.

Nanomaterials enable unparalleled access to the human brain, including the ability to transport materials into the brain 'in analogy with the Trojan horse' and with 'profound implications for the neuropsychopharmacological modulation of behaviour'.[98] This means that the ability to influence, control, manipulate and alter the human brain will only increase. The human rights law framework, whether for optogenetics or similar uses of nanomaterials, provides another set of clear boundaries around the use of such technologies for hostile purposes.

D Right to Food and Water

The right to water was recognised in Article 14(2)(h) of the Convention on the Elimination of All Forms of Discrimination against Women (CEDAW),[99] the CRC,[100] the UDHR[101] and the ICESCR.[102]

97 Office of the United Nations High Commissioner for Human Rights and World Health Organization, *The Right to Health: Fact Sheet No 31* <www.ohchr.org/Documents/Publications/Factsheet31.pdf>.

98 National Research Council, Committee on Military and Intelligence Methodology for Emergent Neurophysiological and Cognitive/Neural Science Research in the Next Two Decades, *Emerging Cognitive Neuroscience and Related Technologies* (National Academies Press, 2008) 135.

99 *International Convention on the Elimination of All Forms of Discrimination against Women*, opened for signature 1 March 1980, 1249 UNTS 13 (entered into force 3 September 1981) art 14(2)(h).

100 *Convention on the Rights of the Child*, opened for signature 20 November 1989, 1577 UNTS 3 (entered into force 2 September 1990) ('*Convention on the Rights of the Child*').

101 *Universal Declaration of Human Rights*, GA Res 217A (III), UN GAOR, 3rd sess, 183rd plen mtg, UN Doc A/810 (10 December 1948).

102 *International Covenant on Economic, Social and Cultural Rights*, opened for signature 16 December 1966, 993 UNTS 3 (entered into force 3 January 1976).

The CRC, Article 24(2)(c) indicates that the right to food and water includes the requirements,

> To combat disease and malnutrition, including within the framework of primary health care, through, inter alia, the application of readily available technology and through the provision of adequate nutritious foods and *clean* drinking water, taking into consideration the dangers and risks of environmental pollution.[103]

The responsibility to protect water is explicitly mentioned by the United Nations Committee on Economic, Social and Cultural Rights (CESCR), which requires that States refrain from 'limiting access to, or destroying, water services and infrastructure as a punitive measure, for example, during armed conflicts in violation of international humanitarian law'.[104] The CESCR goes further to note that this obligation 'includes protection of objects indispensable for survival of the civilian population, including drinking water installations and supplies and irrigation works, protection of the natural environment against widespread, long-term and severe damage and ensuring that civilians, internees and prisoners have access to adequate water'.[105] Any deliberate contamination of water by nanomaterials would be prohibited. Similarly, contaminating water with nanomaterials would be rendered illegal by international law prohibiting poisoning, as discussed in detail in Chapter 3.[106] The right is notably not just to water, but to water that sustains life.

The right to adequate food is enshrined in General Comment No 12 of the CESCR.[107] Governments do not have a responsibility to hand out

103 *Convention on the Rights of the Child* art 24(2)(c), also further detailed in Office of the United Nations High Commissioner for Human Rights and World Health Organization, *The Right to Health: Fact Sheet No 31* <www.ohchr.org/Documents/Publications/Factsheet31.pdf> (emphasis added).

104 Committee on Economic, Social and Cultural Rights, *General Comment No 15: The Right to Water*, 29th sess, Agenda Item 3, UN Doc E/C.12/2002/11 (20 January 2003) [21].

105 Ibid [22].

106 The 1925 Geneva Protocol prohibits the use of 'asphyxiating, poisonous or other gases, and *of all analogous* [emphasis added] liquids, materials or devices' and 'bacteriological methods of warfare', but does not regulate production, storage or transfer. The 1925 Geneva Protocol is still in force and currently has 140 States parties. See United Nations Office for Disarmament Affairs, *Protocol for the Prohibition of the Use in War of Asphyxiating, Poisonous or Other Gases, and of Bacteriological Methods of Warfare: Status of the Treaty* <http://disarmament.un.org/treaties/t/1925>.

107 Committee on Economic, Social and Cultural Rights, *General Comment No 12: The Right to Adequate Food (Art 11)*, 20th sess, Agenda Item 7, UN Doc E/C.12/1999/5 (12 May 1999).

food, but where people are deprived of food for reasons beyond their control (such as toxicity due to nanoparticles, in this instance), governments are responsible for providing food directly. The Food and Agriculture Organization of the United Nations is very specific about what this right includes and what it does not,

> The right to food is not a right to a minimum ration of calories, proteins and other specific nutrients, or a right to be fed. It is about being guaranteed the right to feed oneself, which requires not only that food is available – that the ratio of production to the population is sufficient – but also that it is accessible – i.e., that each household either has the means to produce or buy its own food. However, if individuals are deprived of access to food for reasons beyond their control . . . recognition of the right to life obliges States to provide them with sufficient food for their survival.[108]

In the laws of war, Article 14 of APII prohibits starvation as a method of combat,

> It is therefore prohibited to attack, destroy, remove or render useless, for that purpose, objects indispensable to the survival of the civilian population, such as foodstuffs, agricultural areas for the production of foodstuffs, crops, livestock, drinking water installations and supplies and irrigation works.[109]

The ICRC Commentary states that 'the prohibition on using starvation against civilians is a rule from which no derogation may be made'.[110] The commentary also clarifies that the list is not exhaustive, so that the use of nanomaterials that resulted in toxicity leading to starvation would be prohibited under Article 14. In 2010, the UNGA explicitly stated that there is a human right to water and sanitation, and acknowledged that clean drinking water and sanitation are key to the realisation of all human rights.[111]

[108] Olivier de Schutter, United Nations Special Rapporteur on the Right to Food 2008–2014, cited in Simone Hutter, *Starvation as a Weapon: Domestic Policies of Deliberate Starvation as a Means to an End under International Law* (Brill, 2015) 29.

[109] Yves Sandoz, Christophe Swinarski and Bruno Zimmermann (eds), *Commentary on the Additional Protocols of 8 June 1977 to the Geneva Conventions of 12 August 1949* (Martinus Nijhoff, 1987) 1455–1460.

[110] Ibid 1456.

[111] *The Human Right to Water and Sanitation*, GA Res 264/92, UN GAOR, 64th sess, 108th plen mtg, Agenda Item 48, UN Doc A/RES/64/292 (3 August 2010); Committee on Economic, Social and Cultural Rights, *General Comment No 15: The Right to Water*, 29th sess, Agenda Item 3, UN Doc E/C.12/2002/11 (20 January 2003).

The ubiquitous use of nanomaterials in conflict needs to be reassessed on the basis of new information coming to light regarding the potential toxicity of metallic nanoparticles, regardless of their source. Residual nanoparticles left by thermobaric weapons using nanomaterials that poison or limit the supply of clean water to civilians or combatants would be prohibited under Article 14(2)(h) of the CEDAW,[112] the CRC,[113] the UDHR[114] and the ICESCR.[115] The right to food and water requires food and water that enable human survival, which requires water that is safe to drink. If thermobaric weapons release residual, potentially toxic nanoparticles into the water table or food chain, then such nanomaterial waste would violate the right to clean food and water. As discussed in Chapter 5, the size of nanomaterials, and their ability to permeate food chains and water tables without detection and with virtually no recourse to remove them, poses very particular challenges for the right to food and water. In conclusion, any use of nanomaterials that render food or water toxic would be prohibited.

IV Conclusion

This chapter has analysed the applicability and relevance of international human rights law during conflict to thermobaric weapons, optogenetics and genetic modification. By applying international human rights law to the three specific technologies, this chapter has made it clear that international human rights law, not always the first law to be considered for an Article 36 weapon review, nonetheless has direct relevance to each of the technologies under consideration. The four international human rights legal obligations considered in this chapter are not exhaustive.

Some States already require human rights considerations in Article 36 reviews of weapons, in part because many of their weapons used in armed conflict are also used in peacekeeping or law enforcement

[112] *International Convention on the Elimination of All Forms of Discrimination against Women*, opened for signature 1 March 1980, 1249 UNTS 13 (entered into force 3 September 1981) art 14(2)(h).

[113] *Convention on the Rights of the Child*, opened for signature 20 November 1989, 1577 UNTS 3 (entered into force 2 September 1990).

[114] *Universal Declaration of Human Rights*, GA Res 217A (III), UN GAOR, 3rd sess, 183rd plen mtg, UN Doc A/810 (10 December 1948).

[115] *International Covenant on Economic, Social and Cultural Rights*, opened for signature 16 December 1966, 993 UNTS 3 (entered into force 3 January 1976).

situations that require consideration of relevant human rights.[116] These States include Sweden, Switzerland and the United Kingdom.[117] A failure to consider human rights in the review of weapons may place States at a risk of failure to comply with existing legal obligations of which they 'knew or ought to have known'.[118] States are legally required to consider all of the risks associated with a weapon's use.[119]

States are also required to go beyond the evaluation of a 'single use' of any use of nanomaterials: States must consider the effects of cumulative use of weapons containing nanomaterials on humans to ensure compliance with human rights law obligations, such as potential environmental contamination or potential human health risks following exposure.[120] As discussed in Chapter 3 regarding treaty limitations on the use of thermobaric weapons, a weapon may be found to be appropriate in some situations with limitations, but prohibited in others.[121] It is important that any review of new or modified weapons containing nanomaterials upholds the right to life, the prohibition on torture, the right to health (including mental health) and the right to clean food and water, as each use of nanomaterials may be governed by different areas of human rights. On the other hand, international human rights law does not have implications for all technologies containing nanomaterials: as I have demonstrated in this chapter, the right to life has relevance for the use of thermobaric weapons with nanomaterials and genetic modification, but less so for optogenetics. The prohibition on torture and the right to health are relevant to optogenetics and genetic modification, and any other manipulation of human biology on the nanoscale, but do not have

116 The *1990 United Nations Basic Principles on the Use of Force and Firearms by Law Enforcement Officials* encourage states to review less-lethal weapons used for law enforcement purposes, 'Government and law enforcement agencies should develop a range of means as broad as possible and equip law enforcement officials with various types of weapons and ammunition that would allow for a differentiated use of force and firearms': at [2]. For further commentary see Casey-Maslen, Corney and Dymond-Bass, n 2.

117 Vincent Boulanin, *Implementing Article 36 Weapon Reviews in the Light of Increasing Autonomy in Weapon Systems* (November 2015) SIPRI <www.sipri.org/sites/default/files/files/insight/SIPRIInsight1501.pdf>.

118 *Brincat and Others v Malta* (European Court of Human Rights, Chamber, Application Nos 60908/11, 62110/11, 62129/11, 62312/11, 62338/11, 24 July 2014) [105].

119 *Osman v United Kingdom* [1998] VII Eur Court HR 3124, [116]. See also *O'Keeffe v Ireland* [2014] I Eur Court HR 155, [152].

120 Murray et al, n 2, 172.

121 See, e.g. UK Ministry of Defence, *Manual of the Law of Armed Conflict* (Oxford University Press, 2004) Section 6.2.2.

any relevance for thermobaric weapons with nanomaterials. The human right to food and water is relevant to the potential danger posed by dispersion of nanomaterials in food chains and water cycles and the long-term implications for human health.

As the ability to manipulate the human body at the nanoscale is becoming more advanced and more precise, consideration of international human rights law is becoming increasingly relevant in providing protection from manipulation of the human brain or biology without consent, both in times of war and in times of peace.

7

Conclusion and Recommendations

As early as 2008, Bill Gates expressed his concern to the Stockholm International Peace Research Institute regarding the potential use of various emerging technologies, including the use of nanomaterials, for security,

> there is intensifying awareness around the world of the need to balance the obvious advantages of globalization with its increasingly apparent disadvantages ... This conundrum applies across a widening spectrum of current and emergent technologies – such as nuclear technologies, but especially in the biological sciences, including genetic, engineering, synthetic biology and nanotechnologies.[1]

In this book, I have explored where the balance between our desire for humanity and our desire for security currently rests, outlining the legal parameters set by treaty law, customary international law and principles, environmental law and international human rights law to the use of nanomaterials in war. I have demonstrated where the boundaries and limitations on the use of nanomaterials currently lie, as well as where the boundaries may require clarifying or strengthening to reflect current values, such as in international environmental law, and in the case of biological uses of nanomaterials. In particular, I have argued that States need to agree to prohibit explicitly the hostile use of genetic modification or any other alteration to the human anatomy without consent.

First, in order to ensure compliance with their international law obligations, States are obliged to review any new or modified uses involving nanomaterials under Article 36 to ensure compliance with existing international law. The analysis in this book illustrates that weapons reviews are required for all 'means or methods of warfare'

[1] Bill Gates, 'Introduction' in Stockholm International Peace Research Institute, *2008 SIPRI Yearbook: Armaments, Disarmament and International Security* (Oxford University Press, 2008) 2. The SIPRI report is annual and provides public information about the production, purchase and transfer of arms.

containing nanomaterials to ensure compliance with well-established existing treaties and customary international law and legal principles, environmental law and human rights law. The complexity and diversity of issues raised by each of the different uses of nanomaterials demonstrates exactly why this in-depth consideration is necessary. As already discussed, the tension between the desire for security and humanity is not new; what is new is the speed and scale at which the tools are being developed and interconnected.[2] This speed and scale of development should not be an impediment to thoughtful review and consideration regarding compliance with the law, much of which comprehends the uses of nanomaterials. A similar approach, parsed slightly differently in Crowley's writings of what needs to be done to effectively review (in the case of his book, chemical agents), is as follows,

> *Stage one*: constitutes an examination of the nature of the weapons and technology that are to be controlled . . .
>
> *Stage two*: constitutes an analysis of the full range of potentially applicable international law . . .
>
> *Stage three*: following an analysis of the information derived from stages one and two, a comprehensive strategy is developed to strengthen existing mechanisms and/or introduce new mechanisms to facilitate effective regulation or prohibition of the weapon or weapons-technology of concern.[3]

This type of review is time-consuming and may require multiple experts, including scientists, but it is necessary to effectively understand the applicable law and is very much in line with what I have proposed throughout this book.

Second, my analysis illustrates that not only the laws of war regulate the use of nanomaterials in armed conflict. Treaties and international law and legal principles from environmental law, human rights and even laws of usufruct may apply to different uses of nanomaterials. Lawyers need to

[2] Robert Mathews and Timothy McCormack, 'The Relationship between International Humanitarian Law and Arms Control' in Helen Durham and Tim McCormack (eds), *The Changing Face of Conflict and the Efficacy of International Humanitarian Law* (Martinus Nijhoff, 1999) 70. There is 'a gap between the articulation of commitment to the general principles and the effective application of those general principles to specific weapons categories'.

[3] Michael Crowley, *Chemical Control: Regulation of Incapacitating Chemical Agent Weapons, Riot Control Agents and Their Means of Delivery* (Palgrave Macmillan, 2016) 6–7.

operate outside of their silos and be aware of, and fluent in, other legal discourses.

Third, some existing legal frameworks, such as protection of the environment during armed conflict, are not adequate and require strengthening. In this book, I have shown that even though nanomaterials remain unconsidered in international case law, there is a vast body of existing law that governs different uses of nanomaterials. From treaty law, customary international law and principles, environmental law and international human rights law, I have demonstrated the breadth of applicable law to the use of nanomaterials. As discussed in the introductory chapter of this book, not since the nuclear bomb has the convergence of technological capabilities posed such profound potential for changing how wars are fought, and never has there been such an urgency in consideration of the existing legal frameworks to new technological capabilities used in this way. Nanomaterials differ substantially from other technologies such as nuclear, biological, chemical and robotics. Consideration of their legal limits for use in war is urgent and necessary for each and every use.

Finally, I reiterate throughout the book that regulation for 'nanotechnologies' as if it is a unitary category is unhelpful. Different uses of nanomaterials will attract different laws of war.

As new technologies rapidly develop, are increasingly complex and increasingly interconnected, the type of review applied here to their use in war becomes even more critical to ensure compliance with existing international law.

In conclusion, this chapter makes recommendations for scientists, academia and industry; governments, lawmakers and lawyers; and the armed forces to ensure compliance with their international legal obligations. These recommendations also make suggestions for further research.

I Summary of Findings

In the introductory chapter, the themes and structure of the book were established, as well as the literature review, methodology and the Article 36 legal review requirement that all 'new means and methods' of warfare be assessed for compliance with international law. It is this model that is used to apply the legal frameworks to the three technologies.

Chapter 2 introduced the three technologies, namely thermobaric weapons, optogenetics, and genetic modification with more technical detail, and the reasoning for their selection. This technical detail facilitates a better legal analysis in Chapters 3–6 of the book, including a brief summary of the conclusions of each of the chapters and how each of the legal frameworks prohibits or limits each of the three technologies under consideration.

In Chapter 3, international treaties relevant to regulating the three technologies were considered. Each treaty was then applied individually to the relevant technologies. By considering potentially relevant international law treaties, it was established that weapons systems using or containing nanomaterials are, to a large extent, already prohibited or limited by existing treaty law. International treaty law provides clear limits for the use of most, if not all, aspects of these three technologies. By taking this approach, I conclude that the existing treaty law is relevant to prohibiting or limiting the use of these three uses of nanomaterials: namely, thermobaric weapons with nanomaterials, optogenetics and genetic modification. The use of thermobaric weapons with nanomaterials is not illegal *per se* pursuant to Protocol III of the CCW, the BWC, the CWC or the 1980 Protocol, but the existing legal framework does provide limits to their use. The 1995 Blinding Laser Protocol[4] and the BWC prohibit certain uses and limit other uses of optogenetics. Both the BWC and the CWC prohibit genetic modification of humans in war.

In addition to the treaty law obligations considered in Chapter 3, in Chapter 4 customary law obligations binding State and non-State parties alike were considered. By considering the legal principles of the laws of war, such as the requirement to balance military necessity with the principle of humanity, and the prohibition on superfluous injury and unnecessary suffering, Chapter 4 demonstrates that weapons that are enhanced or 'improved' in their function by nanomaterials require a new review of any 'means or method of warfare'. For example, thermobaric weapons enhanced by nanomaterials may have an intensity and force comparable to a small nuclear weapon (and potentially similarly negative impacts on the environment). These weapons require individual review in light of their enhanced capabilities, and the context in which they will be used. Second, this chapter concluded that the use of nanomaterials in the body is important and requires specific consideration

[4] *Protocol on Blinding Laser Weapons (Protocol IV) to the Convention on Prohibitions or Restrictions on the Use of Certain Conventional Weapons Which May e Deemed to Be Excessively Injurious or to Have Indiscriminate Effects*, opened for signature 13 October 1995, 1380 UNTS 370 (entered into force 30 July 1998) art 1 ('*Protocol IV to the CCW*').

because many bodily functions (such as blood and antibody production) occur at the nanoscale. This means that targeting nanomaterials may mean more specific intervention in the human body, thereby not necessarily undermining the existing law in the way that traditional weapons do. Targeting specific cells may not violate the prohibition on superfluous injury and unnecessary suffering (particularly if the intervention is reversible) or violate the principle of distinction or the rule of precaution. The inclusion of nanomaterials in some 'means or methods' of warfare may in fact make the methods of warfare more targeted and discriminate, and therefore better able to comply with the principles of the laws of war. However, being compliant with international custom or principles does not necessarily mean that the application is permissible *per se*, as discussed in Chapter 5 on environmental law.

Unlike Chapters 2–4, where specific legal frameworks were applied to all three uses of nanomaterials, international environmental law and principles have little relevance to optogenetics and genetic modification, or other uses of nanomaterials to alter human biology. They do, however, have relevance to every other use of nanomaterials, including thermobaric weapons with nanomaterials. Any use of nanomaterials that would release particles into the environment, and in particular, metallic nanoparticles, requires urgent contemplation of the long-term consequences. As Chapter 5 demonstrated, existing international law and principles are inadequate to deal with the risks posed by the as-yet not entirely known toxicity of nanomaterials, as well as the challenges in detecting or removing them from the environment once released. The existing legal standards, which are discussed in detail in Chapter 5, are not suited to the nature of new technologies and materials. I recommend, along with many others, a stronger regime to protect the environment during times of armed conflict that contemplates nanomaterials and their particular properties. The potential long-term, wide-spread and virtually undetectable nature of the toxicity of nanomaterials highlights the deficiencies in international environmental law in protecting the environment during war.

Chapter 6 considered the application of international human rights law: the right to life has relevance for the use of thermobaric weapons with nanomaterials and genetic modification, but less so for optogenetics. The prohibition on torture and the right to health are relevant to optogenetics and genetic modification, and any other manipulation of human biology on the nanoscale, but not to thermobaric weapons with nanomaterials. The human right to food and water is relevant to the potential danger posed by dispersion of nanomaterials in food chains and water cycles in war. The conclusion of Chapter 6 is that to meaningfully undertake an Article 36 review considering the legal obligations of a state during conflict, international human rights legal obligations must be considered. Each different use of nanomaterials will attract different international human rights law, which will therefore require an analysis of different law for each use of nanomaterials.

New or modified 'means or methods' of warfare may violate international treaty law (as discussed in Chapter 3) customary law and principles (as discussed in Chapter 4), international environmental law (as discussed in Chapter 5) and international human rights law. A careful analysis and application of each body of law is required to ensure compliance with, and application of, existing law. Through applying international law to three specific technologies utilising nanomaterials, thermobaric weapons, optogenetics and genetic modification, I have demonstrated that there is a large body of existing international law that already applies to the use of nanomaterials in war. General principles of customary international law limit how weapons can be used, including weapons using nanomaterials.

II Recommendations

First, the metaphorical regulatory wheel does not need to be reinvented for every new and emerging technology, and this includes the use of nanoscale materials. Existing legal frameworks should be referred to in assessments of any future uses of nanomaterials in war, or indeed any new or emerging technology used in a military context. In Chapter 3, I showed where these customary international law principles apply to the three technologies in question. Chapter 4 demonstrates that there are a number of international treaty agreements that have direct relevance for 'means or methods' of warfare containing nanomaterials.

To do this, lawyers need to engage with complicated science to a point where they can meaningfully talk about governing it. In the case of nanomaterials, this means keeping up to date with current scientific research, as knowledge regarding the materials in question changes over time. This sounds like an obvious point, but understanding the technologies is critical for lawyers to meaningfully participate in conversations about governing them. As the rate and scope of technologies continues to rapidly change our lives and challenge our existing legal systems and liberal Western democracies, this ability to engage, ask questions and continue to apply this knowledge to governance is absolutely key not only in ensuring compliance but also to ensure effective governance in future.

Second, before calling for additional law, and in addition to understanding the science, lawyers need to consider areas of the law not necessarily within their immediate specialty and start with the technology as a problem-based approach. A detailed survey and application of the existing scientific and legal landscapes needs to be undertaken for all uses of nanomaterials in war. These themes thread through the entire book and beyond to consideration of other new and emerging technologies if developed or considered. Lawyers need to survey and creatively apply existing law to all new technologies. Regulation and restrictions on use may appear in unusual sources of law, such as the ancient Roman law of usufruct, discussed in Chapter 5. The governance of nanomaterials is bringing together multiple protagonists alongside the developments themselves, not only in the area of science but also within different areas of the legal profession. Lawyers who specialise in the laws of war need to be familiar with human rights law, and traditional human rights lawyers need to have a grasp of the laws of war, just to give one example. Policy makers, safety regulators, industry and NGOs have responded both traditionally and creatively to reduce potential risks to individuals and the environment. I discuss this in more detail in my recommendations for governments, lawmakers and lawyers in this chapter.

Risk management frameworks, codes of conduct and reporting apparatus, interdisciplinary research crossing sectors and geographical boundaries, have profoundly and permanently changed the governance of uses of nanomaterials. This multi-pronged approach sets a new standard not only for the use of nanomaterials in war but also for the use of any new technologies. Expertise from one field is no longer sufficient to ensure compliance with international law. This requirement is symptomatic of new and emerging technologies more broadly, the effective regulation of which requires interdisciplinary and creative governance approaches beyond the role of the specialised traditional legal scholar. Applying international law to the use of nanomaterials in war requires greater awareness and compliance by scientists, academia and industry; governments, lawmakers and lawyers; and armed forces, each of which will be considered separately in the following sections.

A Scientists, Academia and Industry

Scientists, academia and industry develop and create knowledge regarding the risks of specific nanomaterials. For some years, scientists have attempted to categorise and assess risks associated with nanoparticles, but progress has been incremental for several reasons. First, there has not been general agreement on the definition of nanomaterial.[5] As Maynard noted in 2011, '[a] sensible definition has proved hard, if not impossible, to arrive at'.[6] Approaches vary as to whether a definition is possible, useful, or necessary. These contradictory approaches are beyond the scope of discussion in this book, but do indicate that the lack of agreement between experts on how to categorise and define what nanoscale means may compound other challenges of limiting their use.

Despite a lack of consensus within, among others, scientific and academic communities as to how a 'nanomaterial' should be defined for regulatory and policy purposes (if, indeed, it should be), in 2011 the European Commission moved forward with adopting its own definition. According to the Commission Recommendation of 18 October 2011 (2011/696/EU), a 'nanomaterial',

> means a natural, incidental or manufactured material containing particles, in an unbound state or as an aggregate or as an agglomerate and where, for 50% or more of the particles in the number size distribution, one or more external dimensions is in the size range 1 nm-100 nm (Article 2).

Beyond this requirement, scientists need to have a basic knowledge of international legal frameworks to ensure that they are not developing science for purposes contrary to international law.[7]

5 Gary Marchant, *What Is a Nanomaterial?* (22 September 2016) Slate <www.slate.com/articles/technology/future_tense/2016/09/the_difficulty_of_defining_nanomaterials.html>.

6 Andrew Maynard, 'Don't Define Nanomaterials' (2011) 475(7354) *Nature* 31. A contrary view was held by Wickson, who argues that it would be better to have a moratorium on the use of nanomaterials until 'relevant trigger-point attributes can be established. There would still be the problem of defining the point in the life cycle of a nanoproduct at which such attributes should be measured, given that they would be likely to change with time and context': Fern Wickson, 'Technology: Nanomaterials Need Flexible Regulation' (2011) 476(7360) *Nature* 283. A similar moratorium was suggested for genomic engineering and germline gene modification in David Baltimore et al, 'A prudent Path Forward for Genomic Engineering and Germline Gene Modification' (2015) 348(6230) *Science* 36. Although the call for a moratorium is beyond the scope of this book, it is interesting to note the controversy surrounding these developments, and that these types of calls might, in future, give cause to reflect on the definition of the 'dictates of public conscience' under the Martens Clause, contained in the preamble to the 1899 Hague Convention.

7 In 2002, the ICRC launched an appeal supporting this specific approach through its 'Biotechnology, Weapons and Humanity campaign', as noted in Brian Rappert and Catriona McLeish (eds), *A Web of Prevention: Biological Weapons, Life Sciences, and the Governance of Research* (Earthscan, 2007) 4.

> Those in a position to help prevent biotechnology being used for hostile purposes too often focus on only one aspect of the solution, such as the Biological Weapons Convention, bio-safety rules, disease surveillance, or countering 'bio-terrorism'. Seldom is synergy of action achieved between different entities concerned.[8]

Scientists, technologists, engineers and weapons experts need to be part of any legal review team, or at least aware of the legal constraints and requirements that govern their developments, as more complex and less 'traditional' means and methods of warfare are developed.

Different academic fields use vastly disparate terminology and have very individual cultures. Finding a common language for different professions to communicate effectively will be an ongoing challenge. This is a challenge that the use of nanomaterials across disciplines and uses has escalated. Reviews of new or modified 'means or methods' of warfare increasingly require the expertise of not just lawyers but also previously unusual collaborative relationships between scientists from engineering, physics, mathematics, computer science, chemistry, materials science and many other disciplines. For example, a recent biological advance involving a remote-controlled sting-ray robot that is powered by light-activated cells[9] included engineers, biologists, optogenetics experts and an ichthyologist (one who studies fish) to bring the idea to fruition. These are not the traditional actors usually considering the laws of war in their work. This example demonstrates the diverse nature of partnerships in science that may be involved in military developments. Relying on traditional legal reviews of 'means and methods' of warfare is necessary, but not sufficient. Further mechanisms that include the scientists working on the research that may be beyond the scope of the law must be explored. The ICRC notes that there is,

> [A]n obvious need to ensure that all universities offering curricula in life sciences and in chemistry include at least one mandatory session on the risks, the pertinent rules of national and international law and the responsibilities of scientists to prevent the hostile use of their research and its practical applications.[10]

[8] Brian Rappert and Catriona Leish (eds), *A Web of Prevention: Biological Weapons, Life Sciences, and the Governance of Research* (Earthscan, 2007) 4, quoting ICRC Web Prevention Campaign (2003).

[9] Elizabeth Pennisi, 'Robotic Stingray Powered by Light Activated Muscle Cells' (7 July 2016) *Science* <www.sciencemag.org/news/2016/07/robotic-stingray-powered-light-activated-muscle-cells>.

[10] Ibid.

Scientists need to be educated about their legal and ethical responsibilities to create a culture of compliance. A recommended topic for further research would be how to ensure a 'culture of responsibility' within the scientific community to uphold existing international legal responsibilities regarding new and emerging technologies.[11]

1 Potential Dual Use Must Not Undermine Public International Law

Issues that arise in relation to weapons systems that include nanoparticles may be complex. It is important to ensure that legal issues, such as the need for legal review, and concerns about dual use are considered with any weapons system, but particularly those using new technologies and nanomaterials, for all the reasons outlined in previous chapters. The advances that provide better healthcare, monitoring and medicine are the same advances that could also potentially be used for hostile purposes in armed conflict. This dual use potential both heightens the need to identify when reviews of weapons regarding their legality should occur and poses a challenge to the review process in terms of when it should be undertaken and how research should be categorised. Dual use has two definitions. Many legal scholars use the 'civilian use' versus 'military use' definition. The life sciences use a different definition: research with legitimate scientific purpose, the results of which may be misused to pose a threat to the public and/or national security.[12] Dual use remains an ongoing concern for regulation of military use of science. The World Health Organisation (WHO) states that '[d]ual use research of concern (DURC) is life sciences research that is intended for benefit, but which might easily be misapplied to do harm'.[13] Much of science has the potential to be used for both hostile and beneficial purposes. It is necessary to specifically consider dual use in the regulation of individual nanomaterials, as much of it has the potential for dual use.

Science has always had the potential for beneficent or maleficent purposes, but the traditional division between civilian uses and security

[11] *Functional Perspective on the Biological Weapons Convention and Chemical Weapons Convention* (11 December 2006) International Committee of the Red Cross <www.icrc.org/eng/resources/documents/statement/biological-chemical-weapons-statement-111206.htm>.

[12] For example National Institutes of Health, *Dual Use Research of Concern*, Office of Science Policy <https://osp.od.nih.gov/biotechnology/dual-use-research-of-concern/>.

[13] *Dual Use Research of Concern (DURC)*, World Health Organization <www.who.int/csr/durc/en/>.

uses has blurred profoundly. New genetic technologies expand the possibility to modify diverse species, including but not exclusively humans, and raise profound legal, social and ethical issues.

In early 2004, the National Science Advisory Board for Biosecurity (NSABB) was formed to provide guidance on education, regulation and strategies for 'dual use' research. Its agenda included the provision of tools to identify and evaluate the risks and benefits of particular kinds of science. In 2007, NSABB completed a report, *Proposed Framework for the Oversight of Dual-Use Life Sciences Research*, which defined dual research as,

> [A] term to refer in general to legitimate life sciences research that has the potential to yield information that could be misused to threaten public health and safety and other aspects of national security such as agriculture, plants, animals, the environment, and material.[14]

Given that almost all scientific research could fall within this definition, NSABB offered another category of 'dual-use research of concern', which was defined as,

> [R]esearch that, based on current understanding, can be reasonably anticipated to provide knowledge, products, or technologies that could be directly misapplied to pose a threat to public health and safety, agricultural crops and other plants, animals, the environment, or material.[15]

Despite the inevitability of the dual-purpose nature of research, including a multi-billion dollar increase in biodefense research funding in the United States after 2001, 'much of it supporting civilian research',[16] surprisingly little research is censored or held to be a risk.[17]

Particularly in the case of nanomaterials used for advances in neuroscience, the risks of dual use need to be managed very carefully. The

[14] National Science Advisory Board for Biosecurity, Proposed Framework for the Oversight of Dual Use Life Sciences Research: Strategies for Minimizing the Potential Misuse of Research Information (June 2007) <https://osp.od.nih.gov/wp-content/uploads/Proposed-Oversight-Framework-for-Dual-Use-Research.pdf>.

[15] R Terry, 'Addressing Risks of Research Misuse' (Speech delivered at the Dual Use and Codes of Conduct Meeting, Berlin, 2006).

[16] *Biodefense for the 21st Century* (28 April 2004) Office of the Press Secretary, The White House <www.hsdl.org/?view&did=784400>.

[17] Brian Rappert, 'Why Has Not There Been More Research of Concern?' (2014) 2 *Frontiers in Public Health* <www.ncbi.nlm.nih.gov/pmc/articles/PMC4106452/pdf/fpubh-02-00074.pdf>.

CWC incorporates lists of materials that are dual use and limits the quantities in which they can be purchased, sold or transferred across national boundaries. A challenge not particular to, but particularly a feature of, nanomaterials is that, given the literally invisible nature of potentially toxic materials, similar control measures will not be effective for nanomaterials. One such example is virus-like nanoparticles, currently being researched for targeting cancer, but again, with potential dual use.[18] Garage biology (a term used to refer to individuals conducting experiments on their own) also poses a security threat, with its decreasing costs and automation. The extent to which these types of threats remain a risk are considered within the DURC framework mentioned earlier, one in which 'the overall approach is to treat the use of biological weapons as a low probability high impact risk'.[19] Similar frameworks must be developed for nanomaterials, even if they are beyond the range of human sight. Potentially, nanomaterials could be added to the CWC lists of dual use materials as knowledge of their toxicity becomes available.

2 Legal Implications of Chemical and Biological Convergence

The distinction between chemical and biological action blurs at the nanoscale.[20] Experts from the BWC and the CWC meetings need to regularly reiterate that developments in the use of nanomaterials are included within the ambit of both the BWC and the CWC. Nanomaterials can asphyxiate without a chemical action (such as asbestos fibres, which occur on the nanoscale), or assemblies of atoms (nanorobots as described earlier) that can behave like a pathogen.[21] Beyond this blurring of behaviour, the properties of nanomaterials often differ from their regular-scale counterparts, sometimes even when only one component of a material is at the nanoscale.[22] I strongly recommend that the BWC and the CWC,

18 Frank Sainsbury, 'Virus-like Nanoparticles: Emerging Tools for Targeted Cancer Diagnostics and Therapeutics' (2017) 8(12) *Therapeutic Delivery* 1019.

19 Erik Frinking, Paul Sinning and Eva Bontje, *The Increasing Threat of Biological Weapons: Handle with Sufficient and Proportionate Care* (Hague Centre for Strategic Studies, 2017) 32.

20 Mark Wheelis and Malcolm Dando, 'Neurobiology: A Case Study for the Imminent Militarization of Biology' (2005) 87(859) *International Review of the Red Cross* 560.

21 Robert Mathews, 'Chemical and Biological Weapons' in Rain Liivoja and Tim McCormack (eds), *Routledge Handbook of the Law of Armed Conflict* (Routledge, 2016) 229–230.

22 Vladimir Pitschmann and Zdenek Hon, 'Military Importance of Natural Toxins and their Analogs' (2016) 21 *Molecules* 556 <www.mdpi.com/1420-3049/21/5/556/html>.

> prepare statements for endorsement at their respective Review Conferences which confirm that all such novel materials are captured by the prohibition of CBW, even if there are arguments that a particular material may not be covered by the definitions of BW and CW contained in BWC and CWC.[23]

I am also in agreement with suggestions that, in the absence of such clarification, nanomaterials would nevertheless be captured by the language of the 1899 and 1907 Hague Conventions, as well as the Geneva Protocol which prohibits 'poison and poisoned weapons'. This approach is practical and in accordance with the existing customary international law prohibitions on poisons and chemical weapons. Arguing about whether a substance at the nanoscale acts on its chemical or physical properties will seldom change the outcome of the conclusion of a legal review: weaponisation of nanoparticles by any means flies in the face of existing customary international law standards regarding matter at regular scale, and therefore any use of matter in similar ways at the nanoscale would be prohibited.

The Seventh BWC Review Conference in 2011 noted the 'increasing convergence of biology and chemistry and its possible challenges and opportunities for the implementation of the Convention'.[24] In fact, this blurring of behaviour at this scale means that the BWC and the CWC would regulate nanomaterials used within the human body.[25] Further statements from the Review Conference, which would assist in the understanding of the application of the BWC and the CWC to nanomaterial, would serve as a legal source of guidance as to how to interpret the treaty, as discussed earlier in this chapter.[26]

Convergence is not just a matter of behaviour at the nanoscale; it is also an issue across disciplines,

> [c]onvergence is not only the small area of intersection between fields, but also a new research model that represents 'the merging of distinct technologies, processing disciplines, or devices into a unified whole that

[23] Ibid.

[24] *Final Review Document of the Seventh Review Conference, Seventh Review Conference of the States Parties to the Convention on the Prohibition of the Development, Production and Stockpiling of Bacteriological (Biological) and Toxin Weapons and on Their Destruction*, UN Doc BWC/CONF. VII/COW/CRP.2 (5–22 December 2011) 49.

[25] Juan Pablo Pardo-Guerra and Francisco Aguayo Ayala, 'Nanotechnology and the International Regime on Chemical and Biological Weapons' (2005) 2(1) *Nanotechnology Law and Business* 55.

[26] Mathews, n 21, 212–232.

> creates a host of new pathways and opportunities. It involves the coming together of different fields of study – particularly engineering, physical sciences and life sciences – through collaboration among research groups and integration of approaches that were originally viewed as distinct and potentially contradictory.[27]

As nanomaterials have many potential uses across many types of weapons, its regulation with respect to weapons may pose similar challenges to those faced in the civilian sector, where regulation of nanomaterials is separated into categories of use, rather than looking at the behaviour of nanoscale materials as part of a spectrum or pattern. Further, where chemicals behave differently at the nanoscale, and have different (particularly potentially toxic) properties, the BWC and/or the CWC, in many cases, remain applicable, as do general principles of humanitarian law, as discussed in Chapter 3.

The same approach to potential uses of biology needs to be extended to include research in nanomaterials. Much work has been done in this area, including a 2004 appeal by the ICRC for actors in the life sciences to 'promote awareness of the norms against poison and the deliberate spread of disease and the need for preventive action, in conjunction with their responsibilities'.[28] As part of this campaign, the ICRC provided draft model legislation for States, proposed codes of conduct and encouraged awareness of the risks for those working in the life sciences. A similar appeal for those working on nanomaterials, particularly those in the life sciences, would be timely.

Scientists and the academic community need to ensure consistent definitions are used and applied and communicate and share these definitions with defence to ensure consistency. Sharing of information regarding toxicity is also key. This consistency of definitions and sharing of information is important to ensure effective compliance with international law. Scientists, academia and industry have a key role to play in ensuring this compliance.

[27] National Research Council of the National Academies, *Life Sciences and Related Fields: Trends Relevant to the Biological Weapons Convention* (National Academies Press, 2011) 82, citing Phillip Sharp and Robert Langer, 'Promoting Convergence in Biomedical Science' (2011) 333(6042) *Science* 527.

[28] *Biotechnology, Weapons and Humanity* (20 January 2004) International Committee of the Red Cross <www.icrc.org/eng/resources/documents/misc/5vdj7s.htm>.

B Governments, Lawmakers and Lawyers

I have shown how a large body of law already applies to the use of nanomaterials in war. Additional creative regulatory approaches are required for environmental risks posed by the use of nanomaterials even as research is being undertaken. Regulators need to strike a delicate balance between exploratory risk research and regulatory responses. Research does not, and cannot, halt due to unknown risks. The question of how to proceed cautiously in the face of ongoing new scientific information and risks remains. Some parallels can be drawn with the Precautionary Principle, discussed earlier in Chapter 5. These challenges as outlined lead to some very specific conclusions and recommendations regarding the regulation of weapons containing nanomaterials.

Similarly, it is important that lawyers do not get caught up in the hype surrounding new technologies, and in doing so, lose sight of the importance and relevance of the existing legal framework.[29] Technology has always been the hare to the legal tortoise. It usually takes the witnessing of the use of a weapon on the battlefield for States to take steps to prohibit or limit a weapon's use, with limited exceptions.[30]

I call for States and governments to strengthen the existing prohibition on chemical and biological weapons to include materials at the nanoscale, within the existing framework of the Review Conferences of the BWC, and within the Scientific Advisory Board for the CWC. States need to be clear that any materials that contravene the BWC or CWC, whether at the regular, micro or nanoscale, remain prohibited, and reiterate that States will be held to account. The CWC, in particular, which has the ability to inspect, should review its procedures to enable inspections of potentially malevolent research using nanomaterials. This will require greater scrutiny of toxic nanomaterials as their properties become clear, and consideration of mechanisms to quantify or qualify when such matter would fall within the mandate of the CWC. An additional list of prohibited materials at the nanoscale may be necessary in the future to

[29] Gregory N Mandel, 'History Lessons for a General Theory of Law and Technology' (2007) 8(2) *Minnesota Journal of Law, Science and Technology* 551.

[30] With the exception of the use of exploding bullets on humans (prohibited by the *Declaration Renouncing the Use, in Time of War of Explosive Projectiles under 400 grammes Weight*, opened for signature 29 November 1868, 138 CTS 297 (entered into force 11 December 1868)) and more recently, laser weapons (prohibited by *Protocol IV to the CCW*).

ensure that the transfer and use of nanomaterials is compliant with the requirements of the CWC.

Lawyers should not limit themselves to taking the position that the 'law is to be made, but the values and policies that inform this law making should come from elsewhere'.[31] Practical suggestions will need to be made to clarify and strengthen the existing law, and specific suggestions provided for additional methods of governance, including principles, codes of conduct and other forms of governance that will help clarify and strengthen the existing legal framework. It is imperative that lawyers and 'humanities and social sciences have a critical function asking fundamental questions and informing the public'.[32]

1 Overlapping Legal Regimes

The idea of one international legal framework governing the use of nanomaterials in war remains elusive and largely fictional. Modern international law constantly manages multiple legal frameworks that duplicate and overlap each other with their reach. Conflicting legal norms have in some cases developed, and may continue to develop, evidencing the fragmented and, at times, contradictory nature of international legal practice. In 2006, the ILC provided a study on the fragmentation of the law, describing much international law as being accompanied by its own 'ethos'.[33] This 'ethos' between legal regimes, with long and often colourful negotiations and histories, poses a challenge to reconciling the different legal frameworks in many instances. Two well-explored overlapping regimes are human rights and the laws of war. This type of normative and institutional pluralism has been well documented in other areas, including the use of the high seas.[34] In her considerations of fragmentation, Young (2011) proposes an argument for

[31] Kieren Tranter, 'The Law and Technology Enterprise: Uncovering the Template to Legal Scholarship on Technology' (2011) 3(1) *Law, Innovation and Technology* 31. Rain Liivoja discusses this in 'Technological Change and the Evolution of War' (2015) 97(900) *International Review of the Red Cross* 1157. Liivoja suggests that it is typical, but unhelpful, that lawyers traditionally take this position of suggesting reform without suggesting what that reform should be.

[32] Mette Ebbesen, 'The Role of the Humanities and Social Sciences in Nanotechnology Research and Development' (2008) 2(1) *NanoEthics* 1.

[33] Martti Koskenniemi, *Fragmentation of International Law: Difficulties Arising from the Diversification and Expansion of International Law*, International Law Commission, 58th sess, UN Doc A/CN.4/L.682 (13 April 2006) [8], [10] ('*ILC Fragmentation Report*').

[34] Margaret A Young, *Trading Fish, Saving Fish: The Interaction Between Regimes in International Law* (Cambridge University Press, 2011).

a legal framework of regime interaction where there is no regime hierarchy; where the interaction between regimes is 'continuous and constant'; and where the authority of one regime is always contestable. The capacities and duties of intergovernmental organisations and the participation of non-governmental organisations are necessary to take into account when international laws are created, implemented and enforced across multiple regimes.[35] The multiplicity of legal regimes I consider provides the potential for conflicting norms, with the tension between the laws of war and the laws protecting the environment being just one example.

Further, treaties are not uniformly ratified. Different laws aim to perform different functions at different times. In some cases, such as international environmental law, another area of law may provide clarification and support the existing international law: human rights law may provide additional context relevant to determining what constitutes widespread, long-term and severe damage to the environment. Human rights law would prohibit attacks that may be expected to affect the sustainability of an adequate supply of food or water, or any which 'prejudice the health or survival of the population'.[36] This kind of consideration and analysis requires knowledge of multiple legal regimes, and an understanding of their historical interaction. Governments, lawmakers and lawyers have an obligation to ensure awareness of legal regimes and legal frameworks that are not their specialty in order to ensure compliance with the multiple legal regimes addressed in this book, and in order to comply with existing international law.

From analysing the different legal frameworks applicable to three specific uses of nanomaterials in war, it is clear that 'law-making treaties are tending to develop in a number of historical, functional and regional groups which are separate from each other'.[37] In the case of the legal frameworks analysed – namely the laws of war, disarmament treaties,

[35] Margaret A Young, 'Regime Interaction in Creating, Implementing and Enforcing International Law' in Margaret A Young (ed), *Regime Interaction in International Law: Facing Fragmentation* (Cambridge University Press, 2012) 86, 109.

[36] *Protocol Additional to the Geneva Conventions of 12 August 1949, and Relating to the Protection of Victims of International Armed Conflicts (Protocol I)*, opened for signature 8 June 1977, 1125 UNTS 3 (entered into force on 7 December 1978) art 55(1) ('*Additional Protocol I*'). Long-term contamination of food or water would undermine the essential conditions underlying the right to health.

[37] Christopher Jenks, 'The Conflict of Law-Making Treaties' (1953) 30 *British Yearbook of International Law* 401, 403.

environmental law and human rights law – all have developed independently, most frequently without reference or consideration for any of the other areas of law. The treaties range in date from 1925 to 1992, each with a differing number of States parties and each with different reservations, and often supported by 'soft law' instruments, as canvassed in previous chapters. Understanding how these different regimes interact in unseen ways requires 'legal, historical, doctrinal, institutional and sociological' analysis.[38] In many ways, the analysis of the existing applicable law to nanomaterials has used all of these approaches in previous chapters, sometimes more obviously than others. Part of the challenge of writing meaningfully about the international legal framework governing nanomaterials has been negotiating seemingly unrelated areas of law with profoundly different historical roots and cultures. Conversations about limitations on armed conflict undertaken in space also suffer from similar challenges and conflicting and overlapping legal regimes, the relationships of which have been explored in some detail.[39] Lessons should be drawn from other fields where similar overlap and conflict arises in public international law, again, with careful consideration of existing international legal frameworks.

2 Key Challenges for Compliance with Existing Treaties

The BWC and the CWC were drafted well before human manipulation of nanomaterials was possible. That said, this is not an unusual situation as technology is almost always ahead of the law. Developments such as telegraphs and steam trains, all the way through to automated cars, have predated comprehensive legal frameworks. As important as the ability of the law to respond is the ability of the law to be predictable and stable. If new laws were required for every innovation, a complete lack of stability would result, even if it were even possible to keep up with recent rapid technological changes. As has already been noted, technology itself will almost always change more rapidly in response to societal responses than the law.[40] This is not a reason to discount or disregard the law, in fact.

[38] Margaret A Young, 'Introduction: The Productive Friction between Regimes' in Margaret A Young (ed), *Regime Interaction in International Law: Facing Fragmentation* (Cambridge University Press, 2012) 1.

[39] Dale Stephens, 'The International Legal Implications of Military Space Operations: Examining the Interplay between Humanitarian Law and the Outer Space Legal Regime' (2018) 94 *International Law Studies* 75.

[40] Richard Susskind, *The Future of Law: Facing the Challenges of Information Technology* (Clarendon Press, 1996).

Furthermore, technological developments are not going unnoticed or being ignored by States and others. In 2002, in his role as leader of the SIPRI Chemical and Biological Warfare Project, Zanders noted challenges to the OPCW's mandate, singling out nanomaterials in that 'the growing overlap between chemistry and biotechnology as well as the design and production processes based on nanotechnology may be of particular concern'.[41] Other calls have been made by experts in the field, noting that 'strong international action is needed to assess the threats from the new age of biological techniques'.[42]

The laws of war currently already restrict or prohibit many uses of nanomaterials in war, ensuring compliance with existing law. Provisions seeking to control their import, export and use require urgent consideration, whether under existing regimes or by way of new agreements. Practical aspects of enforcing the Geneva Protocol, the BWC and the CWC pose some of the biggest challenges in the context of nanomaterials. Ensuring compliance with existing international legal regulations poses very specific problems different to materials at the regular scale given the different properties at different dimensions and difficulties to detect them.

3 Non-State Actors

To effectively regulate the use of nanomaterials in war, governments, lawyers and academics must also consider their use by non-State actors. I have focused on the regulation of the use of nanomaterials in war. However, the issue of non-State actors is relevant insofar as the obligation is on States to regulate nanomaterials used by non-State actors in times of war.

States are required to pass laws that regulate terrorist groups and corporations. In 1996, the Fourth BWC Review Conference reiterated that the prohibitions contained in the BWC equally applied to acts by terrorist groups.

> Each party is obliged to take measures, in accordance with its constitutional processes, to prohibit and prevent the activities banned by the Convention from taking place within its territory and under its jurisdiction or control anywhere (Article IV) ... [E]ven transnational corporations operating in the territories of non-parties to the Convention are

41 Jean Pascal Zanders, 'The Chemical Weapons Convention and Universality: A Question of Quality over Quantity?' (2002) 4 *Disarmament Forum* 23.

42 Malcolm Dando, 'Find the Time to Discuss New Bioweapons' (2016) 535(7610) *Nature* 9.

> covered by the prohibitions if they remain under the jurisdiction or control of the parties.[43]

An obligation was found to extend not only to terrorist groups but also to corporations. In 2004, UNSCR 1540 explicitly extended the prohibitions on States contained in the Geneva Protocol, BWC and CWC to non-State actors. United Nations Security Council Resolution 1540 requires that all States refrain from providing support to non-State actors, including providing dual use materials.[44] In 2011, the UN Security Council adopted a further resolution, reinforcing the language of the original Resolution, and extending the mandate of the 1540 Committee for a period of 10 years.[45] As already discussed, Security Council Resolutions are binding and, as such, States are in turn required to ensure compliance within their own internal domestic regulation.

Despite having ratified the treaty, many States have not taken the necessary step of ensuring that domestic regulations and regulatory bodies ensure compliance with the obligations to which States are committed under international law. Particularly in relation to the BWC, Goldblat notes,

> Not all parties, however, have taken the steps required to ensure domestic compliance with the Convention. This is all the more regrettable in that biological agents appear to be becoming attractive, for terrorist purposes, to players other than States. According to reliable reports, the Aum Shinrikyo sect, which released nerve gas in a Tokyo subway train, had also been working on the development of biological weapons and in 1995, shortly before the arrest of its leader, was close to completing this programme.[46]

[43] *Final Declaration, Fourth Review Conference of the Parties to the Convention on the Prohibition of the Development, Production and Stockpiling of Bacteriological (Biological) and Toxin Weapons and on Their Destruction*, UN Doc BWC/CONF. IV/9 (25 November to 6 December 1996) pt 2, art IV ('*Fourth Review Conference Final Declaration*'): 'The Conference underlines the importance of Article IV . . . The States Parties recognize the need to ensure, through the review and/or adoption of national measures, the effective fulfilment of their obligations under the Convention in order, inter alia, to exclude the use of biological and toxin weapons in a terrorist or criminal activity'. Jozef Goldblat, 'The Biological Weapons Convention: An Overview' (1997) 37(318) *International Review of the Red Cross* 251, 259.

[44] SC Res 1540, UN SCOR, 59th sess, 4956th mtg, UN Doc S/RES/1540 (28 April 2004).

[45] SC Res 1977, UN SCOR, 66th sess, 6518th mtg, UN Doc S/RES/1977 (20 April 2011) [8], [24].

[46] Goldblat, n 43, 259.

These resolutions, in effect, extend the obligations outlined in the BWC to all states, not just those party to the BWC, and would apply therefore to the use of viruses by any State, individual or corporation with an intention to activate it for hostile use. Whether a virus is 'activated', or whether it remains latent with no apparent effect, the use of any virus without a justification for 'prophylactic, protective or other peaceful purposes' would violate Article 1 of the BWC.[47]

C *Armed Forces*

Defence Forces need to actively seek input from and regularly communicate with scientists, the academic community and industry. The long-term effects that the inclusion of nanoparticles in the weapons systems and processes being analysed in this book will have remains unknown. Little is known about how the particles are absorbed – inhalation, digestion, absorption – and whether the form of absorption will alter the effect of the nanoparticles on the human body. It is very difficult to regulate what you cannot see and cannot define, and the effects of which are uncertain. Very little research has been written on the impact of nanomaterials and health considerations for the military specifically,[48] and the research on the risk of nanomaterials and nanoparticles to humans and to the environment is still in its infancy,[49] and much remains unknown. Limited writing also considers the application of soft law to governing the use of nanomaterials,[50] although how effective this would be in war is questionable. Weapons law is most certainly one of the areas of the laws of war that presents some of the greatest

[47] *Fourth Review Conference Final Declaration*, UN Doc BWC/CONF. IV/9, pt 2, art I.

[48] Jerome Glenn, 'Nanotechnology: Future Military Environmental Health Considerations' (2006) 73(2) *Technological Forecasting and Social Change* 128 is the only example I could find of such research.

[49] Andreas Elsaesser and C Vyvyan Howard, 'Toxicology of Nanoparticles' (2012) 64(2) *Advanced Drug Delivery Reviews* 129; Taryn Rucinski, 'Searching for the Nano-needle in a Green Haystack: Researching the Environmental, Health, and Safety Ramifications of Nanotechnology' (2013) 30(2) *Pace Environmental Law Review* 397; Haji Bahadar et al, 'Toxicity of Nanoparticles and an Overview of Current Experimental Models' (2016) 20 (1) *Iranian Biomedical Journal* 1; Anupam Dhasmana et al, 'Nanoparticles: Applications, Toxicology and Safety Aspects' in Kavin Kesari (ed), *Perspectives in Environmental Toxicology* (Springer, 2017).

[50] Jason Wejnert, 'Regulatory Mechanisms for Molecular Nanotechnology' (2004) 44(3) *Jurimetrics* 323.

challenges.[51] Armed forces can, and should, learn and draw on existing models from the civilian sphere.[52]

Further, particular to the military is often a shroud of secrecy surrounding the ways in which technologies are used and developed.[53] For example, considerations of secrecy will make the open peer review of findings in these areas much more difficult. An unintended consequence of secrecy in the development of some nanomaterials could also fuel public distrust and concerns about non-military developments. This would be so particularly if the term 'nanotechnology' as a whole came to be closely associated with military ends. This culture does not assist in the sharing of information and reduction of risk in the uses of nanomaterials.

III Conclusion

Existing international law comprehends and is capable of effectively governing uses of nanomaterials in war. Nanomaterials do, however, pose particular challenges and risks that are different from more traditional weapons, or even from chemical and biological weapons. I have analysed the applicability of certain areas of the law by reference to three specific technologies that utilise nanomaterials. These specific examples of nanomaterials are reference cases to test the applicability of international law in war. The consideration of other new and emerging technologies is beyond the scope of this book, but exactly this type of thorough legal analysis will be needed not only for nanomaterials but also for other technologies as they rapidly advance.

In the converse, something similar to an Article 36 review for civilian uses of new technologies may also be helpful to ensure compliance with existing law. The regulation of nanomaterials outside of the war context

[51] Steven Haines, 'The Developing Law of Weapons: Humanity, Distinction and Precautions in Attack' in Andrew Clapham and Paola Gaeta (eds), *The Oxford Handbook of International Law in Armed Conflict* (Oxford University Press, 2014) 295.

[52] Kobi Leins and Diana M Bowman, 'Nanomaterials: A Tale of Two Applications' in William Boothby (ed), *New Technologies: The Law in War and Peace* (Cambridge University Press, 2019) 285–314.

[53] The Royal Society, *Nanoscience and Nanotechnologies: Opportunities and Uncertainties* (July 2004) 56 <https://royalsociety.org/~/media/Royal_Society_Content/policy/publications/2004/9693.pdf>.

has been comprehensively considered.[54] Applying this expertise to consider the regulation of the use of nanomaterials in war may be helpful.[55] Developments surrounding the interplay between multiple technologies, such as AI (including sensors, algorithms and data) and the Internet of Things, have made the need to consider the efficacy of existing legal frameworks for governing the individual technologies even more urgent.[56] As the technologies develop rapidly and become more complex, the legal frameworks that govern them require clarification, and, at times, may require additional governance and/or interpretative tools, given their seemingly novel nature. However, before anyone calls for more regulation for any uses of nanomaterials during war, or any new technology, in fact, it is critical that they map the existing legal landscape first. When new governance is contemplated, existing frameworks such as the review conferences of the weapons treaties need to frame these responses. Old regimes, often forgotten but still relevant, such as ENMOD, need to be revived and strengthened to reflect our current understanding of our reliance on the environment. Obviously, there will be resistance to greater accountability from some States – it will be important to connect the different legal regimes and cross-fertilise ideas to ensure that the protection needed for the environment during armed conflict is adequately provided by international law.

The time for clarifying and strengthening the governance of the use of nanomaterials in war is now. The effective regulation of the use of nanomaterials in war to ensure compliance with existing law, and consideration of where the law does not reflect current societal values, remains an urgent task for now and into the future.

[54] Kenneth Abbott, Douglas Sylvester and Garry Marchant, 'Transnational Regulation: Reality or Romanticism?' in Graeme Hodge, Diana Bowman and Andrew Maynard (eds), *International Handbook on Regulating Nanotechnologies* (Elgar, 2010); Graeme Hodge, Diana Bowman and Karinne Ludlow (eds), *New Global Frontiers in Regulation: The Age of Nanotechnology* (Edward Elgar, 2007).

[55] Kobi Leins and Diana M Bowman, 'Nanomaterials: A Tale of Two Applications' in William Boothby (ed), *New Technologies: The Law in War and Peace* (Cambridge University Press, 2019) 285–314.

[56] Aarti Shahani, *Microsoft President Urges Nuclear-Like Limits on Cyberweapons* (16 May 2017) National Public Radio <www.npr.org/sections/alltechconsidered/2017/05/16/528555400/microsofts-president-reflects-on-cyberattack-helping-pirates-and-the-nsa>.

BIBLIOGRAPHY

I Conventions

Amendment to Article I of the Convention on Prohibitions or Restrictions on the Use of Certain Conventional Weapons Which May Be Deemed to Be Excessively Injurious or to Have Indiscriminate Effects, opened for signature 21 December 2001, 2260 UNTS 82 (entered into force 18 May 2004)

Arms Trade Treaty, opened for signature on 3 June 2013 (entered into force 24 December 2014) adopted as *The Arms Trade Treaty*, GA Res 67/234B, UN GAOR, 67th sess, 71st plen mtg, Agenda Item 94, UN Doc A/RES/67/234 B (11 June 2013)

Cartagena Declaration on Renunciation of Weapons of Mass Destruction (signed and entered into force 4 December 1991)

Comprehensive Agreement on Respect for Human Rights and International Humanitarian Law between the Government of the Republic of the Philippines and the National Democratic Front of the Philippines (signed and entered into force 16 March 1998)

Convention (II) with Respect to the Laws and Customs of War on Land and Its Annex: Regulations Concerning the Laws and Customs of War on Land, signed 29 July 1899, 187 CTS 429 (entered into force 4 September 1900)

Convention (IV) with Respect to the Laws and Customs of War on Land and Its Annex: Regulations Concerning the Laws and Customs of War on Land, signed 18 October 1907, 205 CTS 277 (entered into force 26 January 1910)

Convention against Torture and Other Cruel, Inhuman or Degrading Treatment or Punishment, opened for signature 10 December 1984, 1465 UNTS 85 (entered into force 26 June 1987)

Convention Concerning the Protection of the World Cultural and Natural Heritage, opened for signature 16 November 1972, 1037 UNTS 151 (entered into force 17 December 1975)

Convention for the Protection of Human Rights and Dignity of the Human Being with Regard to the Application of Biology and Medicine, opened for signature 4 April 1997, ETS No 164 (entered into force 1 December 1999)

Convention for the Protection of Human Rights and Fundamental Freedoms, opened for signature 4 November 1950, 213 UNTS 221 (entered into force 3 September 1953)

Convention on Biological Diversity, opened for signature 5 June 1992, 1760 UNTS 79 (entered into force 29 December 1993)

Convention on Prohibition or Restrictions on the Use of Certain Conventional Weapons Which May Be Deemed to Be Excessively Injurious or to Have Indiscriminate Effects, opened for signature 10 October 1980, 1342 UNTS 137 (entered into force 2 December 1983)

Convention on the Prohibition of Military or Any Other Hostile Use of Environmental Modification Techniques, opened for signature 10 December 1976, 1108 UNTS 151 (entered into force 5 October 1978)

Convention on the Prohibition of the Development, Production and Stockpiling of Bacteriological (Biological) and Toxin Weapons and on Their Destruction, opened for signature 10 April 1972, 1015 UNTS 163 (entered into force 26 March 1975)

Convention on the Prohibition of the Development, Production, Stockpiling and Use of Chemical Weapons and on Their Destruction, opened for signature 3 September 1992, 1974 UNTS 45 (entered into force 29 April 1997)

Convention on the Prohibition of the Use, Stockpiling, Production and Transfer of Anti-Personnel Mines and on Their Destruction, opened for signature 18 September 1997, 2056 UNTS 211 (entered into force 1 March 1999)

Convention on the Rights of the Child, opened for signature 20 November 1989, 1577 UNTS 3 (entered into force 2 September 1990)

Convention on Wetlands of International Importance Especially as Waterfowl Habitat, opened for signature 2 February 1971, 996 UNTS 245 (entered into force 21 December 1975)

Declaration Renouncing the Use, in Time of War, of Explosive Projectiles under 400 Grammes Weight, signed 29 November 1868, 138 CTS 297 (entered into force 11 December 1868) ('*Declaration of St Petersburg*')

Geneva Convention (I) for the Amelioration of the Condition of the Wounded and Sick in Armed Forces in the Field (First Geneva Convention), opened for signature 12 August 1949, 75 UNTS 31 (entered into force 21 October 1950)

Geneva Convention (II) for the Amelioration of the Condition of Wounded, Sick and Shipwrecked Members of Armed Forces at Sea (Second Geneva Convention), opened for signature 12 August 1949, 75 UNTS 85 (entered into force 21 October 1950)

Geneva Convention (III) Relative to the Treatment of Prisoners of War (Third Geneva Convention), opened for signature 12 August 1949, 75 UNTS 135 (entered into force 21 October 1950)

Geneva Convention (IV) Relative to the Protection of Civilian Persons in Time of War (Fourth Geneva Convention), opened for signature 12 August 1949, 75 UNTS 287 (entered into force 21 October 1950)

Hague Declaration (II) on the Use of Projectiles the Object of Which Is the Diffusion of Asphyxiating or Deleterious Gases, opened for signature 29 July 1899, 187 CTS 453 (entered into force 4 September 1900)

International Convention on the Elimination of All Forms of Discrimination against Women, opened for signature 1 March 1980, 1249 UNTS 13 (entered into force 3 September 1981)

International Covenant on Civil and Political Rights, opened for signature 19 December 1966, 999 UNTS 171 (entered into force 23 March 1976)

International Covenant on Economic, Social and Cultural Rights, opened for signature 16 December 1966, 993 UNTS 3 (entered into force 3 January 1976)

Joint Declaration on the Complete Prohibition of Chemical and Biological Weapons, Argentina-Brazil-Chile (signed and entered into force 5 September 1991)

Optional Protocol to the Convention against Torture and Other Cruel, Inhuman or Degrading Treatment or Punishment, opened for signature 4 February 2003, 2375 UNTS 237 (entered into force 22 June 2006)

Project of an International Declaration Concerning the Laws and Customs of War, signed 27 August 1874 (did not enter into force) <https://ihl-databases.icrc.org/ihl/INTRO/135>

Protocol Additional to the Geneva Conventions of 12 August 1949, and Relating to the Protection of Victims of International Armed Conflicts (Protocol I), opened for signature 8 June 1977, 1125 UNTS 3 (entered into force 7 December 1979)

Protocol Additional to the Geneva Conventions of 12 August 1949, and Relating to the Protection of Victims of Non-International Armed Conflicts (Protocol II), opened for signature 8 June 1977, 1125 UNTS 609 (entered into force 7 December 1978)

Protocol Additional to the Geneva Conventions of 12 August 1949, and Relating to the Adoption of an Additional Distinctive Emblem (Protocol III), opened for signature 8 December 2005, 2404 UNTS 261 (entered into force 14 January 2007)

Protocol for the Prohibition of the Use of Asphyxiating, Poisonous or Other Gases, and of Bacteriological Methods of Warfare, opened for signature 17 June 1925, 94 LNTS 65 (entered into force 8 February 1928)

Protocol on Blinding Laser Weapons (Protocol IV) to the Convention on Prohibitions or Restrictions on the Use of Certain Conventional Weapons Which May Be Deemed to Be Excessively Injurious or to Have Indiscriminate Effects, opened for signature 13 October 1995, 1380 UNTS 370 (entered into force 30 July 1998)

Protocol on Non-Detectable Fragments (Protocol I) to the Convention on Prohibition or Restrictions on the Use of Certain Conventional Weapons Which May Be Deemed to Be Excessively Injurious or to Have Indiscriminate Effects, opened for signature 10 October 1980, 1342 UNTS 137 (entered into force 2 December 1983)

Protocol on Prohibitions or Restrictions on the Use of Incendiary Weapons (Protocol III) to the Convention on Prohibition or Restrictions on the Use of Certain Conventional Weapons Which May Be Deemed to Be Excessively Injurious or to Have Indiscriminate Effects, opened for signature 10 October 1980, 1342 UNTS 171 (entered into force 2 December 1983)

Protocol on Prohibitions or Restrictions on the Use of Mines, Booby-Traps and Other Devices as amended on 3 May 1996 (Protocol II, as amended on 3 May 1996) annexed to the Convention on Prohibitions or Restrictions on the Use of Certain Conventional Weapons Which May Be Deemed to Be Excessively Injurious or to Have Indiscriminate Effects, opened for signature 3 May 1996, 2048 UNTS 93 (entered into force 3 December 1998)

Protocol on Prohibitions or Restrictions on the Use of Mines, Booby-Traps and Other Devices (Protocol II) to the Convention on Prohibitions or Restrictions on the Use of Certain Conventional Weapons Which May Be Deemed to Be Excessively Injurious or to Have Indiscriminate Effects, opened for signature 10 October 1980, 1342 UNTS 137 (entered into force 2 December 1983)

Ratification (with Declarations and Reservations) to Protocol Additional to the Geneva Conventions of 12 August 1949, and Relating to the Protection of Victims of International Armed Conflicts (Protocol I): Algeria, registered 16 August 1989, 1552 UNTS 381 (entered into force 16 February 1990)

Ratification (with Declarations and Reservations) to Protocol Additional to the Geneva Conventions of 12 August 1949, and Relating to the Protection of Victims of International Armed Conflicts (Protocol I): Austria, registered 13 August 1982, 1289 UNTS 302 (entered into force 13 February 1983)

Ratification (with Declarations and Reservations) to Protocol Additional to the Geneva Conventions of 12 August 1949, and Relating to the Protection of Victims of International Armed Conflicts (Protocol I): Australia, registered 21 June 1991, 1642 UNTS 473 (entered into force 21 December 1991)

Ratification (with Declarations and Reservations) to Protocol Additional to the Geneva Conventions of 12 August 1949, and Relating to the Protection of Victims of International Armed Conflicts (Protocol I): Belgium, registered 20 May 1986, 1435 UNTS 367 (entered into force 20 November 1986)

Ratification (with Declarations and Reservations) to Protocol Additional to the Geneva Conventions of 12 August 1949, and Relating to the Protection of Victims of International Armed Conflicts (Protocol I): Canada, registered 20 November 1990, 1591 UNTS 462 (entered into force 20 May 1991)

Ratification (with Declarations and Reservations) to Protocol Additional to the Geneva Conventions of 12 August 1949, and Relating to the Protection of Victims of International Armed Conflicts (Protocol I): France in *Official Records of the Diplomatic Conference on the Reaffirmation and Development of International Humanitarian Law Applicable in Armed Conflicts, Geneva (1974–1977), Volume VII* (Federal Political Department, Bern, 1978)

Ratification (with Declarations and Reservations) to Protocol Additional to the Geneva Conventions of 12 August 1949, and Relating to the Protection of Victims of International Armed Conflicts (Protocol I): Germany, registered 14 February 1991, 1607 UNTS 526 (entered into force 14 August 1991)

Ratification (with Declarations and Reservations) to Protocol Additional to the Geneva Conventions of 12 August 1949, and Relating to the Protection of Victims of International Armed Conflicts (Protocol I): Ireland, registered 12 July 1999, 2073 UNTS 28 (entered into force 19 November 1999)

Ratification (with Declarations and Reservations) to Protocol Additional to the Geneva Conventions of 12 August 1949, and Relating to the Protection of Victims of International Armed Conflicts (Protocol I): Italy, registered 27 February 1986, 1425 UNTS 438 (entered into force 17 August 1986)

Ratification (with Declarations and Reservations) to Protocol Additional to the Geneva Conventions of 12 August 1949, and Relating to the Protection of Victims of International Armed Conflicts (Protocol I): Netherlands, registered 26 June 1987, 1477 UNTS 299 (entered into force 26 December 1987)

Ratification (with Declarations and Reservations) to Protocol Additional to the Geneva Conventions of 12 August 1949, and Relating to the Protection of Victims of International Armed Conflicts (Protocol I): New Zealand, registered 8 February 1988, 1499 UNTS 358 (entered into force 8 August 1988)

Ratification (with Declarations and Reservations) to Protocol Additional to the Geneva Conventions of 12 August 1949, and Relating to the Protection of Victims of International Armed Conflicts (Protocol I): Spain, registered 21 April 1989, 1537 UNTS 389 (entered into force 21 October 1989)

Ratification (with Declarations and Reservations) to Protocol Additional to the Geneva Conventions of 12 August 1949, and Relating to the Protection of Victims of International Armed Conflicts (Protocol I): United Kingdom, registered 28 January 1998, 2020 UNTS 73 (entered into force 28 July 1998)

Rome Statute of the International Criminal Court, opened for signature 17 July 1998, 2187 UNTS 91 (entered into force 1 July 2002)

Statute of the International Court of Justice

Treaty on the Prohibition of Nuclear Weapons, opened for signature 7 July 2017 (entering into force January 2021)

Treaty Relating to the Use of Submarines and Noxious Gases in Warfare, opened for signature 6 February 1922, 25 LNTS 202 (not yet in force)

United Nations Convention on the Law of the Sea, opened for signature 10 December 1982, 1833 UNTS 3 (entered into force 16 November 1994)

Universal Declaration of Human Rights, GA Res 217A (III), UN GAOR, 3rd sess, 183rd plen mtg, UN Doc A/810 (10 December 1948)

Vienna Convention on the Law of Treaties, opened for signature 23 May 1969, 1155 UNTS 331 (entered into force 27 January 1980)

II Cases

Aerial Herbicide Spraying (Ecuador v Colombia) [2013] ICJ Rep 278

Antipenkov v Russia (European Court of Human Rights, Chamber, Application No 33470/03, 15 October 2009)

Armed Activities on the Territory of the Congo (Democratic Republic of the Congo v Uganda) (Judgment) [2005] ICJ Rep 168

Brincat and Others v Malta (European Court of Human Rights, Chamber, Application Nos 60908/11, 62110/11, 62129/11, 62312/11, 62338/11, 24 July 2014)

Čelebići Camp, Prosecutor v Delalić (Zejnil) and ors, Appeal Judgment, Case No IT-96-21-A, ICL 96 (ICTY February 2001)

Certain Activities Carried Out by Nicaragua in the Border Area (Costa Rica v Nicaragua) (Judgment) (International Court of Justice, General List No 150, 2 February 2018)

Colombia Constitutional Court, *Constitutional Case No C-225/95*, 18 May 1995

Corfu Channel (United Kingdom v Albania) (Merits) [1949] ICJ Rep 4

Cyprus v Turkey [2001] IV Eur Court HR 1

Esmukhambetov et al v Russia (European Court of Human Rights, Chamber, Application No 23445/03, 29 March 2011)

Fisheries Jurisdiction Case (Spain v Canada) [1998] ICJ Rep 432

Gabcikovo-Nagymaros Project (Hungary v Slovakia) [1997] ICJ Rep 7

Isayeva v Russia (European Court of Human Rights, Chamber, Application Nos 57947/00, 57948/00 and 57949/00, 24 February 2005)

Kasikili/Sedudu Island (Botswana v Namibia) (Judgment) [1999] ICJ Rep 1045

Legal Consequences for States of the Continued Presence of South Africa in Namibia (South West Africa) notwithstanding Security Council Resolution 276 (1970) (Advisory Opinion) [1971] ICJ Rep 16

Legal Consequences of the Construction of a Wall in the Occupied Palestinian Territory (Advisory Opinion) [2004] ICJ Rep 136

Legal Consequences of the Separation of the Chagos Archipelago from Mauritius in 1965 (Advisory Opinion) (International Court of Justice, General List No 169, 25 February 2019)

Legality of the Threat or Use of Nuclear Weapons (Advisory Opinion) [1996] ICJ Rep 226

Legality of the Use by a State of Nuclear Weapons in Armed Conflict (Advisory Opinion) [1996] ICJ Rep 66

Loizidou v Turkey (1995) 310 Eur Court HR (ser A)

Marab and Ors v IDF Commander in the West Bank and Anor (2008) 133 ILR 332

Military and Paramilitary Activities in and against Nicaragua (Nicaragua v United States of America) (Judgment) [1986] ICJ Rep 14

Military and Paramilitary Activities in and against Nicaragua (Nicaragua v United States of America) (Merits) [1986] ICJ Rep 14

North Sea Continental Shelf (Federal Republic of Germany v Denmark) (Merits) [1969] ICJ Rep 3

Nuclear Tests (Australia v France) (Merits) [1974] ICJ Rep 253

Nuclear Tests (New Zealand v France) (Request for an Examination of the Situation in Accordance with Paragraph 63 of the Court's 1974 Judgment) [1995] ICJ Rep 288

O'Keeffe v Ireland [2014] I Eur Court HR 155

Osman v United Kingdom [1998] VII Eur Court HR 3124

Prosecutor v Boškoski & Tarčulovski (Judgment) (International Criminal Tribunal for the Former Yugoslavia, Appeals Chamber, Case No IT-04-82-A, 19 May 2010)

Prosecutor v Delalić (Judgment) (International Criminal Tribunal for the Former Yugoslavia, Trial Chamber, Case No IT-96-21-T, 16 November 1998)

Prosecutor v Galić (Judgment) (International Criminal Tribunal for the Former Yugoslavia, Trial Chamber I, Case No IT-98-29-T, 5 December 2003)

Prosecutor v Kupreškić (Judgment) (International Criminal Tribunal for the Former Yugoslavia, Trial Chamber, Case No IT-95-16-T, 14 January 2000)

Prosecutor v Martić (Decision) (International Criminal Tribunal for the Former Yugoslavia, Trial Chamber, Case No IT-95-11-R61, 8 March 1996)

Prosecutor v Milošević (Judgment) (International Criminal Tribunal for the Former Yugoslavia, Trial Chamber III, Case No IT-98-29/1-T, 12 December 2007)

Prosecutor v Tadić (Decision on the Defence Motion for Interlocutory Appeal on Jurisdiction) (International Criminal Tribunal for the Former Yugoslavia, Appeals Chamber, Case No IT-94-1-A, 2 October 1995)

Pulp Mills in the River Uruguay (Argentina v Uruguay) (Request for the Indication of Provisional Measures) (2006) 45 ILM 1025

'Request for an Examination of the Situation', *Request for an Examination of the Situation in Accordance with Paragraph 63 of the Court's 1974 Judgment in the Case Concerning Nuclear Tests (New Zealand v France)* (International Court of Justice, General List No 97, 21 August 1995) <www.icj-cij.org/files/case-related/97/7187.pdf>

Ryuichi Shimoda et al v The State (1966) 32 ILR 626 (District Court of Tokyo, Judgment date 7 December 1963)

Santa Domingo Massacre v Colombia (Inter-American Court of Human Rights, Series C No 259, 30 November 2012)

Selvi v State of Karnataka (Supreme Court of India, Criminal Appellate Jurisdiction, 5 May 2010)

Trail Smelter Case (United States v Canada) (1938) 3 RIAA 1905

Tyrer v United Kingdom (1978) 26 Eur Court HR (ser A)

Verbatim Record, *Nuclear Tests (New Zealand v France) (Request for an Examination of the Situation in Accordance with Paragraph 63 of the Court's 1974 Judgment)* [1995] ICJ Rep 288 <www.icj-cij.org/files/case-related/97/097-19950912-ORA-01-00-BI.pdf>

Vinter v United Kingdom [2016] III Eur Court HR 317

Whaling in the Antarctic (Australia and New Zealand (intervening) v Japan) (Judgment) (International Court of Justice, General List No 148, 31 March 2014)

Yugoslavia v United States (1999) 38(4) ILM 1188

III Conference Proceedings/Working Groups/Manuals

Article I: Reinforcing the Core Prohibition of the Biological Weapons Convention: Submitted by the United States of America, Eighth Review Conference of the States Parties to the Convention on the Prohibition of the Development, Production and Stockpiling of Bacteriological (Biological) and Toxin Weapons and on Their Destruction, UN Doc BWC/CONF.VIII/WP.14 (25 October 2016)

Basic Principles for the Protection of Civilian Populations in Armed Conflicts, GA Res 2675 (XXV), UN GAOR, 25th sess, 1922nd plen mtg, UN Doc A/RES/2675(XXV) (9 December 1970)

Charter of Economic Rights and Duties of States, GA Res 3281 (XXIX), UN GAOR, 29th sess, 2315th plen mtg, Agenda Item 48, UN Doc A/RES/29/3281 (12 December 1974)

Charter of the United Nations

Chemical and Bacteriological (Biological) Weapons and the Effects of Their Possible Use: Report of the Secretary-General, 24th sess, Agenda Item 2, UN Doc A/7575/Rev/1 (1 August 1969)

Chemical and Bacteriological (Biological) Weapons, GA Res 32/77, UN GAOR, 32nd sess, 100th plen mtg, Agenda Item 39, UN Doc A/RES/32/77 (12 December 1977)

Chemical and Bacteriological (Biological) Weapons, GA Res 3256 (XXIX), UN GAOR, 29th sess, 2309th plen mtg, UN Doc A/RES/3265(XXIX) (9 December 1974)

Chemical and Bacteriological (Biological) Weapons, GA Res 33/59, UN GAOR, 33rd sess, 84th plen mtg, UN Doc A/RES33/59 (14 December 1978)

Code of Professional Ethics for Science Workers in Cuba: Submitted by Cuba [unofficial English translation], *Eighth Review Conference of the States Parties to the Convention on the Prohibition of the Development, Production and Stockpiling of Bacteriological (Biological) and Toxin Weapons and on Their Destruction*, UN Doc BWC/CONF.VIII/WP.2 (30 September 2016)

Commission on Human Rights, *Study on the Situation of Trade in and Production of Equipment Which Is Specifically Designed to Inflict Torture or Other Cruel, Inhuman or Degrading Treatment, Its Origin, Destination and Forms, Submitted by Theo van Boven, Special Rapporteur on Torture, Pursuant to Resolution 2002/38 of the Commission on Human Rights*, 59th sess, Agenda Item 11(a), UN Doc E/CN.4/2003/69 (13 January 2003)

Torture and Other Cruel, Inhuman and Degrading Treatment: Report of the Special Rapporteur on Torture, Theo Van Boven, 61st sess, Agenda Item 11 (a), UN Doc E/CN.4/2005/62 (15 December 2004)

Committee on Economic, Social and Cultural Rights, *General Comment No 15: The Right to Water*, 29th sess, Agenda Item 3, UN Doc E/C.12/2002/11 (20 January 2003)

General Comment No 14: The Right to the Highest Attainable Standard of Health, 22nd sess, Agenda Item 3, UN Doc E/C.12/2000/4 (11 August 2000)

General Comment No 15: The Right to Water, 29th sess, Agenda Item 3, UN Doc E/C.12/2002/11 (20 January 2003)

General Comment No 12: The Right to Adequate Food (Art 11), 20th sess, Agenda Item 7, UN Doc E/C.12/1999/5 (12 May 1999)

Common Understandings Reached by the Meetings of States Parties during the Intersessional Programme Held from 2012 to 2015, Eighth Review Conference of the States Parties to the Convention on the Prohibition of the Development, Production and Stockpiling of Bacteriological (Biological) and Toxin Weapons and on Their Destruction, UN Doc BWC/CONF.VIII/PC/5 (2 June 2016)

Convention on Prohibitions or Restrictions on the Use of Certain Conventional Weapons Which May Be Deemed to Be Excessively Injurious or to Have Indiscriminate Effect, GA Res 39/56, UN GAOR, 39th sess, 97th plen mtg, Agenda Item 50, Supp No 51, UN Doc, A/RES/39/56 (12 December 1984)

Convention on Prohibitions or Restrictions on the Use of Certain Conventional Weapons Which May Be Deemed to Be Excessively Injurious or to Have Indiscriminate Effects, GA Res 40/84, UN GAOR, 40th sess, 113th plen mtg, Agenda Item 54, Supp No 53, UN Doc A/RES/40/84 (12 December 1985)

Convention on Prohibitions or Restrictions on the Use of Certain Conventional Weapons Which May Be Deemed to Be Excessively Injurious or to Have

Indiscriminate Effects, GA Res 41/50, UN GAOR, 41st sess, 94th plen mtg, Agenda Item 51, Supp No 53, UN Doc A/RES/41/50 (3 December 1986)

Convention on Prohibitions or Restrictions on the Use of Certain Conventional Weapons Which May Be Deemed to Be Excessively Injurious or to Have Indiscriminate Effects, GA Res 45/64, UN GAOR, 45th sess, 54th plen mtg, Agenda Item 64, Supp No 49, UN Doc A/RES/45/64 (4 December 1990)

Convention on Prohibitions or Restrictions on the Use of Certain Conventional Weapons Which May Be Deemed to Be Excessively Injurious or to Have Indiscriminate Effects, GA Res 46/40, UN GAOR, 46th sess, 65th plen mtg, Agenda Item 64, Supp No 49, UN Doc A/RES/46/40 (6 December 1991)

Convention on Prohibitions or Restrictions on the Use of Certain Conventional Weapons Which May Be Deemed to Be Excessively Injurious or to Have Indiscriminate Effects, GA Res 47/56, UN GAOR, 47th sess, 81st plen mtg, Agenda Item 65, Supp No 49, UN Doc A/RES/47/56 (9 December 1992)

Convention on Prohibitions or Restrictions on the Use of Certain Conventional Weapons Which May Be Deemed to Be Excessively Injurious or to Have Indiscriminate Effects, GA Res 48/79, UN GAOR, 48th sess, 81st plen mtg, Agenda Item 75, Supp No 49, UN Doc A/RES/48/79 (7 January 1994)

Convention on Prohibitions or Restrictions on the Use of Certain Conventional Weapons Which May Be Deemed to Be Excessively Injurious or to Have Indiscriminate Effects, GA Res 49/79, UN GAOR, 49th sess, 90th plen mtg, Agenda Item 66, Supp No 49, UN Doc A/RES/49/79 (11 January 1995)

Convention on Prohibitions or Restrictions on the Use of Certain Conventional Weapons Which May Be Deemed to Be Excessively Injurious or to Have Indiscriminate Effects, GA Res 50/74, UN GAOR, 50th sess, 90th plen mtg, Agenda Item 74, Supp No 49, UN Doc A/RES/50/74 (10 January 1996)

Convention on Prohibitions or Restrictions on the Use of Certain Conventional Weapons Which May Be Deemed to Be Excessively Injurious or to Have Indiscriminate Effects, GA Res 51/49, UN GAOR, 51st sess, 79th plen mtg, Agenda Item 75, Supp No 49, UN Doc A/RES/51/49 (8 January 1997)

Convention on Prohibitions or Restrictions on the Use of Certain Conventional Weapons Which May Be Deemed to Be Excessively Injurious or to Have Indiscriminate Effects, GA Res 54/58, UN GAOR, 54th sess, 69th plen mtg, Agenda Item 80, Supp No 49, UN Doc A/RES/54/58 (31 December 1999)

Convention on the Prohibitions or Restrictions on the Use of Certain Conventional Weapons Which May Be Deemed to Be Excessively Injurious or to Have Indiscriminate Effects, GA Res 38/66, UN GAOR, 38th sess, 97th plen mtg, Agenda Item 51, Supp No 47, UN Doc A/RES/38/66 (15 December 1983)

Conventional Weapons Convention, GA Res 52/42, UN GAOR, 52nd sess, 67th plen mtg, Agenda Item 75, Supp No 49, UN Doc A/RES/52/42 (31 December 1997)

Conventional Weapons Convention, GA Res 53/81, UN GAOR, 53rd sess, 79th plen mtg, Agenda Item 75, Supp No 49, UN Doc A/RES/53/81 (8 January 1999)

Draft Articles on the Effects of Armed Conflicts on Treaties, with Commentaries in 'Report on the Work of the International Law Commission Sixty-Third Session (26 April–3 June and 4 July–12 August 2011)' [2011] II(2) *Yearbook of the International Law Commission* 108

Final Declaration, Fourth Review Conference of the Parties to the Convention on the Prohibition of the Development, Production and Stockpiling of Bacteriological (Biological) and Toxin Weapons and on Their Destruction, UN Doc BWC/CONF.IV/9 (25 November–6 December 1996)

Final Review Document of the Seventh Review Conference, Seventh Review Conference of the States Parties to the Convention on the Prohibition of the Development, Production and Stockpiling of Bacteriological (Biological) and Toxin Weapons and on Their Destruction, UN Doc BWC/CONF.VII/COW/CRP.2 (5–22 December 2011)

General and Complete Disarmament, GA Res 2932 A (XXVII), UN GAOR, 27th sess, 2093rd plen mtg, UN Doc A/RES/2932(XXVII) (29 November 1972)

Human Rights Committee, *Consideration of Reports Submitted by States Parties under Article 40 of the Covenant: Concluding Observations of the Human Rights Committee – Israel*, 99th sess, UN Doc CCPR/C/ISR/CO/3 (3 September 2010)

Consideration of Reports Submitted by States Parties under Article 40 of the Covenant: Concluding Observations of the Human Rights Committee – Kosovo (Serbia), 87th sess, UN Doc CCPR/C/UNK/CO/1 (14 August 2006)

Decision: Communication No 45/1979, 15th sess, UN Doc C/CCPR/OP/1 (31 March 1982) ('*de Guerrero v Colombia*')

Decision: Communication No 52/1979, 13th sess, UN Doc CCPR/C/OP/1 (19 July 1981) ('*de Lopez v Uruguay*')

Decision: Communication No 67/1980, 17th sess, UN Doc CCPR/C/17/D/67/1980 (27 October 1982) ('*EHP v Canada*')

Decision: Communication No 429/1990, 47th sess, UN Doc CCPR/C/47/D/429/1990 (29 April 1993) ('*EW v Netherlands*')

Decision: Communication No 1453/2006, 88th sess, UN Doc CCPR/C/88/D/1453/2006 (18 October 2006) ('*Brun v France*')

General Comment No 14: Article 6 (Right to life), 16th sess, UN Doc HRI/GEN/1/Rev.7 (12 May 2004)

General Comment No 14: Article 6, 23rd sess, UN Doc HRI/GEN/1/Rev.1 (2 November 1984)

General Comment No 14: Nuclear Weapons and the Right to Life (Article 6), 16th sess, UN Doc HRI/GEN/1/Rev.6 (12 May 2003)

General Comment No 20: Article 7 (Prohibition of Torture, or Other Cruel, Inhuman or Degrading Treatment or Punishment), 44th sess, UN Doc A/47/40 (10 March 1992)

General Comment No 24: Issues Relating to Reservations Made upon Ratification or Accession to the Covenant or the Optional Protocols thereto, or in Relation to Declarations under Article 41 of the Covenant, 52nd sess, UN Doc CCPR/C/21/Rev.1/Add.6 (4 November 1994)

General Comment No 29: States of Emergency (Article 4), 1950th mtg, UN Doc CCPR/C/21/Rev.1/Add.11 (31 August 2001)

General Comment No. 36 (2018) on Article 6 of the International Covenant on Civil and Political Rights, on the Right to Life, 124th sess, UN Doc CCPR/C/GC/36 (30 October 2018)

General Comment No 36 on Article 6 of the International Covenant on Civil and Political Rights, on the Right to Life (Advanced Unedited Version) <www.ohchr.org/Documents/HRBodies/CCPR/GCArticle6/GCArticle6_EN.pdf>

Human Rights Committee, *Views: Communication No 1275/2004*, 94th sess, UN Doc CCPR/C/94/D/1275/2004 (30 October 2008) ('*Umetaliev and Tashtanbekova v Kyrgyzstan*')

Incendiary and Other Specific Conventional Weapons Which May Be the Subject of Prohibitions or Restrictions of Use for Humanitarian Reasons, GA Res 31/64, UN GAOR, 31st sess, 96th plen mtg, Agenda Item 35, Supp No 39, UN Doc A/RES/31/64 (10 December 1976)

Incendiary and Other Specific Conventional Weapons Which May Be the Subject of Prohibitions or Restrictions of Use for Humanitarian Reasons, GA Res 32/152, UN GAOR, 32nd sess, 106th plen mtg, Agenda Item 38, Supp No 45, UN Doc A/RES/32/152 (19 December 1977)

Inter-American Commission on Human Rights, *Third Report on Human Rights in Colombia*, Organization of American States, Doc No OEA/Ser.L/V/II.102 Doc 9 Rev 1 (26 February 1999)

International Committee of the Red Cross, *Biological Weapons Review Conference: ICRC Statement* (8 November 2016) <www.icrc.org/en/document/biological-weapons-review-conference-statement-icrc>

International Law Commission, *Draft Conclusions of Identification of Customary International Law, with Commentaries*, UN GAOR, UN Doc A/73/10 (2018)

Jacobsson, Marie, *Preliminary Report on the Protection of the Environment in Relation to Armed Conflicts*, UN GAOR, 66th sess, UN Docs A/CN.4/674 (30 May 2014) and A/CN.4/674/Corr.1 (11 August 2014)

Report of the International Law Commission, Sixty-third Session, UN GAOR, 66th sess, Supp No 10, UN Doc A/66/10 (2011) Annex E ('*Protection of the Environment in Relation to Armed Conflicts*')

Second Report on the Protection of the Environment in Relation to Armed Conflicts, UN GAOR, 67th sess, UN Doc A/CN.4/685 (28 May 2015)

Third Report on the Protection of the Environment in Relation to Armed Conflicts, UN GAOR, 68th sess, UN Doc A/CN.4/700 (3 June 2016)

Koskenniemi, Martti, *Fragmentation of International Law: Difficulties Arising from the Diversification and Expansion of International Law*, International Law Commission, 58th sess, UN Doc A/CN.4/L.682 (13 April 2006)

Napalm and Other Incendiary Weapons and All Aspects of Their Possible Use, GA Res 3076 (XXVIII), UN GAOR, 28th sess, 2192nd plen mtg, Agenda Item 34, Supp No 30, UN Doc A/RES/3076(XXVIII) (6 December 1973)

Napalm and Other Incendiary Weapons and All Aspects of Their Possible Use, GA Res 3255 (XXIX), UN GAOR, 29th sess, 2309th plen mtg, Agenda Item 27, Supp No 31, UN Doc A/RES/3255(XXIX)A-B (9 December 1974)

Office of General Counsel, *Department of Defense Law of War Manual* (May 2016) United States Department of Defense <www.defense.gov/Portals/1/Documents/DoD_Law_of_War_Manual-June_2015_Updated_May_2016.pdf>

Peaceful Settlement of Disputes between States, GA Res 37/10, UN GAOR, 37th sess, 68th plen mtg, UN Doc A/RES/37/10 (15 November 1982) annex

Permanent Sovereignty over Natural Resources, GA Res 1803 (XVII), UN GAOR, 17th sess, 1194th plen mtg, UN Doc A/RES/17/1803 (14 December 1962)

Promotion of and Respect for International Humanitarian Law, Organization of American States, GA Res 1565 (XXVIII-O/98), 3rd plen sess, OAS Doc AG/RES 1565 (XXVIII-O/98) (2 June 1998)

Protection of the Environment in Times of Armed Conflict, GA Res 47/37, UN GAOR, 47th sess, 73rd plen mtg, Agenda Item 136, UN Doc A/RES/47/37 (9 February 1993)

Regulation No 2000/15 On the Establishment of Panels with Exclusive Jurisdiction over Serious Criminal Offences, UNTAET, UN Doc UNTAET/REG/2000/15 (6 June 2000)

'Report of the Commission to the General Assembly on the Work of Its Forty-Sixth Session' [1994] II(2) *Yearbook of the International Law Commission*

Report of the Conference of the Committee on Disarmament, Volume I, UN GAOR, 31st sess, Supp No 27, UN Doc No A/31/27 (1976)

Report of the Secretary-General on the Work of the Organization, GA Res 37/67, UN GAOR, 37th sess, 91st plen mtg, UN Doc A/RES/37/67 (3 December 1982)

Report of the Secretary-General Prepared Pursuant to General Assembly Resolution ES-10/13, UN Doc A/ES-10/248 (24 November 2003)

Report of the United Nations Conference on Environment and Development, Rio de Janeiro, 3–14 June 1992, UN GAOR, UN Doc A/CONF.151/26 Vol. I (12 August 1992) annex ('*Rio Declaration on Environment and Development*')

Report of the United Nations Conference on the Human Environment: Stockholm, 5–16 June 1972, UN Doc A/CONF.48/14/Rev.1 (1972) ('*Declaration of the United Nations Conference on the Human Environment*')

Respect for Human Rights in Armed Conflict, GA Res 2444 (XXIII), UN GAOR, 23rd sess, 1748th plen mtg, UN Doc A/RES/2444(XXIII) (19 December 1968)

Respect for Human Rights in Armed Conflicts, GA Res 3102 (XXVIII), UN GAOR, 28th sess, 2197th plen mtg, Agenda Item 96, Supp No 30, UN Doc A/Res/3102(XXVIII) (12 December 1973)

Respect for International Humanitarian Law, Organization of American States, GA Res 1270 (XXIV-O/94), 9th plen sess, OAS Doc AG/RES 1270 (XXIV-O/94) (10 June 1994)

Review of Developments in Science and Technology: Key Points from the 2012–2015 Biological and Toxin Weapons Convention Intersessional Programme: Submitted by the United Kingdom, Eighth Review Conference of the States Parties to the Convention on the Prohibition of the Development, Production and Stockpiling of Bacteriological (Biological) and Toxin Weapons and on Their Destruction, UN Doc BW C/CONF.VIII/WP.17 (1 November 2016)

SC Res 582, UN SCOR, 41st sess, 2666th mtg, UN Doc S/RES/582 (24 February 1986)

SC Res 598, UN SCOR, 42nd sess, 2750th mtg, UN Doc S/RES/598 (20 July 1987)

SC Res 612, UN SCOR, 43rd sess, 2812nd meeting, UN Doc S/RES/612 (9 May 1988)

SC Res 620, UN SCOR, 43rd sess, 2825th mtg, UN Doc S/RES/620 (26 August 1988)

SC Res 687, UN SCOR, 47th sess, 2981st mtg, UN Doc S/RES/687 (8 April 1991)

SC Res 1540, UN SCOR, 59th sess, 4956th mtg, UN Doc S/RES/1540 (28 April 2004)

SC Res 1977, UN SCOR, 66th sess, 6518th mtg, UN Doc S/RES/1977 (20 April 2011)

Scientific and Technological Developments of Relevance to the Convention and the Assessment of Benefits and Risks: Submitted by Switzerland, Meeting of the States Parties to the Convention on the Prohibition of the Development, Production and Stockpiling of Bacteriological (Biological) and Toxin Weapons and on Their Destruction, UN Doc BWC/MSP/2019/MX.2/WP.2 (10 July 2019)

Secretary-General's Bulletin – Observance by United Nations Forces of International Humanitarian Law, UN Doc ST/SGB/1999/13 (6 August 1999)

Statement of the President of the Security Council, UN SCOR, 5705th plen mtg, UN Doc S/PRST/2007/22 (25 June 2007)

Stockholm Declaration of the United Nations Conference on the Human Environment in *Report of the United Nations Conference on the Human Environment*, 21st plen mtg, UN Doc A/CONF.48/14 and Corr.1 (16 June 1972)

The Federal Ministry of Defence of the Federal Republic of Germany, *Humanitarian Law in Armed Conflicts, German Manual, VR II 3* (1992) [trans of: *Humanitäres Völkerrecht in bewaffneten Konflikten* (first published 1992)] <www.humanitaeres-voelkerrecht.de/ManualZDv15.2.pdf>

The Future We Want, GA Res 66/288, UN GAOR, 66th sess, 123rd plen mtg, Agenda Item 19, UN Doc A/RES/66/288 (11 September 2012)

The Human Right to Water and Sanitation, GA Res 264/92, UN GAOR, 64th sess, 108th plen mtg, Agenda Item 48, UN Doc A/RES/64/292 (3 August 2010)

Towards a Global Pact for the Environment, GA Res 72/277, UN GAOR, 72nd sess, Agenda Item 14, UN Doc A/RES/72/277 (14 May 2018)

Transforming Our World: The 2030 Agenda for Sustainable Development, GA Res 70/1, UN GAOR, 70th sess, 4th plen mtg, Agenda Items 15 and 116, UN Doc A/RES/70/1 (21 October 2015)

United Kingdom Ministry of Defence, *The Manual of the Law of Armed Conflict* (Oxford University Press, 2004)

United Nations Compensation Commission, *Governing Council Decision 7: Criteria for Additional Categories of Claims*, UN SCOR, 3rd sess, 18th mtg, UN Doc /AC.25/1991/7/Rev.1 (17 March 1992)

United Nations Compensation Commission Governing Council, *Report and Recommendations Made by the Panel of Commissioners Concerning the Fifth Instalment of 'F4' Claims*, UN Doc S/AC.26/2005/10 (30 June 2005)

United Nations Conference on Prohibitions or Restrictions of Use of Certain Conventional Weapons Which May Be Deemed to Be Excessively Injurious or to Have Indiscriminate Effects, GA Res 33/70, UN GAOR, 33rd sess, 84th plen mtg, Agenda Item 49, Supp No 45, UN Doc A/RES/33/70 (14 December 1978)

United Nations Conference on Prohibitions or Restrictions of Use of Certain Conventional Weapons Which May Be Deemed to Be Excessively Injurious or to Have Indiscriminate Effects, GA Res 34/82, UN GAOR, 34th sess, 97th plen mtg, Agenda Item 41, Supp No 46, UN Doc A/RES/34/82 (11 December 1979)

United Nations Conference on Prohibitions or Restrictions of Use of Certain Conventional Weapons Which May Be Deemed to Be Excessively Injurious of to Have Indiscriminate Effects, GA Res 35/153, UN GAOR, 35th sess, 94th plen mtg, Agenda Item 43, Supp No 48, UN Doc A/RES/35/153 (12 December 1980)

United Nations Conference on Prohibitions or Restrictions of Use of Certain Conventional Weapons Which May Be Deemed to Be Excessively Injurious or to Have Indiscriminate Effects, GA Res 36/93, UN GAOR, 36th sess, 91st plen mtg, Agenda Item 52, Supp No 51, UN Doc A/RES/36/93 (9 December 1981)

United Nations Conference on Prohibitions or Restrictions of Use of Certain Conventional Weapons Which May Be Deemed to Be Excessively Injurious or to Have Indiscriminate Effects, GA Res 37/79, UN GAOR, 37th sess, 98th plen mtg, Agenda Item 51, Supp No 51, UN Doc A/Res/37/79 (9 December 1982)

United States Department of Army, *Field Manual No. 3-36 Electronic Warfare* (9 November 2012) <https://fas.org/irp/doddir/army/fm3-36.pdf>

World Charter for Nature, GA Resolution 37/7, UN GAOR, 48th plen mtg, UN Doc A/RES/37/7 (28 October 1982)

IV Conference Papers

Altmann, Jürgen and Mark Gubrud, 'Risks from Military Uses of Nanotechnology: The Need for Technology Assessment and Preventive Control' (Paper presented at Nanotechnology – Revolutionary Opportunities and Societal Implications, 3rd JOINTEC-NSF Workshop on Nanotechnology, Lecce, Italy, 31 January–1 February 2002) <https://e3.physik.tu-dortmund.de/p&d/pubs/riskmilnt_lecce.pdf>

Defence Science Institute and Defence Science and Technology Organisation, Symposium: 'Future Technologies for Personal Protection', 7–8 November 2013

Feynman, Richard, 'There's Plenty of Room at the Bottom' (Paper presented at American Physical Society, Pasadena, 29 December 1959) <www.pa.msu.edu/~yang/RFeynman_plentySpace.pdf>

Kibong, Kim, 'Thermobarics: Promises, Challenges, and Recommendations' (Paper presented at 7th Joint Bombs/Warheads & Ballistics Symposium, Monterey, United States, 2004)

Kica, Evisa and Ramses Wessel, 'Transnational Arrangements in the Governance of Emerging Technologies: The Case of Nanotechnology' (Paper presented at ECPR Standing Group on Regulatory Governance Conference, Barcelona, 25–27 June 2014) <http://reggov2014.ibei.org/bcn-14-papers/67-218.pdf>

Koval, Romona, 'On the Whispering of Bones', Speech delivered at Wheeler Centre Gala Night: Stories for the Dead, Melbourne, Australia, 26 February 2017

Kritsiotis, Dino, 'An Uncensored History of International Law' (Lecture delivered at Master of Laws program, The University of Melbourne, 2 June 2018)

Mathews, Robert, 'The 1980 Convention on Certain Conventional Weapons: A Useful Framework Despite Earlier Disappointments' (Paper presented at the Australian Defence Force Conference on 'Pushing the Envelope: The

ADF Contribution to International & Operations Law', University of Melbourne, 20–22 February 2002)

Sassòli, Marco, 'Transnational Armed Groups and International Humanitarian Law' (Occasional Paper series No 6, Program on Humanitarian Policy and Conflict Research, Harvard University, Winter 2006)

Secretariat of the Convention on Biological Diversity, 'United Nations Convention on Biological Diversity' (Paper presented at Twelfth Conference of the Parties, Pyeongchang, Republic of Korea, 29 September–17 October 2014)

United Nations Office for Disarmament Affairs (UNODA), 'Final Document of the Seventh Review Conference' (Paper presented at Seventh Review Conference of the States Parties to the Convention on the Prohibition of the Development, Production and Stockpiling of Bacteriological (Biological) and Toxin Weapons and Their Destruction, Geneva, Switzerland, 5–22 December 2011)

Wang, Jun and Peter Dortmans, 'Nanotechnology: Selected Topics and Potential Military Application' (Paper presented at Land Warfare Conference, Melbourne, Australia, 27–30 September 2004) <http://dspace.dsto.defence.gov.au/dspace/handle/1947/2559>

V Books

Abbott, Kenneth, Douglas Sylvester and Garry Marchant, 'Transnational Regulation: Reality or Romanticism?' in Graeme Hodge, Diana Bowman and Andrew Maynard (eds), *International Handbook on Regulating Nanotechnologies* (Elgar, 2010)

Ach, Johann and Beate Luttenberg (eds), *Nanobiotechnology, Nanomedicine and Human Enhancement* (Lit Verlag, 2008)

Akhavan, Jackie, *The Chemistry of Explosives* (Royal Society of Chemistry, 2004)

Allhof, Fritz and Patrick Lin (eds), *Nanotechnology & Society* (Springer, 2008)

Alston, Philip and Ryan Goodman, *International Human Rights: Text and Materials* (Oxford University Press, 2013)

Altmann, Jürgen, 'Preventing Hostile and Malevolent Use of Military Technology After 15 Years of the US National Nanotechnology Initiative' in Maurizio Martellini and Andrea Malizia (eds), *Cyber and Chemical, Biological, Radiological, Nuclear, Explosive Challenges* (Springer, 2017)

Military Nanotechnology: Potential Applications and Preventive Arms Control (Routledge, 2006)

Austin, Jay and Carl Bruch (eds), *The Environmental Consequences of War: Legal, Economic, and Scientific Perspectives* (Cambridge University Press, 2000)

Baskin, Toney and John Holcomb, 'Bombs, Mines, Blast, Fragmentation and Thermobaric Mechanisms of Injury' in Peter Mahoney et al (eds), *Ballistic Trauma: A Practical Guide* (Springer, 2nd ed, 2005)

Bassiouni, M Cherif, *A Manual on International Humanitarian Law and Arms Control Agreements* (Transnational Publishers, 2000)

Benameur, Laila, Liu Wei and Alain Botta, 'Genotoxicity of Nanoparticles' in Bharat Bhushan (ed), *Encyclopedia of Nanotechnology* (Springer, 2012)

Bernauer, Thomas, *The Projected Chemical Weapons Convention: A Guide to Negotiations in the Conference on Disarmament* (United Nations, 1990)

Bertolotti, Mario, *The History of the Laser* (Institute of Physics Publishing, 2005)

Berube, David, *Nano-Hype: The Truth behind the Nanotechnology Buzz* (Prometheus Books, 2006)

Besson, S, 'Theorizing the Sources of International Law' in S Besson and J Tasioulas (eds), *The Philosophy of International Law* (Oxford University Press, 2008)

Best, Geoffrey, *Humanity in Warfare* (Columbia University Press, 1980)

Bjorge, Eirik and Cameron Miles (eds), *Landmark Cases in Public International Law* (Hart Publishing, 2018)

Blix, Hans, 'Means and Methods of Combat' in *Henry Dunant Institute, International Dimensions of Humanitarian Law* (Martinus Nijhoff, 1988)

Boothby, William (ed), *New Technologies: The Law in War and Peace* (Cambridge University Press (2019)

Conflict Law: The Influence of New Weapons Technology, Human Rights and New Actors (Asser Press, 2014)

The Law of Targeting (Oxford University Press, 2012)

Weapons and the Law of Armed Conflict (Oxford University Press, 2009)

'The Law of Weaponry: Is It Adequate?' in Michael Schmitt and Jelena Pejic (eds), *International Law and Armed Conflict: Exploring the Faultlines* (Martinus Nijhoff Publishers, 2007)

Bothe, Michael et al, *The New Chemical Weapons Convention: Implementation and Prospects* (Kluwer, 1998)

New Rules for Victims of Armed Conflict: Commentary on the Two 1977 Protocols Additional to the Geneva Conventions of 1949 (Martinus Nijhoff, 1982)

Bowman, Michael and Dino Kritsiotis (eds), *Conceptual and Contextual Perspectives on the Modern Law of Treaties* (Cambridge University Press, 2018)

Bradley, Curtis, *Custom's Future: International Law* (Cambridge University Press, 2016)

Bratspies, Rebecca, 'Trail Smelter's (Semi) Precautionary Legacy' in Rebecca Bratspies and Russell Miller (eds), *Transboundary Harm in International Law* (Cambridge University Press, 2006)

Cahier, Phillipe, 'La Charte des Nations Unies et les Etats tiers' [in French] in Antonio Cassese (ed), *Current Problems of International Law: Essays on UN Law and on the Law of Armed Conflict* (A Giuffrè, 1975)

Capco, David and Yongsheng Chen (eds), *Nanomaterials: Impacts on Cell Biology and Medicine* (Springer, 2014)

Čapek, Karel, R.U.R. (Rossum's Universal Robots) (Claudia Novack trans, Penguin Books, 2004) [trans of: R.U.R. (Rossumovi Univerzální Roboti (first published 1920)]

Carson, Rachel, *Silent Spring* (Houghton Mifflin, first published 1962, 2002 ed)

Carter, Matt and Jennifer Shieh, *Guide to Research Techniques in Neuroscience* (Elsevier, 2nd ed, 2015)

Casey-Maslen, Stuart, Neil Corney and Abi Dymond-Bass, 'The Review of Weapons under International Humanitarian Law and Human Rights Law' in Stuart Casey-Maslen (ed), *Weapons under International Human Rights Law* (Cambridge University Press, 2014)

Casey-Maslen, Stuart, *Weapons under International Human Rights Law* (Cambridge University Press, 2014)

Cassese, Antonio (ed), *The Human Dimension of International Law: Selected Papers* (Oxford University Press, 2008)

The New Humanitarian Law of Armed Conflict (Editoriale Scientifica, 1979)

Charlesworth, Hilary, 'Law-making and Sources' in James Crawford and Martii Koskienniemi (eds), *The Cambridge Companion to International Law* (Cambridge University Press, 2012)

Christiansen, Sonja Boehmer, 'The Precautionary Principle in Germany: Enabling Government' in Tim O'Riordan and James Cameron (eds), *Interpreting the Precautionary Principle* (Earthscan, 1994)

Clapham, Andrew and Paola Gaeta (eds), *The Oxford Handbook of International Law in Armed Conflict* (Oxford University Press, 2014)

Coleman, Stephen, 'Ethical Challenges of New Military Technologies' in Hitoshi Nasu and Robert McLaughlin (eds), *New Technologies and the Law of Armed Conflict* (Asser Press, 2014)

Corn, Geoffrey et al (eds), *The Law of Armed Conflict: An Operational Approach* (Wolters Kluwer, 2012)

Crawford, James, *Brownlie's Principles of Public International Law* (Oxford University Press, 2012)

Crowley, Michael, *Chemical Control: Regulation of Incapacitating Chemical Agent Weapons, Riot Control Agents and Their Means of Delivery* (Palgrave Macmillan, 2016)

Dando, Malcolm, *A New Form of Warfare: The Rise of Non-lethal Weapons* (Brasseys, 1996)

Darcy, Shane, *Judges, Law and War* (Cambridge University Press, 2016)

Davison, Neil, *'Non-Lethal' Weapons* (Palgrave, 2009)

De Grasse Tyson, Neil and Avis Lang, *The Unspoken Alliance between Astrophysics and the Military: Accessory to War* (W W Norton & Company, 2018) de Hemptinne, Jérôme, 'Challenges Regarding the Protection of Animals during Warfare' in Anne Peters (ed), *Studies in Global Animal Law* (Springer, 2020)

De Schutter, Olivier, United Nations Special Rapporteur on the Right to Food 2008–14, *cited in Simone Hutter, Starvation as a Weapon: Domestic Policies of Deliberate Starvation as a Means to an End under International Law* (Brill, 2015)

Del Monte, Louis A, *Nanoweapons: A Growing Threat to Humanity* (University of Nebraska Press, 2017)

Delissen, Astrid and Gerard Tanja (eds), *Humanitarian Law of Armed Conflict: Challenges Ahead* (Martinus Nijhoff, 1991)

Detter, Ingrid, *The Law of War* (Ashgate Publishing, 2013)

Dhasmana, Anupam et al, 'Nanoparticles: Applications, Toxicology and Safety Aspects' in Kavin Kesari (ed), *Perspectives in Environmental Toxicology* (Springer, 2017)

Dinstein, Yoram, 'The Principle of Proportionality' in Kjetil Mujezinović Larsen, Camilla Guldahl Cooper and Gro Nystuen (eds), *Searching for a 'Principle of Humanity' in International Humanitarian Law* (Cambridge University Press, 2012)

International Law of Belligerent Occupation (Cambridge University Press 2009)

Dörr, Oliver and Kirsten Schmalenbach (eds), *Vienna Convention on the Law of Treaties: A Commentary* (Springer, 2012)

Doswald-Beck, Louise, 'Human Rights Law and Nuclear Weapons' in Gro Nystuen, Stuart Casey-Maslen and Annie Golden Bersagel (eds), *Nuclear Weapons under International Law* (Cambridge University Press, 2014)

'Humanitarian Law in Future Wars' in Michael Schmitt and Leslie Green (eds), *The Law of Armed Conflict: Into the Next Millennium* (US Naval War College, 1998)

Drexler, K Eric, *Engines of Creation* (Oxford University Press, 1990)

Engines of Creation: The Coming Era of Nanotechnology (Anchor Press, 1986)

Drexler, Kim, *Radical Abundance: How a Revolution in Nanotechnology Will Change Civilization* (Perseus Books, 2013)

Dugué, Guillaume, Walther Akemann and Thomas Knöpfel, 'A Comprehensive Concept of Optogenetics' in Thomas Knöpfel and Edward Boyden (eds), *Optogenetics: Tools for Controlling and Monitoring Neuronal Activity* (Elsevier, 2012)

Dunworth, Treasa, *Humanitarian Disarmament: An Historical Enquiry* (Cambridge University Press, 2021)

Dworkin, Ronald, *Law's Empire* (Harvard University Press, 1986)

Eide, Asbjörn, 'Internal Disturbances and Tensions' in Henry Dunant Institute, *International Dimensions of Humanitarian Law* (Martinus Nijhoff, 1988)

Elshtain, Jean (ed), *Just War Theory* (New York University Press, 1992)

Emanuelli, Claude, *International Humanitarian Law* (Éditions Yvon Blais, 2009)
Falk, Richard, *Revitalizing International Law* (Iowa State University Press, 1989)
Faunce, Thomas, *Nanotechnology for a Sustainable World* (Edward Elgar, 2012)
Fleck, Dieter (ed), *The Handbook of International Humanitarian International Law* (Oxford University Press, 2008)
'Environment: Legal and Policy Perspectives' in Hazel Fox and Michael A Meyer (eds), *Effecting Compliance* (British Institute of International and Comparative Law, 1993)
Fox, Hazel and Michael A Meyer (eds), *Effecting Compliance* (British Institute of International and Comparative Law, 1993)
Fries, Amos and Clarence West, *Chemical Warfare* (McGraw Hill, 1921)
Frinking, Erik, Paul Sinning and Eva Bontje, *The Increasing Threat of Biological Weapons: Handle with Sufficient and Proportionate Care* (Hague Centre for Strategic Studies, 2017)
Gardiner, Richard, *Treaty Interpretation* (Oxford University Press, 2015)
Gasman, Lawrence, *Nanotechnology: Applications and Markets* (Artech House, 2006)
Gates, Bill, 'Introduction' in Stockholm International Peace Research Institute, *2008 SIPRI Yearbook: Armaments, Disarmament and International Security* (Oxford University Press, 2008)
Gill, Terry and Dieter Fleck (eds), *The Handbook of the International Law of Military Operations* (Oxford University Press, 2010)
Gillard, Emanuela-Chiara, 'Protection of Civilians in the Conduct of Hostilities' in Rain Liivoja and Tim McCormack (eds), *Routledge Handbook of the Law of Armed Conflict* (Routledge, 2016)
Goldblat, Jozef, *Agreements for Arms Control: A Critical Survey* (Taylor & Francis, 1982)
Göring, Hermann, *Trial of the Major War Criminals before the International Military Tribunal, Nuremberg, 14 November 1945–1 October 1946* (1947)
Gowlland-Debbas, Vera, 'The Right to Life and the Relationship between Human Rights and Humanitarian Law' in Christian Tomuschat, Evelyne Lagrange and Stefan Oeter (eds), *The Right to Life* (Martinus Nijhoff, 2010)
Green, Leslie, *The Contemporary Law of Armed Conflict* (Manchester University Press, 2008)
Grotius, Hugo, *De Jure Belli ac Pacis Libri Tres* (1625) quoted in John O'Connor, *Good Faith in International Law* (Dartmouth, 1991)
Haber, Ludwig Fritz, *The Poisonous Cloud: Chemical Warfare in the First World War* (Clarendon Press, 1986)
Haines, Steven, 'The Developing Law of Weapons: Humanity, Distinction and Precautions in Attack' in Andrew Clapham and Paola Gaeta (eds), *The Oxford Handbook of International Law in Armed Conflict* (Oxford University Press, 2014)

Hakimi, Monica, 'Custom's Method and Process: Lessons from Humanitarian Law' in Curtis A Bradley (ed), *Custom's Future: International Law in a Changing World* (Cambridge University Press, 2016)

Harding, Ronnie, 'Toxics, Industry and Precaution: What Role for Science' in Ronnie Harding and Elizabeth Fisher (eds), *Perspectives on the Precautionary Principle* (Federation Press, 1999) 209

Heller, Kevin Jon, 'The Use and Abuse of Analogy in IHL' in Jens Ohlin (ed), *Theoretical Boundaries of Armed Conflict and Human Rights* (Cambridge University Press, 2016)

Henckaerts, Jean-Marie and Louise Doswald Beck, *Customary International Humanitarian Law* (Cambridge University Press, 2005)

Henderson, Ian, *The Contemporary Law of Targeting: Military Objectives, Proportionality and Precautions in Attack under Additional Protocol I* (Martinus Nijhoff, 2009)

Higgins, Polly, *Eradicating Ecocide* (Shepheard-Walwyn, 2015)

Hitz, Breck, James Ewing and Jeff Hecht, *Introduction to Laser Technology* (IEEE Press, 4th ed, 2012)

Hodge, Graeme, Diana Bowman and Andrew Maynard (eds), *International Handbook on Regulating Nanotechnologies* (Edward Elgar, 2010)

Hodge, Graeme, Diana Bowman and Karinne Ludlow (eds), *New Global Frontiers in Regulation: The Age of Nanotechnology* (Edward Elgar, 2007)

Hollis, D B (ed), *The Oxford Guide to Treaties* (Oxford University Press, 2012)

Houdy, Philippe, Marcel Lahmani and Francelyne Marano, *Nanoethics and Nanotoxicology* (Springer, 2010)

Hull, Matthew and Diana Bowman, *Nanotechnology Environmental Health and Safety: Risks, Regulation and Management* (Elsevier, 2nd ed, 2014)

Hull, William, *The Two Hague Conferences and Their Contributions to International Law* (Athenaeum Press, 1908)

Hulme, Karen, *War Torn Environment: Interpreting the Legal Threshold* (Brill Academic, 2004)

Humphreys, Stephen, 'Structural Ambiguity: Technology Transfer in Three Regimes' in Margaret A Young (ed), *Regime Interaction in International Law: Facing Fragmentation* (Cambridge University Press, 2012)

Hunt, Geoffrey and Michael Mehta, *Nanotechnology: Risks, Ethics and Law* (Routledge, 2013)

International Committee of the Red Cross, *Commentary on the First Geneva Convention: Convention (I) for the Amelioration of the Condition of the Wounded and Sick in Armed Forces in the Field* (Cambridge University Press, 2017)

The Geneva Conventions of 12 August 1949 – Commentary (1952–1960) vols I–IV

The Geneva Conventions of 12 August 1949 - Commentary: IV Geneva Convention Relative to the Protection of Civilian Persons in Times of War (1958)

International Court of Justice Yearbook 1999–2000 (United Nations Publications, 2002)

International Institute for the Unification of Private Law, *UNIDROIT Principles of International Commercial Contracts* (UNIDROIT, 2004)

Johnson, James Turner, *Just War Tradition and the Restraint of War: A Moral and Historical Inquiry* (Princeton University Press, 1981)

Joseph, Sarah and Melissa Castan, *The International Covenant on Civil and Political Rights: Cases, Materials, and Commentary* (Oxford University Press, 3rd ed, 2013)

Joseph, Sarah, Jenny Schultz and Melissa Castan, *The International Covenant on Civil and Political Rights: Cases, Materials and Commentary* (Oxford University Press, 2012)

Jungk, Robert, *Brighter than a Thousand Suns: A Personal History of the Atomic Scientists* (Houghton Mifflin Harcourt, 1958)

Kalshoven, Frits and Liesbeth Zegveld, *Constraints on the Waging of War* (ICRC, 2001)

Kalshoven, Frits, *Reflections on the Law of War* (Martinus Nijhoff, 2007)

Klabbers, Jan, 'Treaties and Their Preambles' in Michael J Bowman and Dino Kritsiotis (eds), *Conceptual and Contextual Perspectives on the Modern Law of Treaties* (Cambridge University Press, 2018)

Klapötke, Thomas, *Chemistry of High-Energy Materials* (de Gruyter, 2011)

Kolb, Robert and Richard Hyde, *An Introduction to the Law of Armed Conflicts* (Hart Publishing, 2008)

Kosal, Margaret, *Nanotechnology for Chemical and Biological Defense* (Springer, 2009)

Le Bouthillier, Yves, 'Article 32 Supplementary Means of Interpretation' in Olivier Corten and Pierre Klein (eds), *The Vienna Convention on the Law of Treaties: A Commentary* (Oxford University Press, 2011)

Lee, Steven, 'Weapons of Mass Destruction: Are They Morally Special?' in Larry May (ed), *War: Essays in Political Philosophy* (Cambridge University Press, 2008)

Lefebure, Victor, *The Riddle of the Rhine: Chemical Strategy in Peace and War* (Collins Clear-Type, 1921)

Leins, Kobi and Diana Bowman, 'Nanomaterials: A Tale of Two Applications' in William Boothby (ed), *New Technologies: The Law in War and Peace* (Cambridge University Press, 2019) 285

Leins, Kobi, *Environmental Law in War: Legal Limitations on Harming the Environment during Armed Conflict* (Monash University, 2001)

Levi-Faur, David and Hanna Comaneshter, 'The Risks of Regulation and the Regulation of Risks: The Governance of Nanotechnology' in Graeme Hodge, Diana Bowman and Karinne Ludlow (eds), *New Global Regulatory Frontiers in Regulation: The Age of Nanotechnology* (Edward Elgar, 2007) 149

Liivoja, Rain and Andres Saumets (eds), *The Law of Armed Conflict: Historical and Contemporary Perspectives* (Tartu University Press, 2012)

Liivoja, Rain, Kobi Leins and Tim McCormack, 'Emerging Technologies of Warfare' in Rain Liivoja and Tim McCormack (eds), *Routledge Handbook of the Law of Armed Conflict* (Routledge, 2016)

Mahoney, Peter (ed), *Ballistic Trauma a Practical Guide* (Springer, 2nd ed, 2005)

Marchant, Gary, Kenneth Abbott and Braden Allenby (eds), *Innovative Governance Models for Emerging Technologies* (Edward Elgar, 2013)

Martin, Francisco et al (eds), *International Human Rights and Humanitarian Law: Treaties, Cases, & Analysis* (Cambridge University Press, 2006)

Mathews, Robert and Timothy McCormack, 'The Relationship between International Humanitarian Law and Arms Control' in Helen Durham and Timothy McCormack (eds), *The Changing Face of Conflict and the Efficacy of International Humanitarian Law* (Martinus Nijhoff, 1999)

Mathews, Robert, 'Chemical and Biological Weapons' in Rain Liivoja and Tim McCormack (eds), *Routledge Handbook of the Law of Armed Conflict* (Routledge, 2016)

Matsuura, Jeffrey, *Nanotechnology Regulation and Policy Worldwide* (Artech House, 2006)

Maynard, Andrew and Jack Stilgoe (eds), *The Ethics of Nanotechnology, Geoengineering and Clean Energy* (Routledge, 2017)

McBride, Sean, 'The Legality of Weapons of Social Destruction' in C Swinarski (ed), *Studies and Essays on International Humanitarian Law and Red Cross Principles in Honour of Jean Pictet* (Martinus Nijhoff, 1984)

McNeill, J R, 'Global Environmental History: The First 150,000 Years' in J R McNeill and E S Mauldin (eds), *A Companion to Global Environmental History* (Wiley-Blackwell, 2012)

Meron, Theodor, 'Human Rights in Time of Peace and in Time of Armed Strife: Selected Problems' in Thomas Burgenthal (ed), *Contemporary Issues in International Law: Essays in Honor of Louis B Sohn* (NP Engel, 1984)

Meyer, Michael and Hilaire McCoubrey (eds), *Reflections on Law and Armed Conflicts* (Kluwer Law, 1998)

Ministry for Foreign Affairs, *The International Peace Conference, The Hague, May 18–July 29 1899* (Martinus Nijhoff, 1907)

Monica, John, Geert Van Calster and Patsa Agapi, 'A Nanotechnology Legal Framework' in Matt Hull and Diana M Bowman (eds), *Nanotechnology*

Environmental Health and Safety: Risks, Regulation and Management (Elsevier Science, 2nd ed, 2014)

Moore, William, *Gas Attack!: Chemical Warfare 1915–1918 and Afterwards* (Leo Cooper, 1987)

Mulhall, Douglas, *Our Molecular Future: How Nanotechnology, Robotics, Genetic and Artificial Intelligence Will Transform Our World* (Prometheus Books, 2002)

Murashov, Vladimir and John Howard (eds), *Nanotechnology Standards* (Springer, 2011)

Murray, Daragh et al (eds), *Practitioners' Guide to Human Rights Law in Armed Conflict* (Oxford University Press, 2016)

Nasu, Hitoshi and Robert McLaughlin (eds), *New Technologies and the Law of Armed Conflict* (Asser Press, 2014)

National Research Council, Committee on Military and Intelligence Methodology for Emergent Neurophysiological and Cognitive/Neural Science Research in the Next Two Decades, *Emerging Cognitive Neuroscience and Related Technologies* (National Academies Press, 2008)

National Research Council, Committee on Toxicologic and Radiologic Effects from Exposure to Depleted Uranium During and After Combat Committee on Toxicology, *Review of Toxicologic and Radiologic Risks to Military Personnel from Exposure to Depleted Uranium during and after Combat* (National Academies Press, 2008)

National Research Council of the National Academies, *Review of the Federal Strategy for Nanotechnology-Related Environmental, Health, and Safety Research* (National Academies Press, 2009)

Ndiaye, Tafsir and Ruediger Wolfrum (eds), *Law of the Sea, Environmental Law and Settlement of Disputes* (Martinus Nijhoff, 2007)

Nowak, Manfred and Elizabeth McArthur, *The United Nations Convention against Torture: A Commentary* (Oxford University Press, 2008)

Nowak, Manfred, 'Torture and Other Cruel, Inhuman or Degrading Treatment or Punishment' in Andrew Clapham and Paola Gaeta (eds), *The Oxford Handbook of International Law in Armed Conflict* (Oxford University Press, 2014)

UN Covenant on Civil and Political Rights: CCPR Commentary (NP Engel, 2nd ed, 2005)

O'Donnell, Erin, *Legal Rights for Rivers: Competition, Collaboration and Water Governance* (Routledge, 2019)

O'Riordan, Tim, James Cameron and Andrew Jordan, 'The Evolution of the Precautionary Principle' in Tim O'Riordan, James Cameron and Andrew Jordan (eds), *Reinterpreting the Precautionary Principle* (Cameron May, 2001)

Pais, Abraham, *Subtle Is the Lord: The Science and the Life of Albert Einstein* (Oxford University Press, 2005)

Payne, Cymie and Peter Sand (eds), *Gulf War Reparations and the United Nations Compensation Commission: Environmental Liability* (Oxford University Press, 2011)

Payne, Cymie, 'Developments in the Law of Environmental Reparations: A Case Study of the UN Compensation Commission' in Carsten Stahn, Jens Iverson and Jennifer Easterday (eds), *Environmental Protection and Transitions from Conflict to Peace: Clarifying Norms, Principles and Practices* (Oxford University Press, 2017)

'Legal Liability for Environmental Damage: The United Nations Compensation Commission and the 1990–1991 Gulf War' in Carl Bruch, Carroll Muffett and Sandra Nichols (eds), *Governance, Natural Resources and Post-Conflict Peacebuilding* (Routledge, 2016)

Pearson, Alan, Marie Isabelle Chevrier and Mark Wheelis (eds), *Incapacitating Biochemical Weapons* (Lexington Books, 2007)

Peel, Jacqueline, *Science and Risk Regulation in International Law* (Cambridge University Press, 2010)

Permanent Court of International Justice: Advisory Committee of Jurists, *Procès-verbaux of the Proceedings of the Committee, June 16th–July 24th, 1920, with Annexes* (Van Langenhuysen, 1920)

Perna, Laura, *The Formation of the Treaty Law of Non-International Armed Conflicts* (Brill, 2006)

Plant, Glen (ed), *Environmental Protection and the Law of War: Elements of a 'Fifth Geneva' Convention on the Protection of the Environment in Times of Armed Conflict'* (Bellhaven, 1992)

Prasad, Shiv Kant, *Advanced Nanotechnology* (Discovery Publishing House, 2008)

Rappert, Brian and Catriona McLeish (eds), *A Web of Prevention: Biological Weapons, Life Sciences, and the Governance of Research* (Earthscan, 2007)

Rappert, Brian and Michael Selgelid (eds), *On the Dual Uses of Sciences and Ethics Principles, Practices and Prospects* (ANU Press, 2013)

Rappert, Brian, 'Education for the Life Sciences' in Brian Rappert and C McLeish (eds), *A Web of Prevention: Biological Weapons, Life Sciences and the Future Governance of Research* (Earthscan, 2007)

Remdani, Noureddine, *Polymer Nanocomposites for Advanced Engineering and Military Applications* (IGI Global, 2019)

Richardson, Ben, *Time and Environmental Law: Telling Nature's Time* (Cambridge University Press, 2017)

Riedel, Eibe, Gilles Giacca and Christophe Golay (eds), *Economic, Social and Cultural Rights in International Law: Contemporary Issues and Challenges* (Oxford University Press, 2014)

Roberts, Adam and Richard Guelf (eds), *Documents on the Laws of War* (Oxford University Press, 3rd ed, 2000)

Robinson, Julian Perry, 'The Negotiations on the Chemical Weapons Convention: An Historical Overview' in Michael Bothe, Natalino Ronzitti and Allan Rosas (eds), *The New Chemical Weapons Convention: Implementation and Prospects* (Kluwer Law International, 1998) 17

Rogers, A P V, *Law on the Battlefield* (Manchester University Press, 3rd ed, 2012)

Rogers, Ben, Sumita Pennathur and Jesse Adams (eds), *Nanotechnology: Understanding Small Systems* (Taylor and Francis, 2nd ed, 2011)

Rose, Kenneth, *One Nation Underground: The Fallout Shelter in American Culture* (New York University Press, 2001)

Sandoz, Yves, Christophe Swinarski and Bruno Zimmermann (eds), *Commentary on the Additional Protocols of 8 June 1977 to the Geneva Conventions of 12 August 1949* (Martinus Nijhoff, 1987)

Sands, Phillippe and Jacqueline Peel, *Principles of International Environmental Law* (Cambridge, 2012)

Sands, Phillippe, *Lawless World: America and the Making and Breaking of Global Rules* (Penguin, 2005)

Sassòli, Marco, *Antoine Bouvier and Anne Quinne, How Does Law Protect in War?* (ICRC, 3rd ed, 2011)

Sattler, Klaus (ed), *Handbook of Nanophysics: Nanomedicine and Nanorobotics* (CRC Press, 2011)

Saxon, Dan (ed), *International Humanitarian Law and the Changing Technology of War* (Martinus Nijhoff, 2013)

Schabas, William, 'The Right to Life' in Andrew Clapham and Paola Gaeta (eds), *The Oxford Handbook of International Law in Armed Conflict* (Oxford University Press, 2014)

Schindler, Dietrich (ed), *The Laws of Armed Conflicts: A Collection of Conventions, Resolutions and other Documents* (Martinus Nijhoff, 1988)

Schlütter, Birgit, *Developments in Customary International Law* (Martinus Nijhoff, 2010)

Schmitt, Michael N and Jelena Pejic (eds), *International Law and Armed Conflict: Exploring the Faultlines* (Martinus Nijhoff, 2007)

Schmitt, Michael N and Leslie Green (eds), *The Law of Armed Conflict: Into the Next Millennium* (US Naval War College, 1998)

Schmitt, Michael, 'Military Necessity and Humanity in International Humanitarian law: Preserving the Delicate Balance' in Michael Schmitt, *Essays on War and Law at the Faultlines* (Springer, 2012)

'The Law of Targeting' in Elizabeth Wilmshurst and Susan Breau (eds), *Perspectives on the ICRC Study on Customary International Humanitarian Law* (Cambridge University Press, 2007)

'War, Technology, and the Law of Armed Conflict' in Anthony Helm (ed), *The Law of War in the 21st Century: Weaponry and the Use of Force* (Naval War College, 2006)

'War and the Environment: Fault Lines in the Prescriptive Landscape' in Jay Austin and Carl Bruch (eds), *The Environmental Consequences of War: Legal, Economic and Scientific* (Cambridge University Press, 2000)

Schulz, Mark and Vesselin Shanov (eds), *Nanomedicine: Design of Particles, Sensors, Motors, Implants, Robots and Devices* (Artech House, 2009)

Schwab, Klaus, *The Fourth Industrial Revolution* (World Economic Forum, 2016)

Scobbie, Iain, 'Natural Resources and Belligerent Occupation: Mutation through Permanent Sovereignty' in Stephen Bowen (ed), *Human Rights, Self-Determination and Political Change in the Occupied Palestinian Territories* (Martinus Nijhoff, 1997)

Shelley, Toby, *Nanotechnology: New Promises, New Dangers* (Fernwood Publisher, 2006)

Shipbaugh, Calvin et al, 'Nano-Enabled Components and Systems for Biodefense' in Neelina H Malsch (ed), *Biomedical Nanotechology* (Taylor and Francis, 2005)

Singer, Peter and August Cole, *Ghost Fleet: A Novel of the Next World War* (Houghton Mifflin Harcourt, 2015)

Singer, Peter, *Military Robots and the Law of War* (Brookings, 2009)

Slayton, Rebecca, *Arguments that Count* (Massachusetts Institute of Technology, 2013)

Sloan, Elinor, *The Revolution in Military Affairs: Implications for Canada and NATO* (McGill-Queen's University Press, 2002)

Sorel, Jean-Marc, 'Article 31 General Rule of Interpretation' in Olivier Corten and Pierre Klein (eds), *The Vienna Conventions on the Law of Treaties: A Commentary* (Oxford University Press, 2011) 804

Sparrow, Rob, 'The Social Impacts of Nanotechnology: An Ethical and Policy Analysis' in Andrew Maynard and Jack Stilgoe (eds), *The Ethics of Nanotechnology, Geoengineering and Clean Energy* (Routledge, 2017) 179

Ssenyonjo, Manisuli, *Economic, Social and Cultural Rights in International Law* (Hart Publishing, 2009)

Stachan, Hew and Andreas Herberg-Rothe (eds), *Clausewitz in the Twenty-First Century* (Oxford University Press, 2007)

Stirling, Dale, *The Nanotechnology Revolution: A Global Bibliographic Perspective* (Pan Stanford Publishing, 2018)

Stock, Thomas, 'Chemical and Biological Weapons: Developments and Proliferation' in Stockholm International Peace Research Institute, *1993 SIPRI Yearbook: World Armaments and Disarmament* (Oxford University Press, 1993)

Stoltzenberg, Dietrich, *Fritz Haber: Chemist, Nobel Laureate, German, Jew* (Chemical Heritage Foundation, 2004)

Susskind, Richard, *The Future of Law: Facing the Challenges of Information Technology* (Clarendon Press, 1996)

Suy, Eric, 'Le Préambule' in Emile Yakpo and Tahar Boumedra (eds), *Liber Amicorum Judge Mohammed Bedjaoui* (Kluwer, 1999)

Szasz, Paul, 'The International Law Concerning Weapons of Mass Destruction' in Sohail Hashmi and Steven Lee (eds), *Ethics and Weapons of Mass Destruction* (Cambridge University Press, 2004)

'The Existing Legal Framework, Protecting the Environment during International Armed Conflict' in Richard Grunawalt, John King and Ronald McClain (eds), *Protection of the Environment during Armed Conflict* (Naval War College, 1996) 278

Terry, R, 'Addressing Risks of Research Misuse' (Presentation to Dual Use and Codes of Conduct Meeting, Berlin, 2006)

Thakur, Vijay Kumar and Manju Kumari Thakur, *Handbook of Sustainable Polymers: Structure and Chemistry* (Taylor and Francis, 2016)

Turns, David, 'Military Objectives' in Rain Liivoja and Tim McCormack (eds), *Routledge Handbook of the Law of Armed Conflict* (Routledge, 2016)

US National Research Council Committee for the Review of ONR's Air and Surface Weapons Technology Program, *2002 Assessment of the Office of Naval Research's Air and Surface Weapons Technology Program* (National Academies Press, 2002)

US National Research Council of the National Academies, *Life Sciences and Related Fields: Trends Relevant to the Biological Weapons Convention* (National Academies Press, 2011)

Van der Wolf, René and Willem-Jan van der Woolf (eds), *Laws of War and International Law* (Wolf Legal Publishers, 2002)

Verwey, W, 'Observation on the Legal Protection of the Environment in Times of International Armed Conflict' in A-C Kiss and Johan Lammers (eds), *Hague Yearbook of International Law Vol 7* (Brill, 1994) 36

Von Clausewitz, Carl, *On War* (Princeton, 1976)

Von Deimling, Berthold, *Aus der Alten in die Neue Zeit: Lebenserinnerungen von Berthold von Deimling* (Verlag Ullstein, 1930)

Waldock, Sir Humphrey, 'Third Report on the Law of Treaties [1964] II' *Yearbook of the International Law Commission 58*, cited in Richard Gardiner, Treaty Interpretation (Oxford University Press, 2008)

Walzer, Michael, *Just and Unjust Wars: A Moral Argument with Historical Illustrations* (Basic Books, 1977)

Wang, Jun and Peter Dortmans, *A Review of Selected Nanotechnology Topics and the Potential Military Applications* (Department of Defence, 2004)

Weber, Marvin, *Handbook of Laser Wavelengths* (CRC Press, 1999)

Weinberger, Sharon, *The Imagineers of War: The Untold Story of DARPA, the Pentagon Agency that Changed the World* (Vintage Books, 2017)

Westing, Arthur, *Ecological Consequences of the Second Indochina War* (Almqvist & Wiksell International, 1976)

Wheelis, Mark, Lajos Rozsa and Malcolm Dando (eds), *Deadly Cultures: Biological Weapons since 1945* (Harvard University Press, 2006)

White, Gillian, 'The Principle of Good Faith' in Vaughan Lowe and Colin Warbrick (eds), *The United Nations and the Principles of International Law: Essays in Memory of Michael Akehurst* (Routledge, 1994) 230

Whitman, Jim, 'Nanotechnology and Dual Use Dilemmas' in Brian Rappert and Michael Selgelid (eds), *On the Dual Uses of Science and Ethics: Principles, Practices and Prospects* (ANU Press, 2013)

Wilmshurst, Elizabeth and Susan Breau, *Perspectives on the ICRC Study on Customary International Humanitarian Law* (Cambridge University Press, 2007)

Wong, Wilson, *Emerging Military Technologies: A Guide to the Issues* (Praeger Security International, 2013)

Yearbook of The International Court of Justice 1999–2000 (United Nations, 2000)

Young, Margaret A, 'Fragmentation and International Environmental Law' in Lavanya Rajamani and Jacqueline Peel (eds), *Oxford Handbook of International Environmental Law* (Oxford University Press, 2nd ed, forthcoming) <https://papers.ssrn.com/sol3/papers.cfm?abstract_id=3441535>

'Introduction: The Productive Friction between Regimes' in Margaret A Young (ed), *Regime Interaction in International Law: Facing Fragmentation* (Cambridge University Press, 2012)

'Regime Interaction in Creating, Implementing and Enforcing International Law' in Margaret A Young (ed), *Regime Interaction in International Law: Facing Fragmentation* (Cambridge University Press, 2012)

Trading Fish, Saving Fish: The Interaction between Regimes in International Law (Cambridge University Press, 2011)

Zegveld, Liesbeth, *Accountability of Armed Opposition Groups in International Law* (Cambridge University Press, 2002)

VI Journal Articles

Abbott, Kenneth and Duncan Snidal, 'Strengthening International Regulation through Transnational New Governance: Overcoming the Orchestration Deficit' (2009) 42 *Vanderbilt Journal of Transnational Law* 501

Abbott, Kenneth, Gary Merchant and Douglas Sylvester, 'A Framework Convention for Nanotechnology?' (2006) 36 *Environmental Law Reporter* 10931

Abbott, Linda and Andrew Maynard, 'Exposure Assessment Approaches for Engineered Nanomaterials' (2010) 30(11) *Risk Analysis* 1634

Adelman, David, 'Scientific Activism and Restraint: The Interplay of Statistics, Judgment, and Procedure in Environmental Law' (2004) 79(2) *Notre Dame Law Review* 497

Akande, Dapo, 'Nuclear Weapons, Unclear Law? Deciphering the *Nuclear Weapons* Advisory Opinion of the International Court' (1998) 68(1) *British Yearbook of International Law* 165

Akhtarkhavari, Afshin, 'Environmental Principles and the International Court of Justice' (2009) 28 *Australian Year Book of International Law* 101

Aldrich, George, 'Progressive Development of the Laws of War: A Reply to Criticisms of the 1977 Geneva Protocol I' (1986) 26 *Virginia Journal of International Law* 693

Allenby, Braden R, 'Are new Technologies Undermining the Laws of War?' (2014) 70(1) *Bulletin of the Atomic Scientists* 21

Altmann, Jürgen, 'Military Uses of Nanotechnology: Perspectives and Concerns' (2007) 35 *Security Dialogue* 61

'Military Uses of Nanotechnology: Too Much Complexity for International Security?' (2004) 23 *Complexity* 62

Altmann, Jürgen and Mark Gubrud, 'Anticipating Military Nanotechnology' (2004) 23 *IEEE Technology and Society Magazine* 328

Ananthaswamy, Anil, 'The March of the Motes' (2003) 179(2409) *New Scientist* 26

Andrew, David, 'Thermobaric Munitions and Their Medical Effects' (2003) 12(1) *Australian Military Medicine* 9

Backstrom, Alan and Ian Henderson, 'New Capabilities in Warfare: An Overview of Contemporary Technological Developments and the Associated Legal and Engineering Issues in Article 36 Weapons Reviews' (2012) 94(886) *International Review of the Red Cross* 483

Bahadar, Haji et al, 'Toxicity of Nanoparticles and an Overview of Current Experimental Models' (2016) 20(1) *Iranian Biomedical Journal* 1

Baker, Roozbeh B, 'Customary International Law in the 21st Century: Old Challenges and New Debates' (2010) 21 *European Journal of International Law* 173

Balbus, John M et al, 'Meeting Report: Hazard Assessment for Nanoparticles: Report from an Interdisciplinary Workshop' (2007) 115(11) *Environmental Health Perspectives* 1654

Baltimore, David et al, 'A Prudent Path Forward for Genomic Engineering and Germline Gene Modification' (2015) 348(6230) *Science* 36

Bauer, Keith, 'Wired Patients: Implantable Microchips and Biosensors in Patient Care' (2007) 16(3) *Cambridge Quarterly of Healthcare Ethics* 281

Bean, James, 'Enhanced Blast Weapons and Forward Medical Treatment' (April–June 2004) *US Army Medical Department Journal* 48

Benkoski, Jason et al, 'Systems Engineering at the Nanoscale' (2012) 8373 *International Society for Optical Engineering* <https://arizona.pure.elsevier.com/en/publications/systems-engineering-at-the-nanoscale>

Bennett Moses, Lyria, 'How to Think about Law, Regulation and Technology: Problems with "Technology" as a Regulatory Target' (2013) 5(1) *Law, Innovation and Technology* 1

Boothby, William, 'How Will Weapons Reviews Address the Challenges Posed by New Technologies?' (2013) 52(1) *Military Law and the Law of War Review* 58

Borm, Paul J A et al, 'The Potential Risks of Nanomaterials: A Review Carried out for ECETOC' (2006) 3(1) *Particle and Fibre Toxicology* 11

Bothe, Michael et al, 'International Law Protecting the Environment during Armed Conflict: Gaps and Opportunities' (2010) 92(879) *International Review of the Red Cross* 569

Boverhof, Darrell R et al, 'Comparative Assessment of Nanomaterial Definitions and Safety Evaluation Considerations' (2015) 73(1) *Regulatory Toxicology and Pharmacology* 137

Bowman, Diana and Graeme Hodge, 'A Small Matter of Regulation: An International Review of Nanotechnology Regulation' (2007) 8 *Columbia Science and Technology Law Review* 1

Bowman, Diana and Jake Gatof, 'Reviewing the Regulatory Barriers for Nanomedicine: Global Questions and Challenges' (2015) 10(21) *Nanomedicine* 3275

Bowman, Diana and Michael G Bennett, 'The Current State of Australia's Evolving Approach to Regulating Nanotechnologies' (2013) 9(4) *Nanotechnology Law and Business* 330

Bowman, Megan and Geert van Calster, 'Does REACH Go too Far?' (2007) 2(9) *Nature Nanotechnology* 525

Bradley, Lucas, 'Regulating Weaponized Nanotechnology: How the International Criminal Court Offers a Way Forward' (2013) 41 *Georgia Journal of International and Comparative Law* 723

Brar, Satinder Kaur et al, 'Engineered Nanoparticles in Wastewater and Wastewater Sludge: Evidence and Impacts' (2009) 30(3) *Waste Management* 504

British Defence Doctrine (JWP-0-01) in Anthony Rogers, 'Zero-casualty Warfare' (2000) 82(837) *International Review of the Red Cross* 165

Brownlie, Ian, 'A Survey of International Customary Rules of Environmental Protection' (1973) 13 *Natural Resources Journal* 179 <http://digitalrepository.unm.edu/cgi/viewcontent.cgi?article=3333&context=nrj>

Bunker, Robert (ed), 'Nonlethal Weapons: Emerging Requirements for Security Strategy' (INSS Occasional Paper 15, *Institute for Foreign Policy Analysis*, 1996) <www.hsdl.org/?view&did=1145>

Buzea, Cristine, Ivan Pacheco and Kevin Robbie, 'Nanomaterials and Nanoparticles: Sources and Toxicity' (2007) 2(4) *Biointerphases* 17 <https://link.springer.com/content/pdf/10.1116/1.2815690.pdf>

Cassese, Antonio, 'The Martens Clause: Half a Loaf or Simply Pie in the Sky?' (2000) 11(1) *European Journal of International Law* 187

Cello, Jeronimo, Aniko V Paul and Eckard Wimmer, 'Chemical Synthesis of Poliovirus cDNA: Generation of Infectious Virus in the Absence of Natural Template' (2002) 297(5583) *Science* 1016

Charlesworth, Hilary, 'Customary International Law the Nicaragua Case' (1984) 11 *Australian Yearbook of International Law* 1

'Chemical Weapons' (1986) 11 *United Nations Disarmament Yearbook* 241

Chong et al, Amy, 'Non-invasive Optical Inhibition with a Red-Shifted Microbial Rhodopsin' (2014) 17(8) *Nature Neuroscience* 1123

Chun-xiao, Li and Qian Hai-li, 'A Double-Edged Sword: CRISPR-Cas9 Is Emerging as a Revolutionary Technique for Genome Editing' (2015) 2 *Military Medical Research* 25

Chuong, Amy S et al, 'Noninvasive Optical Inhibition with a Red-Shifted Microbial Rhodopsin' (2014) 17(8) *Nature Neuroscience* 1123

Claggett, Brice and O Thomas Johnson Jr, 'May Israel as a Belligerent Occupant Lawfully Exploit Previously Unexploited Oil Resources of the Gulf of Suez?' (1978) 72(3) *American Journal of International Law* 558

'Commission on the Responsibility of the Authors of the War and Enforcement of Penalties' (1920) 14(1/2) *American Journal of International Law* 95

Coupland, Robin and Kobi-Renée Leins, 'Science and Prohibited Weapons' (2005) 308(5730) *Science* 1841

Coupland, Robin, '"Non-Lethal" Weapons: Precipitating a New Arms Race' (1997) 315(7100) *British Medical Journal* 72

'The Effect of Weapons: Defining Superfluous Injury and Unnecessary Suffering' (1996) 3 *Medicine and Global Survival* <www.ippnw.org/pdf/mgs/3-coupland.pdf>

Craik, Alastair Neil, 'The Duty to Cooperate in International Environmental Law: Constraining Discretion through Due Respect' (2020) <https://dx.doi.org/10.2139/ssrn.3596981>

Cusato, Eliana, 'From Ecocide to Voluntary Remediation Projects: Legal Responses to Environmental Warfare in Vietnam and the Spectre of Colonialism' (2018) *Melbourne Journal of International Law* 19(2) 494

Cyranoski, David, 'CRISPR Gene-editing Tested in a Person for the First Time' (2016) 539(7630) *Nature* 479

Dando, Malcolm, 'Find the Time to Discuss New Bioweapons' (5 July 2016) 535 *Nature* 9

Daoust, Isabel, Robin Coupland and R Ishoey, 'New Wars, New Weapons? The Obligation of States to Assess the Legality of Means and Methods of Warfare' (2002) 84(846) *International Review of the Red Cross* 354

Doroudchi, Mohammed Mehdi et al, 'Virally Delivered Channelrhodopsin-2 Safely and Effectively Restores Visual Function in Multiple Mouse Models of Blindness' (2011) 19(7) *Molecular Therapy* 1220

Douglas, Shawn, Ido Bachelet and George Church, 'A Logic-Gated Nanorobot for Targeted Transport of Molecular Payloads' (2012) 335(6070) *Science* 831

Draper, G I A D, 'Role of Legal Advisers in Armed Forces' (1978) 18(202) *International Review of the Red Cross* 6

Droege, Cordula, '"In Truth the Leitmotiv" – The Prohibition of Torture and Other Forms of Ill-Treatment in International Humanitarian Law' (2007) 89 (867) *International Review of the Red Cross* 515

Drucker, Merrit, 'The Military Commander's Responsibility for the Environment' (1989) 135 *Environmental Ethics* 135

Dugué, Guillaume, Walther Akemann and Thomas Knöpfel, 'A Comprehensive Concept of Optogenetics' (2012) 196 *Progress in Brain Research* 1

Duruigbo, Emeka, 'Permanent Sovereignty and Peoples' Ownership of Natural Resources in International Law' (2006) 38(1) *George Washington International Law Review* 33

Duxbury, Geoffrey et al, 'Quantum Cascade Semiconductor Infrared and Far-Infrared Lasers: From Trace Gas Sensing to Non-Linear Optics' (2005) 34 *Chemical Society Reviews* 921

Ebbesen, Mette, 'The Role of the Humanities and Social Sciences in Nanotechnology Research and Development' (2008) 2(1) *NanoEthics* 1

Elsaesser, Andreas and C Vyvyan Howard, 'Toxicology of Nanoparticles' (2012) 64 (2) *Advanced Drug Delivery Reviews* 129

Ewing, Russell, 'The Legality of Chemical Warfare' (1927) 61 *American Law Review* 58

Fenno, Lief, Ofer Yizhar, and Karl Deisseroth, 'The Development and Application of Optogenetics' (2011) 34 *Annual Review of Neuroscience* 389

Fenrick, William J, 'The Conventional Weapons Convention: A Modest but Useful Treaty' (1990) 279 *International Review of the Red Cross* 498

'The Rule of Proportionality and Protocol I in Conventional Warfare' (1982) 98 *Military Law Review* 102

Fry, James, 'Contextualized Legal Reviews for the Methods and Means of Warfare: Cave Combat and International Humanitarian Law' (2006) 44(2) *Columbia Journal of Transnational Law* 453

Giannardi, Cristina and Daniele Dominici, 'Military Use of Depleted Uranium: Assessment of Prolonged Population Exposure' (2003) 64(2/3) *Journal of Environmental Radioactivity* 227

Gilman, Ryan, 'Expanding Environmental Justice after War: The Need for Universal Jurisdiction over Environmental War Crimes' (2011) 22(3) *Colorado Journal of International Environmental Law and Policy* 447

Gleick, Peter, 'Water and Conflict: Fresh Water Resources and International Security' (1993) 18 *International Security* 79

Glenn, Jerome, 'Nanotechnology: Future Military Environmental Health Considerations' (2006) 73(2) *Technological Forecasting and Social Change* 128

Goldblat, Jozef, 'The Biological Weapons Convention: An Overview' (1997) 37 (318) *International Review of the Red Cross* 251

Gómez, Javier, 'The Law of Air Warfare' (1998) 38(323) *International Review of the Red Cross* 347

Grant, Simon and John Quiggin, 'Bounded Awareness, Heuristics and the Precautionary Principle' (2013) 93 *Journal of Economic Behavior & Organization* 17

Grau, Lester and Timothy Smith, 'A "Crushing" Victory: Fuel-Air Explosives and Grozny 2000' (2000) 84(8) *Marine Corps Gazette* 30

'Guidelines for Military Manuals and Instructions on the Environment in Times of Armed Conflict' (1996) 36(311) *International Review of the Red Cross* 231

Haagen, Paul, 'A Hamburg Childhood: The Early Life of Herbert Bernstein' (2003) 13 *Duke Journal of Comparative and International Law* 7

Hansen, Steffen Foss et al, 'Late Lessons from Early Warnings for Nanotechnology' (2008) 3(8) *Nature Nanotechnology* 444

Hathaway, O et al, 'Which Law Governs during Armed Conflict? The Relationship between International Humanitarian Law and Human Rights Law in Armed Conflicts' (2012) 96(6) *Minnesota Law Review* 1883

Hodge, Graeme, Andrew Maynard and Diana Bowman, 'Nanotechnology: Rhetoric, Risk and Regulation' (2014) 41(1) *Science and Public Policy* 1

Hoet, P H, I Brüske-Hohlfeld and O V Salata, 'Nanoparticles: Known and Unknown Health Risks' (2004) 2(1) *Journal of Nanobiotechnology* 12

Horowitz, Michael, 'Coming Next in Military Tech' (2014) 70 *Bulletin of the Atomic Scientists* 54

Hourcle, Laurent, 'Environmental Law of War' (2001) 25(1) *Vermont Law Review* 653

Howard, Sean, 'Nanotechnology and Mass Destruction: The Need for an Inner Space Treaty' (2002) 65 *Disarmament Diplomacy* <www.acronym.org.uk/old/archive/dd/dd65/65op1.htm>

Hulme, Max, 'Preambles in Treaty Interpretation' (2016) 164(5) *University of Pennsylvania Law Review* 1281

Huskisson, Darren, 'The Air Bridge Denial Program and the Shootdown of Civil Aircraft under International Law' (2005) 56 *The Air Force Law Review* 98

Hutchinson, Terry and Nigel Duncan, 'Defining and Describing What We Do: Doctrinal Legal Research' (2012) 17(1) *Deakin Law Review* 83

International Committee of the Red Cross, 'A Guide to the Legal Review of New Weapons, Means and Methods of Warfare: Measures to Implement Article 36 of Additional Protocol I of 1977' (2006) 88(864) *International Review of the Red Cross* 931

Iyer, Shrivats Mohan et al, 'Virally Mediated Optogenetic Excitation and Inhibition of Pain in Freely Moving Nontransgenic Mice' (2014) 32(3) *Nature Biotechnology* 274

Jenks, Christopher, 'The Conflict of Law-Making Treaties' (1953) 30 *British Yearbook of International Law* 401

Jevglevskaja, Natalia, 'Weapons Review Obligation under Customary International Law' (2018) 94 *International Law Studies* 186

Kahn, Jennifer, 'Nano's Big Future' (2006) 209(6) *National Geographic* 98

Kalinich, John et al, 'Embedded Weapons-grade Tungsten Alloy Shrapnel Rapidly Induces Metastatic High-grade Rhabdomyo-sarcomas in F344 Rats' (2005) 113(6) *Environmental Health Perspective* 729

Kalshoven, Frits, 'The Conventional Weapons Convention: Underlying Legal Principles' (1990) 279 *International Review of the Red Cross* 510

'Reaffirmation and Development of International Humanitarian Law Applicable in Armed Conflicts: The Diplomatic Conference, Geneva, 1974–1977, Part II' (1978) 9 *Netherlands Yearbook of International Law* 117

Kelly, Joseph, 'Gas Warfare in International Law' (1960) 9 *Military Law Review* 1

Kim, Kyung Man et al, 'Optogenetic Mimicry of the Transient Activation of Dopamine Neurons by Natural Reward Is Sufficient for Operant Reinforcement' (2012) 7(4) *PLoS One* <https://doi.org/10.1371/journal.pone.0033612>

Klabbers, Jan, 'International Legal Histories: The Declining Importance of *Travaux Préparatoires* in Treaty Interpretation' (2003) 50(3) *Netherlands International Law Review* 267

Kosal, Margaret, 'The Security Implications of Nanotechnology' (2013) 66(4) *Bulletin of the Atomic Scientists* 58

Kosta, Eleni and Diana Bowman, 'Treating or Tracking? Regulatory Challenges of Nano-Enabled ICT Implants' (2011) 33(2) *Law and Policy* 256

Kuran, Timur and Cass R Sunstein, 'Availability Cascades and Risk Regulation' (1999) 51(4) *Stanford Law Review* 683

Laurila-Pant, Mirka et al, 'How to Value Biodiversity in Environmental Management?' (2015) 55 *Ecological Indicators* 1

Lawrence, Jessica and Kevin Heller, 'The First Ecocentral Environmental War Crime: The Limits of Article 8(2)(b)(iv) of the Rome Statute' (2007) 20 *Georgetown International Environmental Law Review* 61

Lefebure, Victor, 'Chemical Warfare: The Possibility of Its Control' (1921) 7 *Transactions of the Grotius Society* 153

Leins, Kobi, 'Shining a Regulatory Spotlight on New Lasers: Regulation of the Use of Nanolaser Technologies in Armed Conflict' (2016) 56 *Jurimetrics* 261

Levie, Howard, 'Humanitarian Restrictions on Chemical and Biological Weapons' (1982) 13 *University of Toledo Law Review* 1192

Liivoja, Rain, 'Technological Change and the Evolution of War' (2015) 97(900) *International Review of the Red Cross* 1157

Lijnzaad, Liesbeth and Gerard Tanja, 'Protection of the Environment in Times of Armed Conflict: The Iraq–Kuwait War' (1993) 40(2) *Netherlands International Law Review* 169

Lin, Dayu et al, 'Functional Identification of an Aggression Locus the Mouse Hypothalamus' (2011) 470(7333) *Nature* 221

Ludlow, Karinne, 'Hitting the Mark or Falling Short with Nanotechnology Regulation?' (2009) 27(11) *Trends in Biotechnology* 615

Maher, Barbara et al, 'Magnetite Pollution Nanoparticles in the Human Brain' (2016) 113(39) *Proceedings of the National Academy of Sciences of the United States of America* 10797

Maiman, Theodore H, 'Stimulated Optical Radiation in Ruby' (1960) 187(4736) *Nature* 493

Mandel, Gregory N, 'History Lessons for a General Theory of Law and Technology' (2007) 8(2) *Minnesota Journal of Law, Science and Technology* 551

Marchant, Gary, Douglas Sylvester and Kenneth Abbott, 'What Does the History of Technology Regulation Teach Us about Nano Oversight?' (2009) 37(4) *Journal of Law, Medicine and Ethics* 724

Marchant, Gary and Kenneth W Abbott, 'International Harmonization of Nanotechnology Governance through "Soft Law" Approaches' (2013) 9(4) *Nanotechnology Law & Business* 393

Marcus, David, 'Famine Crimes in International Law' (2003) 97(2) *American Journal of International Law* 245

Mathews, Robert, 'WMD Arms Control Agreements in the Post-September 11 Security Environment: Part of the Counter-Terrorism Toolbox' (2007) 8(2) *Melbourne Journal of International Law* 292

Maynard, Andrew et al, 'Is Novelty Overrated?' (2014) 9(6) *Nature Nanotechnology* 409

'Old Materials, New Challenges?' (2014) 9(9) *Nature Nanotechnology* 658

'Don't Define Nanomaterials' (2011) 475(7354) *Nature* 31

'Safe Handling of Nanotechnology' (2006) 444(7117) *Nature* 267

McClelland, Justin, 'The Review of Weapons in Accordance with Article 36 of Additional Protocol I' (2003) 85(850) *International Review of the Red Cross* 397

McCormack, Tim and Meredith Hagger, 'Regulating the Use of Unmanned Combat Vehicles: Are General Principles of International Humanitarian Law Sufficient?' (2012) 21(2) *Journal of Law, Information and Science* 74

McCormack, Tim, 'A Non-Liquet on Nuclear Weapons: The ICJ Avoids the Application of General Principles of International Humanitarian Law of Armed Conflict' (1997) 316 *International Review of the Red Cross* 76

McCormack, Timothy, 'International Law and the Use of Chemical Weapons in the Gulf War' (1990–1991) 21(1) *California Western International Law Journal* 1

Melzer, Nils, 'Keeping the Balance between Military Necessity and Humanity: A Response to Four Critiques of the ICRC's interpretative Guidance on the Notion of Direction Participation in Hostilities' (2010) 42 *New York University Journal of International Law and Politics* 831

Mendelson, Maruice, 'The Formation of Customary International Law' (1998) 272 *Receuil des Cours*

Meron, Theodor, 'The Martens Clause, Principles of Humanity and Dictates of Public Conscience' (2000) 94(1) *The American Journal of International Law* 78

Merrills, John, 'Two Approaches to Treaty Interpretation' (1969) 4 *Australian International Law* 55

Meselson, Matthew, 'Averting the Hostile Exploitation of Biotechnology' (2000) 48 *CBW Conventions Bulletin*

Miller, Alexandra et al, 'Neoplastic Transformation of Human Osteoblast Cells to the Tumorigenic Phenotype by Heavy Metal Tungsten Alloy Particles: Induction of Genotoxic Effects' (2001) 22(1) *Carcinogenesis* 115

Miller, Mark et al, 'Inhaled Nanoparticles Accumulate at Sites of Vascular Disease' (2017) 11 *ACS Nano* 4542

Mitchell, Andrew, 'Good Faith in WTO Dispute Settlement' (2006) 7(2) *Melbourne Journal of International Law* 339

Mohamed, Ahmed, Hasem Mostafa and Sherif Elbasuney, 'Nanoscopic Fuel-rich Thermobaric Formulations: Chemical Composition Optimization and Sustained Secondary Combustion Shock Wave Modulation' (2015) 301 *Journal of Hazardous Materials* 491

Moore, Daniel, 'Nanotech in Warfare: Some Ethical Concerns' (2012) 23 *Nano: The Magazine for Small Science* 14

Morrison, Philip and Kosta Tsipis, 'Rightful Names' (2003) 59(3) *Bulletin of the Atomic Scientists* 77

Moses, Lyria Bennett, 'How to Think about Law, Regulation and Technology: Problems with "Technology" as a Regulatory Target' (2013) 5(1) *Law, Innovation and Technology* 1

Nasu, Hitoshi and Thomas Faunce, 'Nanotechnology and the International Law of Weaponry: Towards International Regulation of Nano-Weapons' 20 (2009) *Journal of Law, Information and Science* 21

Nasu, Hitoshi, 'Nanotechnology and Challenges to International Humanitarian Law: A Preliminary Legal Assessment' (2012) 94(886) *International Review of the Red Cross* 653

Nelson, Ray, 'Nano-technology and Biotechnology for Future Defense' (2015) 3 (22) *Space & Missile Defense Report* cited in Jefferson Reynolds, 'Collateral Damage on the 21st Century Battlefield: Enemy Exploitation and the Law of Armed Conflict, and the Struggle for a Moral High Ground' (2005) 56 *The Air Force Law Review* 1

Nixdorff, Katherine et al, 'Dual-Use Nano-neurotechnology: An Assessment of the Implications of Trends in Science and Technology' (2018) 37(2) *Politics and the Life Sciences* 180

Oberdörster, Günter, Eva Oberdörster and Jan Oberdörster, 'Nanotoxicology: An Emerging Discipline Evolving from Studies of Ultrafine Particles' (2005) 113 (7) *Environmental Health Perspectives* 823

Oberdörster, Günter et al, 'Principles for Characterizing the Potential Human Health Effects from Exposure to Nanomaterials: Elements of a Screening Strategy' (2005) *Particle and Fibre Toxicology* <https://doi.org/10.1186/1743-8977-2-8>

'Increased Pulmonary Toxicity of Ultrafine Particles' (1990) 21(3) *Journal of Aerosol Science and Technology* 381

Öberg, Marko Divac, 'The Legal Effects of Resolutions of the UN Security Council and the General Assembly in the Jurisprudence of the ICJ' (2006) 16(5) *The European Journal of International Law* 879

Okorodudu-Fubara, Margaret, 'Oil in the Persian Gulf War: Legal Appraisal of an Environmental Warfare' (1992) 23 *St Mary's Law Journal* 123

Ostrov, Nili et al, 'Design, Synthesis and Testing toward a 57-codon Genome' (2016) 353(6301) *Science* 819

Pardo-Guerra, Juan Pablo and Francisco Aguayo Ayala, 'Nanotechnology and the International Regime on Chemical and Biological Weapons' (2005) 2(1) *Law and Business* 55

Parks, W Hays, 'Means and Methods of Warfare' (2006) 38 *George Washington International Law Review* 511

'Classification of Chemical-Biological Warfare' (1981–1982) 13 *University of Toledo Law Review* 1165

Parsons, Rymn James, 'The Fight to Save the Planet: U.S. Armed Forces, "Greenkeeping," and Enforcement of the Law Pertaining to Environmental Protection during Armed Conflict' (1998) 10(2) *Georgetown Environmental Law Review* 441

Payne, Cymie, 'UN Commission Awards Compensation for Environmental and Public Health Damage from 1990–91 Gulf War' (2005) 9(25) *American Society for International Law* <www.asil.org/insights/volume/9/issue/25/

un-commission-awards-compensation-environmental-and-public-health-damage>

Peel, Jacqueline, 'Science and Risk Assessment in International Law: Learning from the WTO SPS Experience' (2004) 98 *Proceedings of the Annual Meeting (American Society of International Law)* 283

Pinson, Robert, 'Is Nanotechnology Prohibited by the Biological and Chemical Weapons Conventions?' (2004) 22(2) *Berkeley Journal of International Law* 279

Pitschmann, Vladimir and Zdenek Hon, 'Military Importance of Natural Toxins and Their Analogs' (2016) 21 *Molecules* 556 <www.mdpi.com/1420-3049/21/5/556/html>

Plascencia-Villa, German, et al, 'High-resolution Analytical Imaging and Electron Holography of Magnetite Particles in Amyloid Cores of Alzheimer's Disease' (2016) 6 *Scientific Reports* <www.nature.com/articles/srep24873>

Pleus, Richard, 'Rethinking Dose in a Nano-World' (May 2013) *Chemistry in Australia* 16

Rappert, Brian, 'Why Has Not There Been More Research of Concern?' (2014) 2 *Frontiers in Public Health* 74 <http://journal.frontiersin.org/article/10.3389/fpubh.2014.00074/full>

Reynolds, Glenn, 'Nanotechnology and Regulatory Policy: Three Phases' (2003) 17 (1) *Harvard Journal of Law and Technology* 179

'Environmental Regulation of Nanotechnology: Some Preliminary Observations' (2001) 31 *Environmental Law Institute* 10681

Rhea, Harry, 'The Commission on the Responsibility of the Authors of the War and on Enforcement of Penalties and Its Contribution to International Criminal Justice after World War II' (2014) 25 *Criminal Law Forum* 147

Roberts, Guy, 'The New Rules for Waging War: The Case against Ratification of Additional Protocol I' (1985) 26 *Virginia Journal of International Law* 109

Roco, Mihail C, 'International Perspective on Government Nanotechnology Funding in 2005' (2005) 7(6) *Journal of Nanoparticle Research* 707

Roedel, Erik et al, 'Pulmonary Toxicity after Exposure to Military-relevant Heavy Metal Tungsten Alloy Particles' (2012) 259(1) *Toxicology and Applied Pharmacology* 74

Rucinski, Taryn, 'Searching for the Nano-needle in a Green Haystack: Researching the Environmental, Health, and Safety Ramifications of Nanotechnology' (2013) 30(2) *Pace Environmental Law Review* 397

Sainsbury, Frank, 'Virus-like Nanoparticles: Emerging Tools for Targeted Cancer Diagnostics and Therapeutics' (2017) 8(12) *Therapeutic Delivery* 1019

Sales, Louise, 'Corporate Influence over Nanotechnology Regulation' (2014) 121 *Chain Reaction* 37

Schmitt, Michael N and Jeffrey Thurnher, 'Out of the Loop: Autonomous Weapon Systems and the Law of Armed Conflict' (2013) 4 *Harvard National Security Journal* 231

Schmitt, Michael N, 'Green War: An Assessment of the Environmental Law of International Armed Conflict' (1997) 22(1) *Yale Journal of International Law* 1

'Military Necessity and Humanity in International Humanitarian Law: Preserving the Delicate Balance' (2010) 50(4) *Virginia Journal of International Law* 795

Schoiswohl, Michael, 'Human Rights and Disarmament: A Blind Date or Shotgun Marriage?' (2013) 15(1) *Austrian Review of International and European Law* 109

'September 11 Terrorist Panel Discussion' (2002) 34(2) *Case Western Reserve Journal of International Law* 149

Sharp, Phillip and Robert Langer, 'Promoting Convergence in Biomedical Science' (2011) 333(6042) *Science* 527

Shelley-Egan, Clare, Diana Bowman and Douglas Robinson, 'Devices of Responsibility: Over a Decade of Responsible Research and Innovation Initiatives for Nanotechnology' (2017) *Science, Engineering and Ethics* <www.ncbi.nlm.nih.gov/pubmed/29019058>

Shelton, Dinah and Alexandre Kiss, 'Martens Clause for Environmental Protection' (2000) 30(6) *Environmental Policy and Law* 285

Shipbaugh, Calvin, 'Offense-Defense Aspects of Nanotechnologies: A Forecast of Potential Military Applications' (2006) 34(4) *Journal of Law, Medicine and Ethics* 741

Shipway, Andrew, Eugenii Katz and Itamar Willner, 'Nanoparticle Arrays on Surfaces for Electronic, Optical, and Sensor Applications' (2000) 1(1) *ChemPhysChem* 18

Sidiropoulos, Themistoklis et al, 'Ultrafast Plasmonic Nanolasers Near the Surface Plasmon Frequency' (2014) 10 *Nature Physics* 870

Sjöstedt, Britta and Anne Dienelt, 'Enhancing the Protection of the Environment in Relation to Armed Conflicts: Draft Principles of the International Law Commission and Beyond' (2020) 10(1) *Goettingen Journal of International Law* 13

Solow, Andrew and Stephen Polasky, 'The Endangered Species Act as a Tool to Conserve Biological Diversity' (1999) 14 *Choices* 17

Som, Claudia et al, 'The Importance of Life Cycle Concepts for the Development of Safe Nanoproducts' (2010) 269 *Toxicology* 160

Sparrow, Robert, 'The Social Impacts of Nanotechnology: An Ethical and Political Analysis' (2009) 6(1) *Journal of Bioethical Enquiry* 13

Steffen, Will et al, 'Planetary Boundaries: Guiding Human Development on a Changing Planet' (2015) 347(6223) *Science* 736

Stephens, Dale, 'The International Legal Implications of Military Space Operations: Examining the Interplay between Humanitarian Law and the Outer Space Legal Regime' (2018) 94 *International Law Studies* 75

Stewart, Frances, 'Root Causes of Violent Conflict in Developing Countries' (2002) 324(74333) *British Medical Journal* 342

Stylianou, Andreas and Michael A Talias, 'The "Magic Light": A Discussion on Laser Ethics' (2015) 21(4) *Science and Engineering Ethics* 979

Tabassi, Lisa, 'Impact of the CWC: Progressive Development of Customary International Law and Evolution of the Customary Norm against Chemical Weapons' (2004) 63 *The CBW Conventions Bulletin* 1

Themistoklis, Sidiropoulos P H et al, 'Ultrafast Plasmonic Nanowire Lasers Near the Surface Plasmon Frequency' (2014) 10(11) *Nature Physics* 870

Ticehurst, Rupert, 'The Martens Clause and the Laws of Armed Conflict' (1997) 37 (317) *International Review of the Red Cross* 125

'The Advisory Opinion of the International Court of Justice on the Legality of the Threat or Use of Nuclear Weapons' (1996) 2(1) *War Studies Journal* 107

Tobin, John, 'Seeking Clarity in Relation to the Principle of Complementarity: Reflections on the Recent Contributions of Some International Bodies' (2007) 8(2) *Melbourne Journal of International Law* 356

Tranter, Kieren, 'The Law and Technology Enterprise: Uncovering the Template to Legal Scholarship on Technology' (2011) 3(1) *Law, Innovation and Technology* 31

Trzciński, Waldemar and Lotfi Maiz, 'Thermobaric and Enhanced Blast Explosives: Properties and Testing Methods' (2015) 40(5) *Propellants, Explosives, Pyrotechnics* 632

Türker, Lemi, 'Thermobaric and Enhanced Blast Explosives (TBX and EBX)' (2016) 12 *Defence Technology* 423

US Army War College, *Summary Report on Biotechnology Workshop 2020 (29 and 30 May 1996, document number 96-6963)* cited in Jan Van Aken and Edward Hammond, 'Genetic Engineering and Biological Weapons' (2003) 4 *EMBO Reports* S57

US Department of Army Legal Service Agency, *The Desert Storm Assessment Team's Report to the Judge Advocate General of the Army* (1992) cited in Michael Schmitt, 'Green War: An Assessment of the Environmental Law of International Armed Conflict' (1997) 22(1) *Yale Journal of International Law* 1

US Joint Chiefs of Staff, *Joint Urban Operations JP 3-06* (20 November 2013) cited in Isabel Robinson and Ellen Nohle, 'Proportionality and Precautions in Attack: The Reverberating Effects of Using Explosive Weapons in populated Areas' (2016) 98 *International Review of the Red Cross* 107

Van Aken, Jan and Edward Hammond, 'Genetic Engineering and Biological Weapons' (2003) 4 *EMBO Reports* S57

Van der Heijden, A et al, 'Modification and Characterization of (Energetic) Nanomaterials' (2003) 71(2) *Journal of Physics and Chemistry of Solids* 59

Van der Sande, Meike et al, 'Sub-Chronic Toxicity Study in Rats Orally Exposed to Nanostructured Silica' (2014) 11(8) *Particle and Fibre Toxicology* <https://doi.org/10.1186/1743-8977-11-8>

Van Est, Rinie and Dirk Stemerding, 'Governance Strategies for Living Technologies: Bridging the Gap between Stimulating and Regulating Technoscience' (2013) 19(3) *Artificial Life* 437

Wagner, Wendy, 'Commons Ignorance: The Failure of Environmental Law to Produce Needed Information on Health and the Environment' (2004) 53 (6) *Duke Law Journal* 1619

Wallach, Evan, 'A Tiny Problem with Huge Implications: Nanotech Agents as Enablers or Substitutes for Banned Chemical Weapons: Is a New Treaty Needed?' (2009) 33(3) *Fordham International Law Journal* 860

Wedgwood, Ruth, 'The Enforcement of Security Council Resolution 687: The Threat of Force against Iraq's Weapons of Mass Destruction' (1998) 92(4) *American Journal of International Law* 724

Wejnert, Jason, 'Regulatory Mechanisms for Molecular Nanotechnology' (2004) 44 (3) *Jurimetrics* 323

Wexler, Lesley, 'Limiting the Precautionary Principle: Weapons Regulation in the Face of Scientific Uncertainty' (2006) 39(2) *University of California Davis Law Review* 459

Wheelis, March, 'Will the "New Biology" Lead to New Weapons?' (2004) 34(6) *Arms Control Today* 6

Wheelis, Mark and Malcolm Dando, 'Neurobiology: A Case Study of the Imminent Militarization of Biology' (2005) 87(859) *International Review of the Red Cross* 560

Whitman, Jim, 'The Arms Control Challenges of Nanotechnology' (2011) 32(1) *Contemporary Security Policy* 99

Wickson, Fern, 'Technology: Nanomaterials Need Flexible Regulation' (2011) 476 (7360) *Nature* 283

Widdows, Kelvin, 'Security Council Resolutions and Non-Members of the United Nations' (1978) 27 *International and Comparative Law Quarterly* 459

Wildegger-Gaissmaier, Anna, 'Aspects of Thermobaric Weaponry' (April 2003) 4 (1) *Australian Defence Force Health* 3

Young, Margaret A and Sebastian Sullivan, 'Evolution through the Duty to Cooperate: Implications of the Whaling Case at the International Court of Justice' (2015) 16(2) *Melbourne Journal of International Law* 15

Young, Margaret A, 'The WTO's Use of Relevant Rules of International Law: An Analysis of the Biotech Case' (2007) 56(4) *The International and Comparative Law Quarterly* 907

Yuzon, Ensign Florencio J, 'Deliberate Environmental Modification through the Use of Chemical and Biological Weapons: "Greening" the International

Laws of Armed Conflict to Establish an Environmentally Protective Regime' (1996) 11(5) *American University International Law Review* 793

Zanders, Jean Pascal, 'The Chemical Weapons Convention and universality: A Question of Quality over Quantity?' (2002) 4 *Disarmament Forum* 23

Zawadzki, Przemysław and Agnieszka K Adamczyk, 'Personality and Authenticity in Light of the Memory-modifying Potential of Optogenetics' (2020) *Nanoethics* <https://doi.org/10.1007/s11569-020-00377-1>

Zhang, Haiyuan et al, 'Processing Pathway Dependence of Amorphous Silica Nanoparticle Toxicity: Colloidal vs Pyrolytic' (2012) 134(38) *Journal of the American Chemistry Society* 15790

Ziolkowski, Richard W, 'Metamaterials: The Early Years in the USA' (2014) 1 *EJP Applied Metamaterials* 1

VII Press Releases/News/Web

Acharya, Subhojyoti, *Is Narco Analysis a Reliable Science? – Present Legal Scenario India* (19 February 2008) Legal Service India <www.legalserviceindia.com/article/l176-Narco-Analysis.html>

Arkin, William, Damian Durrant and Marianne Cherni, *On Impact: Modern Warfare and the Environment: A Case Study of the Gulf War* (1991) Greenpeace <www.greenpeace.org/international/Global/international/planet-2/report/1991/6/on-impact-modern-warfare-and.pdf>

Article 36, *Article 36 Reviews and Addressing Lethal Autonomous Weapons Systems* (April 2016) <www.article36.org/wp-content/uploads/2016/04/LAWS-and-A36.pdf>

Nanoweapons (November 2017) <www.article36.org/wp-content/uploads/2017/11/Nano-Final-17Nov17.pdf>

Backgrounder on Russian Fuel Air Explosives ("Vacuum Bombs") (1 February 2000) Human Rights Watch <www.hrw.org/report/2000/02/01/backgrounder-russian-fuel-air-explosives-vacuum-bombs>

Baker, Betsy, 'Hague Peace Conferences (1899 and 1907)' (November 2009) *Max Planck Encyclopedia of Public International Law* <http://opil.ouplaw.com/view/10.1093/law:epil/9780199231690/law-9780199231690-e305>

Bertell, Rosalie, *Depleted Uranium as a Weapon of War* (August 1999) <www.begegnungszentrum.at/texte/bertell/bertell2-du.htm>

Biodefense for the 21st Century (28 April 2004) Office of the Press Secretary, The White House <www.hsdl.org/?view&did=784400>

Biotechnology, Weapons and Humanity (20 January 2004) International Committee of the Red Cross <www.icrc.org/eng/resources/documents/misc/5vdj7s.htm>

Boulanin, Vincient, *Implementing Article 36 Weapon Reviews in the Light of Increasing Autonomy in Weapon Systems* (November 2015) SIPRI <www.sipri.org/sites/default/files/files/insight/SIPRIInsight1501.pdf>

Brondizio, E S et al (eds), 'Global Assessment Report on Biodiversity and Ecosystem Services of the Intergovernmental Science-Policy Platform on Biodiversity and Ecosystem Services' (2019) *IPBES* <https://ipbes.net/global-assessment>

Brueck, Hilary, 'This Tiny Robot Team Could Help Stop the No. 1 Killer in America' (12 January 2016) *Fortune* <http://fortune.com/2016/01/12/artery-clearing-nanobot/>

Bugnion, François, *From Solferino to the Birth of Contemporary International Humanitarian Law* (22 April 2009) International Committee of the Red Cross <www.icrc.org/eng/assets/files/other/solferino-bugnion-icrc.pdf>

Campaign to Stop Killer Robots <www.stopkillerrobots.org>

Carlson, Lonnie and Margaret Kosal, *Preventing Weapons of Mass Destruction Proliferation – Leveraging Special Operational Forces to Shape the Environment* (January 2017) Joint Special Operations University <www.hsdl.org/?view&did=798283>

Cho, Eun Seon et al, 'Graphene Oxide/Metal Nanocrystal Multilaminates as the Atomic Limit for Safe and Selective Hydrogen Storage' (2016) *Nature Communications* <www.nature.com/articles/ncomms10804.pdf>

Chodos, Alan (ed), *Einstein Predicts Stimulated Emission* (August 2005) American Physical Society <www.aps.org/publications/apsnews/200508/history.cfm>

Clapper, James, *Statement for the Record: Worldwide Threat Assessment of the US Intelligence Community* (9 February 2016) Office of the Director of National Intelligence <www.dni.gov/files/documents/SASC_Unclassified_2016_ATA_SFR_FINAL.pdf>

Conko, Gregory and Henry I Miller, 'WTO and Biotech Food: Who Really Won?' (26 February 2006) *Competitive Enterprise Institute* <https://cei.org/opeds_articles/wto-and-biotech-food-who-really-won/>

Coupland, Robin (ed), *The SIrUS Project: Towards a Determination of Which Weapons Cause "Superfluous Injury or Unnecessary Suffering"* (1997) International Committee of the Red Cross <www.loc.gov/rr/frd/Military_Law/pdf/SIrUS-project.pdf>

Dambrot, Stuart Mason, *Your Brain on Mesh: Injectable Flexible Probe Melds with Neurons, Causes Little or No Chronic Immune Response* (5 July 2017) Phys Org <https://phys.org/news/2017-07-brain-mesh-flexible-probe-melds.html>

Dando, Malcolm, 'Science, Technology, and the Bioweapons Treaty' (13 May 2011) *Bulletin of the Atomic Scientists* <https://thebulletin.org/science-technology-and-bioweapons-treaty>

Daniels, Jeff, *Mini-nukes and Mosquito-like Robot Weapons Being Primed for Future Warfare* (17 March 2017) CNBC <www.cnbc.com/2017/03/17/mini-nukes-and-inspect-bot-weapons-being-primed-for-future-warfare.html>

De Saussure, Hamilton, *Military Objectives*, Crimes of War Project <www.crimesofwar.org/a-z-guide/military-objectives>

Defence Intelligence Agency, 'Future Threat to the Soldier System, Volume I; Dismounted Soldier: Middle East Threat' (September 1993) cited in *Backgrounder on Russian Fuel Air Explosives ('Vacuum Bombs')* (1 February 2000) Human Rights Watch <www.hrw.org/report/2000/02/01/backgrounder-russian-fuel-air-explosives-vacuum-bombs>

Defense Advanced Research Projects Agency, 'Atoms to Product: Aiming to Make Nanoscale Benefits Life-Sized' (Media Release, 22 August 2014) <www.darpa.mil/news-events/2014-08/22>

Dense Inert Metal Explosive (DIME) (2017) Global Security <www.globalsecurity.org/military/systems/munitions/dime.htm>

Dual Use Research of Concern (DURC), World Health Organization <www.who.int/csr/durc/en/>

EU Consults on Nanomaterial Definition: Revision of Recommendation Three Years Late (19 September 2017) ChemicalWatch <https://chemicalwatch.com/59016/eu-consults-on-nanomaterial-definition>

European Commission, Nanoscience and Nanotechnologies: An Action Plan for Europe 2005–2009 (2005) European Commission Community Research and Development Information Service <https://cordis.europa.eu/pub/nanotechnology/docs/action_plan_brochure.pdf>

Ferber, Dan, *Cloaked DNA Nanodevices Survive Pilot Mission* (22 April 2014) Harvard Medical School <http://hms.harvard.edu/news/cloaked-dna-nanodevices-survive-pilot-mission-4-22-14>

Functional Perspective on the Biological Weapons Convention and Chemical Weapons Convention (11 December 2006) International Committee of the Red Cross <www.icrc.org/eng/resources/documents/statement/biological-chemical-weapons-statement-111206.htm>

Gartner, John, 'Military Reloads with Nanotech' (21 January 2005) *MIT Technology Review* <www.technologyreview.com/news/403624/military-reloads-with-nanotech>

Genesis Nanotechnology <http://genesisnanotech.com/wp-content/uploads/2014/12/Applications-of-Nanomaterials-Chart-Picture1.jpg>

Ghosh, Shona, 'One of Europe's Most Influential Investors Gave a Brutal Example of How AI Could Wipe out White-Collar Jobs' (13 June 2017) *Business Insider UK* <http://uk.businessinsider.com/fred-destin-artificial-intelligence-will-wipe-out-white-collar-jobs-2017-6?r=US&IR=T>

Gross, Michael, 'The Pentagon's Push to Program Soldiers' Brains' (November 2018) *The Atlantic* <www.theatlantic.com/magazine/archive/2018/11/the-pentagon-wants-to-weaponize-the-brain-what-could-go-wrong/570841/?utm_source=eb>

Hall, Stephen S, 'Neuroscience's New Toolbox' (17 June 2014) *MIT Technology Review* <www.technologyreview.com/featuredstory/528226/neurosciences-new-toolbox>

Hambling, David, *Cancer Worries for New U.S. Bombs, DefenseTech* (22 May 2006) Military.com <www.military.com/defensetech/2006/05/22/cancer-worries-for-new-u-s-bombs>

'Deadly Blast from the Past', *The Guardian* (online), 18 January 2001, <www.theguardian.com/science/2001/jan/18/technology2>

Hearn, Kelly, *Future Soldiers Could Get Enhanced Minds* (19 March 2001) United Press International <www.geocities.ws/marksrealm/project457.html>

Henschke, Adam, '"Supersoldiers": Ethical Concerns in Human Enhancement Technologies' on International Committee of the Red Cross, *Humanitarian Law & Policy* (3 July 2017) <http://blogs.icrc.org/law-and-policy/2017/07/03/supersoldiers-ethical-concerns-human-enhancement-technologies-2/>

Homeland Defense and Security Information Analysis Centre, *State of the Art Report: Uses of Nanotechnology on Surfaces for Military Applications* (17 October 2016) <www.hdiac.org/system/files/20161017_HDIAC_SOAR_Nanotech_FINAL_reduced%20size.pdf>

How to Tell When a Nanoparticle Is out of Shape (21 December 2016) National Institute of Standards and Technology <https://m.phys.org/news/2016-12-nanoparticle.html>

Institute for Soldier Nanotechnologies <http://isnweb.mit.edu/what-is-isn.html>

Instructions for the Government of Armies of the United States in the Field (Lieber Code) (24 April 1863) <https://ihl-databases.icrc.org/ihl/INTRO/110>

International Committee of the Red Cross, *Practice Relating to Rule 50. Destruction and Seizure of Property of an Adversary* (2017) <https://ihl-databases.icrc.org/customary-ihl/eng/docs/v2_rul_rule50>

The Geneva Conventions of 1949 and Their Additional Protocols (29 October 2010) <www.icrc.org/eng/war-and-law/treaties-customary-law/geneva-conventions/overview-geneva-conventions.htm>International Committee of the Red Cross, *Customary IHL – Rule 1. The Principle of Distinction between Civilians and Combatants* (2005) <https://ihl-databases.icrc.org/customary-ihl/eng/docs/v1_cha_chapter1_rule1>

Customary IHL – Rule 14. Proportionality in Attack (2005) <https://ihl-databases.icrc.org/customary-ihl/eng/docs/v1_cha_chapter4_rule14>

Customary IHL – Rule 22. Principle of Precautions against the Effects of Attacks (2005) <https://ihl-databases.icrc.org/customary-ihl/eng/docs/v1_rul_rule22>

Customary IHL – Rule 70. Weapons of a Nature to Cause Superfluous Injury or Unnecessary Suffering (2005) <https://ihl-databases.icrc.org/customary-ihl/eng/docs/v1_rul_rule70>

Customary IHL – Rule 73. Biological Weapons (2005) <https://ihl-databases.icrc.org/customary-ihl/eng/docs/v1_rul_rule73>

Customary IHL – Rule 74. Chemical Weapons (2005) <https://ihl-databases.icrc.org/customary-ihl/eng/docs/v1_rul_rule74>

Customary IHL – Rule 79. Weapons Primarily Injuring by Non-Detectable Fragments (2005) <https://ihl-databases.icrc.org/customary-ihl/eng/docs/v1_rul_rule79>

Customary IHL – Rule 85. The Use of Incendiary Weapons against Combatants (2005) <https://ihl-databases.icrc.org/customary-ihl/eng/docs/v1_rul_rule85>

Customary IHL – Rule 86. Blinding Laser Weapons (2005) <https://ihl-databases.icrc.org/customary-ihl/eng/docs/v1_rul_rule86>

Customary IHL Database <https://ihl-databases.icrc.org/customary-ihl/eng/docs/home>

International Committee of the Red Cross, *Protocol Additional to the Geneva Conventions of 12 August 1949, and relating to the Protection of Victims of International Armed Conflicts (Protocol I), 8 June 1977* <https://ihl-databases.icrc.or5g/applic/ihl/ihl.nsf/INTRO/470?OpenDocument>

International Court of Justice, 'Legality of Use of Force: The Court Extends by One Year the Time-limits for the Filing by Yugoslavia of Written Statements on the Preliminary Objections Made by the Respondent States' (Press Release, 23 February 2001) <www.icj-cij.org/files/case-related/107/107-20010223-PRE-01-00-EN.pdf>

Joannopoulos, John and Francis Davis, *Institute for Soldier Nanotechnologies* (18 June 2015) Massachusetts Institute of Technology <http://web.mit.edu/annualreports/pres15/2015.18.06.pdf>

Johnson, Dexter, *Nanoparticles Found in Brains Come from External Sources* (8 September 2016) IEEE Spectrum <http://spectrum.ieee.org/nanoclast/semiconductors/materials/nanoparticles-found-in-brains-comes-from-external-sources>

Joy, Bill, *Why the Future Doesn't Need Us* (1 April 2000) Wired <www.wired.com/2000/04/joy-2/>

Kivivali, Lea, *Swinburne Researchers Mimic Butterfly Wing for Compact New Technology* (1 June 2016) Swinburne Institute of Technology <www.swinburne.edu.au/news/latest-news/2016/06/swinburne-researchers-mimic-butterfly-wing-for-compact-new-technology.php>

Lawand, Kathleen, *A Guide to the Legal Review of New Weapons, Means and Methods of Warfare: Measures to Implement Article 36 of Additional Protocol I of 1977* (November 2006) International Committee of the Red Cross <www.icrc.org/en/publication/0902-guide-legal-review-new-weapons-means-and-methods-warfare-measures-implement-article>

Le Club des Juristes, *Draft Project Global Pact for the Environment* (24 June 2017) International Union for Conservation of Nature <www.iucn.org/sites/dev/files/content/documents/draft-project-of-the-global-pact-for-the-environment.pdf>

Legal Issues Arising from the War in Afghanistan and Related Anti-Terrorism Efforts (2002) Human Rights Watch <www.hrw.org/campaigns/september11/ihlqna.htm>

Lentzos, Filippa, Catherine Jefferson and Claire Marris, 'The Myths (and Realities) of Synthetic Bioweapons' (18 September 2014) *Bulletin of the Atomic Scientists* <https://thebulletin.org/myths-and-realities-synthetic-bioweapons7626>

Lewis, Jim, *Nanotechnology for Heart Repair Advances* (29 September 2011) Foresight Institute <https://foresight.org/nanotechnology-for-heart-repair-advances>

Liivoja, Rain, *Chivalry without a Horse: Military Honour and the Modern Law of Armed Conflict* (ENDC Proceedings, Volume 15, 2012) <www.ksk.edu.ee/wp-content/uploads/2012/12/KVUOA_Toimetised_15_3_Liivoja.pdf>

Ludlow, Karinne, Diana Bowman and Graeme Hodge, *A Review of Possible Impacts of Nanotechnology on Australia's Regulatory Framework: Final Report* (September 2007) <www.researchgate.net/profile/Graeme_Hodge/publication/265997359_A_Review_of_Possible_Impacts_of_Nanotechnology_on_Australia%27s_Regulatory_Framework/links/54b511d00cf28ebe92e4b974/A-Review-of-Possible-Impacts-of-Nanotechnology-on-Australias-Regulatory-Framework.pdf>

Macoubrie, Jane, *Informed Public Perceptions of Nanotechnology and Trust in Government* (2005) Woodrow Wilson International Centre for Scholars <www.pewtrusts.org/~/media/legacy/uploadedfiles/wwwpewtrustsorg/news/press_releases/nanotechnologies/nanotech0905pdf.pdf>

Marchant, Gary, *What Is a Nanomaterial?* (22 September 2016) Slate <www.slate.com/articles/technology/future_tense/2016/09/the_difficulty_of_defining_nanomaterials.html>

Marquand, Robert and Nicholas Blanford, 'Gaza: Israel under Fire for Alleged White Phosphorus Use' (14 January 2009) *Christian Science Monitor* <www.csmonitor.com/World/Middle-East/2009/0114/p07s01-wome.html>

McCall, Maxine, *Nanoparticles and Nanosafety: The Big Picture* (6 February 2014) The Conversation <http://theconversation.com/nanoparticles-and-nanosafety-the-big-picture-22061>

McCoy, Darryl, Marco Arrigoni and Nigel Gallaher, *Optogenetics Research Drives New Laser Technologies* (6 January 2015) Laser Focus World <www.laserfocusworld.com/articles/print/volume-51/issue-06/biooptics-world/biooptics-features/optogenetics-optogenetics-research-drives-new-laser-technologies.html>

Melzer, Nils, *Interpretative Guidance on the Notion of Direct Participation in Hostilities under International Humanitarian Law* (2009) International Committee of the Red Cross <https://www.icrc.org/eng/assets/files/other/icrc-002-0990.pdf>

Mulvaney, Paul, *From Roman Nanocrystals to New Gold Catalysts* (24 November 2009) Stories of Australian Science <http://stories.scienceinpublic.com.au/2010/roman-nanocrystals>

Nanotechnology Now <www.nanotech-now.com/images/military_uses.gif>

Nasu, Hitoshi, *The Future of Nanotechnology in Warfare* (4 July 2013) Global Minds <www.theglobaljournal.net/article/view/1132>

National Academy of Sciences and National Academy of Medicine, *Human Genome Editing: Science, Ethics and Governance* (February 2017) <http://nationalacademies.org/cs/groups/genesite/documents/webpage/gene_177260.pdf>

National Institutes of Health, *Dual Use Research of Concern*, Office of Science Policy <https://osp.od.nih.gov/biotechnology/dual-use-research-of-concern/>

National Science Advisory Board for Biosecurity, *Proposed Framework for the Oversight of Dual Use Life Sciences Research: Strategies for Minimizing the Potential Misuse of Research Information* (June 2007) <https://osp.od.nih.gov/wp-content/uploads/Proposed-Oversight-Framework-for-Dual-Use-Research.pdf>

National Science and Technology Council, *NNI Supplement to The President's Budget for Fiscal Year 2017* (31 March 2016) Executive Office of The President of the United States <www.nano.gov/node/1573>

O'Donnell, Erin, *Constructing the Aquatic Environment as a Legal Subject: Legal Rights, Market Participation, and the Power of Narrative* (PhD Thesis, The University of Melbourne, 2017) <http://hdl.handle.net/11343/191749>

O'Donnell, Erin, Michelle Maloney and Christine Parker, *New Developments in the Legal Status of Rivers* (11 August 2017) University of Melbourne <http://law.unimelb.edu.au/__data/assets/pdf_file/0007/2516479/Legal-rights-for-rivers-Workshop-Report.pdf>

OECD Environment Directorate: Joint Meeting of the Chemicals Committee and The Working Party on Chemicals, Pesticides and Biotechnology, Silicon Dioxide: Summary of the Dossier 71 (2016) <www.oecd.org/officialdocuments/publicdisplaydocumentpdf/?cote=env/jm/mono(2016)23&doclanguage=en>

Office of the Prosecutor, *Policy Paper on Case Selection and Prioritisation* (15 September 2016) International Criminal Court <www.icc-cpi.int/itemsDocuments/20160915_OTP-Policy_Case-Selection_Eng.pdf>

Office of the United Nations High Commissioner for Human Rights and World Health Organization, *The Right to Health: Fact Sheet No 31* <www.ohchr.org/Documents/Publications/Factsheet31.pdf>

Organisation for Economic Co-operation and Development, *Publications in the Series on the Safety of Manufactured Nanomaterials* (2018) <www.oecd.org/env/ehs/nanosafety/publications-series-safety-manufactured-nanomaterials.htm>

Report of the OECD Workshop on the Safety of Manufactured Nanomaterials: Building Co-operation, Co-ordination and Communication (2005) <www.oecd.org/officialdocuments/publicdisplaydocumentpdf/?cote=ENV/JM/MONO(2006)19&docLanguage=bi>

Organisation for the Prohibition of Chemical Weapons, *Convergence of Chemistry and Biology: Report of the Scientific Advisory Board's Temporary Working*

Group (27 June 2014) <www.opcw.org/fileadmin/OPCW/SAB/en/TWG_Scientific_Advsiory_Group_Final_Report.pdf>

Note by the Director-General: Report of the Scientific Advisory Board on Developments in Science and Technology (28 February 2008) <www.opcw.org/fileadmin/OPCW/CSP/RC-2/en/RC-2_DG.1-EN.pdf>

Reports <www.opcw.org/about-opcw/subsidiary-bodies/scientific-advisory-board/documents/reports/>

Osborn, Kris, *Navy Declares Laser Weapons Ready to Protect Ships in Persian Gulf* (2015) Military.com <www.military.com/daily-news/2014/12/10/navy-declares-laser-weapons-ready-to-protect-ships-in-persian.html>

Owens, Brian, 'Silver Makes Antibiotics Thousands of Times More Effective' (2013) *Nature* <www.nature.com/news/silver-makes-antibiotics-thousands-of-times-more-effective-1.13232>

PBS, 'Cave War', *News Hour with Jim Lehrer*, 10 December 2001 <www.pbs.org/newshour/bb/asia/afghanistan/caves12-10.html>

Pennisi, Elizabeth, 'Robotic Stringray Powered by Light Activated Muscle Cells' (7 July 2016) *Science* <www.sciencemag.org/news/2016/07/robotic-stingray-powered-light-activated-muscle-cells>

'President Obama Announces New Executive Actions to Fulfill our Promises to Service Members, Veterans, and Their Families' (Media Release, 26 August 2014) <www.whitehouse.gov/the-press-office/2014/08/26/fact-sheet-president-obama-announces-new-executive-actions-fulfill-our-p>

Puscas, Ioana, 'Governing Nanotechnology: Persistent Fragmentation?' (3 October 2014) *Global Policy Journal* <www.globalpolicyjournal.com/blog/03/10/2014/governing-nanotechnology-%E2%80%93-persistent-fragmentation>

Reardon, Sara, 'Light Controlled Genes and Neurons Poised for Clinical Trials' (19 May 2016) *Nature* <www.nature.com/news/light-controlled-genes-and-neurons-poised-for-clinical-trials-1.19886>

Royal Society, *Nanoscience and Nanotechnologies: Opportunities and Uncertainties* (July 2004) <https://royalsociety.org/~/media/Royal_Society_Content/policy/publications/2004/9693.pdf>

Russo, Deborah, *The Use of Proportionality in the Recent Case-Law of the ICJ* (4 June 2015) SSRN <https://ssrn.com/abstract=2614316>

Sargent Jr, John, *The National Nanotechnology Initiative: Overview, Reauthorization, and Appropriations Issues* (16 December 2014) US Congressional Research Service <www.fas.org/sgp/crs/misc/RL34401.pdf>

Secretary-General's Message on International Day for Preventing Exploitation of Environment in Armed Conflict (6 November 2012) United Nations Secretary-General <www.un.org/sg/en/content/sg/statement/2012-11-06/secretary-generals-message-international-day-preventing-exploitation>

Security Council Report, *Protection of Civilians in Armed Conflict* (December 2013) <www.securitycouncilreport.org/atf/cf/%7B65BFCF9B-6D27-4E9C-8CD3-CF6E4FF96FF9%7D/cross_cutting_report_3_protection_of_civilians_2013.pdf>

Shahani, Aarti, *Microsoft President Urges Nuclear-Like Limits on Cyberweapons* (16 May 2017) National Public Radio <www.npr.org/sections/alltechconsidered/2017/05/16/528555400/microsofts-president-reflects-on-cyberattack-helping-pirates-and-the-nsa>

Shaver, David, *High Energy Liquid Laser Area Defense System (HELLADS)*, Defense Advanced Research Projects Agency <www.darpa.mil/news-events/2015-05-21-2>

Siddique, Haroon, 'British Researchers Get Green Light to Genetically Modify Human Embryos', *The Guardian* (online), 2 February 2016, <www.theguardian.com/science/2016/feb/01/human-embryo-genetic-modify-regulator-green-light-research>

Smalley, David, 'Historic Leap: Navy Shipboard Laser Operates in Persian Gulf' (Media Release, 10 December 2014) <www.onr.navy.mil/Media-Center/Press-Releases/2014/LaWS-shipboard-laser-uss-ponce.aspx>

Sparrow, Rob, Symposium on the Ethical, Legal and Social Implications of Emerging Military Technologies, PREMPT, Melbourne, 29–30 May 2017

Sparrow, Robert, 'Ethics as a Source of Law: The Martens Clause and Autonomous Weapons' on International Committee of the Red Cross, *Humanitarian Law & Policy* (14 November 2017) <http://blogs.icrc.org/law-and-policy/2017/11/14/ethics-source-law-martens-clause-autonomous-weapons/>

Storm, Christian, 'Inside the Secret Cave Hideouts Used by Syrian Rebels and Families' (11 March 2015) *Business Insider Australia* <www.businessinsider.com.au/syrian-secret-cave-hideouts-2015-3>

Subcommittee on Nanoscale Science, Engineering, and Technology, Committee on Technology, and National Science and Technology Council, *NNI Supplement to The President's Budget for Fiscal Year 2017* (31 March 2016) The National Nanotechnology Initiative, Executive Office of The President <www.nano.gov/node/1573>

Switek, Brian, *Beautiful Skull Spurs Debate on Human History* (19 October 2013) National Geographic <http://news.nationalgeographic.com/news/2013/10/131017-skull-human-origins-dmanisi-georgia-erectus/>

The Global Network of Science Academics, *The Biological and Toxin Weapons Convention: Implications of Advances in Science and Technology* (2015) <https://royalsociety.org/~/media/policy/projects/biological-toxin-weapons-convention/bwc-trends-booklet.pdf>

The Laws of War on Land, signed 9 September 1880 <https://ihl-databases.icrc.org/ihl/INTRO/140?OpenDocument>

The Nobel Peace Prize in Chemistry 2016, Nobelprize.org <www.nobelprize.org/nobel_prizes/chemistry/laureates/2016/>

The Royal Society, *Brain Waves Module: Neuroscience, Society and Policy* (January 2011) <https://royalsociety.org/~/media/Royal_Society_Content/policy/publications/2011/4294974932.pdf>

Trapp, Ralph, 'Advances in the Life Sciences: Between Hype and Caution' (Workshop on the Eighth Review Conference of the Biological Weapons Convention, Geneva, 19 September 2016) <www.unog.ch/80256EDD006B8954/(httpAssets)/2735DBE154902ADBC1258035002C1F09/$file/Trapp+Science+and+technology.pdf>

Travis, John, 'And Science's 2015 Breakthrough of the Year Is . . .' (17 December 2015) *Science* <www.sciencemag.org/news/2015/12/and-science-s-breakthrough-year>

Trial Chambers: The Prosecutor v Stanislav Galič – Case No. IT-98-29-T – "Judgement and Opinion" (5 December 2003) International Criminal Tribunal for the Former Yugoslavia <www.icty.org/x/file/Legal%20Library/jud_supplement/supp46-e/galic.htm>

United Nations Environment Programme, *Protecting the Environment during Armed Conflict: An Inventory and Analysis of International Law* (2009) United Nations <www.un.org/zh/events/environmentconflictday/pdfs/int_law.pdf>

United Nations General Assembly, 'Speakers Consider Criteria for Area-Based Management Tools, as Negotiations on Draft Treaty to Protect Marine Biodiversity Enter Third Day' (Media Release, 21 August 2019) <www.un.org/press/en/2019/sea2111.doc.htm>

United Nations Office for Disarmament Affairs, *Convention on the Prohibition of the Development, Production and Stockpiling of Bacteriological (Biological) and Toxin Weapons and on Their Destruction: Status of the Treaty* <http://disarmament.un.org/treaties/t/bwc>

Convention on the Prohibition of the Development, Production, Stockpiling and Use of Chemical Weapons and on Their Destruction: Status of the Treaty <http://disarmament.un.org/treaties/t/cwc>

Protocol for the Prohibition of the Use in War of Asphyxiating, Poisonous or Other Gases, and of Bacteriological Methods of Warfare: Status of the Treaty <http://disarmament.un.org/treaties/t/1925>

University of York Centre for Industry Education Collaboration, *The Essential Chemical Industry – Online* <www.essentialchemicalindustry.org/images/stories/160_nanotech/03-16-nano_Fig_03.jpg>

Uppsala Conflict Data Program Database, Uppsala University <http://ucdp.uu.se/>

Vöneky, Silja, 'A New Shield for the Environment: Peacetime Treaties as Legal Restraints of Wartime Damage' (2003) *Review of European, Comparative and International Environmental Law* <https://doi.org/10.1111/1467-9388.00229>

Wassenaar Arrangement on Export Controls for Conventional Arms and Dual-Use Goods and Technologies: Public Documents, Volume 1, Founding Documents (February 2017) <www.wassenaar.org>

Watts, Sir Arthur, *Israeli Wall Advisory Opinion (Legal Consequences of the Construction of a Wall in the Occupied Palestinian Territory* (February 2007) Max Planck Encyclopedia of Public International Law <http://opil.ouplaw.com/view/10.1093/law:epil/9780199231690/law-9780199231690-e150>

Wax, Naomi, 'Ideas & Trends; Notes from Underground', *The New York Times* (online), 25 November 2001, <www.nytimes.com/2001/11/25/weekinreview/ideas-trends-notes-from-underground.html>

Weidner, Kristna, *Nanomotors Are Controlled for the First Time, within Living Cells* (11 February 2014) Penn State News <http://news.psu.edu/story/303296/2014/02/10/research/nanomotors-are-controlled-first-time-inside-living-cells>

Whittle, Richard, 'Silent, Invisible, Deadly: The Weapon that Could Change Warfare', *New York Post* (online), 27 December 2015, <http://nypost.com/2015/12/27/air-force-will-test-first-aircraft-mounted-laser-weapon-in-january>

Yin, Hao et al, 'Structure-guided Chemical Modification of Guide RNA Enables Potent Non-viral *in vivo* Genome Editing' (2017) *Nature Biotechnology* <http://nature.com/articles/doi:10.1038/nbt.4005>

Zyga, Lisa, *Microbots Can Clean up Polluted Water* (11 April 2016) Phys Org <https://phys.org/news/2016-04-microbots-polluted.html>

INDEX

For EU product safety concerns, contact us at Calle de José Abascal, 56–1°, 28003 Madrid, Spain or eugpsr@cambridge.org.

www.ingramcontent.com/pod-product-compliance
Ingram Content Group UK Ltd.
Pitfield, Milton Keynes, MK11 3LW, UK
UKHW021948310326
469558UK00021B/848

* 9 7 8 1 1 0 8 7 9 9 8 4 3 *